MARK

THE IVP NEW TESTAMENT COMMENTARY SERIES

RONALD J. KERNAGHAN

GRANT R. OSBORNE, SERIES EDITOR

D. STUART BRISCOE AND HADDON ROBINSON,
CONSULTING EDITORS

IVP Academic

An imprint of InterVarsity Press
Downers Grove, Illinois

InterVarsity Press
P.O. Box 1400, Downers Grove, IL 60515-1426
World Wide Web: www.ivpress.com
E-mail: email@ivpress.com

InterVarsity Press® is the book-publishing division of InterVarsity Christian Fellowship/USA®, a
movement of students and faculty active on campus at hundreds of universities, colleges and
schools of nursing in the United States of America, and a member movement of the International
Fellowship of Evangelical Students. For information about local and regional activities, write
Public Relations Dept., InterVarsity Christian Fellowship/USA, 6400 Schroeder Rd., P.O. Box 7895,
Madison, WI 53707-7895, or visit the IVCF website at <www.intervarsity.org>.

Design: Cindy Kiple
Images: Einzug in Jerusalem—Entry into Jerusalem by Wilhelm Morgner at Museum am Ostwall,
Dortmund, Germany. Erich Lessing/Art Resource, NY.

ISBN 978-0-8308-4002-1

Printed in the United States of America ∞

Library of Congress Cataloging-in-Publication Data

Kernaghan, Ronald J.
    Mark/Ronald J. Kernaghan, Grant R. Osborne.
        p. com—(The IVP New Testament commentary series)
Includes bibliographical references (p.   ).
ISBN 978-0-8308-1702-0 (cloth: alk. paper)
1. Bible. N.T. Mark—Commentaries.   I. Osborne, Grant R.   II. Title
BS2585.53.K47 2007
226.3'07—dc22
                                                    2006101576

P   17   16   15   14   13   12   11   10   9   8   7   6   5   4   3   2   1
Y   24   23   22   21   20   19   18   17   16   15   14   13   12   11   10

To Paul (in memoriam) and Marilyn Byer,
*mentors, teachers and friends
to generations of students around the world*

General Preface

In an age of proliferating commentary series, one might easily ask why add yet another to the seeming glut. The simplest answer is that no other series has yet achieved what we had in mind—a series to and from the church, that seeks to move from the text to its contemporary relevance and application.

No other series offers the unique combination of solid, biblical exposition and helpful explanatory notes in the same user-friendly format. No other series has tapped the unique blend of scholars and pastors who share both a passion for faithful exegesis and a deep concern for the church. Based on the New International Version of the Bible, one of the most widely used modern translations, the IVP New Testament Commentary Series builds on the NIV's reputation for clarity and accuracy. Individual commentators indicate clearly whenever they depart from the standard translation as required by their understanding of the original Greek text.

The series contributors represent a wide range of theological traditions, united by a common commitment to the authority of Scripture for Christian faith and practice. Their efforts here are directed toward applying the unchanging message of the New Testament to the ever-changing world in which we live.

Readers will find in each volume not only traditional discussions of authorship and backgrounds, but useful summaries of principal themes and approaches to contemporary application. To bridge the gap between commentaries that stress the flow of an author's argument but skip over exegetical nettles and those that simply jump from one difficulty to another, we have developed our unique format that expounds the text in uninterrupted form on the upper portion of each page while dealing with other issues underneath in verse-keyed notes. To avoid clutter we have also adopted a social studies note system that keys references to the bibliography.

We offer the series in hope that pastors, students, Bible teachers and small group leaders of all sorts will find it a valuable aid— one that stretches the mind and moves the heart to ever-growing faithfulness and obedience to our Lord Jesus Christ.

Author's Preface

This commentary is one voice in a long conversation. It began in the late 1960s as Paul Byer, a campus staff worker with InterVarsity Christian Fellowship, led students, seminary and university professors, and pastors in weeklong inductive studies in the Gospel of Mark. Most of the early conversation included people from the western United States. Today the conversation also includes village folk, students, pastors and professors in Africa, Latin America, Asia and Europe. The conversation takes place in dormitories, rustic conference centers, fellowship halls, inexpensive hotels, simple village structures with roofs but no walls, and homes. It is not a conversation that ignores either the larger community of faith or the insights of modern scholarship. Those voices are welcomed and tempered by the concerns of people from diverse cultures and classes. There are few grants or scholarships for the events that draw people together over long distances. Most of those who attend pay for the travel and accommodations themselves or raise the funds from family and friends. What draws the participants together is an encounter with Jesus Christ through the words of the Gospel of Mark.

Paul Byer was a lifelong student of the Bible, and he was an extraordinarily creative person. Among his many insights two stand out as foundational. The first was his insistence that chapter and verse numbers were often an obstacle to reading the story. At the very least, they interrupt the flow of the narrative, and in some cases they interfere with the story. Mark 9:1 is a case in point: it belongs structurally to the conversation between Jesus and his followers that began in 8:27, but the decision to begin a new chapter after 8:38 removes 9:1 from its natural context and connects it to the story of the transfiguration. In all probability the scribe who inserted the system of chapter and verse divisions interpreted Jesus' saying about the coming of the kingdom of God with power in light of the story that follows.

The interpretation of any text is no simple task. Good interpretation pays attention to the social, historical and cultural contexts of the original document, just as it must also take into account the circumstances and assumptions of the interpretive community. Every reading is an act of interpretation, whether the reader is a medieval scribe, skeptic, pietist or professor, and the division of the text into verses, paragraphs and chapters is itself a fundamental act of interpretation. In fact, it is an interpretation that colors every subsequent reading. Paul introduced us to the study of biblical texts without verses, paragraphs and chapters in order to engage the Gospel more directly. His approach has become known as the manuscript method of Bible study. From the first moments in a manuscript study with Paul Byer, students of every persuasion were encouraged to ask questions and probe whatever came to mind for whatever insight might be found in the text under consideration. It was a demanding engagement that discouraged ready-made answers and opened intriguing possibilities.

Second, Paul wanted to see beyond the printed text. Trained as an architect, Paul encouraged his students to look for pictures in the words. Years ago this was a far-sighted approach to interpreting the Gospel that lay outside the concerns of the academic community. More recently, though, biblical scholars have begun to pay attention to the idea that the Gospels were not written to be read alone. They were written to be read aloud, typically in a congregational setting, to an audience that was largely illiterate or semiliterate. People with limited reading skills process information concretely. They hear words and turn them into images without thinking about the process. After hearing a story, they are far more likely to want to act it out than to discuss it dispassionately, and dramatizing a text produces its own intriguing insights.

We must be careful not to assume that thinking concretely and finding pictures in the Gospel are important only for those who strain to read. There is good reason to believe that images are also becoming more important in literate societies (Stephens 1998: 10, 11). Newspaper subscriptions, for example, have been declining for years, and people are turning increasingly to the internet for news. The internet, of course, is a medium based on images and visual metaphors. Images have become gateways to spirituality for people with advanced degrees, and churches which cannot find the images in the gospel may find themselves on the outside looking in.

A manuscript study with Paul Byer was uncommonly empowering. Looking back over the thirty years we worked together, I would have to say that I never heard him say *no*. It was not that he lacked convictions, discernment or confidence. On the contrary, he believed that asking questions was supremely important, and he understood the many reasons people are afraid to voice them. Part of Paul's genius was his gift for affirmation. He could turn people whose education, social standing or stages of healing made them an improbable group into a community of equals who made exciting discoveries together. Some pastors excel at telling people what God expects of them. Many spiritual mentors have the gift of helping someone listen to God in the stillness of his or her heart. Paul had the rare gift of helping us learn how to listen to God together.

When I was invited by Jim Hoover at InterVarsity Press to write this commentary, I had no idea how difficult it would be. I thought it would be done in three years—and my contract with IVP is now approaching its nineteenth anniversary. Jim asked me to bring some insights from the manuscript studies of Mark into the commentary. That has proven to be a task that was much more complex than I had ever imagined. This is an ongoing conversation with a life of its own. Much of it is open-ended by design, and although there is a broad consensus on many points, there is also a good deal of friendly disagreement. Furthermore, the conversation is not restricted to members of one group, language or class. It includes voices from many cultures and economic strata. The questions and insights of folk who cannot read stand side by side with the historical judgments and disciplined exegesis of printed commentaries. There are many voices, and choosing which ones to reproduce has not been an easy task. In the end, this commentary itself is only one voice. I cannot claim to speak for the others, but I hope that I have listened well.

Introduction

Until the middle of the nineteenth century Matthew was considered to be the earliest Gospel. That assessment can be traced back to the leaders of the early church, and Matthew's place at the opening of the New Testament owes much to that point of view. There is, however, a considerable historical gap between that testimony and the timeframe within which the canonical Gospels were written. In the nineteenth century most, if not all, of the judgments of the early church were called into question, and the priority of Matthew came under close scrutiny for the first time.

It had been assumed, for example, that the Matthew listed in the title of the Gospel was the disciple named in Matthew 10:3. There is no internal evidence in the Gospel to support that assumption, and the evidence of the later church was found to be questionable. Mark, on the other hand, is firmly connected to Peter in the early church, a point which will be taken up in the next section.

Also important in the reassessment of Matthew's priority were close textual studies of the material which Matthew and Mark share. If corresponding passages from these two Gospels are set next to each other, Mark's are seen to be almost invariably longer. That observation supports the idea that Mark—not Matthew—was written first. It is easier to understand why Matthew would have shortened Mark's material than to explain why Mark would have lengthened Matthew's, especially since Mark's Gospel is the shorter overall.

Furthermore, in terms of the internal and external controversies which the early church faced, the Gospel of Matthew is consistently more explicit and expansive. Mark's engagement of Jewish opponents contains nothing like Matthew's characteristic formula, "You have heard it said/but I tell you." Similarly, Matthew's presentation of Jesus' ministry as the fulfillment of Scripture is much more explicit than Mark's. And a comparison of Jesus' prophecy in Matthew 24 and Mark 13 shows Matthew repeatedly using the word *parousia*, while Mark does not use it at all. Observations like these have led to the modern consensus that Mark was written before Matthew. It is easier to see why Matthew would have wanted to refine Mark's work than to explain why Mark would have wanted to undo Matthew's.

By the early part of the twentieth century, then, the Gospel of Mark was thought to be the most primitive of the canonical Gospels. For much of the last century the author of the Gospel of Mark was thought to be little more than an editor of questionable skill who merely cut and pasted pieces of tradition together. Willi Marxsen was the first to argue that Mark was a theologian in his own right. That assessment of Mark was accepted in principle and extended in new directions by Theodore J. Weeden, Ralph P. Martin, Ched Meyers and Rudolf Pesch among others. Today there is a great interest in understanding the nature of Mark's theological accomplishment.

☐ Authorship

According to the first church historian, Eusebius, this Gospel was written by Mark, who collected and interpreted material from Peter's sermons (1989:49, 154). Church tradition has subsequently identified this Mark as John Mark, known to us from Acts 12:12. The reliability of Eusebius's testimony has been challenged on several grounds (Edwards 2002:6-7). Eusebius, for example, wrote somewhere in the late third or early fourth century and named Papias, a bishop of Hierapolis in the early second century, as his source. So there is a gap of up to two hundred years between Eusebius's record and the source he claimed. Furthermore, Eusebius stated that Matthew was the earliest Gospel, a judgment that most New Testament scholars deny. Today the Gospel of Mark is generally accepted as the first Gospel to have been written down. Thus, the gap between Eusebius and his source, coupled with the well-founded doubt about his historical judgment, leads to questions about his attribution of this Gospel to Mark.

Traditions about Mark's authorship cannot be accepted uncritically, of course, but there are good reasons for crediting Eusebius on this point. Despite an extensive number of early manuscripts, there is no other attribution for this Gospel. Furthermore, it circulated in the first century along with other Gospel traditions, which makes it improbable that this Gospel circulated without a title. Since "According to Mark" is the only title the book has had, the tradition of Mark's authorship may actually go back to the first century (France 2002:40).

☐ Audience, Date and Place of Origin

Eusebius points to Rome as the place where the Gospel of Mark was written, and until the middle of the twentieth century most scholars accepted that Mark wrote for congregations in and around Rome. In the latter half of that century, however, newer studies, many of which were based in the social sciences, reevaluated the internal evidence in the Gospel and identified Syria or Palestine as a more likely point of origin. Most of the internal evidence from the Gospel itself can be argued either way. The use of Latin words like the name Legion in 5:9 can point in either direction. Those who argue for a Roman origin cite these Latinisms in their favor. Since Roman troops were stationed in Palestine, cities were founded in honor of the emperor in Palestine; and since Roman merchants traveled through Asia Minor, Latin words undoubtedly made their way into common speech.

Likewise, mining the text for information about the socioeconomic conditions of Mark's audience is inconclusive. The stories that Mark records reflect patterns of life in an advanced agrarian society (Waetjen 1989:5). Yet much of the Mediterranean world in the first century could be described as an advanced agrarian society both before and after the fall of Jerusalem. Furthermore, 1 Corinthians 1:26 suggests that the gospel appealed to the underclasses throughout the Mediterranean world, a point supported by the frequent appeals to slaves in Pauline literature. A sympathetic portrait of the underclasses would have had an appeal throughout the Roman Empire, and that portrait may have been grounded in Mark's sources, irrespective of where the Gospel was written.

Mark's emphasis on the suffering of Jesus has often been seen as indirect support for a Roman origin. The suffering of early Christians in Rome under Nero was horrific, and this Gospel's call to stand firm to the end (13:13) would have both warned and encouraged them. Yet believing communities throughout the empire must also have been alarmed as the stories of martyrdom spread, and the same word of encouragement could have applied almost anywhere. If there is a case to be made here, it is that the suffering of Christians in Rome was worse than it was elsewhere in the empire, and their need for encouragement was greater.

One remaining piece of evidence favors a Roman origin: the presence of Aramaic expressions that Mark translates into Greek with one exception. The exception is the name Barabbas in 15:7. All other Aramaisms, including the name Bartimaeus in 10:46, are translated. That Mark translates the Aramaic words but not the Latin ones suggests that the Gospel was not written for a Palestinian or Syrian audience, because Aramaic was widely spoken in those areas. The translated Aramaic words support a Roman origin. On balance, more is to be said for a Roman origin, but much of the evidence is ambiguous, and there is certainly room for caution. It is quite possible that Mark was acquainted with more than one Christian community and wrote for a wider audience (Bauckham 1998:44).

Three other pieces of internal evidence offer clues about the date of composition. The first is the editorial comment in 7:19: "In saying this, Jesus declared all foods clean." Here is a point where the Evangelist steps out of his role as narrator to speak directly to the audience. For the narrator to move out of character in this way suggests that arguments about what was clean or unclean were a matter of considerable concern for the Evangelist and his church. And that in turn suggests that the Gospel was written before the final rift between church and synagogue.

Similarly, the narrator steps out of his normal role again in 13:14: "Let the reader understand." The reader in this case is probably the person who read the Gospel aloud to the congregation. The surrounding verses are a summons to flee when the destruction of the temple in

Jerusalem was imminent. The reader is to watch for the sign of the figure that stood where he or it should not be and then to warn the congregation to flee the disaster that was coming. The community that would have been most directly endangered by the temple's destruction would have been the church in Jerusalem, but there is no evidence that Mark wrote for them. The destruction of the temple would have been a matter of grave concern to followers of Jesus throughout the empire, particularly those who were still in synagogues or had come out of them. This warning would have been compelling if it were given before Jerusalem was sacked. It makes little sense after the fact.

Finally, one other notable feature of the prophecy against the temple points to an earlier rather than a later date of composition: neither the prophecy nor the rest of the Gospel contains any reference to ruins of the temple being burned. After the Roman troops pulled the temple down, they burned its ruins—and Mark makes no mention of this event. This Gospel was probably written, then, with the fate of the temple still unresolved (Dodd 1961:44 n. 2). Mark 13 does not have the character of a prophecy composed after the fact, and there is no internal evidence in the rest of the Gospel to contradict that observation. Taken together, these three Markan features support an early date of composition, sometime before the destruction of the temple. Whether the date can be pinned down any more precisely to a point before or after Peter's death in Rome is problematic. There is no internal evidence either way, and the witness of later Christian writers is mixed.

The two editorial comments at 7:19 and 13:14 are not the only places where Mark's interaction with his audience is instructive. Throughout the Gospel, Mark's style is open-ended and interactive. At the beginning of the Gospel (1:1) and near its ending (15:39), Jesus is declared to be the Son of God. In between these affirmations, though, Jesus is presented indirectly for the most part. For example, in 1:2-14 Mark does not identify John the Baptist as the voice crying in the wilderness, nor does he specify that Jesus was the one about whom John prophesied. Those meanings have to be inferred by those who hear the Gospel. The testimony of the unclean spirits about Jesus is direct, but its value is suspect since it culminates in the charge that Jesus himself was possessed and cast out demons by the power of Beelzebub

(3:22). Peter's confession (8:29) leads to an argument, a command to be silent and a rebuke. And although Jesus claims the title Messiah before the Sanhedrin (14:62), he is reticent on the same subject before Pilate (15:2-5). Throughout the Gospel the Evangelist treats the identity of Jesus as an open question about which the audience has to make a decision. Mark tells the story of Jesus not simply to instruct but to elicit a response.

At times the audience is placed in the position of the first disciples. Nowhere is this way of addressing his readers and hearers clearer than in the parables of Mark 4. We are told that Jesus spoke many things in parables and explained everything privately to his disciples. The first parable in this section is explained, and we can see or hear the explanation. The next four parables, however, are reproduced in the Gospel without explanation. This narrative device leaves the audience as people who themselves hear the parable but must ask Jesus what it means. The unstated assumption is that Jesus still speaks to his followers. Their questions, their lack of understanding, can be addressed in the same way that the first disciples' lack of understanding was addressed because Jesus still speaks.

Mark presents the resurrection of Jesus in similar terms. In this Gospel no one sees the risen Lord without going to Galilee, "where you will see him, just as he told you" (16:7). Here the original followers of Jesus are placed in the same position as his later ones. The assumption, clearly stated here, is that Jesus will appear to those who hear his words and act upon them. Mark invites his audience to encounter Jesus not only as a figure in a story they hear, but as a living presence who still speaks and appears to them.

In this interaction there are no hints of a particular audience. This dynamic is set up without reference to any specific group of people. The people who encounter Jesus in this way might be Romans, Jews, Athenians, Ephesians or the residents of Spain for that matter. Ultimately for Mark the Gospel of Jesus Christ is not the property of any one group of people. It is to be proclaimed to the whole world, a theme that is underscored in the prophecy about the temple (13:10) and in the story of the unnamed woman who anointed Jesus (14:9). If Mark had one eye fixed on a particular audience like Roman Christians as he wrote, he had the other eye focused on the whole world. We might call Mark a bifocal Gospel. It can be read through one lens as speaking to a limited group of disciples, but it also invites a larger audience to meet the risen Jesus just as his early followers did. Mark was after all an evangelist.

☐ The Gospel as Parable

In this commentary the shorter ending of the Gospel is accepted as original and intentional. There is no compelling evidence of any other original ending, and the longer endings are demonstrably later. Kähler's observation that Mark was a passion story with a long introduction (1988:80) leads to the thought that this Gospel was written backward. In other words, this so-called long introduction serves the purpose of preparing us for the ending. As Martin suggests, the shadow of the cross falls across the entire Gospel (1972:117). Yet it is not just the cross that interprets the rest of the Gospel. Mark's treatment of the resurrection is also woven into the fabric of his account of the ministry of Jesus.

Mark treats the resurrection as a parable. It comes to us as a word—but even so, not as the report of an event that ties up all the loose ends that the preceding stories have introduced. It is open-ended. At the end of this Gospel none of the disciples has seen the risen Jesus. Peter in all his bitter remorse has yet to meet him. Not even the women who went to the tomb have seen him. Instead of joy there is fear, and the good news that does not need to be kept secret is not told. The narrative simply stops, but that is not the end of the Gospel. If it were, there would be no Gospel.

Several recent commentators argue that Mark is a self-referential story much like a modern novel (Waetjen 1989:1). Unlike a modern novel, though, that reaches its conclusion when the conflicts generated in the story are resolved, Mark does not resolve the conflicts. Instead, 16:8 highlights the biggest conflict of all, the one Jesus introduced when he said, "Whoever loses his life for me and for the gospel will save it" (8:35). In this Gospel the resolutions for Peter, the two women and the audience are postponed indefinitely.

Mark's Gospel lacks what might be called a proper ending. It does not conform to the canons of modern literary criticism, and it is only self-referential to a degree. The allusion to Alexander and Rufus (15:21), who play absolutely no part in the narrative, moves the horizon of the narrative far beyond the stopping point of the story. There would be no point in mentioning them if they were not known to Mark's audience. They must have been connected in some unspecified way to the early church. In mentioning them so late in the story, Mark offers a picture of the community of faith after the resurrection. Mark's Gospel then does not stand apart from history. It begins even before the appearance of Jesus with the covenant theology of Isaiah, and as the story stops the Evangelist provides glimpses of the way it shapes history.

Much the same thing can be said about the role of the women who first appear as followers of Jesus in 15:40-41. The word *followers* is not used lightly there. It is the same language that describes Jesus' male adherents as disciples. In the patriarchal world of first-century Palestine it is not surprising to find men as apostles, but to meet women described as disciples is. How that tension is to be resolved is left as a mystery in 16:8, and yet the women receive the same invitation to follow Jesus to Galilee that the men receive. This, too, is a conflict that the Gospel resolves after the story stops.

Mark's treatment of the resurrection has implications for the broader question of the relationship between the four canonical Gospels. Given Mark's preference for the open-ended story, any argument from silence about the relationship between this Gospel and other Gospel traditions must be regarded with suspicion. If Mark is content to bring the story to an end without telling all he knows, what justification is there for assuming that he tells all he knows about its beginning or for that matter about any particular episode?

The resurrection is not the only miracle that Mark treats as a parable. In fact, all of the other miracle stories in this Gospel have a parabolic quality to them. They are all open-ended. They appear at points in the narrative to raise or underscore conflicts of value, and they are interwoven with secrecy motifs. All the secrecy motifs have a hint of irony about them, but in two cases the irony is inescapable. The healing of the deaf man (7:31-37) was an impossible secret to keep, just as the resurrection of Jesus was a story that somehow got out despite the women's silence. It would not be going too far to describe the entire Gospel as a parable. It is a compelling story, unfolding in an open-ended fashion, engaging its audience intentionally about the most fundamental values in life and inviting us to make a decision of enormous consequence.

Outline of Mark

9:2-13 _____ The Transfiguration
9:14-29 _____ A Near-Resurrection Experience
9:30-50 _____ The Second Prediction of Jesus' Passion
10:1-12 _____ Creation, Marriage and Divorce
10:13-16 _____ Jesus Blesses the Children
10:17-31 _____ Entitlement and Wealth
10:32-45 _____ The Third Passion Prediction
10:46-52 _____ The Blind Man Who Saw

11:1—13:37_____ Faith in the City
11:1-11 _____ The Entry into Jerusalem
11:12-25 _____ Jesus Condemns the Temple
11:27—12:12 ___ A Question of Authority
12:13-17 _____ Land and Loyalty
12:18-27 _____ The God of the Living
12:28-34 _____ The Greatest Commandment
12:35-44 _____ David's Lord and the House of God
13:1-37 _____ A Prophecy About the Temple

14:1—16:8_____ The Cross as the Gateway to the Future
14:1-11 _____ At the Home of Simon the Leper
14:12-31 _____ Jesus and God's Covenant
14:32-42 _____ The Son of Man in the Hands of Sinners
14:43-52 _____ Judas's Betrayal of Jesus
14:53-72 _____ Jesus' Trial Before the Elders of Israel
15:1-15 _____ Jesus, Pilate and the Crowd
15:16-39 _____ Jesus' Humiliation and Death
15:40—16:8 ____ The Empty Tomb

COMMENTARY

☐ **Promise, Fulfillment and Conflict (1:1—3:6)**
The Gospel of Mark opens on a note that is fundamentally different from that of the other three Gospels. Mark records no account of Jesus' birth, no angelic appearances to Mary and Joseph, and no heavenly scene before creation. Instead, there is a prophecy and a messenger. The prophecy was hundreds of years old, and some people might prefer to call it merely a memory. For Mark, however, it was much more than even a living memory. For this messenger represented the next step toward its fulfillment.

The Time Is Fulfilled (1:1-15) In 1963 Martin Luther King Jr. led a march on Washington, D.C., and proclaimed, "I have a dream." His speech electrified the nation, and the march on Washington proved to be a turning point in the American civil-rights movement. It forced a reluctant citizenry to face a living legacy of racial oppression. People who challenge the structures of society, however, receive a mixed reception at best. No matter how large their following or impressive their credentials, men and women who speak forcefully against a nation's sins make powerful enemies. Some of their enduring opposition comes from the same spiritual communities that nurtured them. In the American church King was welcomed in some quarters as a prophet. Yet some church members agreed with former FBI director J. Edgar

Hoover that King was a dangerous Communist who wanted to subvert the American way of life. And regrettably some in the church thought that King simply had to be stopped. Decades after his assassination the hostility endures: although he is the only minister whom the American government has honored with a national holiday, some churches from California to Maine do not observe his birthday.

The Beginning of the Good News (1:1-3) The Gospel of Mark opens with an old and powerful dream: the promise that God would act again in history to save the Jewish people. The first verse, which does not have a period in the Greek text, may have been the original title: *The beginning of the gospel about Jesus Christ, the Son of God.* It contains two terms that were guaranteed to rekindle this ancient hope: *good news* and *Christ.* Our English word *Christ* is derived from the Greek word for *Messiah* or *anointed one.* It refers to a person who has been appointed to accomplish God's redemptive purpose. And the words *good news* or *gospel* recall the prophecy of Isaiah 40:1-11, which promises that a people destroyed by war will rejoice because of the good news about what God has promised to do for them.

This uncomplicated opening might lead us to suppose that reading the Gospel of Mark was a straightforward matter. Yet even the first verse discloses a richness of meaning if we ask about its contribution to the unfolding story. What, for example, does the word *beginning* signify? Does it refer to a few verses at the opening of the Gospel that introduce a preamble to the ministry of Jesus Christ (Guelich 1989:11-12)? If that were so, we would expect to find other sections of the Gospel that were set off in a similar way. Or perhaps the Gospel itself is only the beginning of the good news of Jesus. That would be a particularly interesting possibility if we discovered later on that no point draws all the strands of the story together into a neat and tidy

---

1:1 The NIV's choice of words is misleading. The Greek text carries a range of meanings that the translators have chosen to truncate. A better translation would be *The good news of Jesus Christ.* The Greek text can mean either *the good news that Jesus proclaimed* or *the good news about Jesus.* The Gospel does present the good news about Jesus (1:1; 15:39; 16:16), but Jesus did not preach about himself. In between

ending. Then we might conclude that the Gospel of Mark is only the beginning of a story that continues beyond the place where the narrative stops.

On the other hand, this opening might direct our attention not ahead, but backward to some earlier point when the good news began. And in fact, the next verse draws us back to the book of Isaiah. Isaiah was composed hundreds of years before Jesus preached his first sermon, and yet it is the point at which the story opens. It looks very much as though the Evangelist did not understand the Gospel as something brand new. It is the continuation of something that God had been doing for a long time.

This reference to Isaiah, however, is not as simple and straightforward as it might first appear. In fact, the first part of Mark 1:2 does not come from Isaiah at all but from the Greek version of Exodus 23:20, where God promises to send an angelic messenger ahead of the twelve tribes to prepare the way for their entry into the Promised Land. Much later at the close of the prophetic era in Malachi 3:1 these words were used again to predict the appearance of another messenger whose task is to announce the coming of the Lord. And the last words of the book of Malachi (4:5-6) reveal that this messenger will be none other than Elijah, who did not die but was taken to be with God. In between the conquest of the Promised Land and the end of the prophetic era is the promise of Isaiah 40:3, quoted here in part in Mark 1:3, about a messenger who heralds the return of the Jewish exiles from Babylon.

These opening verses depict in broad strokes the entire sweep of Israel's history after the exodus. The messenger of Exodus 23:20 had come, and over a period of two hundred years the people of Israel had gained control of the land. They lost the land in a series of wars with Assyria and Babylon in the sixth, seventh and eighth centuries B.C. In

the opening verse and the climactic scene of the crucifixion Mark is careful to show us what Jesus proclaimed.

1:1 An interesting problem occurs with the term *Son of God*, which is missing from several early manuscripts. It is easier to see why a later editor might have inserted it than to explain why it would have been dropped if it had belonged to the earliest manuscript.

587 B.C. Jerusalem was completely destroyed, and Babylon became the new cultural center for the people of Judah. The messenger of Isaiah 40 had prophesied that the exiles would return from Babylon, that Jerusalem would be restored and that God would once again become the king and protector of Judah. This prophecy was one of several that encouraged the hope that God would restore the sovereignty of the royal house and extend the borders of Judah to the boundaries of the kingdom of David. In 538 B.C. the first exiles returned to Jerusalem, but the people of Judah did not regain their independence until 140 B.C. They lost it again in 63 B.C., when Jerusalem surrendered to Roman General Pompey. Yet by the end of that century the work of rebuilding Jerusalem was complete except for the construction of a new temple on the scale of the one Solomon had built.

As Mark's Gospel opens, a grand, new temple funded by the ruthless Herod the Great was still under construction. The people of Judah were once again subject to a foreign power, and the temple was being built from the fortune of a king whose only passion was power. The great promise of the messenger of Isaiah 40 had yet to be realized, and the messenger of Malachi 3:1 had not appeared in any sense.

John the Baptist Appears (1:4-8) Then John the Baptist appeared in the desert preaching a baptism of repentance for the forgiveness of sins. Hundreds of years had passed since the last prophet had spoken in Judah, when a new voice summoned everyone to leave Jerusalem and come to the wilderness. People streamed out of the cities in mass to gather by the banks of the River Jordan to hear something new. But who was John the Baptist? Was he a messenger or prophet? Was he a member of the lunatic fringe? After all, even two thousand years ago a man living in the desert on a diet of grasshoppers and wild honey would not have been regarded as a pillar of the community. And what was John's relationship to the community? Did he hope to strengthen it, reform it or destroy it?

In light of the importance of the messengers alluded to in 1:2-3, it is surprising that Mark does not answer this question directly. The narrative moves abruptly from the promises and expectations to the ministry of John, suggesting without actually stating that John is the fulfillment of these hopes. If we look carefully at the relationship between those prophecies and John's ministry, however, we discover that this is not a foregone conclusion.

In Isaiah 40:3, for example, preparing the way of the Lord means building a highway in the wilderness for God to lead the exiles back from Babylon to rebuild Jerusalem. John was not building a highway, and the exiles had already returned. In fact, John did just the opposite. He called the residents of Jerusalem to come out of the city and return to the wilderness. Furthermore, the message of Isaiah 40:3 is, "In the desert prepare the way for the LORD." But in Mark 1:4 the words *in the desert* have been placed outside the quotation marks and reinterpreted to specify the locale of John's ministry. John was a voice *calling in the wilderness: "Prepare the way for the Lord."* He did not say: "In the desert prepare the way for the Lord." And even then John did not actually cry out: "Prepare the way for the Lord." He stood in the desert apart from the mainstream of first-century Jewish life and cried: "Repent."

What is the connection then between John and the conflation of prophecies in Mark 1:2-3? Three clues help us appreciate who John was and what he did. In the first place, John preached in the wilderness, and the reference to Isaiah 40:3 leads us to expect something to happen there. Second, John was a messenger. He announced the coming of someone who would do what no human being had done before: baptize people with the Holy Spirit. Both the messengers of Isaiah 40:3 and Malachi 3:1 were supposed to announce the coming of someone greater than themselves, although in both cases the one who would come after them was God. In Isaiah 40:1-11 God comes to reestablish his kingship over Israel. In Malachi 3:1 God comes to judge and purify the temple. Finally, the physical description of John bears some striking similarities to Elijah. John ate locusts and wild honey and wore clothing made of camel hair instead of the fine fabrics of the city. Like Elijah in 1 Kings 17:1-6 he was a man of the wilderness.

The context certainly suggests that John is the long-awaited messenger, but if we follow this line of thought, we need to be clear about where it leads. First, John the Baptist was fulfilling more than one role. Not only was he fulfilling the role of Elijah as prophesied in Malachi 3:1, he was also enacting the role of the messenger in Isaiah 40:1-11, a prophecy that had spawned a hope only partly realized. Second, as the messenger of Isaiah 40:1-11 his task was to prepare for the return of God's rule. How did he prepare the way of the Lord? It was not by building a highway in the desert, but by calling everyone to repent and be baptized. Third, as the messenger of Malachi 3:1 John was to announce that God was coming to judge and purify the temple. And if his mission failed, if the people turned insincerely or incompletely, then God had promised to strike the land with a curse in Malachi 4:5-6. John's ministry was beset by a cluster of awesome and disturbing possibilities.

We often say that when God acts in history the inspired writings that follow tell us what the events mean. In this case that relationship is more complex. After the disappointing results of the return from Babylon, the activity of God in the ministry of John the Baptist tells us how to read the prophecy of Isaiah 40:3. Eventually that reinterpretation itself became part of the inspired writings. So the relationship between God's Word and the events of history is more fluid and dynamic than we might like to contemplate, for it means that we must discern God's purpose not only in what we read but also in what we see God doing in our time. That thought invites the difficult question of whether we see God doing anything at all.

In this passage we find two themes in John's preaching. The first was forgiveness mediated through repentance. For John repentance was not a private matter; it was a public matter expressed through baptism in the Jordan River. The idea of being baptized for the forgiveness of sin is interesting on several counts. Since the exodus there had been ways by which the people of God could receive forgiveness, and at this time the avenues of forgiveness all led to the temple in Jerusalem. They were sanctioned by the Mosaic law, which had become the cornerstone of Judaism after the exile. John, however, had nothing to do with the temple at all. He was not a priest. He did not require sacrifices or sin offerings or prayers in the temple. He turned his back on the established institutions of religion and called the people of God to the desert, where he challenged them to do something that no leader of Israel had ever asked before: he summoned them to be baptized for the forgiveness of their sin.

How baptism came to be associated with the forgiveness of sins is problematic. It is suggested that the ceremonial washings of the Qumran community or the practice of baptizing Jewish proselytes might have served as a model for John's baptism (Oepke 1964:537). Although the possibility that John might have been influenced by these practices cannot be discounted, he does not appear to follow any precedent (Guelich 1989:17-18).

There is another possibility, if we use the word *baptism* as a guide. Perhaps it is not from the past but from the future that John derived his practice. That is to say, the origin of his baptism might not be found in what went before it, but in what followed. This at any rate is the way John seems to have understood things. His baptism was anticipatory. It was the forerunner of the baptism of the Holy Spirit. His practice of baptism was unique because of the singular character of the event to which it pointed.

This is the second great theme of John's preaching. Repentance and baptism for forgiveness of sins are strictly preliminary acts. They were the means by which people prepared for the coming of the *one more powerful than I, the thongs of whose sandals I am not worthy to stoop down and untie.* The person who was to come after John would do something that neither he nor any other human figure in Israel's history had been able to do: he would baptize with the Holy Spirit. The prophets, judges and occasionally the kings of Israel were people upon whom the Spirit of God rested briefly, but human beings were not agents through whom God's Spirit was given. The outpouring of the Spirit of God prophesied in Joel 2:28, for example, is something that God alone does. Previously, we might have assessed the strength of judges or the ministry of prophets by the amount of God's Spirit that they possessed. The one who came after John, however, would be distinguished not by the Spirit of God that he possessed, but by the Spirit of God that he bestowed.

It would be easy to underestimate the import of John's preaching. There was much more at stake than the personal piety of a few people or even a few thousand people. John's preaching and the response it drew shook the foundation of the nation. It raised the question whether the existing social order could survive. If God had opened a means of forgiveness that had nothing to do with the temple or priesthood, what was to become of the temple? If one had to come out of the cities to meet God, then what role would Jerusalem play in God's work in history? If baptism, which is not even mentioned in the Torah, was the new standard for repentance, what was the purpose of the law? In short, could the central institutions of Judaism survive the coming of the one who would baptize with the Holy Spirit?

In Hebrew and Aramaic the word *repent* simply means to "turn." Depending up the context it can mean "turn around," "turn away from" or "turn toward." In the opening verses of Mark, what does John's call to repent mean? It means to turn around and look for God in the desert. It means in some sense to turn away from a fixation with the temple and the law. And it means to turn in eager expectancy toward the baptism of the Holy Spirit, which the coming one would bring.

Having come this far, we should go on to ask a series of questions that cannot be answered at this point in our exploration of the Gospel of Mark. It would be unthinkable not to ask what the baptism of the Holy Spirit is, where and when it occurs, and how it takes place—for this experience and the encounter with the one who brings it is the whole point of John the Baptist's ministry. If, as most students of the New Testament think, Mark wrote the earliest Gospel, we cannot assume that the answer to this question is to be found in some later document. On the contrary, it is more logical to assume that the Evangelist intends for us to find answers to questions that his story prompts in what he wrote. At this point, though, it is not even clear what the baptism of the Holy Spirit is. This is one of the many places in the Gospel of Mark where we achieve the most clarity if we approach the text as though we were reading or hearing it for the first time. The best way to answer questions like these is to keep reading the Gospel, to look for places where Mark repeats words or themes related to this text and to discover his meaning inductively.

The Baptism of Jesus (1:9-11) Mark introduces Jesus in the same way he introduced John the Baptist. Jesus simply appears without fanfare, genealogy or credentials, and if there is some ambiguity about John's identity, there is also something of a mystery about who Jesus is. The earlier references to Isaiah 40:3 and Malachi 3:1 suggest that John

---

1:10 Unfortunately, the NIV obscures the connection between the baptism and the

was the messenger, yet both of those passages indicate that the messenger prepares the way for God. So, who is Jesus? Is he the one to whom the prophecies ultimately point? Is he another messenger or prophet? Or is he someone outside the realm of expectations delineated by Isaiah and Malachi?

The first clue appears in Mark 1:1, which identifies Jesus as *the Son of God*. A second one appears in 1:9-10 when Jesus was baptized and the Spirit descended on him *like a dove*. Except for John's prophecy in 1:8, this is the only place in this Gospel where the words *baptism* and *Spirit* appear in the same context. The baptism of Jesus is clearly connected with the Spirit of God, but the one thing that John prophesied about the one who was to come after him is never referred to again. Furthermore, in Mark no one other than Jesus seems to perceive what was happening. When the heavens opened, Jesus saw the Spirit descend, and the voice from heaven spoke to him personally without the slightest indication that John or anyone else heard it. This scene is the only connection between John's preaching and Jesus. Mark is content to leave his audience with several open questions: If Jesus is the one whom John expected, what is the baptism of the Holy Spirit, who receives it, and when does it take place? The juxtaposition of material is highly suggestive but not in itself conclusive. It is more an invitation than an emphatic declaration. In this respect Mark's presentation of Jesus is similar to the invitations to "come and see" in John 1:39, 46.

There is, on the other hand, a clear connection between Jesus and the prophecies of Isaiah. In the description of Jesus' baptism Mark uses an expression that appears in only one other place in the Bible: the verb "to tear open" also occurs in Isaiah 64:1, where the prophet calls upon God to rend the heavens and come down and rebuild a desolated kingdom. Isaiah 64 is an anguished plea for God to forgive the sins of the people of Judah, secure its prosperity and establish justice in the world.

The words that accompanied the descent of the dove are actually a collection of texts from the Psalms, the book of Genesis and the later part of Isaiah. They contain three striking statements: (1) *You are my*

---

temptation by choosing not to translate the Greek word *euthys,* which is often translated "immediately."

Son, (2) *whom I love,* and (3) *with you I am well pleased.* The affirmation *You are my Son* comes from Psalm 2:7, an enthronement psalm or hymn used in Israel at religious ceremonies whose highpoint was the ascension of the king to his throne. The coronation of a new king would have been an occasion on which this psalm would have been used. These words point to Jesus as the one through whom God's reign would be established.

Second, Jesus is the one whom God loves. Other translations use the single word *beloved,* and it is easier to see the connection to Genesis 22:2 if we use that expression here. In that passage God told Abraham to take his only son, the beloved, to Mount Moriah to offer as a sacrifice. On various occasions in the Old Testament other people are referred to as those whom God loved: David is identified as the king whom God loves forever (Ps 89:28, 33), and the nation of Israel is called God's beloved (Jer 12:7; Hos 11:1). In texts like these we find a cluster of themes related to love, covenant, faithfulness, promise and restoration. These same themes are interwoven throughout the story of Isaac and Abraham on Mount Moriah. The designation of Jesus as God's beloved evokes all these themes. It presents Jesus as the one through whom God's promises would be fulfilled. It affirms that God would be faithful to him, and without specifying a role it suggests that Jesus would have something essential to do with God's covenant.

The final affirmation from heaven is drawn from another set of texts. The phrase *with you I am well pleased* comes from the description of God's servant in Isaiah 42:1. Again several people in the Old Testament are referred to as the servant of the Lord: David (Is 37:35), Daniel (Dan 6:20), and Moses (2 Chron 1:3). One of the most interesting occurrences of this term is the designation of King Nebuchadnezzar of Babylon as God's servant (Jer 27:6; 43:10).

In this case something even more amazing transpires, for the words *with you I am well pleased* have a very precise application. They refer initially not to any servant of God, but to the suffering ser-

---

1:11 That Jesus fulfilled the role of the suffering servant has long been a staple of Christian theology. Recently, though, some Christian voices have raised anew the

vant portrayed in Isaiah 40—55, who brings justice to the nations. According to Isaiah 43:10 the suffering servant is none other than the nation of Israel. In Mark 1:11, however, the suffering servant is not the nation of Israel, but Jesus. The application of this language to Jesus means that God has designated him as the one who would fulfill the role that had first been given to Israel. This is the second place in the opening scenes of Mark where something that God does reinterprets what God said years before.

Mark begins with a conflated prophecy that frames the history of Israel. In the sweep of events from the exodus to the return of the exiles one theme is given particular prominence: the picture of God coming to save the people who have suffered judgment, drawn from Isaiah 40:3. The voice from heaven also employed a conflation of three texts whose themes are the rule of God, covenant and redemptive suffering. Each of these themes is well attested in biblical and intertestamental literature. What is new here is the implied connection between the coming of God's reign and redemptive suffering. Mark does not at this point spell out what sort of relationship he sees between Psalm 2:7, Genesis 22:2 and Isaiah 42:1 except for his applying all three texts to Jesus. How these themes relate to each other will be developed as the story unfolds. It is enough for now to observe that these are the opening themes of the Gospel, to become alert to stories where they reappear and to recognize the prominence of Isaiah in the development of Mark's theology. A good case can be made for treating the prophecies of Isaiah as the lens through which Mark views the saving acts of God in history.

In the first eleven verses of Mark then we encounter two almost contradictory ways of telling a story. At several points Mark is content to suggest who Jesus and John are by the way he edits and arranges the material he has received. At other points, though, he is direct. Yet even when the voice from heaven affirmed Jesus' identity it is not clear that anyone else heard what was said. Two implications may be drawn from these narrative techniques. Mark is, first of all, convinced that God speaks and acts in history, and he expects his audience to decide

---

question whether the continued suffering of the Jewish people still plays a role in God's redemptive plan (Soulen 1996:151).

what to do with what it sees and hears. Mark has highlighted a profound set of dreams and promises and set them next to the ministry of John the Baptist and the appearance of Jesus. On the evidence of Mark 1:1-11 it might not be too difficult to define the broad outlines of meaning that the Evangelist saw here. And yet we need to remember that Mark does not tell us what it all means. He shows us the material and invites us to decide for ourselves.

Second, although Mark places the audience in the role of interpreter, reading and hearing the Gospel is not a simple exercise of subjectivity. What we might make of this story is clearly important, but the story is also clearly bigger than its audience. Profound changes were in the making, and those changes were not limited to what we might think they mean. Mark leaves it to us to work out who Jesus and John were, but the heavens have been torn open and God has spoken. Even if the other characters in the story did not hear the voice, Mark's audience does. Even if the reader glosses over the allusions to the Law, the Writings and the Prophets, they remain subtly woven into the story line. They point backward to promises God has made and forward to their fulfillment. In the end Mark does not invite us to decide what the Gospel means, but to find our place in the unfolding good news. The Gospel of Mark is not the unsophisticated story it is sometimes mistaken to be. Its message is complex and nuanced. It addresses the deepest human needs and beckons us to follow a little bit further along.

The Temptation of Jesus (1:12-13) Sometimes through either familiarity or carelessness we read parts of the Bible without realizing what they actually say. This is one of those passages. Mark recounts Jesus' temptation with such brevity that we are likely to overlook what is missing. There is no indication of the issues involved in this confrontation with Satan, nor does Mark tell us how Jesus fared. Mark records only that the Spirit sent Jesus out, that he was in the wilderness forty days tempted by Satan, that he was with wild animals and that angels attended him.

1:12 The word *euthys* translated "at once" is a very important element of the narrative structure of Mark, a point that the NIV obscures by translating it variously: "without delay," "just then," "quickly" and "as soon as" within the space of the next fifteen verses. The NIV also omits the word entirely in its rendering of 1:10, where the word appears for the first time.

It is difficult to imagine that the story of Jesus' temptation circulated in the early church without some resolution of the conflict between Jesus and Satan, so it is more likely that Mark chose to omit whatever ending he found in the material he had before him. We cannot help but wonder why Mark left this out. At this point there are two pertinent observations. First, telling the story in this way keeps the audience in suspense. We expect to find a resolution somewhere, and that expectation prompts us to read the rest of the Gospel more carefully.

Second, in Mark we know so little about the temptation that 1:12-13 cannot stand as an independent episode. These verses are presented as the continuation of the story of Jesus' baptism. There is no break between these two events, which are closely connected by the word *euthys* in 1:10 and 1:12. In this case the separation of 1:12-13 as a discrete paragraph was an editorial decision made by someone who thought he or she was reading one of the other Gospels. Without a resolution the temptation appears simply as the consequence of Jesus' baptism. That may be the most important inference we can draw from the way Mark presents the temptation. Mark is concerned primarily to show the connection between the baptism of the Holy Spirit and Jesus' encounter with Satan. What matters most is not that we know how Jesus fared, but that we see that the baptism of the Holy Spirit led to a confrontation with the forces of evil.

The Spirit of God drove Jesus into the desert, and the Greek word translated "sent out" is a particularly forceful term. It appears most often in reports of the exorcisms that Jesus performed, where it is translated "cast out." Jesus' venture into the wilderness is described almost as though it were an expulsion. In this regard there is an interesting ambiguity about the word translated "desert," which can refer to a place of solitude, a place away from the cities and towns, or a dry wasteland. John baptized in a place far enough away from the cities to be called a desert, but near enough so that crowds of people could move back and forth without much apparent discomfort. Mark 1:5 depicts a massive

---

1:13 The verb *attend*, which the NIV translates "serve" in 10:45 or "care for his needs" in 15:41, is a highly significant term in this Gospel. Since Jesus was fasting, it may be best to take the word *angel* in the sense of "messenger" and see the angels as attending Jesus by sustaining him with God's word.

movement of people that would have been impossible without reliable sources of food and water and probably without secure means of passage. The Spirit drove Jesus out beyond the kind of place where John ministered to a place where he was alone except for the angels who attended him and the wild animals. There he was tempted by Satan.

Mark's inclusion of *wild animals* in the temptation story is variously explained as an allusion to Jesus as the second Adam (Waetjen 1989:75-76) or to the persecution that Christians in Rome experienced during Nero's reign (Best 1965:8-9). Such interpretations should be regarded cautiously. While they are not implausible in themselves, there is little, if anything, in the rest of this Gospel to support them. The presentation of Jesus as the second Adam is a prominent theme in Luke, but there is no explicit depiction of Jesus in these terms in Mark. Furthermore, the wild animals appear only in this passage. They are not mentioned in the apocalyptic discourse of Mark 13 at all, where the testing of Jesus' disciples is a central theme. On balance, it is better to take this reference as an indication that Jesus was alone, a theme that comes to a climax during the crucifixion. Except for the presence of the angels and wild animals Jesus was alone in his temptation (Lane 1974:61). There was no human comfort or support, and in that loneliness he was tempted by Satan.

This description leads to another measurement of the difference between John and Jesus. As a wilderness figure, John challenged the fundamental structures of first-century Judea. Despite whatever was wrong with them, however, Jesus came to confront something more fundamental. This temptation not only distinguishes Jesus from John. It also defines the scope of his ministry. He would not be dealing with a set of concerns that pertained only to the people of Judah. He had come to confront evil in all its forms.

We hear a great deal today from preachers who insist that having the Holy Spirit is the key to getting what we want out of life. In fact, unless you are especially adept at manipulating your remote control, you cannot avoid hearing something about the gospel of health and wealth. It is standard fare on most of the Christian television channels. There are indications that Christians in the early church believed that their faith would shield them from suffering and help them acquire the things they most wanted (Martin 1972:117-20). Mark's presentation of

Jesus' baptism and temptation does not offer any encouragement to advocates of a "me-first" Christianity. Marks draws too strong a connection between the baptism of the Spirit and the confrontation with evil for anyone to be glib about having the Holy Spirit.

The Gospel Jesus Proclaimed (1:14-15) The kingdom of God is an expression that embodied the hopes of the Jewish people that God would one day remove all evil from the world and inaugurate a new, unprecedented age of blessing, prosperity and joy. This hope was nourished by a number of important Old Testament texts, and it touched every area of life. It was spiritual because the power of sin would be destroyed and Yahweh would be universally worshiped as the one true God (Is 11:9). It was political in that God's people would be released from the power of the various Gentile governments that had afflicted them with so much suffering through the course of history (Dan 7:13-14, 22, 25). War and the lust for power would be replaced by the politics of peace (Is 9:7). It was an economic hope because the new world would know nothing of poverty, hunger, famine or deprivation (Is 32:1-8; 35:1-2). The world would be so transformed that children could play safely with lions, bears and poisonous snakes (Is 11:6-8). The kingdom of God expresses the hope for a world in which the powers of sin, death and darkness are replaced by peace, justice and the worship of the one true God. In essence, it is the hope that the rule of God would be restored over all of creation.

Yet here at the beginning of Jesus' ministry we encounter a disturbing paradox. If, as Jesus proclaimed, the kingdom of God is near, how is it that John the Baptist, who appeared as the herald of Jesus' message, was arrested and eventually put to death? According to Mark 1:14 it was not the forty days in the wilderness, but John's arrest that marked the start of Jesus' ministry. If the rule of God were about to be restored over creation, we would expect things to work out differently.

The Greek verb translated "is near" can mean either "has arrived" or "has almost arrived." Since either translation is possible, we must look at the context for clues that point to Mark's meaning. The first one is found in Jesus' announcement that the time has come (or is fulfilled). The time that is fulfilled is the time of waiting, and this observation implies that the kingdom of God is actually here (Beasley-Murray 1986:73). If the kingdom were not here, the time of waiting would not be over.

On the other hand, John's arrest is a precursor of Jesus' death. That is to say, if the kingdom of God is really present, how is it possible that innocent people still suffer and die? This observation suggests that the kingdom is either not present or not completely present. If we take both statements seriously, that is, without allowing either one to negate the other, then we arrive at the conclusion that the kingdom of God has actually come into history, although we are still waiting for its complete realization (Schnackenburg 1971:141-42). As we look more closely in the following sections at Jesus' ministry, we will try to figure out inductively what it means to affirm that the kingdom of God is actually, though not completely, here.

For this reason Jesus called people to repent and believe. John had called people to embrace the new thing God was doing. With Jesus, embracing this new thing becomes even more complex for he invites us to turn away from our expectations about how the rule of God comes. Believing the gospel means affirming what God does, particularly when our expectations are not met. There is a fundamental tension between the hopes that Jesus' ministry generated and the course of events as they unfolded according to God's will. The need for repentance did not disappear when John's ministry came to an end. On the contrary, the call to repent and believe was essential to Jesus' ministry.

Repenting and believing are as important for Jesus' modern followers as they were for his first ones. Jesus' gospel was not packaged into a personal version for those who seek inner peace and a social version for those who want to change the world. In Mark the personal and social dimensions of the gospel are inseparable. The kingdom of God addresses us personally, just as it addresses the structures of our life together. Picking and choosing the aspects of the gospel we like is a matter for repentance, just as embracing those aspects of the gospel that make us anxious is a matter for faith.

An Exposition of Authority (1:16-39) In the fall of 1989 a stunning series of events transformed Central and Eastern Europe. The Communist Party ended its persecution of Solidarity, and Poland became the first multiparty country in the Warsaw Pact. Czechoslovakia quickly followed suit, and the hopes for freedom that had been so brutally crushed by Russian tanks in 1968 suddenly blossomed into a democratically elected government. Then the Berlin Wall fell. Erich Honecker, the ironfisted leader of East Germany, was arrested and charged with corruption. And in Romania after government security forces had slaughtered an estimated ten thousand unarmed demonstrators, that country's former dictator Nicolae Ceausescu was executed with his wife on Christmas Day.

Many people on both sides of the Iron Curtain had long hoped to witness the collapse of communism. Yet the collapse of communism came as a surprise despite a vast array of spies and electronic surveillance systems. The victory celebrations in the West, however, were muted as states like California struggled to recover from the impact of drastically reduced spending for national defense. Then the euphoria in the East turned quickly into confusion as the level of unemployment quickly rose above thirty percent in many places, and the liberated peoples struggled to adjust to life in a free-market economy. It was an exceptional period of history when extraordinary events moved ahead with their own momentum.

Jesus Calls Four Disciples (1:16-20) What kind of time was Jesus talking about when he traveled through Galilee proclaiming that *the time has come* (1:15)? Even a casual reading of 1:16-34 demonstrates the Evangelist's concern with time. Expressions like *at once* (1:18), *without delay* (1:20), *just then* (1:23), *quickly* (1:28) and *as soon as* (1:29) appear with surprising frequency. The effect is even more pronounced in Greek, because these terms are all translations of the same word: *euthys*. In fact, it appears so often that the NIV translators chose to omit it entirely on two occasions: once in 1:21, where the text could read "immediately on the Sabbath," and again in 1:30, where the text could read "and they told him about her at once."

What kind of immediately is this? Is it a time of urgency, emergency or crisis? What energy drives this new sense of time? In each case this new sense of time is connected with something Jesus says or does. In 1:16-20, for example, Jesus appeared unannounced and called Simon and Andrew who followed him immediately. Then Jesus saw two other fishermen, James and John, whom he immediately called. Few other details of these encounters are evident. We can deduce, for example, that Simon and Andrew worked without benefit of a boat, standing in the shoals and casting their nets in the shallow waters (Waetjen 1989:79). James and John, on the other hand, were part of a family business that owned a boat. They worked with their father, Zebedee. Nothing here indicates that Jesus had any prior contact with these people or that they knew anything about him. In the Gospel of John several men who eventually follow Jesus are either in the company of John the Baptist or are introduced to Jesus before they become his disciples. Mark, on the other hand, describes only a Judean ministry for John the Baptist, and there is no indication that these four Galilean fishermen had encountered either him or Jesus before they were called.

Furthermore, Jesus did not invite the four fishermen to follow him. The words "come, follow me" are in the imperative mood. It was a command, and the four men reacted as though they had been issued orders by a superior officer. Where they were going is not clear at this point, nor is it clear what they would be doing. Jesus had said only that he would make them fishers of men, a metaphor that is difficult to define with precision. In a poetic depiction of judgment Habakkuk 1:14-15 compares people to fish caught in nets. It is certainly possible that Jesus was calling Simon and Andrew to play a role in preparing for the judgment at the end of this age when the kingdom of God arrives in all its fullness, but at this point it is difficult to be certain. In the early chapters of Mark forgiveness is a more prominent theme than judgment.

Only two things are clear from this account. If we cannot say where Jesus would take the four men, we do know something about what they left. One pair of brothers, Peter and Andrew, walked away from their nets and at least temporarily from positions at the low end of the socioeconomic scale. The other two brothers left a boat, their father and the family business. It is as though the encounter between Jesus and the four fishermen had been pared down to make a single impression: the person who spoke was a figure of enormous authority.

Here is at least a partial answer to the question about what kind of time this is. It is a time when someone exercised an awesome authority. If we ask where this authority came from, we can follow the word *euthys* back to its first occurrence in 1:10, when Jesus came up from the water and immediately saw heaven being torn open and the Spirit descending on him like a dove. Things happened immediately around Jesus because he was empowered by the Spirit of God.

Mark portrays Jesus as someone vested with the authority to make tremendous demands upon people, who so far respond as though they recognize implicitly Jesus' right to do this. In the context of Jewish expectations about the duties of sons and the authority of fathers, we have to wonder whether becoming a disciple of Jesus might not have been viewed as a violation of the commandment to honor father and mother (Ex 20:12). There is no indication that Jesus consulted Zebedee or any other member of the families of these four. He simply spoke and Zebedee's sons followed him.

On the other hand, these four fishermen did exactly what Jesus expected people to do when they heard the gospel: repent and believe. When they left their boats and careers, they repented in a profound way, for repentance is not essentially a matter of ceasing to commit a particular sin. The fundamental meaning of repentance is to turn away from what we are doing and embrace what God is doing wholeheartedly. That is exactly what Simon, Andrew, James and John did. When they acknowledged Jesus' authority, they acted with faith. They put their futures and the livelihood of their families in his hands.

Jesus in the Synagogue (1:21-28) The exposition of Jesus' authority continues in the account of his teaching in the synagogue. Although we are told repeatedly in this passage that Jesus taught in the synagogue, there is not very much here to help us understand what he said apart from the introductory comment of 1:14-15. As in 1:16-20, the narrative is abbreviated so that the reader receives only a single impression—that Jesus taught with authority.

At first glance, the statement that he taught with authority might be taken as a description of his style. It could be a way of saying that Jesus was a dynamic and compelling speaker. As the story unfolds, though, it is not the way he spoke that is important; it is what happens when he taught. In this instance his presence provoked a confrontation with the demonic. Jesus cast the evil spirit out, and with an appalling convulsion the evil spirit obeyed him. After the exorcism Mark repeats the reference to Jesus' amazing authority. Jesus' teaching was much more than a collection of novel or encouraging ideas. It was an exercise of power. The powers of darkness perceived in his teaching a challenge to their dominion. The authority of Jesus was displayed as those powers were first silenced and then banished. What distinguishes Jesus' teaching is this combination of word and event, something which becomes an increasingly important theme as Mark's account of the gospel proceeds.

A second important theme also appears in this passage for the first time. During the exorcism Jesus ordered the evil spirit to be silent. All the exorcisms that Mark describes are characterized both by unwelcome declarations that the demonic powers make and by Jesus' commands for them to be silent. Ever since William Wrede's study of Mark at the beginning of the twentieth century, scholars have associated several distinctive features of this Gospel with the idea of secrecy. Among those features are the parables, various commands for the observers of other miracles to be silent and Jesus' rebuke of Peter in 8:33. Wrede found no credible evidence in the gospel traditions that Jesus had used the term *Messiah* about himself. The various secrecy themes, Wrede argued, were attempts to read back into the gospel stories an identity that Jesus had not claimed, but which the church nevertheless believed to be true.

There is much to be said for interpreting these expressions of secrecy together, but Wrede's theory is not convincing. The major difficulty is the two points in the passion story where Jesus' messianic identity is explicitly affirmed: once on Jesus' lips in the trial before the Sanhedrin (14:62) and again on the sign that hung on his cross (15:26). On Wrede's reading both affirmations would have to be late insertions made by the early church. How late they were is not the point. The difficult point for Wrede's thesis is the assertion that they would have been made at all. If those parts of the passion story were insertions, then the gospel traditions were either so poorly remembered or so poorly formed that there would have been no need to elaborate a complex set of secrecy motives. If the living memory of the early church was so easily shaped that some editor could simply put words like that in Jesus' mouth, no Markan subterfuge would have been required. Wrede's messianic secret is an overly complicated solution for a simple problem. The explanation for the secrecy themes must be sought elsewhere.

Jesus' preaching and teaching were not inspirational in the typical sense of that word. He did not dispense hopeful thoughts. His sermons and teachings were expositions of power. They were confrontational, and when he spoke, something happened. Contemporary preachers might do well to reflect on Mark's portrayal of Jesus. There is nothing wrong at all with words of encouragement. Hope is a fragile thing for some people, and the gospel is surely a message of hope. Yet sermons devoid of any call for change fall short of the model of Jesus. The kingdom of God is not a prop for the status quo; it is the power of God at work in history to bring wholeness and healing to people and the structures of power and culture in which they live. An often told story about eighteenth-century evangelist George Whitefield reflects this perspective on preaching. Whitefield was an amazingly popular preacher who spoke to crowds of thousands of people, frequently in open fields. At one point when Whitefield was asked how he knew if he had preached a good sermon, he replied that it was easy—either someone got saved or someone got angry. That is not a bad description of what happens when Jesus preaches in this Gospel.

Jesus Heals on the Sabbath and Afterward (1:29-34) The healing of Simon's mother-in-law opens several new perspectives on Jesus' authority. On the one hand, this miracle demonstrates his authority over disease, and since Simon's mother-in-law was the beneficiary of his power to heal, this story suggests that Jesus did not exercise his authority capriciously. That is to say, he did not call the fishermen to repent and believe without any regard for the people to whom they were bound. In this incident Jesus solved a problem that might have remained unsolved if he had not appeared on the scene. If Peter had stayed with his nets, he could not have solved it himself. As the story unfolds, Simon's mother-in-law was the first of many people about whom he presumably cared and whom Jesus healed. On the other hand, however, the inhabitants of Capernaum are portrayed in a curious hesitation. With the single exception of Peter's household the villagers did not bring their sick ones to Jesus until sundown, well after the conclusion of services in the synagogue and apparently some time after word had spread about this extraordinary healing. Why did they wait?

Mark makes a point of assuring his audience that the sun had set (1:32). Sundown signified the end of the Sabbath and the beginning of a new day. Unlike people of the modern world, Peter's contemporaries used sundown to demarcate one day from its successor. It seems that the good people of Capernaum felt that it was inappropriate for them to bring their sick friends and relatives to Jesus before the Sabbath had ended. Precisely why they were concerned is not evident. The Sabbath controversies that figure so prominently in 2:18—3:6 have not yet materialized. Still, there is a discernible tension between the old ways of life that are regulated by the Sabbath and the presence of Jesus through whom things happen immediately, without regard for the rhythm of the week. We should not overlook that in the Gospel of Mark Jesus performed his first two miracles immediately on the Sabbath.

Is it by accident that this impressive demonstration of Jesus' authority is set against the backdrop of the Sabbath? In all probability these miracles were already connected with the Sabbath well before Mark wrote (Guelich 1989:120). They belong to an early part of the Christian tradition. Nevertheless, there is a striking similarity between this embryonic conflict and the tension that has already surfaced between John the Baptist and the leaders of first-century Judaism (1:4-8). Taken together with Jesus' call to repent and believe, these two early antitheses raise the question whether the power that Jesus brings into the world is compatible with the existing structures and institutions of Judaism. Or to pose the question in the sharpest possible terms, is it possible that the authority of Jesus, so impressively displayed on the Sabbath, comes from the same God who created the Sabbath and made it holy? Is the God who created the Sabbath for rest, recreation and worship also the one who is at work so immediately in Jesus?

Jesus' Agenda (1:35-39) In this developing portrait of Jesus' authority we find a new and perhaps surprising note. Jesus rose very early the next morning to find a place to be alone and pray. The juxtaposition of Jesus' praying and exercising power is particularly interesting. In our world prayer is often neglected by active people who are simply too busy. It sometimes seems that the people who get things done and the people who pray belong in two different groups. Furthermore, I have to admit that I am more likely to get up early to pray *before* I undertake a formidable task, rather than *after* it has come to a successful conclusion. Here, however, the busiest person—the one who has already accomplished incredible things—got up before dawn to pray.

There is not very much here to indicate what Jesus was praying about. No words from his prayer have been handed down to us. The text simply sets his desire to be alone and pray against the desire of the villagers to find him and presumably experience again some display of his power. The only pointer to a larger meaning is the phrase *a solitary place* (1:35).

Behind this English expression is the same Greek word translated desert in the brief account of the temptation (1:12). As we have seen, Mark's account of the temptation is striking on two counts: it tells neither how Jesus was tempted nor how he fared. One explanation for this curiosity is that Mark wanted his readers to see the temptation as something that continued throughout Jesus' ministry (Mauser 1963:100). And on this reading when Mark places Jesus in the desert, the wilderness or a solitary place (all of which translate the same Greek word), he may be telling us something about the ways in which Jesus was tempted.

If that is so here, we do not have to look far to discover what is at stake. We might state the issue like this: should the expectations of the people of Capernaum form the framework for the exercise of Jesus' authority, or should he act according to some other set of priorities? That Jesus prayed at this point indicates that he is committed to letting God set his agenda. So at the end of his prayer when there were still people to be healed, he explained why he had come out: *Let us go somewhere else . . . so I can preach there also (1:38).*

As brief as it is, this picture of Jesus at prayer is very instructive. Every person has some measure of power. The fundamental issue is not how we can obtain more, but how we use what we have. Praying as Jesus did is a tremendous statement about power. In God's original design we were created to exercise authority as stewards. Whether we pray about the things that are within our power to do reveals a great deal about us. In this sense we might even speak of prayer as a barometer of faith. In prayer we submit our will to God's. If we do not pray, it is quite possible that we are operating on our own agenda and have refused our proper role as stewards.

This section draws to a close with a brief summary: *So he traveled throughout Galilee, preaching in their synagogues and driving out demons* (1:39). This is the second time in two verses that Mark emphasizes Jesus' preaching mission. Yet except for the brief outline of his message in 1:15, we do not have a sample of his preaching. In fact, it is not until the beginning of Mark 4 that Mark lets Jesus speak long enough to give us anything like a sermon. Is it not strange to find this insistence on the importance of preaching and then to observe Jesus doing everything except preaching?

Could it be that Mark intends to tell us what Jesus preached by showing us what he did? Could these miracle stories also be sermons? There is a very good reason for thinking that this is actually so, for the one sample of Jesus' preaching that we have announces that the time has come and that the kingdom of God is near. We have already seen that the way in which the stories in 1:16-39 are told reflects the first theme. These events are connected in a rapid-fire narrative that indicates that the time has come for something new.

In a similar way the stories also demonstrate that the kingdom of God is near. They show the power of the kingdom making its presence felt in the world. It makes new demands on people. It comes against the powers of evil, and it frees people from illness. In a remarkable way this is the climax of the initial exposition of Jesus' authority. In the interplay between what Jesus proclaims and what he does, we see an awesome demonstration of power: what he proclaims happens, and it happens immediately.

Here we find the key to understanding the role of miracles in the Gospel of Mark. They are his words taking shape among the historical, social, spiritual and political forces that shape the world. They are sermons that become events. In one way or another they are all expressions of his fundamental proclamation that the kingdom of God is near. Without the miracles his preaching would be another collection of encouraging words, suitable perhaps for greeting cards or occasions when something inspirational needed to be said. But Jesus did not come to offer the world an anthology of inspirational sentiment. He came with a message of power, and that power is displayed in the miracles. For this reason his words and actions are inseparable.

For much of the last one hundred years we have made the mistake of playing Jesus' words against his deeds. We have in the church today people who do not think miracles happen anymore, as well as people who think they never did. We have Christians who think his acts of compassion are all that matter and people who think his teaching is the only thing that mattered. Yet the good news that the kingdom of God is near was fundamental to everything Jesus did and said. If, after all, none of this happened, then his words are just that—so many words. On the other hand, if these things really happened, then we may be living in a time we do not understand.

Three Healings (1:40—2:17) One morning an elderly man walked into my office and wrote out a check for one thousand dollars. He handed it to me and said, "I simply want to thank the church. You were very kind to my son." Then he turned to leave. I had no idea what he was talking about, so I asked him to stay and tell me about his son. He spoke with great difficulty about the son he had buried the week before. His son had died of AIDS. The family had not been present when he died. In fact there had not been any communication between the rest of the family and the son for several years, even though they all lived in the same city. The family had learned of the death of the son from two members of our church who had visited him daily for the last three months of his life to feed, bathe and do household chores for him.

Jesus and the Leper (1:40-45) By all the canons of common sense the encounter between Jesus and the leper should not have happened. In fact, it was not just a matter of common sense. The law of Moses forbids it. The leper was unclean, and he made everything he touched unclean. There were, of course, many things that could make a person unclean, but the laws regarding the range of skin diseases that are categorized as leprosy are particularly harsh. Leprosy was considered to be highly contagious and usually incurable. Lepers had to live away from clean people, and a natural home for them was the garbage dumps of the ancient world, where they could eke out a meager living. By the first century they were required to wear bells around the necks. If someone approached them on the road, they were required to call out, *Unclean! Unclean!* at the top of their voices so that no one would make contact with them accidentally (Lev 13:45). This leper broke the law to approach Jesus.

Leprosy cut its victims off from members of their own family. It also cut them off from the community of faith. Unclean people could not enter the temple or synagogue to worship or offer sacrifices (2 Chron 26:21). These harsh measures nevertheless had some justification in that they protected the health of the larger community. And yet it is the epitome of alienation in a religious community for people to find themselves in a position where they must break the law of God to get help.

There are no tinkling bells in this story, no cries of unclean, no furtive stepping away. The leper said, If you are willing, you can make me clean. He did not question Jesus' power, but he had no way of gauging how the healer would receive him. Under the law of Moses, Jesus might very well have rebuked him and walked away in anger. In fact, that is probably what Jesus should have done if he had belonged to any of the major religious parties of first-century Judaism. The question was whether Jesus would step outside the provisions of the law to help him.

The implications of the leper's question, however, take us much further than that. This desperate man wanted Jesus to heal him of his disease and free him from its awful consequences. The leper wanted to be restored, and that was the province of the temple priests. By observing the stipulations and rituals of the law, a priest could declare someone clean. Yet Jesus was not a priest, had no particular standing in the temple and was operating outside the guidelines of the law. For Jesus to heal the leper on these terms is to put himself above the law and priests.

1:41 An interesting textual variant states that Jesus was not moved by compassion but by anger to heal the leper, leaving open the question of what he might have been angry about (Martin 1972:121; Taylor 1974:87).

1:44 It is possible to translate the last words differently. Instead of *as a testimony to*

Jesus not only healed the leper. He stretched out his hand and touched him. If the leper should not have approached Jesus, Jesus should not have touched him either. Even looking at life from a modern perspective, we know what happens when something clean touches something unclean: both come away dirty. This time, however, both came away clean, although that was too big a leap for the people of Galilee to make in one bound. As the account of this healing spread, Jesus could not openly enter a town. It is hard to tell exactly what happened. We do know that the leper failed to present himself to a priest, as Jesus had instructed him (1:44-45). We do not know, however, whether the leper punctuated the report he spread around with the statement, "He touched me," or whether he said something like, "Jesus made me clean, and I don't need a priest." In either case the consequences for Jesus were striking. Because of the misperception that he was unclean, he could not enter the places where clean people lived (Lane 1974:87).

Here we must disagree with the Jesus Seminar, which dismisses this account as a late creation of the church on the grounds that it "belongs to the narrative strategy of Mark, but it has no basis in Jesus' life or thought" (Funk et al. 1993:43). This so-called strategy is the theory of a messianic secret devised to answer the question why people did not recognize Jesus as the Messiah while he was alive. Even in this one story, however, the theory has some obvious weak points. In the first place the secret was not kept. The leper ignored Jesus' instructions and spread the news. As soon as the secrecy motif is introduced, Mark records that the leper defied Jesus' instructions and told everyone he met. For that reason Jesus could not openly enter a town. He had touched a leper, and in the calculus of Jewish purity codes Jesus himself had become unclean. The instructions to keep silent make perfectly good sense on their own. The theory of a messianic secret read back into the accounts of Jesus' ministry makes absolutely no sense as a narrative strategy in this account. It falls apart before the story ends.

them we might read "as a testimony against them," giving the story a very different character. The later reading underscores Jesus' escalating confrontation with the law. There is some ambiguity here, but in most cases where it occurs the underlying Greek construction usually means "to them."

Second, there is nothing specifically messianic about this incident. In contrast to the exorcisms, no voice cried out to reveal Jesus' identity, nor was there any particular expectation that the Messiah would heal lepers. Furthermore, given Mark's portrayal of the ministry of John the Baptist outside the structures of the temple and the growing tension between Jesus and the law, it is more likely that 1:44 was part of the tradition Mark received. It is improbable that he created it (Guelich 1989:75-76).

The healing of the leper is laced with tremendous irony, and this irony suggests a different way to understand the theme of secrecy. Normally, when something clean touches something unclean both are rendered dirty. Even today it is common sense not to let something clean come in contact with something dirty. I have, for example, a self-imposed rule for bringing clothes home from the cleaners: I do not allow the clothes to touch the outside of my car. That entire set of expectations in the ancient and modern worlds is overturned here. When Jesus touched the leper, the leper became clean. For perhaps the first time in history someone who was clean touched someone who was unclean, and both came away clean.

This is the second account of a miracle in which the theme of secrecy occurs together with a clash of values. The first one was the exorcism in the synagogue, which was followed by a number of healings after the Sabbath had ended (1:29-34). The picture of a man with an unclean spirit disrupting worship in the synagogue is rife with irony. And the sick people who delayed approaching Jesus acted upon another set of values that were curiously at odds with his ability to heal. In neither of these accounts did the command to be silent keep the word about Jesus from spreading. As the news about Jesus spread, the tension between his authority and the traditions of the people increased. This connection between secrecy and irony characterizes most, if not all, of the miracle stories in this Gospel. As we proceed through the text, we will explore the possibilities it presents.

One more thing can be said about this healing. In a very real sense the leper is a model of repentance. That is not to suggest that his leprosy was the consequence of some sin. Rather, the leper symbolizes our alienation from God. Here is a person who could not even enter

God's house. He was thoroughly ostracized. Within the prescriptions of the law there was nothing he could do to make himself acceptable. His only hope was expressed in the plea, *If you are willing*. This is true repentance—not simply a change of thought or affection, but an unqualified turning to ask if we can be made clean. Ultimately, there is no other basis on which we can approach God.

Jesus and the Paralytic (2:1-12) In the ancient world, poverty and disease went hand in hand. Beggars were often disabled or chronically ill. It is not clear that the man whose friends carried him to Jesus on a mat was a beggar, but the picture Mark draws is reminiscent of street scenes from around the globe today. Our world is not immune to the numbing cycle of poverty and illness, and there are some signs that the circle is widening. In the richest nation in the modern world many people live without health insurance of any kind. To no one's surprise those people come from the poorer segment of American society. Whether we have become a kinder and gentler world is an open question.

In the folk traditions of first-century Galilee one other feature of human life was closely associated with disease: sin. Many of the people listening to Jesus preach in that house would have assumed that the man who lay on the mat had committed a sin for which God had judged him. This account begins, however, on a different note. It was not the man's sin that prompted Jesus to act but the faith of his four friends.

They came because Jesus was preaching about the kingdom of God, and whenever he preached, the kingdom of God drew near: lepers were made clean, the sick were healed, the powers of darkness fled, and ordinary people found new direction for their lives. It is obvious from the intrusive behavior of these four men that they expected something powerful to happen when Jesus preached, which was exactly what he was doing when they began to tear the roof apart.

As compelling as it might have seemed to the paralytic, however, the experience of walking on two legs would not have prepared him for the kingdom of God. His healing would have been another sign that the rule of God had come near, but how near it would come to him was an open question. People who walk on two legs can do some very evil things. If the kingdom of God implies a world released from the grip of evil, how could the paralytic, or anyone else for that matter, qualify for admission? Surely one of the lessons of the last one hundred years is the enormous capacity we have for doing evil. How could we exist in a world of undiminished good?

It may seem as though Jesus' declaration that the paralytic's sins were forgiven is an abrupt departure from the developing line of this story. Ever since Bultmann's *History of the Synoptic Tradition,* many New Testament scholars have viewed the story of the paralytic as the product of two separate traditions that were clumsily pasted together (1972:331). At some point, the argument runs, a miracle story became entwined with another story about Jesus' forgiving sins, producing what appears to some commentators as an awkward, disjointed account. This assessment, however, overlooks the way the Evangelist uses the miracles as enacted sermons and ignores the content of Jesus' preaching.

When Jesus said, *Son, your sins are forgiven,* he gave the man on the mat the key to entering a world that was bigger than the world where everyone else walked, earned a living and held a place of some respect in the social order. Jesus qualified him for the rule of God. The very first step in dealing with our talent for evil is to find forgiveness. Without forgiveness we would be locked into a troubling cycle of sin, guilt, shame, anger and more sin. Jesus' claim to forgive sin is not an arbitrary intrusion of a foreign element into this narrative; it is part of the logic of his preaching.

It was a staggering claim, and we should understand it not only as a further exposition of Jesus' authority but also as another sign of the diminishing role of the temple. This is the second time in the Gospel when a prophetic figure opens a means of forgiveness outside the cultic center in Jerusalem. John the Baptist had called people to the desert to receive a baptism of repentance for the forgiveness of sins (1:4). And here in the village of Capernaum in rural Galilee Jesus declared that the Son of Man came to forgive sin on earth. Furthermore, Jesus' declaration follows a revelation of his power to make clean irrespective of the authority of the priests in the temple. Mark opens by quoting a few lines from the well-known prophecy in Isaiah 40:3-5,

---

2:10 Mark's expression *Son of Man (hyios tou anthrōpou)* refelcts the LXX translation of the Aramaic *bar enash* ("son of man") of Daniel 7:13 and its Hebrew equivalent *ben*

which describes a great leveling process: "Every valley shall be raised up, every mountain and hill made low." As Mark's presentation of Jesus unfolds, it begins to appear that Mount Zion is one of the high places that might be brought down.

Jesus used no symbolic medium like water, but he did offer a demonstration for the astounding claim he had made. Jesus healed the paralytic's body as a sign that his sins had been forgiven. Furthermore, Jesus made a claim that went well beyond anything John the Baptist had said. John did not claim to forgive sin. Even though he offered a surprising new mode of forgiveness, the means of forgiveness remained unchanged: people repented and God forgave them. Repentance, of course, was central to Jesus' message, yet he did not call this man to repent. Jesus simply pronounced his sins forgiven. Then in response to the silent objection that only God could forgive sin, Jesus claimed to have that authority himself.

Furthermore, in asserting his claim to forgive sin, Jesus used a term that has not appeared in the Gospel before: *Son of Man,* an idiomatic expression that has been the subject of considerable discussion. It appears in several places outside the Gospels, where it has different meanings. In Psalm 8:4, for instance, "son of man" simply means a human being. Throughout the book of Ezekiel God addresses the prophet as "son of man." A third possibility is identified by Geza Vermes in extrabiblical material where "son of man" simply means "I" (1967:321).

A fourth possibility appears in Daniel 7:13, where one like a son of man appears before the throne of God to receive authority and dominion over all the nations and people of the world. This is an interesting passage on two counts. Daniel's son of man is strictly a heavenly figure who appears at the end of history. Nowhere in the book of Daniel does he appear on earth, and according to Daniel 7:27 the term is corporate. In that text the one like a son of man is the saints of the Jewish people who suffered on earth for their faithfulness to God. At the end of history they will receive the authority and dominion that is given to the one "like a son of man" in Daniel 7:13.

---

adam found in Psalm 8:4 (8:5 Heb and LXX) and frequently throughout Ezekiel.

Their sovereignty, power and greatness is his kingdom.

In Mark 2:10 Son of Man appears as a title. What did it mean when applied to Jesus? When Jesus presented his justification for claiming to forgive sins, he also claimed to be this heavenly figure. None of the other possible precedents for what he says have anything to do with forgiving sins. That power is implied, however, when God delegates to Daniel's one like a son of man authority and dominion over all the people of the world. Furthermore, only against this background do the words *on earth* make any sense. They would have no meaning if Jesus were speaking as any human being or as a prophet. In any of those cases the words on earth would be redundant. Against the background of Daniel 7:13, however, they add a new dimension to the meaning of forgiveness, for if the paralytic's sins were forgiven then, he would stand before the Son of Man at the end of history without fear.

Many scholars deny that Jesus ever made a claim like this. John Dominic Crossan, for example, argues that Jesus never even referred to himself as the Son of Man. In his judgment there is only one instance in the earliest gospel traditions where the expression Son of Man appears in two independent strands. In the other cases, he maintains, it appears to be a later addition (1994:50).

Several objections from this lengthy debate are still pertinent. For example, no one other than Jesus uses this title in all the gospel traditions. It is the only one used frequently, some sixty-five times in the canonical Gospels, and it always appears on his lips—with one exception, John 12:34, where someone from the crowd hears him use the title and asks what it means. There is no evidence in Acts or the Epistles that the early church ever called Jesus the Son of Man (Ladd 1974:146), a particularly difficult fact to explain when compared to the number of times that the titles *Christ* and *Son of God* appear. If the early church first applied the term Son of Man to Jesus, as it supposedly also did with the titles Son of God and Messiah, why does this title appear nowhere else but on the lips of Jesus?

There is some evidence that indicates that the term has some claim to authenticity. In the parallel accounts of Mark 8:27 and Luke 9:18, Jesus refers to himself in the first-person singular, but in Matthew 16:13 he says the Son of Man. It is easier to explain why Mark and Luke would change

Son of Man to I than to account for a change in the other direction. All three Evangelists wrote in the context of the church's mission to the Greco-Roman world, where the term Son of Man would not have been readily understood. Given that Matthew was writing to an audience composed of Jewish and Gentile converts, his use of "Son of Man" makes perfectly good sense. Mark 8:27 and Luke 9:18 are evidence that the church recognized the problem and took steps to mitigate it.

It is one thing to claim the power to forgive sin. That only requires a touch of megalomania, a phenomenon observed with surprising frequency in our own time. Jesus' claim to forgive sin was not, however, an idle boast. He understood the objection that the teachers of the law harbored unspoken in their hearts, so he posed a question: *Which is easier: to say to the paralytic, "Your sins are forgiven," or to say, "Get up, take your mat and walk"?* Then he told the man on the mat to get up and walk. In this account Jesus gave a visible justification for a claim to an invisible power. At the point when the paralytic stood up, the world of tangible forms served as a sign for a spiritual truth. The man's physical disease symbolized his spiritual condition, and Jesus' power to heal his body authenticated the claim to restore his standing before God.

When Jesus touched the leper, he shattered the social and religious conventions of his day. A new power had entered the world. It was the power to make people clean. It was not dependent upon the laws and rites of the temple. It operated outside the jurisdiction of the recognized religious authorities. Here that new power pressed its claim one step further. No physical condition rendered this man unfit to stand before God. The problem was sin, and Jesus did not make him clean by healing his body; Jesus made him clean by forgiving his sin.

If this story had had any other outcome, the question of blasphemy might have been raised with considerable justification. If this new revelation of power had drawn people away from God, it would have been damnable. If it had caused people to question God's goodness, doubt God's integrity or harden their hearts, a charge of blasphemy would have been in order. This encounter, though, did not end with a display of unholy arrogance. On the contrary, when the paralytic rose from his mat all the witnesses, including apparently Jesus' critics, praised God.

Jesus' claim to forgive sin was undoubtedly a controversial subject when the Evangelist wrote this Gospel. That Mark included an incident which highlights the issue suggests as much. In a larger sense, though, more is at stake than the question of Jesus' authority. We misread this text if our curiosity is satisfied when the paralytic stood up. There is a deeper tension here than the one between Jesus and the temple, for the clear witness of Mark is that Jesus did not act alone. He proclaimed the good news that God's rule was at hand. His words became acts of power that substantiated his preaching, and all the people who watched these sermons happen praised God. As Mark tells the story, God was behind everything Jesus did.

In at least one important way this passage challenges basic assumptions about sin, disease and health in our context as well. The paralytic did not owe his condition to a sin he had committed. Jesus did not forgive his sin as a prelude to healing him. On the contrary, Jesus overturned the wisdom of his day when he healed the man to prove that his sin was forgiven. In this Gospel sin is not the cause of disease, but healing is a sign of forgiveness. One might even say that health is a sign of grace.

If health is a sign of grace, what witness is appropriate for people who claim to be forgiven? In our world health is increasingly treated as a bartered commodity. Wealthier people have access to services that are denied to the rest of the world. This situation is often justified as an economic necessity, but that point of view is a far cry from the gospel's. People in the West are among the wealthiest people in the world. What we do with our money and our stake in the political system is part of our witness, and one day God will call the Western churches to account for it. What will we say—that we were witnesses for the wisdom of the day or that we held health to be a sign of grace?

An Outrageous Gospel (2:13-17) In 1988 George H. W. Bush campaigned for a kinder, gentler America. As the Cold War stumbled toward a conclusion, however, his hope proved to be illusive. The peace dividend arrived in red ink. The American economy soured, unemployment rose to post-Depression-era highs and a new wave of violence racked urban centers in North America. The one remaining superpower was tormented by a wave of self-doubt as voices across the country asked, "What is wrong with America?" A new wave of media pundits pointed their fingers at the traditional scapegoats: immigrants, ethnic minorities, the urban poor and hardened criminals. Many Christians found comfort in their angry denunciations.

The Pharisees, who make their first appearance here, were ardent nationalists. For them as well as other Jewish patriots, Jesus' behavior in Mark 2:13-17 was absolutely outrageous. When he called a tax collector to become one of his disciples, Jesus cast his lot with the people who symbolized everything that ardent nationalists thought was wrong with the Promised Land. Tax collectors were Jewish people who worked for Rome. They bought a franchise that gave them the exclusive right to collect taxes in a particular area. The Roman government stipulated how much money it expected in taxes and supplied soldiers to enforce the process of collection. Rome, however, did not set a limit on how much tax could be collected from a particular franchise. The tax collectors themselves assessed the total amount that would be collected in their district. The difference between what was actually collected and what was sent to Rome was what belonged to the tax collector. The home of Levi, where Jesus ate on this occasion, was surely not an incommodious shack.

For the Pharisees in particular, the people described as sinners were another symptom of the same problem. Let us be clear, though. The sinners who were present at Levi's house were not necessarily moral monsters. Although there may have been some rough characters in the company Jesus kept, the term sinners essentially referred to people who did not keep the provisions of the covenant law. They did not frequent the synagogues or temple. They may have taken God's name in vain. They did not wash their hands as soon as they came home from a shopping trip. They associated with non-Jewish people and did not keep the Sabbath. By and large the people called sinners were no worse than many of us. They simply did not pay much attention to covenant law. As far as the Pharisees were concerned, if there were any rabble who might reasonably be blamed for the sorry state of affairs in first-century Galilee and Judea, it was the people with whom Jesus associated.

There is no chronological connection between this story and the preceding account of Jesus and the paralytic. Mark simply introduces it with the words *once again Jesus went out beside the lake*. It is not a healing story, yet several themes connect this incident with the earlier ones. Jesus was once again in conflict with the teachers of the law. The occurrence of the word *sinners* recalls an important theme from the story about the paralytic. Then, too, despite the fact that Jesus did not heal anyone in this passage, he described what he was doing as the work of a doctor. Furthermore, if we examine the three stories of the leper, the paralytic, and the tax collectors and sinners together, we can discern a very interesting progression. In his encounter with the leper Jesus healed a disease. When the paralytic was lowered through the roof, Jesus first pronounced his sins forgiven and then healed his body. Here we find Jesus keeping company with sinners and speaking as a doctor. These three events lead us from the physical realm where Jesus' power to heal can be seen to the spiritual domain where his authority is more difficult to verify. Mark shows Jesus treating the most deplorable disease, leprosy, and the most deplorable social sin, the calculating greed of people who profit from the oppression of their own kind.

In this brief series of events Mark has recreated a moving exposition of Jesus' preaching. As Jesus proclaimed the kingdom of God, he healed the worst of diseases, opened a new avenue of forgiveness and gathered together a fellowship of people whom the religious elite considered incorrigible and perhaps irredeemable. The Pharisees expected sinners to be destroyed when the kingdom of God came, but Jesus did not show the slightest interest in pronouncing judgment upon the unclean, the irreligious or the morally bankrupt. His intention was clear. He had come to heal and restore. Inviting tax collectors and sinners to accompany his preaching tour through Galilee was a sign that he had a very different idea about the kingdom of God. These three stories leave the reader with the single impression that Jesus came to make people whole.

Jesus' metaphor about the doctor is comforting, but his closing comment has an edge to it. There is no hint of the Pharisees' reaction to the declaration *I have not come to call the righteous, but sinners*. As zealous guardians of the law, the Pharisees believed that they would be among the first to benefit when the kingdom of God arrived. Jesus left them, however, with the kind of remark that they would have found difficult to hear as a compliment. If the Pharisees took offense at the people Jesus gathered, he took offense at their presumption of righteousness.

There is more than a little presumption when someone poses the question, Who is to blame for society's ills? It is easy in retrospect to see the Pharisees' presumption. It is harder, perhaps, to see our own. Jesus was less concerned with finding someone to blame and more concerned with how to save the whole lot of us. His vision was inclusive. Given the religious and political context of his day, his vision was scandalously inclusive. In fact, it invites the question whether we have heard the gospel whenever we look for scapegoats.

Parables About the New and Old (2:18-22) It is not clear who posed the question about fasting to Jesus, nor is it clear what their intention was. Mark simply describes them as some people, a nonspecific reference that is insufficient to connect them with any of the groups mentioned in the Gospel. It is also impossible to tell whether they had come to argue or simply to request information. That Mark refers to the Pharisees and John's disciples twice in two lines suggests, however, that this was more than polite conversation. The question might well imply that Jesus was neglecting an important duty to which any person concerned about righteous conduct should attend. In any event, Mark included this encounter in a collection of controversy stories in which Jesus made increasing use of parables. As the tension accompanying his ministry escalated, parables became Jesus' primary means of engaging his opponents.

The Pharisees and the followers of John the Baptist were not natural allies. The Pharisees, who had no great love for Herod the Great, who had built the temple, nevertheless held the temple and the religious structures associated with it in considerable esteem. John the Baptist, on the other hand, showed little if any regard for it. The one point they had in common was their hope for the kingdom of God. Here again, though, their paths diverged. For the Pharisees strict adherence to the law was the key that would inaugurate the rule of God. John, on the other hand, saw their observance of the law as perfunctory and superficial. He called the Pharisees to come to the Jordan River with the rest of Judea to repent and be baptized. Thoroughgoing repentance was for John the essential step before the arrival of the one whom God was sending.

The question about fasting has to be considered in the contexts of these conflicting views about the coming of the kingdom of God. The Pharisees fasted because texts like Leviticus 16:29 list fasting as one of the covenant obligations. John's disciples might have observed any particular fast that was stipulated in the law, but it is doubtful that their practice would have included the weekly fasts that had become part of the Pharisees' tradition. Since no particular day of fasting is indicated here, we might conclude that John's disciples were fasting for another reason. John was in prison awaiting execution, and they were probably fasting in the hope that God would secure his release. The arrest and possible death of this prophet would have seemed to them incompatible with the arrival of the rule of God. Jesus, on the other hand, preached that the kingdom of God had arrived, and neither he nor his disciples were fasting at that time. Fasting then could be understood as a way of demonstrating one's commitment to the covenant, a form of prayer, a way of grappling with God's will or as something that was not necessary in that situation.

Jesus' response would not have improved the Pharisees' opinion of him, and it might well have been disconcerting to John's disciples. It is doubtful that either party would have agreed that it was not a time for fasting. They might also have found additional ground for concern in the terms that Jesus employed, for in the language of this parable it was not the arrival of an event like a wedding or the announcement of a new law that accounted for his practice. It was the presence of a person, the bridegroom, that justified a different sort of practice. That phrasing points to Jesus himself as the reason that his disciples did not fast. They could not fast because he was with them. The implications of this parable are stunning. It is as though Jesus was claiming to be the fulfillment of the covenant, the revelation of God's will or the focal point for expressions of devotion. Yet this is all treated indirectly. Jesus did not go quite so far as to assert those claims, but the parable points toward them. As it stands in our text, the parable does not claim to introduce a new kind of time that invalidates everything that went before it. It does not go so far as to suggest that a permanent change in the nature of time has occurred. It relates everything to the presence of the bridegroom. The time was different because he was present.

The Son of Man Is Lord of the Sabbath (2:23-28) "If your grandmother could see what you let your boys do on the Sabbath," observed my mother one Sunday afternoon as we sat quietly drinking coffee in the living room, "she would roll over in her grave." She was right. My grandmother had been a strict Calvinist, and Sundays in her home had been an ordeal of holiness. Our two young sons, on the other hand, suffered from no lack of energy or enthusiasm on Sundays. It may be an act of providence that my grandmother did not live to celebrate the Sabbath with her great-grandchildren.

Traditions change with time. The years between the return from exile in Babylon and the ministry of Jesus, however, had not seen a loosening of traditions about the Sabbath, but a tightening. In exilic and postexilic Judaism the Law was elevated above the Writings and the Prophets so that the regulations about the Sabbath were accorded the utmost seriousness. One of the most striking texts in this regard is Jeremiah 17:24-25, where God promises that kings will sit on David's throne and that Jerusalem will never be destroyed if the people of Judah keep the Sabbath day holy by not doing any work on it. Several centuries later Rabbi Shim'on ben Jochai taught that Israel's redemption would come when all the people kept only two Sabbaths perfectly (Lohse 1971:8). By the time Jesus began to preach in the synagogues of Galilee, the Pharisees had developed an inflexible connection between the Sabbath traditions and the hope that the Messiah would come.

The question that the Pharisees put to Jesus was not a simple request for an informed opinion. It was an accusation that the disciples were acting outside the limits of the law. At issue was the commandment not to do any work on the Sabbath, and the disciples might have violated the Pharisees' tradition in either of two ways. Plucking a handful of grain could have been considered harvesting, something specifically prohibited in Exodus 34:21. Alternatively, since most people had to walk to complete any kind of errand, the Pharisees had defined how far someone could walk on the Sabbath without working. A stroll of about half a mile was permitted, but a greater distance was considered work. The text does not say how much grain they plucked, whether they ate it or how far they walked. We simply read the accusation that the disciples did something unlawful on the Sabbath.

This is an important observation, for it shows that the controversy was not about the violation of a particular Sabbath tradition, but about the importance of the Sabbath itself. This controversy is part of the conflict between the old and new. In this case the new is Jesus' proclamation that the kingdom of God is near. The old is the expectation that keeping the law, especially the traditions about the Sabbath, is the factor that determines when the rule of God would appear on earth. For the Pharisees it was inconceivable that the reign of God would be ushered in by someone who did not revere the law as they did.

Jesus' response was neither gentle nor conciliatory. He invoked the story of David taking the consecrated bread from the sanctuary at Nob for his own provision, observing that David's action was unlawful because he was not a priest and therefore was forbidden to eat the bread on the altar. Actually, the account of David's actions at Nob in 1 Samuel 21 is a much more troubling story than we would suspect from the language of Jesus' answer. Eating the consecrated bread was by no means the worst thing David did at Nob, which Jesus underscored by adding a couple of ironic touches of his own.

David had not gone to Nob on a whim. He was fleeing for his life, and the man who was trying to kill him was King Saul. David was in such a hurry to get away that he had set out without food or weapons. He went to the sanctuary at Nob, not far from Saul's palace, to get help. The priest who met him seems to have been aware of the trouble brewing between David and the king, for he trembled when they met. Afraid of what this meeting might mean, the priest asked David why he had come alone. David lied. In fact, he told two calculated lies. He claimed that he was on a secret mission for Saul and that he had arranged to meet his own men later on. There is no mention of David's men elsewhere in 1 Samuel 21, and the story does not leave room for a larger group of David's followers. His plan was to flee to the Philistine city of Gath and beg Israel's enemies for refuge. Therefore he asked

Ahimelech, the priest who met him, for five loaves of bread—just about enough to get David to Gath all by himself.

First Samuel 21 is a complex narrative. Ahimelech gave David the consecrated bread and the only weapon that was housed in the sanctuary at Nob, the sword of Goliath, the mighty enemy whose death at David's hand had precipitated the king's fits of jealous rage. It was a national treasure. It was too big for David to use as a weapon, but it was something David might have used to ingratiate himself into Gath since that was the city from which Goliath had come. When Saul heard what had happened, he concluded that Ahimelech had helped David escape. Consequently, King Saul authorized the killing of eighty-five priests and all the other people, cattle, dogs and sheep who lived in Nob. The sole survivor was Abiathar, son of Ahimelech.

Of course, most of this lies under the surface of Jesus' reply, but he added other comments that draw us into the larger story. In Mark 2:25 he referred to David's companions, ironically pointing to one of the lies David told. And in 2:26 Jesus said that David ate the consecrated bread in the days of Abiathar the high priest. Abiathar was not the high priest then. The elder members of his family were in charge of the sanctuary at Nob. Abiathar is listed with Zadok in 2 Samuel 8:17 as a leading figure after David conquered Jerusalem. Abiathar was the sole survivor of the slaughter at Nob, an ironic reference to the consequences of David's lies.

The kingdom of David was the model for the dreams of independence in first-century Judaism. Thus, with this brief but scathing reference to David, Jesus dismissed the entire theological structure upon which the Pharisees had built their hopes. David himself had broken the law, and an entire Israelite village had consequently been annihilated. Pharisaic rigor was not the premise on which the kingdom of David was founded, nor was it the appropriate measure of Jesus and his followers. The kingdom of God would not come at some point in the distant future when all Israel kept the Sabbath perfectly. Ironically, the reign of God was already present, but the Pharisees did not see it.

If the appeal to David's conduct was provocative, the assertions Jesus made about the Sabbath were incendiary. His claim that *the Sabbath was made for man, not man for the Sabbath* would not have appeased these critics. Most of the texts that speak about the purpose of the Sabbath state that it is holy to the Lord. Exodus 16:23-27 is a case in point, and Exodus 20:8-11 actually goes a long way toward saying that the Sabbath is for the Lord. There are, on the other hand, a few passages like Exodus 16:29, which say that the Lord has given the Sabbath to humans. Exodus 31:14 takes this line of thought one step further by stating that the Sabbath is holy to humans. It is not too far from Exodus 31:14 to what Jesus set forth in Mark 2:27, but Jesus did not cite a text from the Mosaic law to justify his pronouncement. He asserted it without qualification or warrant and proceeded to advance an astounding claim: *So the Son of Man is Lord even of the Sabbath.*

There is no explanation, apology or argument, but within the Gospel of Mark it is the conclusion of an implicit logic. This is the second time Jesus has referred to himself as the Son of Man. The first occasion was 2:1-12, when Jesus healed a man who had been lowered through a roof on a stretcher to prove that the Son of Man had authority on earth to forgive sins. If he has the right as the Son of Man to forgive sins on earth, then he also has authority over people. And if the Sabbath was made for people, then it follows that the Son of Man has authority over it.

The Son of Man is an eschatological figure drawn from Daniel 7:13-14 to whom God gives authority over all peoples of the world at the end of history. That is good news for people of conscience, because it means that the wrongs of history will be set right. Before that day comes, however, something unexpected has happened to nurture this hope. Someone from eternity entered our space and time. The Son of Man who can forgive sins on earth is also the Lord of the Sabbath in this age.

Our study of this text leaves one difficult issue unresolved. How can a day that is holy to God also be a day for us? That is a problem every child who grows up in the community of faith understands implicitly. Despite the profound differences between Jesus and the Pharisees, nothing suggests that he did not also consider the Sabbath to be holy to God. It would be wrong to see Jesus setting people and God against each other. On the contrary, the opening chapters of this Gospel portray Jesus preaching and acting as an expression of the authority of the kingdom of God. His claim to be Lord of the Sabbath should be understood in the same way. That is to say, the Sabbath finds its place within the proclamation of the rule of God. It does not define or circumscribe the kingdom. The rule of God is fundamental. The Sabbath is secondary insofar as it finds its true meaning within the context of the kingdom of God. How the Sabbath is to be observed in practical terms is not addressed here. This passage merely exposes the problem and sets the stage for Jesus' next visit to a synagogue.

It should be clear by now that we are not looking at something which grows out of the spiritual hunger of individual Christians. The case for the Son of Man as Lord of the Sabbath is not an argument from experience. The authority Jesus exercised and the claims he made about himself are demonstrations of the rule of God. Everything he did and said was subordinated to the message summarized in 1:15: "The time has come. The kingdom of God is near. Repent and believe the good news!" The logic that leads from the Son of Man who forgives sins to the Lord of the Sabbath is not the logic of the Evangelist; it is the logic of the kingdom of God, and it is grounded in the preaching of Jesus.

Conflict in the Synagogue (3:1-6) Several years ago our church joined other congregations to purchase and reequip an old drilling rig. It cost fifty thousand dollars, even with donated parts and labor. Once the rig was ready we drove it to Baja California to provide small impoverished communities their first safe supply of drinking water. After drilling three wells in one community, where the average wage is about two dollars a day, we began to take members of our church to Baja California to build houses. Each simple 400-square-foot home cost about $2,500 and had no plumbing or electricity. In the winter the people sleep puppy-dog style on the floor to keep warm.

The first trip or two did not create much of a stir. Over the years, though, as we kept going down for weekend construction projects, a vocal group of disgruntled members objected that we were spending too much time and money on other people and neglecting the needs in our own community. So we became part of a local shelter program for homeless people. We provided food and lodging in our social hall for short periods at a time. Then the same group of folks who had objected to the water project demanded to know why we had to bring homeless people into the neighborhood and let them stay in our church.

As Jesus entered the synagogue in 3:1, the lines of engagement were already sharply drawn. He had come to keep the Sabbath. His opponents had come to look for something to use against him. The conduct of his disciples had come unsuccessfully under hostile scrutiny in the previous story, so here his growing group of enemies hoped to find solid justification for accusing Jesus himself. They wanted to see if they could catch Jesus defiling the Sabbath. They considered healing to be a form of work. Thus in this unnamed synagogue two competing views of holiness collided—with fatal consequences.

On this Sabbath Jesus found a man with a shriveled hand in the company of people who would have been content if he had retained his disability for one more day. Had Jesus waited until sundown to heal this man, he would have avoided giving further offense to his critics. The Pharisees who were present considered healing to be a form of work, a violation of Exodus 34:21. To be sure, the Torah contains provisions for exceptional circumstances. Nothing in this passage, however, indicates that the man with the shriveled hand faced an emergency (Lohse 1971:24).

Jesus had declared that the Sabbath was made for man, and he criticized the Pharisees for holding the Sabbath laws and traditions so rigidly that people became servants of the Sabbath (2:27). The Old Testament consistently presents the Sabbath as a day that belongs to God. In Numbers 15:32-36, for example, a man is put to death because he gathered sticks on the Sabbath. There is every indication that Jesus also held the Sabbath to be holy to God, even though he rejected the Pharisees' interpretation of the Mosaic law. His presence in the synagogue demonstrates his respect for the Sabbath.

At the beginning of this Gospel the Evangelist turns to the book of Isaiah to summarize the pivotal junctures in Israel's history. As frequently as themes from Isaiah appear in Mark, we could call Isaiah the beginning of the Gospel. Isaiah 58 is an illuminating critique of the practices of fasting (Is 58:1-12) and keeping the Sabbath (Is 58:13-14).

The prophet condemns the people for doing as they pleased, a charge that appears in Isaiah 58:3 and then again twice in Isaiah 58:13. The problem with their fasting, as regular and self-debasing as it was, happened to be the same problem with the Sabbath, as somber and holy as that was: the people of Judah took God too lightly; they exploited their workers, made laws that favored the wealthy and bound the poor with chains of injustice (Is 58:3). In short, the people who had nice homes and plenty to eat had turned their backs on the rest of God's people (Is 58:7).

There is no threat of punishment in this prophecy, but there is a promise: if the people of Judah will stop doing what pleases them and do instead what pleases God (58:13), God will turn their Sabbaths into days of joy and feasting (58:14). This is not just a call for personal repentance; it is a call for social reform, for laws that insure that everyone is treated fairly. God expects more than a level playing field where the strongest and smartest thrive at the expense of the weaker and slower. God expects a social order that works for everyone.

Furthermore, the Sabbath that God promises is a day that is truly for God and for people. Such a Sabbath would be holy to God because God would be honored. It would be holy to the people of Judah because joy and contentment would fill their world. This is a moral view of the Sabbath, which is not narrowly based on the specific stipulations that pertain to the Sabbath itself. It is based on the whole Mosaic law. Even better, it is based on the will of God as revealed through the law.

Mark 3:1-6 has several points of contact with Isaiah 58. In the first place, the man who came to the synagogue with a shriveled hand was in all probability poor. To be a victim of a chronic illness or disability in that time meant a life of poverty, unless one had the rare blessing of belonging to a wealthy family. In the ancient world, where much of the population existed as peasants (Waetjen 1989:6), any sort of disability amounted to social and economic disenfranchisement. Releasing a poor man from the shackles of his disability is a way of honoring the Sabbath and making it a delight (Is 58:13).

Furthermore, the Pharisees' insistence on observing the details of the Sabbath while overlooking the weightier matter of doing good or evil recalls the denunciation of formal and somber religion that overlooks God's passion for justice in Isaiah 58:5, 13. As it turns out in this instance, someone was plotting to do evil. After Jesus healed the man, the Pharisees went out and plotted Jesus' death immediately. Although the NIV omits it in Mark 3:6, the word *immediately* is important because it indicates that the Pharisees were acting with malice on the Sabbath.

The extent of their malice shows in their choice of allies. The Herodians were people associated with Herod's court, and under any other circumstances the Pharisees would have had little to do with them. The Pharisees were ardent nationalists who resented the presence of Roman soldiers on the land God had promised to give to Abraham's children. This Herod made a career of courting favor from Rome, and he is the one who had John the Baptist thrown in jail. Seeking an alliance with this Herod was an act of malicious compromise.

If it was not against the letter of the law for the Pharisees to embark on this course of action, it was certainly against the spirit of the law. That more than anything else, perhaps, demonstrates the bankruptcy of their position. For in claiming to uphold the letter of the law they set themselves against God. Their reverence for the law has rendered it useless as a tool for understanding the will of God. There is a new way of understanding God's will—in the person of Jesus, in the things he says and does. It was preposterous for the Pharisees to argue about violations of Sabbath law when God was doing mighty things before their eyes, which they would not acknowledge due to the hardness of their hearts.

The Sabbath of Isaiah 58 is profoundly moral. It shares with Mark 3:1-6 both a passion for breaking the chains of oppression and for the prospect of joy. Yet it would not be accurate to call Jesus' view of the Lord's Day essentially moral. It is, rather, eschatological. The moral concerns of Isaiah's prophecy are anchored in the past, in the covenant God made with the people of Israel at the exodus. The moral concerns of Jesus are anchored in the future, when the kingdom of God comes in its fullness. The Sabbath that Jesus celebrates has something not found in its counterpart. On the eschatological Sabbath we not only celebrate as the chains of oppression are broken. We also rejoice in the healing that Jesus brings because it is a sign that God will make all things new.

What is left of the Sabbath? In the Western world the Lord's Day has certainly become a day for us. It is our day off—a day for soccer, roller hockey, catching up with work around the house, softball, golf, shopping and televised sports. And once or twice a month, perhaps, it is a day to spend an hour in worship. For an increasing number of people, going to church has become irrelevant or boring. We are missing the joy in worship. Is the answer to be found in the attempt to make worship more exciting? Neither the Gospel of Mark nor the prophecies of Isaiah encourage us to hope that we can reclaim the Sabbath as a day for God and people by improving our technique and form. Joy comes when we open our hearts and let the things that move God move us too.

☐ The Power of God in Parable and Miracle (3:7—6:6)

The plot to destroy Jesus resulted in a profound change in his ministry. In its aftermath much of what had been open and easily accessible became more difficult to comprehend. Teaching rather than preaching became his primary mode of communication, and parables emerged as his primary means of teaching. The connection between word and event that illuminated his earlier preaching is still important, but in the following material the miracles themselves become noticeably parabolic.

Jesus and the People of God (3:7-35) On July 6, 1415, John Hus was burned at the stake after a church court condemned him for preaching against corrupt clergy. In 1536 William Tyndale was convicted of heresy for translating large parts of the Bible into English and for advocating the doctrine of justification by faith. He was strangled and his body was subsequently burned. In April 1521 Martin Luther was hauled before an ecclesiastical tribunal in the city of Worms and examined about his supposedly heretical views on the sacraments, the authority of the clergy and the nature of salvation. According to church tradition Luther said, "Here I stand. I cannot do otherwise." Jesus, unlike these later reformers, withdrew after a group of religious leaders had decided to eliminate him.

What are the implications of Jesus' withdrawal? Was it a polite escape from a troublesome confrontation? Was it a retreat, an interlude to reassess the situation or perhaps a gesture expressing his desire to find some middle ground of accommodation? The answer depends on what he withdrew from. He might have withdrawn from one village or synagogue in Galilee. He might have withdrawn from the entire region of Galilee. Or he might have withdrawn from the synagogues themselves. The last possibility represents a decision of enormous consequences, because from the beginning of the Gospel the Evangelist has described Jesus' mission in terms of preaching the good news about the kingdom of God in the synagogues of Galilee (1:14, 39).

Withdrawal and Expansion (3:7-12) Jesus withdrew to the lake, that is, to the Sea of Galilee, so he did not withdraw from the region. There is, no indication in the preceding account about the location of the synagogue where the conflict between Jesus and his opponents became deadly. We cannot say with any degree of certainty whether he ever returned to that particular village, but we can say that Jesus was through with the synagogues. From this point on they do not figure in his preaching or teaching ministry. On only one other occasion did he enter a synagogue (6:1-6). With this single exception Jesus turned his back on the synagogues. He has withdrawn from the institution that had been the center of Jewish religious and cultural life for hundreds of years.

There had been no council of elders or rabbis. No vote had been taken. No public announcement had been made. Yet Jesus regarded his treatment at this one synagogue as though it spoke for the entire system. Is there a warrant for his sweeping rejection of the synagogues? Two things distinguish the confrontation in 3:1-6. In the first place, the opposition to him has gone far beyond criticism and objection. It has hardened into a plot to destroy him. Although the word translated "kill" can also mean "destroy someone's credibility," the Pharisees' alliance with the Herodians signals a lethal intention. Furthermore, the conspiracy between the Pharisees and Herodians elevated the conflict to a new level. Up to this point Jesus had faced opposition from religious groups such as the scribes (2:6), the scribes of the Pharisees (2:16) and the Pharisees (2:24). Now for the first time representatives of the royal family have taken a position against him.

Why the Herodians became interested in this conspiracy is not clear at this point in the Gospel. The reasons for the Pharisees' hostility are evident, but a motivation for the Herodians to join the plot does not appear until 6:6-29. The opposition to Jesus has assumed the classical proportions faced by the prophets of ancient Israel and Judah. A faction associated with the royal family has aligned itself with representatives of a religious party to kill him. In response Jesus withdrew from the synagogues.

The material in 3:7-12 is often referred to as a summary, and it is true that Mark is painting with broad brush strokes. The text is very general and does not contain a reference to any single thing that Jesus said or did. Yet some caution is required here. First of all, these verses not only summarize what Jesus did in the preceding chapters of the Gospel. They look forward, as well as backward, and they introduce some new material.

Jesus' withdrawal to the lake signals an important change in his evangelistic strategy. The synagogue was no longer the place where he preached the good news. The references to familiar themes like the popularity of Jesus as a healer and exorcist indicate that his appeal had not suffered. The size of the crowd (3:9) is much larger than anything Mark has described before, and for the first time Mark portrays a vast following of people from outside of Galilee. These crowds came from Judea, Jerusalem, Idumea, and the regions across the Jordan and around Tyre and Sidon (3:8), besides the villages of Galilee. This area includes the original allotments of the twelve tribes and the territory over which the house of David ruled. Yet several of these areas— Idumea, Transjordan, Tyre and Sidon—were not Jewish territories in the first century, nor were Tyre and Sidon part of David's kingdom. These verses show Jesus drawing a following from beyond the geographic boundaries that were associated with the nation of Israel. The size of the crowds, then, is another indication that the rift with the synagogue did not diminish his ministry.

The description of Jesus' ministry becomes retrospective only in 3:10-12 with the brief references to the large number of people he healed and a more detailed summary of the exorcisms he had performed. The passage concludes with the words *but he gave them strict orders not to tell who he was*. The Evangelist has now provided enough information for us to attempt an explanation of why Jesus commanded the demonic powers to be silent. At the very beginning of his ministry Jesus entered a synagogue and encountered a man who was possessed (1:23), and certain things have become clear since then. First, the encounter with the demonic is part of a larger pattern of conflict that happened whenever Jesus proclaimed the kingdom of God. As we have seen in 1:21-28 and 1:35-39, these exorcisms are a kind of enacted sermon.

When the demons identified him as the Holy One of God (1:24) or the Son of God (3:11), they were not trying to do him any favors. Their declarations were a form of opposition—a variation of a prominent feature found in extrabiblical exorcism accounts in which a struggle occurs between the exorcist and demon. Typically when the exorcist discovers the name of the demon, the exorcism proceeds. In this case the demons used a similar tactic to resist Jesus: they exposed his identity in an attempt to assert their own power and frustrate the exorcism. It is an indication of the nearness of the kingdom of God that their tactic was useless. Jesus first disarmed them by commanding silence, and then he cast them out. The power of evil was broken, and this is a compelling sign of the imminent triumph of God's reign.

Jesus Calls the Twelve (3:13-21) Names are subtle but firm reminders of family traditions. My middle name is John, a name I share with my grandfather and great-grandfather. It is a very common name, and my parents created no stir when they gave it to me. They were simply honoring a family tradition. When my great-grandfather was born in Ireland more than a century ago, however, the situation was quite different. His parents' decision to name him John rather than Sean embodied a set of cultural, political and religious allegiances that symbolized the forces that divided that nation. Outside of Ireland today few people understand the dynamics of their choice. In my case, however, it is interesting to consider what my extended family might have thought if my parents had decided to call me Juan. Names are also reminders of cultural boundaries.

Jesus renamed three of his followers. By itself, perhaps, the renaming of Simon as Peter and the characterization of James and John as Sons of Thunder may appear to be of only minor interest. The renaming, however, does not stand alone; it is part of a much profounder change that almost slips by unnoticed. The most revealing question about this passage comes from the last verse: why did Jesus' family think he was out of his mind? This is the first time any other members of his family have made an appearance in the Gospel of Mark, and there has been no previous hint of conflict with his relatives. What has happened to make his family conclude that he was crazy?

Lane argues that Jesus' being so busy that he did not have time even to eat accounts for the family's concern (1974:139). This is an improbable explanation. Busy people may be harassed, pressured, fatigued or greatly stressed, but they are not psychotic. Even if that were so, this explanation only invites the question. The pressure from the crowds is greater than anything we have seen before. What has happened to draw this kind of attention to Jesus?

Just before his family arrived, Jesus went up to a mountain away from the crowds and called twelve of his followers to be with him, to preach and to have authority to drive out demons (3:13-19). This is the second time Jesus has called people to do something. In 1:16-20 he called four men to follow him. That was a command to reorder their lives around the imperative of the gospel, to turn and believe that the kingdom of God was at hand. The call of the Twelve in 3:14, though, has a markedly different character. It was not a demand. It was a commissioning to share his authority. The Twelve were to be with him, to proclaim the gospel and to drive out demons.

Mark has already summarized Jesus' ministry in similar terms, but the synagogues that had been central to his initial strategy have ceased to be a factor in his public ministry. Instead of a place for proclaiming the gospel, there were now other people to share in the preaching. In a sense the Twelve replaced the synagogues. The conflict with the synagogues was not something from which Jesus withdrew in defeat. He responded to the growing opposition by expanding his ministry by a factor of twelve. Mark does not depict a meek and mild Jesus. The Jesus we meet in these pages responded to opposition with a dramatic expansion of his ministry. In addition to his growing appeal, Jesus' opponents now had twelve more heralds of the kingdom of God to contend with.

If the apostles have taken the place of the synagogues, is it significant that Jesus appointed twelve of them? Would it have made any difference if he had chosen ten or fifteen? This question is all the more interesting because the number quickly becomes a title. On only one other occasion is the term *apostles* used (6:30). In the Gospel of Mark the ones with whom Jesus chose to share his authority are typically referred to as the Twelve. Twelve, of course, is the number of the tribes of Israel. To associate it in any way with the kingdom of God was to evoke deep nationalistic and religious passions. Other prophets and rabbis had their schools of interpretation and their followers. Yet no matter how deeply they had left their mark on the faith of the people of Israel, none of them had commissioned twelve.

It is also true that the ten tribes of the northern kingdom had disappeared. The Assyrians conquered Israel in 721 B.C. They deported large numbers of Israelites, imported other conquered peoples to Israel and forced the remaining Israelites to marry the newly arrived immigrants. The Samaritans, whom the people of Judah despised as half-breeds, were all that was left of those ten tribes within the historical borders of Israel when Jesus began to preach. Despite the tribes of the northern kingdom having been destroyed by years of deportation and forced assimilation, the prophets looked forward to the restoration of the entire people of Israel. The dry bones of Ezekiel 37:11-14 are not the skeletons of individual people awaiting resurrection. They symbolize what was left of a nation God had judged. The prophecy that the bones would live again expressed the hope that the whole nation of Israel, all twelve tribes, would be restored. Texts like Zephaniah 3:13-15, Zechariah 9:13 and Micah 2:12 express a similar promise.

Four salient points help us understand the importance of Jesus' commissioning the Twelve. First, Jesus was preaching and demonstrating the gospel in such a way that the people of Galilee could experience the presence of the kingdom of God. Second, Jesus had turned away

---

3:21 The Greek expression that Mark uses means "to be beside oneself." It is often used to describe ecstatic experiences when people are not in their right minds. It

from the one institution that had served as the political, cultural and religious center for the people of Israel who had survived the exile. Although he continued to address himself to the Jewish people, he did so now as John the Baptist had done: he spoke from a position outside the institutions of Judaism. Third, there was a prophetic quality about his rejection of the synagogues and his preaching that would have encouraged speculation about the revival of the nation of Israel. And, finally, Jesus was preaching in Galilee, which was itself part of the territory that had originally belonged to tribes of the northern kingdom.

Against this background it looks very much as though Jesus was establishing a new nation when he appointed the Twelve. If his family thought he was setting up a new regime, then from a certain point of view their conviction that he was out of his mind is understandable. What Jesus did went well beyond the boundaries of safe and socially acceptable behavior: it is the behavior of either a megalomaniac or a human being so uniquely gifted that the institutions of first-century Judaism could not contain him. Jesus was intent upon fundamentally reshaping the people of God, and when that reshaping proved to be impossible within the existing structures of Judaism, Jesus created new ones.

If Jesus was laying the foundation for a new people of God, who are they? What would the citizenry of this new nation look like? These are not questions that the Evangelist answers directly at this point, but some features can be deduced from the description Mark provides of the Twelve. The Twelve were people who had turned away from whatever they were doing before they met Jesus, and they believed the gospel. To be sure, nothing here is as dramatic as the picture of four men leaving their nets, boats and family in 1:16-20. Yet their being appointed to be with Jesus implies a radical rearrangement of their other priorities. They would not be with the other people who had a claim on them, and they would not be pursuing their former occupations for the foreseeable future.

In this regard, it is highly suggestive that the first three people whom Jesus called are listed with new names. Peter, of course, is the Greek

---

can carry the connotation of being delusional or out of touch with reality. Either of those meanings is possible.

equivalent of Cephas. Both names mean rock or stone. The name Cephas does not appear in this Gospel, and up to this point Mark has referred to this disciple only as Simon. This text is the last occasion when Mark calls him Simon. Throughout the rest of this Gospel this disciple is called Peter. Mark does not treat the name Peter as simply one more way to refer to Simon. This renaming is more like a change of identity, for Simon receives not only a new name but a new profession and a new place. Peter stands at the head of the list of apostles.

It is not too difficult to discern the significance of James and John's new name: Sons of Thunder. Unlike the name Peter this one is thoroughly Semitic, and calling them Sons of Thunder is a way of describing their character (Anderson 1976:118). These two men were apparently capable of sudden and explosive outbursts of anger. Mark's reference to their new name suggests that having a reverent and pious demeanor is not a prerequisite for belonging to the new people of God.

One other member of the Twelve is singled out for special attention. Rather surprisingly, Mark identifies Judas Iscariot as the one who betrayed him. One of the distinguishing features of this Gospel is its early references to Jesus' death (Martin 1972:141). Mark does not scatter these references around pointlessly. The first intimation of his death (1:14) establishes a connection between the beginning of Jesus' ministry and the arrest of John the Baptist. What function does this one play?

Mark does not offer a direct answer, but the context of this passage is suggestive. The appointment of the Twelve follows Jesus' rejection of the synagogues and precedes the description of the enormous crowds that came from all the surrounding areas, some of which were outside the historical boundaries of Israel and Judah. Simon, to whom Jesus gave a Gentile name, is mentioned first, and Judas Iscariot, who betrayed him, is named last. Their appointment symbolizes a fundamental reshaping of the people of God. Mark has crafted this material to cast Jesus' death against the backdrop of the formation of a new nation. He implies a connection between Jesus' death and the formation of a new nation without specifying yet what the connection is. At this point Mark is content to imply that the death of Jesus is connected to the formation of a new people.

Jesus treated religious institutions not only as centers of spiritual life, but also as centers of power. When it became clear that the synagogues would not embrace the gospel, he turned away from them and created a new center of power: he appointed twelve people to be with him and share his authority. His standard of judgment was not the success or vitality of the institution. It was whether the synagogues would embrace the good news of the kingdom of God.

In America today it is hard to find much loyalty to religious institutions. Some of Jesus' modern followers change churches almost as easily as they change clothes. Among the many explanations for attending or leaving a particular congregation are music, the quality of programs for children and youth, and the ability of the preacher. It is rare to find anyone who uses the kingdom of God as a yardstick for measuring a church, and that is a source of some concern. Is it possible that we have invested so much time and energy in understanding how the gospel is good news for us that we have lost sight of what the gospel actually is?

Blasphemy Against the Holy Spirit (3:22-30) The opposition to Jesus reasserted itself in a new and dreadful way. A group of scribes arrived from Jerusalem, perhaps indicating an orchestrated response to his ministry. They came in the hope of discrediting him once and for all by accusing him publicly of being in league with the devil. It is not hard to discern something that might have made that charge believable. Whenever Jesus cast them out, the unclean spirits called him "the Holy One of God" or "the Son of God." Their declarations went far beyond the affirmations anyone in the crowds had made about him, and they are the kind of statements that would have been kept alive in the public imagination. The testimony of the demonic powers offered a plausible way to undermine Jesus' growing popularity. It was the seed of an unholy idea.

Once again, however, Jesus refused to let his critics define the terms of the argument. He responded in parables, a strategy that was soon to become his standard method of communicating. Jesus had used parables before as ways of responding to entrenched opposition. In this encounter he took the parable form one step further as an instrument of conflict. As he moved from one metaphor to another, the parables became an instrument of judgment.

These brief parables all expose the absurdity of the scribes' attempt to discredit Jesus. The accusation, Jesus pointed out, was manifestly ridiculous: How can Satan drive out Satan? He answered his own question with the observation that kingdoms or houses divided against themselves are self-destructive. Today we might say that a business that works against itself is doomed to failure. Then he provided three brief parables that make the same point. If good things are happening to people through what Jesus has done, then Satan must have empowered someone to work against him. And if Satan's power was working against itself, then his kingdom was crumbling.

The parable about binding the strong man in 3:27 goes even further. It suggests that someone even stronger than Satan has appeared (Gundry 1993:174). This observation effectively turned the tables on Jesus' opponents. They had admitted implicitly that Jesus drove out demons. In the absence of any other credible explanation, the only remaining possibility was that Jesus was more powerful than Satan. Mark does not specify where and how Jesus might have gained mastery over Satan, but from his first encounter with unclean spirits they feared him as the Holy One of God. In any case, the implication of 3:27 is clear: Jesus had the power to release Satan's captives. Once again in the face of increasing opposition Jesus made another assertion of his authority.

Mark 3:28-30 breaks new ground. Jesus had crossed the boundaries established by the purity codes. He had eaten with tax collectors and sinners. He had publicly forgiven sin. So it is not surprising that he could say, *All the sins and blasphemies of men will be forgiven them.* With the declaration that one will not be forgiven, however, Jesus broached a subject he had not hinted at before. At this point the parables in Mark are directly linked to judgment.

What is the blasphemy against the Holy Spirit, and who, if anyone, has committed this sin? Few people have not wrestled with the thought that they have done something that cannot be forgiven. The good news is that the things that typically plague our hearts can be forgiven. Neither unfaithfulness, betrayal, embezzlement nor even murder is blasphemy against the Holy Spirit. That sin is something the teachers of the law had just committed. They had accused Jesus of being in league with Satan. To identify the work of God as the work of the devil is to blaspheme against the Holy Spirit; it is the ultimate blindness, the point from which there is no turning back.

The New Family (3:31-35) If Mark were writing for dramatic effect, the previous encounter with the scribes from Jerusalem might have made a fitting climax for a sustained exposition of Jesus' authority. The Evangelist has presented us with a picture of someone whose personal charisma and sense of authority have provoked both a plot and an actual attempt to destroy him. He seems, though, to be writing for a different purpose, for he now introduces a new and unexpected point of conflict—the family. As Jesus' mother and brothers stood outside the house where he was teaching, they expected him to honor his obligations to the family and come out to them. He refused and sent a vexing answer back.

The obligations of a son in a Jewish family were considerable. It was a son's duty to honor his father and mother. In the Wisdom Literature it is clear that honoring parents means obeying what they teach and respecting their authority, even as an adult. We do not know what concerns Jesus' family carried with them that day or what plans they may have had other than to talk with him. If we look back over Mark 1—3, however, we might suspect that the following items would have been on the agenda. In the first place Jesus was not pursuing a career and did not have a stable income (1:39). Therefore he may not have been contributing sufficiently to the family's finances. Second, Jesus kept bad company (2:15). Even worse, he had offended the leading religious authorities (2:23-27; 3:1-6, 22). It could be said that his recent activities border on the irresponsible, and some members of his family had already tried to restrain him. There were no signs of improvement. All indications pointed to the probability that things were going to get worse.

With these or similar concerns the responsible members of the family, his mother and brothers, stood outside the house where he was and sent word for him to come out. Jesus replied, *Who are my mother and my brothers?* Then he looked at the people sitting with him and said, *Here are my mother and my brothers! Whoever does God's will is my brother and sister and mother.*

That was a radical assertion. Jesus rejected both the traditional authority and structure of the family and then provided his own definition of the family. The new family is a company of people not bound by ties of blood, but by a commitment to doing God's will. This statement recalls the harsh language of Matthew 10:35-37: "For I have come to turn 'a man against his father, a daughter against her mother.' . . . Anyone who loves his father or mother more than me is not worthy of me." Rejecting the expected role of your parents may even look like hatred (Lk 14:26). Jesus held out for a higher responsibility, a more pressing claim. For him, doing the will of God superseded any other obligation. And this, of course, leads us to wonder where his natural family stood in the escalating confrontation between the new and the old.

Once again we see the impact of the new upon the world. What God was doing through Jesus could not be contained in the old structures of life. It was no longer possible to assume that what God expects of people would necessarily be mediated through the structures of family, nation or even ethnic group. It is quite possible that Mark was writing to Christians in Rome who faced enormous pressure from their families because of their faith in Jesus. This passage is a reminder of the absolute claim on us that God has.

It is also a call to think of ourselves first as part of a new family, a new people, a new set of relationships that have come into being because of the good news about the kingdom of God. This is what we might call a spiritual truth that took concrete form in the life of the early church. Jesus' declaration in Mark 3:35 is the reason there is so much talk about brothers and sisters and children in the Pauline and Johannine Epistles. This new reality proved to be more compelling than the natural sociology of the early Christians in cities like Colossae. Jesus did not come to bring a kind of spirituality that was celebrated only on Sunday mornings inside the walls of a building where it could never affect anything else. Jesus brought something new into the world that transforms all of our relationships. We might pose this issue in the practical realities of our time by asking this question: How should Christians in the West respond when we hear about Palestinian Christians being forcibly evicted from their homes without compensation, jailed without trial or summarily deported?

God made a covenant with Israel, and God does not abandon a

covenant even when people break it (Torrance 1992:27-28). Divine forgiveness means that God finds ways to renew the covenants people break. Whether the people of Israel had broken the covenant again is an issue that Mark has not yet clarified. What has emerged, though, is the question who belongs to the family of God. If this family now includes anyone who does the will of God—including non-Jewish people—do the same standards of love and fairness apply to all?

Parables of the Kingdom of God (4:1-34) Following a series of heart problems, a friend of mine, whose name also happens to be Mark, decided that he needed to lose a lot of weight. In consultation with a doctor and weight-loss counselor, Mark set himself the goal of losing 150 pounds. When he had shed about 80 pounds, he was able to wear several well-tailored suits that had hung unused in his closet for some time. It gave him a lot of pleasure to wear those suits again, but his counselor did not share his enthusiasm. She told him to throw them all away. He was appalled at the idea. Those suits were worth a great deal of money, and he felt that he deserved a reward for his hard work. His counselor refused to explain or justify her instruction. In response to Mark's repeated complaints, she had only one thing to say: "Get rid of those clothes."

The counselor had given him a parable. It was not obscure or packed with difficult symbolism. It was very simply stated, yet it made no sense to my friend initially. It just made him angry. It took Mark several days to get past his anger, and then he realized that the counselor was right. His only argument was with himself. Losing the next 70 pounds would be more difficult than losing the first 80, and those suits represented a temptation to be satisfied with what he had already accomplished. If the counselor had allowed herself to be drawn into an argument, my friend would have been fighting with the wrong person, and he might never have faced the decision he needed to make. So, gritting his teeth, Mark threw the clothes away.

The parables in chapter four signal a new direction in Jesus' ministry, but they are not the first ones we have seen. Jesus had used parables in arguing with his critics and enemies (2:17, 19-22; 3:23-27), but preaching the good news had been his primary way of communicating with his larger audience. From this point on, however, Jesus spoke to the crowd in parables even when he was talking about the kingdom of God, a point the Evangelist underscores in 4:34.

The earlier parables are brief, simple and open-ended. The parable of the soils, by contrast, is long, complex and allegorical. Furthermore, between the parable in 4:3-9 and its interpretation in 4:13-20 is a disturbing quotation from Isaiah 6:9-13, with what many scholars see as predestinarian overtones, which suggests that this particular parable is a model for understanding all the others. We have to wonder then what accounts for this change. Why has an instrument of controversy and confrontation replaced open proclamation as the way Jesus spoke about the kingdom of God?

Ears to Hear (4:1-9) The crowd heard many things, all in parables (4:2), and the last parable Jesus told them was the parable of the soils. Then either Jesus moved away or the crowd dispersed, and he was left alone with a smaller group of people, which included the Twelve. This smaller group learned the explanation of the parable of the soils (4:14-20) and received another set of parables (4:21-32). Most of the original audience did not hear the other parables, nor did it learn the meaning of the parable of the soils. The last thing those people heard was a story about something farmers normally do each spring.

This parable would be completely unremarkable except for two features. The first is the pair of instructions to listen that frame it: Jesus said, *Listen* (4:3) and *He who has ears to hear, let him hear* (4:9). Both the verbs listen and hear are in the imperative mood. They are not invitations or declarations. They are commands, and no other parable in this Gospel is framed at both ends with an order to listen. These two commands indicate that this parable is of special importance.

Second, the parable contains an interesting description of sowing, but a farmer who hoped to harvest a crop would never plant a field like this. He would sow the seed and then plow it into the ground or cover it with more soil. In the natural order of things a farmer who plants a field as this sower does would produce only one thing—a feast for the birds. It has been argued that plowing a field after sowing was a typical practice in the Mediterranean world and should be as-

---

4:8 Harvests as bountiful as the parable of the soils describes were not unknown, as

sumed here (Payne 1978:127). Edwards, on the other hand, finds the evidence mixed. He maintains, on the contrary, that a field was ordinarily plowed before sowing, and he finds much less support for the practice of plowing a field after it had been sown (2002:128). There is, in any event, nothing in the parable about covering the seed or plowing the field. Even more to the point, the principal figure in this parable is not introduced to us as a farmer, but as a sower. That is to say, the parable directs us to look at the activity of this one particular sower and not to typical patterns of farming, whatever they might have been. Mark 4:3-9 recounts an annual rite of spring with which the crowd was familiar. Many of them were peasant farmers, and they knew that planting a field in this manner would never yield a crop of one hundred, sixty or even thirty times the amount of seed that was sown. That is a point underscored by 4:13-20, where as much as three quarters of the labor comes to naught (Edwards 2002:128). Jesus used a familiar image from the life of rural peasants to tell an extremely improbable story, which he commanded his audience to hear as he began and ended. Simply put, this is a parable about hearing, but it is not after all a simple matter (Cranfield 1963:151).

The Secret of the Kingdom of God (4:10-12) The terms of verses 10-12 cast a different light on this parable, indeed on Jesus' entire ministry. They signal a permanent change in the way he interacted with the crowds that followed him. Now there were insiders and outsiders. Those on the inside received a secret that was withheld from those on the outside, and it appears that Jesus spoke in parables precisely so the outsiders would not understand what he said.

Many commentators find here a new and decidedly predestinarian emphasis in the Gospel of Mark. Schweizer, for example, argues that the Evangelist added these verses to explain the lackluster results of the church's preaching (1970:93). More than a full generation had passed since Jesus' resurrection, and there were still many more people who did not believe in Jesus than there were people who believed in him. Mark, so the argument runs, adapted the parables of Jesus to explain why unbelief was so predominant. In short, the preaching of the

---

records from the fertile grain fields in North Africa show (White 1964:301).

early church was not more successful because God had hardened people's hearts. They did not believe because they could not. God did not intend for them to believe, and so Jesus spoke in parables to conceal the truth from them. In this interpretation those on the outside are the people whom God predestined not to believe.

The words *they may be ever seeing but never perceiving, and ever hearing but never understanding; otherwise they might turn and be forgiven* are some of the harshest words in the Bible. Whether this is the language of predestination, however, is debatable. Neither Jesus nor Mark was the first to use them. They are a quotation from Isaiah 6:9-13. In that prophecy they are not words of predestination but of judgment. Despite God's faithfulness and nurturing, the people of Judah had cultivated a social system that was rife with exploitation and violence (Is 5:7). Ultimately, God called Isaiah to declare that it was time for judgment. The opening chapters of Isaiah depict a nation under judgment, but the judgment had not achieved its purpose. The people of Judah were still not listening to God. The next stage in God's judgment was that they would be ever seeing, but never perceiving (Is 6:9). That is to say, God did to the people of Judah something they had already done to themselves. God confirmed their sin by imprisoning them in a pattern of disobedience. They had not listened, so now they could no longer make sense out of what they heard. Still to come was the destruction of the people, until only a remnant was left. The surviving group was to be a holy remnant through which the people of God would grow and flourish again.

There is one telling similarity between the meaning of these words in Isaiah and in Mark: in both cases the institutions of God's people had proven resistant to doing the will of God. In Isaiah the places of worship had been corrupted so that the practice of religion masked the sin of the people. Even the offerings they made to God were an expression of their sin (Is 1:10-17). In Mark the synagogues to which Jesus took the good news about the kingdom of God had turned against him. His message was no longer welcome there, and he had abandoned the synagogues as a place to proclaim and demonstrate the gospel.

4:12 The likelihood that Jesus used the words from Isaiah 6:9-13 is indicated by their

On the other hand, it is not at all clear that Mark is working with the concept of a holy or righteous remnant. In Isaiah's prophecy God's judgment led to the formation of a righteous remnant and the rebirth of a holy people. In Mark when Jesus left the synagogue he founded a new people with a new structure for the family that was built upon doing God's will. The first person named as a leader of this new people, however, was a Jewish man to whom Jesus gave a Gentile name. Whether the new family had anything essentially Jewish about it is an open question. In fact, it existed in tension with the demands and obligations of a typical Jewish family. Jesus defined the new family in the face of his natural family's attempt to assert its authority over him. Furthermore, that the people of God would be purified by the punishment they suffer (Is 40:2) does not appear anywhere in Mark's treatment of this theme. So as Mark develops the concept of a new people of God, it is not clear that this is an exclusively Jewish group. And if it is not a Jewish group, it does not conform to the paradigm of the holy remnant.

Clarity about who the people of God are is one of the things we would expect if the Evangelist were advocating predestination. This is not, though, a subject on which Mark is clear. In this collection of sayings the word *disciples* appears only in Mark 4:34: *When he was alone with his own disciples, he explained everything.* Who were these disciples? At this point in the Gospel Jesus' followers are an unspecified group of people who expand and contract without elaboration. We know that at least twelve of them were Jewish men, because they are named in 3:16-19, but that is about all that can be said. What distinguishes them is their relationship with Jesus—not their conduct or spirituality. After Mark 4, for instance, the theme of hardened hearts becomes a prominent topic in this Gospel, and it is used especially of people inside the circle of Jesus' disciples. It appears subsequently in connection with the Twelve (6:52; 8:17-18). Faith, then, is not something Mark treats in a deterministic way, and the difficult words of 4:11-13 are a statement about judgment and not about predestination.

Even so, it is one thing to say that the primary institution of first-

being one of the few sayings attributed to Jesus that appear in all four Gospels (Mt 13:13; Lk 8:10; Jn 9:39).

century Judaism was opposed to what God was doing in Jesus. It is another thing to say that the people who listened to Jesus speak beside the Sea of Galilee had done something to deserve God's judgment. What is this judgment, and why has it come upon these people? The judgment is that they will see but not perceive and listen but not understand. It is the same kind of thing that happened to the people to whom Isaiah spoke, a confirmation of what they had already done themselves. They have heard the word without acting upon it. They listened to the parables, they heard Jesus instruct them to pay attention, and then they went away. The ones who came to understand the parables were those who came with the Twelve to Jesus when he was alone. They heard the parable of the soils. They heard the commands to listen. They paid attention. They realized that they were hearing a story that did not make sense by itself, so they asked Jesus what the parable meant. In short, they heard the word and acted on it. They did the very thing that the parable describes.

Is it fair for this judgment to fall so quickly? In Isaiah 6:9-13 a considerable period of time separates faithless act from judgment. There had been a multitude . . . of sacrifices (Is 1:11) and a succession of New Moons, Sabbaths and convocations (Is 1:13); and Jerusalem, which was once a city of faithfulness, had become a harlot (Is 1:21). Judgment did not come as soon as the people of Judah acted falsely. Years passed, while God spoke through the prophets. In Mark 4:11-13, however, judgment seems to fall almost instantly. Either the people who listened to the parables acted upon what they heard at that moment or their hearts were hardened.

Two points need to be made. First, the distance between act and judgment may not be as short as it appears. Before matters reached this point Jesus had gone throughout Galilee preaching about the kingdom of God in the synagogues (1:14, 39). This was not the first time Jesus had addressed the people who lived in Galilee. Furthermore, when he preached in the synagogues his message centered around four themes: the time is fulfilled, the kingdom of God is at hand, repent, and believe the gospel (1:15). Even before the rift between Jesus and the synagogues developed, the people of Galilee were living in a time of crisis that required decisive action. The kingdom of God was at hand, and the people who heard the good news had to decide what they were going to do about it. Once the gospel had left the synagogue, the need to act became even more critical. If the kingdom of God was at hand and if the structures of first-century Jewish life were aligning themselves against it, then listening to Jesus' words without believing them was itself an act of serious consequence. It was the kind of time that demands action. So after proclaiming the good news openly through preaching and acts of power all over Galilee, Jesus began to speak in a way that makes understanding and acting inseparable.

This line of thought leads to the most difficult question in this passage. What is the secret of the kingdom of God? Jesus' first comment to the people who asked him about the parable was, *The secret of the kingdom of God has been given to you.* Previously we have examined the aftermath of that statement, but we have not addressed what the secret is. And here we face a formidable challenge because, whatever the secret is, Mark does not tell us (Carlston 1975:101), at least not directly.

It is possible, of course, that Mark simply forgot to include it. One of the recurring judgments against this Evangelist is that he was not in control of his material (Nineham 1968:29-30). Within the bounds of modern biblical criticism that possibility cannot be overlooked. Given the subtle attention to detail that Mark has taken in developing the theme of the kingdom of God, however, this would be a curious omission indeed. His exposition of this theme is not only subtle, it is also indirect.

For example, the subject of Jesus' preaching was the kingdom of God, but Mark never presents his audience with a sermon. These parables, most of which were told privately, are the most extensive collection of Jesus' sayings Mark has provided so far. After introducing the theme in 1:15, though, he shows us Jesus acting with a unique authority. Later in 1:39 we find a justification for viewing the miracles as examples of Jesus' preaching. That is to say, although Mark does not give us the text of Jesus' preaching, he does give us enacted sermons. Then as the impact of Jesus' ministry grows, Mark gives us a parable about the tension between the new and the old, as well as a series of encounters that define it. If Mark's style is inherently indirect, then the omission of something essential is unlikely to be a proof of his clumsiness. It is much more likely to be an example of his artistry.

Here, however, after treating his audience as though they were part of those on the inside, he now treats the audience as part of the crowd. We read (or hear) something that pricks our interest, but we do not know what it means. He puts us in the position of having to ask what the secret of the kingdom is. And this is not the only point where Mark presents Jesus or the kingdom of God in this way. After the parable of the soils, for which he provides the interpretation, Mark relates four more parables—all without an explanation. The parable of the seed growing by itself and the mustard seed are the first explicit teaching Mark provides about the kingdom of God. His treatment of this theme is consistent. Despite the seminal importance of this material, the Evangelist is content to present it again indirectly.

What then is the secret of the kingdom of God? In Jesus' preaching, parables and miracles, the kingdom of God had arrived in a form that no one had expected (Guelich 1989:232; Ladd 1974:94). Jesus did not exhort young Jewish men and their fathers to expel the Roman oppressors from the Promised Land. He did not call pious Jews who lived in the Diaspora to colonize Israel again. His miracles did not demonstrate political cunning, and Jesus did not call the Roman troops dogs. Even at this early stage in the Gospel the power of God was at work to heal, restore and reconcile. To believe the gospel Jesus brought meant holding visions of national dominance and freedom loosely.

The Parable of the Soils Explained (4:13-20) True to form, the interpretation of the parable begins with two questions: the rhetorical *Don't you understand this parable?* and the open-ended *How then will you understand any parable?* The first question does not require an answer, while the second does not receive an answer until 4:33-34. Those verses restrict the circle of understanding to the disciples, to whom he explained everything. Those who read the Gospel are brought only partially into this process of hearing and understanding. Mark provides the interpretation for the parable of the soils, but leaves the other four parables in 4:21-32 unexplained. We are left to ponder how to understand them.

The interpretation casts the parable as an allegory. Most of its details have some larger meaning outside the parable itself. The seed is the word, and in the context of this Gospel it could be either a word about the kingdom or any word of God. The soil refers to four different kinds of people. The birds represent Satan. The scorching sun symbolizes trouble and persecution. The thorns point to the cares of the world. And the good soil is the people who hear, accept and produce.

Everyone hears the same word initially. The good soil, however receives the word in a way that the other three do not. The Greek word translated "accept" (4:20) is an intensive verb that can also mean "acknowledge as true" or even "love." This is a parable about hearing, and out of the large crowd that came to listen, one smaller group can be distinguished from the rest. It was composed of those who accepted what they had heard and acknowledged that they did not understand it. Presumably, the rest of the crowd either reached the same conclusion or decided that the parable had no significance. Those who became disciples, however, did something else. They acted upon what they heard and asked what it meant.

Finally, the productivity of the good soil is connected to perseverance. None of the other soils persevere. The rocky soil produces only a brief spurt of growth, while the soil with thorns produces growth that is eventually choked out. Nothing, though, prevents the growth of the seed in good soil. If the kingdom of God has come in an unexpected way, then those who receive it must accept a word that contradicts their hopes, act on this word in some manner and persevere in embracing the word when other avenues of fulfillment open to them. Believing and repenting were the responses Jesus expected. So acting on the word might also be called the secret of the kingdom of God. Ultimately, to act on Jesus' word is to do the will of God, an idea that has already found expression in 3:31-35. Here, however, doing the will of God is to take a relatively small step. To do the will of God is to ask what the parables mean.

We live in the age of instant gratification. That expectation is even built into our technology. In designing microchips for computers, a principle called Moore's Law states that every year and a half the number of transistors that can be built into a microprocessor will double. What pushes the drive to double our computing speed and power every eighteen months? It is the same drive that makes us complain about having to wait in a line at amusement parks. That cultural expectation has made its way into the church. We expect to have everything on demand and on our terms. Accordingly, religious sociologists often describe this as the era of the consumer church.

That is not the way Mark presents Jesus. Faith for him is not one of the consumer goods. We do not grow on demand. We do not experience God by scheduling time in our personal organizers. And we do not have all our questions answered before Jesus asks us to make a commitment. The Jesus we meet in this Gospel cannot be understood until we begin to act on his word, and then his word sets the agenda. Perhaps we ought to exercise some caution in attempting to build churches that cater to the consumer mind-set.

Parables About Parables (4:21-25) "Do you know what I like best about your church?" the mother of the bride gushed at the end of a rehearsal. "You don't have a big old cross cluttering up the sanctuary. I can't begin to tell you how relieved I am." She had not been to church in years. She would have preferred to have had the wedding in a park, but her daughter and future son-in-law had insisted on a Christian church. "Instead," she continued, "you have this gorgeous stained-glass window that fills the room with light. I just love it."

She was right about the stained-glass window, but wrong about the cross. About fourteen feet wide and nearly twenty-five feet high, the window is a stunning impressionistic representation of the interplay of light and water elegantly crafted in four panels. The two upper panels extend ten feet down from the roofline, and beneath them are two longer panels reaching down another fifteen feet. Its southern exposure does fill the sanctuary with light. But the four panels are connected by two large, intersecting beams of dark wood that stretch from side to side and from the top to the bottom of the window.

Do you bring in a lamp, Jesus asked (4:21), to put it under a bowl or a bed? Instead, don't you put it on its stand? Those two rhetorical questions would provoke no dissent. The nature of light is to reveal, illuminate and expose. His next two comments, however, would not prompt universal agreement: *For whatever is hidden is meant to be disclosed, and whatever is concealed is meant to be brought out into the open.* This is a paradoxical pair of affirmations with which an array of international leaders might disagree. In politics at least, more often than not the purpose of hiding something is to keep it hidden. Whether a secret is hidden in order for it to be revealed depends upon who is speaking and what is being hidden.

The speaker in this case is Jesus, and the question is, What has he hidden? In the Gospel of Mark the only thing that Jesus has hidden is his teaching about the kingdom of God, and he has hidden it in parables. These verses then are actually a collection of sayings about parables. They affirm two things that stand together in considerable tension. The first is that Jesus has not come to hide himself (Schweizer 1970:98), the kingdom of God (Anderson 1976:136) or even his message (Gundry 1993:212). Second, 4:22 paradoxically affirms that the purpose of hiding something is to reveal it. And after these two assertions we encounter once again the command to pay attention.

Mark has done similar things before. All of Mark 3, for example, revolves around a set of questions and arguments that the Evangelist does not resolve. It is up to the audience to decide why Jesus' family thought he was crazy (3:21), why he appointed twelve apostles (3:14) and why he dismissed his mother and brothers in such striking terms (3:33-35). At this point, however, Mark moves beyond the style of indirect communication that asks the reader to decide what something means. He has divided the characters into two groups of people: those on the inside and those on the outside. The insiders learn the meaning of the parables. The outsiders are left with the unexplained parables, and we are on the outside. Mark does not tell us directly what the secret of the kingdom of God is. He does not tell us how to resolve the tension between the light that illuminates and the things that are hidden in order to be revealed. Furthermore, he does not tell us the meaning of either the parable about the seed growing by itself or the parable about the mustard seed.

We are not, though, left to our own devices. Mark has already given us in his own terms a way to learn the meaning of the parables. It is found in the interplay between Jesus and the people who came to ask him about the parable of the soils: *Don't you understand this parable?* he asked in 4:13. *How then will you understand any parable?* They understood the parables by asking Jesus what his sayings meant. That is the way Mark leaves open for his audience to pursue. Built into the fabric of this Gospel is the assumption that Jesus still speaks. The one who explained the parables to his first followers is also present for later generations of people who are drawn to follow him.

The parable of the measure (4:24-25) develops a similar theme. It, too, is about the way we listen. The meaning of this parable might become clearer if we picture what would have happened when someone went to purchase flour in a Galilean town. The price of flour would have been fixed at so much per measure. When the customer produced the money, the merchant would have produced the measure, filled it carefully and given the proper amount to the customer. Imagine how the transaction would change if the buyer supplied the measure, and the price remained fixed no matter what the measure was. Customers would bring the largest measures they could find, and every day would be bargain day!

That is not, of course, the way things normally work, but that reversal of the expected order of things lies at the center of this small parable. When he told a parable, Jesus was not the one who determined how much the hearer received. The listener was! With the measure you use, it will be measured to you—and even more. The measure is the way people listened to the parables, and the way they listened determined what they would take away from an encounter with Jesus. In other words, parables are a way of teaching that requires a response from the listener. A simple hearing is not enough for a person to understand. Hearing, affirming and acting are inseparable.

Jesus elaborated on the last three words, and even more, by saying: *Whoever has will be given more; whoever does not have, even what he has will be taken from him* (4:25). In terms of this statement the people who have are the ones who hear the word, welcome it and act on it in some way. Those people receive even more. In this context what they receive is more of Jesus' words. The people who respond to Jesus' words get something back that is out of all proportion to their response. On the other hand, the people who fail to welcome or respond to what they hear walk away from something they did not understand and quickly forget all about it. They lose what they had.

The larger passage (4:1-34) is built around the principle contained in 4:24-25. The people who respond are the ones who recognize that they do not understand what the parables mean and ask about them. They are the ones with the Twelve who question Jesus about the parables after the crowd has gone (4:10). They receive not only the explanation of the parable of the soils, but the secret of the kingdom of God and a general explanation of how all the parables are to be understood.

The parables of Jesus then are instruments of judgment. The words Jesus speaks are not like other words we hear and about which we make judgments. We decide whether those words are appealing, true, helpful or worthwhile. It is not going too far to say that we assume the right to judge them. The words of Jesus, on the other hand, judge us. If we respond in faith and obedience, God gives us more. If we disregard them, we lose what we might already have had.

Parables are the language of faith. What is distinctive about faith, from Mark's perspective, is indicated in the parable of the soils. Faith is welcoming the word, receiving it with joy, letting it take root, and above all else persevering in the face of adversity. It is not something that originates in us. Like Paul in Romans 10:17, Mark thinks of faith as originating with the Word of God. Insofar as faith involves hearing and acting, the parables are a way of communicating that is particularly suited to what Mark wants to communicate. Faith involves both hearing and acting, and Jesus' parables are figures of speech that provoke a response. One kind of response leads to judgment, while another kind leads to more faith.

We might also think of parables in terms of the distinction that is sometimes drawn between objective and subjective faith. Objective faith refers to what we believe. The Apostles' Creed, the Westminster Confession and the Barmen Declaration are examples of objective faith. Subjective faith, on the other hand, refers to how we believe; it is a matter of the affections and encompasses the elements of trust, personal commitment, perseverance and loyalty that we have in mind when we say that someone is a faithful person.

In the last 150 years a number of theological systems have been built upon either the objective or subjective aspect of faith. As Mark presents them, however, the parables of Jesus are a medium for faith in which the objective and subjective elements are treated as an indivisible whole. There is something objective that Jesus wants to talk about:

the word or, more precisely, the word about the kingdom of God. But the people who hear the parables cannot understand what is being said unless they exercise the subjective elements of faith. From this point forward in the Gospel, Jesus does not put his teaching out so that it can be understood objectively. The word about the rule of God is not a matter for idle curiosity. To understand the gospel people must respond by welcoming, acting and persevering.

Two Parables about the Kingdom of God (4:26-34) The parables about the seed growing by itself and the mustard seed address expectations about the kingdom of God that were held by Jesus' contemporaries. Many of them thought of the kingdom of God primarily in terms of the land of Israel, and some held that the land would have a new Jewish king when the people obeyed the law completely. The Gospel of Mark does not depict the kingdom of God in these terms at all. Judgment had not fallen on evil and hypocritical people. Jerusalem and Judah were still occupied by a foreign power. The poor and oppressed were still poor and oppressed, and yet some things had changed. A new power had appeared in the person of Jesus to heal the sick, break the hold of demonic forces and bring God's love and forgiveness directly to people who were outside the law.

The parable of the seed growing by itself compares the kingdom of God to the growth of a seed. The seed grows in stages according to its own timetable (Dahl 1952:141-43), and the arrival of the harvest is not the result of human activity: *All by itself the soil produces grain.* In this parable soil does not refer to people, nor does the growth of the seed depend upon human activity. Soil is simply the medium in which growth takes place. How it grows is a mystery. The seed has a life of its own, and the farmer can sleep in this knowledge. This parable suggests that the kingdom of God does not arrive all at once and that its coming is more a matter of God's grace than of our obedience. This is a significant departure from the rabbinic teachings we examined in connection with 2:23—3:6, in which the obedience of all the people of

---

4:32 Based on similar language in the Greek version of Ezekiel 31:6, Markus suggests that the birds in the parable of the mustard seed symbolize the Gentiles (1999:324). There is, however, no fixed symbolism attached to birds in biblical liter-

Israel was the precondition for the arrival of the kingdom of God. In this parable Jesus distinguishes his teaching about the kingdom of God in several ways: the rule of God is more like the growth of a plant than a geographic entity; it does not wait for perfect obedience; and it does not arrive all at once. For these reasons many scholars prefer to speak of the rule of God rather than the kingdom of God.

The parable of the mustard seed points to another surprise. The popular expectation in the first century envisioned the kingdom arriving as a cataclysmic event. Jesus' contemporaries would have been more likely to compare it to a thunderstorm than a mustard seed, but there is nothing overwhelming or abrupt about a mustard seed. It is so small as to be insignificant, but it eventually produces a plant so large that the birds of the air take refuge in its shade. This parable contrasts a small and unexpected beginning with a much larger consummation. This comparison leads in turn to the possibility that the kingdom of God might be present, although unnoticed by people looking for something else.

At the end of this collection of parables the Evangelist adds the comment that Jesus taught the crowd with many other parables like these as much as they could understand (4:33). This comment rounds out the narrative nicely by summarizing some of the ideas that Jesus first stated in 4:10-13. In one sense it is a fitting conclusion to the things Mark has shown us about Jesus in chapter four. In another sense, however, it is a provocative statement in its own right, for it leaves Mark's readers with the disturbing question of what we are able to understand.

We live in an age of negotiated commitments. The contract is more important than the handshake, and in some cases a written prenuptial agreement defines the meaning of the promises that a bride and groom exchange at their wedding. We want to know all the contingencies before we make a commitment. Jesus speaks in parables, on the other hand, and no one understands what he says before making a commitment. Understanding comes as people respond to what they hear. Those who follow him and ask questions learn the meaning of what he

---

ature, as a comparison with Mark 4:4-15 demonstrates, and this parable does not exhibit any of the allegorical characteristics of the parable of the soils.

has said and receive more. Then what they receive opens up a whole new set of possibilities for even more hearing and acting.

Faith for Mark is more like an adventure whose terms unfold as we pursue it. It cannot be understood from a distance, and we are never in control of what happens. Our part is to listen and act, and then listen and act again and again. That alone is an unnerving thought for people living in a postmodern world. In our thoughts and dreams the self is invariably at the center of things, but in this adventure the self has been dislodged. There is something or someone else at the center of things whom we can neither define nor control. We are invited to follow along when we have only an inkling of where we are going.

Jesus Rebukes the Wind (4:35-41) Extending twenty-five miles from the back of Glendora, California, all the way up to Mount Baldy Village, Glendora Mountain Road is one of the premier bicycling roads in America. I am definitely not one of the premier cyclists in America, but I enjoy the challenge of the ride. Several years ago I had a close encounter with a very large tow truck as I was racing back down GMR. It almost convinced me to give up the sport. I remember watching the five-foot-high front wheel roll past, inches away from my head as I sped toward a three-point landing on my knees and chin. Everything happened so quickly that I did not have time to be afraid before slamming into the asphalt. It occurred to me, in an objective way, as I tumbled over the handlebars that I might die, but it was not until afterward, when I tried unsuccessfully to stand up, that I felt the fear. The decision to start riding again was not easy, and for the next year and a half I flinched every time I spotted a car coming toward me.

It would be easy to dismiss the fear of the people in the boat with Jesus by asserting that they should have realized who he was. At least four of them were fishermen, and two of them, James and John, were skilled in handling boats on this lake. And if Jesus were asleep in the pilot's seat, as the reference to a cushion suggests (Waetjen 1989:112), then their plight was even more serious. The wind was driving the waves over the boat, the ship was filling up with water, and the person sitting in the pilot's seat was fast asleep. If those fishermen thought they were in trouble, there was in all probability something to fear.

At this point in the development of the story none of Jesus' followers understood who he was. They had seen his dynamic teaching (1:21-28), witnessed his power to heal the worst of diseases (1:40-45), heard him claim to be the Son of Man with power on earth to forgive sin (2:10), watched him confound his enemies (2:23-28), received authority to cast out unclean spirits (3:15) and learned his parables (4:1-34). Yet his claim to be the Son of Man must have been confusing since there is no reference in the Old Testament to the Son of Man appearing on earth. He is an eschatological figure who appears only at the end of history. Furthermore, nowhere in the Old Testament is the Son of Man ever associated with the Messiah or the Son of God. And as far as their new authority is concerned, it was a power the Twelve had yet to test. To expect the disciples to understand who Jesus was is stretching things a good deal.

What then did Jesus expect of them? His rebuke in 4:40 indicates that faith is the issue. But if their fear is not to be undervalued and if it is too early to expect them to perceive Jesus' identity, then what does it mean to believe? Doubt, which is usually cast as the opposite of faith, is not part of this story, nor does it appear in the following accounts. In fact, in the miracle stories of 4:35—5:43 the opposite of faith is always fear. This is no small distinction. It is common to affirm, for instance, that faith is necessary in order to see or experience a miracle. That idea is consistent to some extent with the notion that doubt is the opposite of faith. In the account of Jesus' calming the storm, however, the disciples were rescued by a miracle even though they lacked faith. If fear is the opposite of faith, how do we believe?

There is a new kind of tension in this pericope. The earlier miracles contained seeds of conflict that matured into intractable opposition. Here, however, there is a lot of tension, but neither the teachers of the law, the leaders of the synagogues nor the traditions of the people are anywhere in evidence. The tension in this event is between Jesus and his own followers. Their fear of death and his undisturbed sleep generate the conflict. Jesus slept unconcerned, while they bailed furiously in fear of their lives.

Unlike the earlier miracles, this one has two focal points. The first one is consistent with all the earlier accounts in that it demonstrates the power of the kingdom of God. When Jesus rebuked the sea and commanded the wind to be silent, he revealed a new aspect about the kingdom of God. He spoke to the storm as though it were a demonic power (Guelich 1989:267). As he had already demonstrated his authority over the demonic powers in people, here Jesus revealed his authority over the demonic or chaotic in nature.

That much is clear when he rebuked the wind. That rebuke is followed by a second one, and the abrupt words he spoke to his disciples signal two fundamental changes in the form of the miracle story. Instead of ending on a note of praise, as the healing of the paralytic did (2:12), this one ends in fear. The disciples were terrified, even more afraid after Jesus spoke to them than they had been during the storm. Terrified they asked: *Who is this? Even the wind and the waves obey him!* The account of this miracle does not have a conclusion that resolves all the points of tension. In fact, if we take the comment that Jesus accompanied them *just as he was, in the boat* (4:36) as an indication of the disciples' settled view of Jesus, there is more confusion and less resolution at the end of the story than at its beginning.

Mark has cast the shadow of the cross over the entire structure of the Gospel. The arrest of John the Baptist (1:14) and the plot to destroy Jesus (3:6) are signposts to Golgotha. Later on it becomes clear that following Jesus means following him to Jerusalem and taking up one's own cross. Here for the first time the disciples confronted the possibility that following Jesus might cost them their lives. They were saved because Jesus was incredibly more powerful than they had thought. So they were left with the question of who he is.

In short, unlike the previous accounts of miracles this one ends with a question, has a hidden meaning and invites the followers of Jesus to come to terms with their fear of death, something they might otherwise avoid. In the earlier part of Mark 4, Mark portrays Jesus teaching exclusively through a form of speech that has these same qualities. The parables are open-ended, contain a hidden meaning and provoke people into coming to terms with something they might otherwise avoid. The basic features of Jesus' parables have taken root in this story, and this is the Evangelist's signal that the miracles are no longer direct expositions of the kingdom of God. Like Jesus' teaching, the miracles have also become indirect. They are enacted parables about the kingdom that increasingly raise questions about who Jesus is and what it means to believe.

If the miracles are parables, we have an answer to the question of what Jesus expected of the people in the boat with him. It was on the basis of his word, *let us go over to the other side,* that they found themselves in this predicament. Jesus expected them to ask something like the question in 4:10. That is to say, he did not expect them to leap over their fear and confusion to confess him as Messiah and Son of God. He expected them to ask him what to do or how to pray or where they could turn. That was the kind of thing they did when they asked him what his parable meant, but fear had turned their faith into sarcasm. The question *don't you care if we drown?* is not the stuff of faith—it is an accusation.

The dynamic tension between fear and faith is still an important, if often overlooked, component of spirituality. In 1984 Jerry Levin, the CNN bureau chief in Beirut, was kidnapped on his way to work. For more than a year he was held hostage by powerful men who objected violently to the way the United States was employing its forces in Lebanon. Tethered to a radiator for fourteen months by a chain so short that he could not stand up straight, Jerry reexamined the premises by which he had lived. A convinced agnostic for most of his life, Jerry had thought that Jesus' ideas about how people should live were too flimsy for the harsh realities of life. Day after day as his captors used his fear of death to humiliate him, however, Jerry began to see that constantly escalating violence was no solution for international disputes. The Sermon on the Mount, he realized, was not wishful thinking. It was the only reasonable response to an absurd world. And so in an absolutely hopeless situation Jerry Levin found faith: "It was a shrinking . . . millionth of a second, on one side of which I did not believe and on the other side I did" (Levin 1989:188). Since his conversion Jerry and Sis Levin have both served as activists for peace in Israel and in the occupied territories.

Jesus Casts Out a Legion (5:1-20) In 1997 Rev. Wylie Drake was put on trial for sheltering homeless people at his church. Night after night he served food and allowed an indeterminate number of folks to sleep beneath a covered patio, defying building codes and restraining orders from the city of Buena Park, California. Neighbors complained that the homeless people frightened them, did not bother to use indoor toilets and posed a threat to their safety. Drake eventually reached an accommodation with the city that allowed him to keep the shelter open. He agreed to hire security guards and to build a permanent structure to house the homeless on church property. Two years passed quietly and Drake did not make the headlines again until May 21, 1999, when Jack Leonard reported that Drake had applied for a permit to carry a concealed weapon. Although professing a belief in nonviolence, Drake applied for the permit because the homeless population includes "dangerous criminals on probation and parole" (*Los Angeles Times*, May 21, 1999).

The man who lived in a cemetery and ran to fall at Jesus' feet must have presented another terrifying spectacle to the people who had spent a night on the lake. Mark 5:2 specifies that Jesus got out of the boat. The disciples, it seems, did not. Like some of the mentally ill who make up a large percentage of the modern homeless population, the man in the cemetery was driven by powerful self-destructive impulses that he could not control. The opening verses of this chapter describe in some detail a human being who was an appalling collection of contradictions. He was an antisocial outcast who did not stray far from the centers of population. He lived in the place of the dead, within screaming distance of a tormented village. He abused himself either because of a fascination with death or because of morbid impulses that he could not control, yet he went on living. He could not be bound even with iron shackles, but he was not free in any sense. When he ran from the tombs to fall at Jesus' feet without saying a word, the demoniac presented Jesus with another contradiction. Falling at someone's feet was an act of submission, supplication or even worship (Greeven 1968:763). Yet as soon as Jesus ordered the demonic powers to leave, the man opposed him with the words: *What do you want with me, Jesus, Son of the Most High God?*

No other incident in the Gospels is quite like this one. The prolonged introduction of the demoniac in 5:1-5 has no parallel in this Gospel. The story line is awkward and jumbled. Chronologically, the material in 5:8 when Jesus first spoke to the demoniac should proceed the defiant words of 5:7. Furthermore, the story has several unique elements. Never before have the demonic powers refused to leave when Jesus commanded them. Nowhere else does he encounter a spiritual power whose name suggests a company of Roman soldiers. Finally, this is the only exorcism in which the unclean spirits bargain for territorial rights.

These features raise a series of questions that may be unanswerable. Why, for example, did Jesus bargain with the demonic powers? How were they able to resist him? What purpose was served by allowing them to enter the swine? If they are unanswerable, the important point is to appreciate the puzzling effect they create. The awkward story line, the shocking description of the man who fell at Jesus' feet, the power of the legion to resist Jesus and the bewildering questions about what Jesus did all heighten the elements of fear in the story. The entire episode has been crafted so that the reader receives an overwhelming impression of fear, a feature that is still palpable after Jesus restored the man to his right mind.

The lingering fear is apparent in the villagers' request that Jesus leave the area. Why they would make a request like this is not difficult to understand. The exorcism he had performed had resulted in the destruction of a herd of pigs. The economic impact of this miracle is staggering. Furthermore, whatever can be said about the legion of unclean spirits, Jesus had not sent them out of the territory. They were still there, possibly seeking a new host after the demise of the swine. One man had been set free, but the price of his freedom might well have been more than the community wanted to pay.

There is a certain security in knowing where evil is. To tie evil to a name or location creates the hope that it can be avoided. Before Jesus cast out the demonic host, the local people had a kind of awful security. They knew where evil was, and despite the screams in the night they knew how to avoid it. Avoid the man, and you could avoid the evil. Because of what Jesus did, though, this system no longer worked. Jesus' presence constituted a threat to the structure of their community. The people of this region faced the choice of embracing Jesus and trusting his authority to order and protect them or asking him to leave and await the return of something with which they were already familiar. Not surprisingly they asked him to leave.

Crossan puts forth a novel reinterpretation of the passage. He thinks that the encounter between Jesus and the legion of unclean spirits was a late creation of the early church, perhaps only a few years before the destruction of temple when the tension between Jerusalem and Rome was at its height. Taking his cue from the word *legion,* Crossan proposes that the unclean spirits symbolize the Roman oppression of the Jewish people and that the story presents Jesus as the one who challenges the power of Rome. The argument that colonial oppression can lead to mental illness is unquestionably modern, but Crossan thinks there are enough indicators in this incident to establish that people in the first century could appreciate the connection. In the final analysis, he maintains, this is essentially a story about political rather than spiritual oppression (1994:88-89).

Crossan is a gifted writer, but even his elegant prose cannot cover up the flaws in this argument. In the first place, there is nothing Jewish about the story, and except for the suggestive word *legion* nothing could place it in the tension between Rome and Jerusalem. Second, Jesus' opponents in the Gospel of Mark are Jewish: he offended the Pharisees and teachers of the law; he was forced out of the synagogues; and the historical event that led to his death took place in Jerusalem. Even though this Gospel was probably written about the time when Jerusalem was destroyed, a period that also included the persecution of Christians in Rome, Mark consistently presents Jesus' opponents as the people who were vested in the social, political and religious structures of first-century Judaism. Why Mark would include a supposedly late fabrication that stands so thoroughly at odds with his own point of view is inexplicable. If there were a connection between political oppression and demonic possession in the minds of first-century folk, Mark is completely unaware of it.

The implications of this exorcism may be far-reaching, but the issues and power structures Jesus engaged here are local and spiritual. At the end of this encounter they come to focus on the man who had been possessed. He is the most alienated person to appear so far in Mark's Gospel, and the people who came to see what had happened were more concerned about the death of the pigs than about his restoration. They felt no joy at the release of an oppressed man. There was only fear about the future.

It would have been perfectly understandable if Jesus had said, "Come—follow me." Yet even though the restored man asked to accompany him, Jesus denied him. It is easy to understand why the man wanted to leave; it is harder to understand why Jesus would not let him go along. Instead, Jesus told him to tell his family what the Lord had done for him, and without any further instruction or training he became a gospel preacher. He told people throughout the Decapolis what Jesus had done for him. If we stick strictly to the language of this account, it appears that this Gentile was the first person to proclaim that Jesus was Lord.

Jesus left the people of the area with a living parable. He honored their request that he leave, but he also left behind a man who kept telling what had happened to him and the pigs. The people of the Decapolis heard a remarkable story from a man whose continued wholeness was a challenge to their way of living. Whenever he told his story the same questions about the value of a completely marginalized person, the threat of economic disaster and the place of evil were present just below the surface. Had something truly good happened? Should they fear his words or believe them? Those questions would be addressed when Jesus returned to the area.

Sometimes we invite people to follow Jesus without giving them any idea that accepting his invitation may be costly. In our eagerness to offer them hope and healing we may understate the ways faith will change them, underestimate the power and entrenched structures of evil or explain away the tension between faith and fear. That is certainly not the way Mark and Jesus proclaimed the gospel. Mark highlights the healing at the same time that he probes the tension between faith and fear. He presents Jesus' words and ministry as parables that offer the hope of the gospel in simple terms, while he also shows how an encounter with Jesus changes the structures of life. The tension between faith and fear may be with us for most of our lives. Whenever we take a risk for the gospel, we may also find something to fear. Our responsibility is neither to shy away from fear nor to make ourselves numb to it. Our challenge is to act in faith even when we are afraid. That is a challenge we cannot meet alone.

Jesus Heals Two Daughters (5:21-43) Nothing demands more from a pastor than ministering to a family that has lost a child. Phillip was eight years old when he crawled into his mother's arms just before dawn and breathed his last breath. His brave, five-year struggle against cancer had come to an end, but the spiritual battle facing his family was far from over. They did not attend our church, but his devastated parents came to us because their pastor had warned them that their son would be healed only if their faith was perfect. When Phillip died they were crushed. They believed his death was their fault. And his eleven-year-old sister went to sleep at night and dreamed of going to heaven to be with her brother.

The miracle stories that follow the collection of parables in 4:1-34 all deal with impossible situations. They remind us of what a fragile thing hope is, and they portray the dialectic of belief as a struggle between faith and fear. Neither Jairus, whose twelve-year-old daughter lay at home at the point of death, nor the unnamed woman, whose hemorrhage had proven incurable despite twelve years of care under many doctors, was hopeless, but they were both desperate.

It was a sign of Jairus's desperation that he even came to Jesus. He was a ruler of the synagogue, and the breach between Jesus and the synagogues had become irreparable. Leading members of the synagogues had conspired to kill him. Jairus met Jesus outside the structure of the synagogues. The full measure of Jairus's desperation became apparent when he bowed down publicly at Jesus' feet and begged for the life of his daughter. It is unlikely that Jairus's approach to Jesus would have increased his standing in the synagogue.

A secretive desperation drove the woman who touched Jesus (5:27). Her hemorrhage made her unclean, and according to the law of Moses anyone whom she touched would also become unclean (Lev 15:19-30). So she approached him from behind, hidden among the crowd, while

---

5:22 As an *archisynagōgos* Jairus was a man of considerable prominence in his community. In addition to his standing in the community as a whole, he would also have

the questions about Jairus and Jesus filled everyone else's thoughts. She hoped to escape notice and not to incur any more shame. She wanted merely to touch Jesus' clothing, be healed and steal away unnoticed. That would set the stage for her to perform the rituals of purification and reenter society without embarrassment.

As this procession was jostling its way toward Jairus's house, Jesus stopped abruptly and asked: *Who touched my clothes?* The disciples thought it was a ridiculous question. The woman who had been healed thought it was a terrifying question, and she came forward trembling with fear. We do not know what Jairus thought. He, too, might have been rendered unclean, and before they could get moving again, he received word that his daughter had died.

Jesus' question sets him apart from modern superstars. It demonstrates his sensitivity to faith rather than to popular acclaim. They make room in their busy schedules for photo opportunities, power lunches and interviews with the media. The first priority on their agenda is enhancing their public image. If that had been Jesus' concern, he might have been better advised to reach Jairus's house without delay. Healing the daughter of an important person like Jairus could have paid great dividends in public exposure. If she died because he stopped along the way, however, his reputation might suffer.

It is easy to sympathize with the bewilderment of Jesus' disciples. There were undoubtedly a lot of people bumping and clutching at Jesus. The idea of distinguishing one particular person in that crowd would naturally seem impossible. On the other hand, though, their bewilderment confirms their dwindling perception. The parables of Mark 4, for which they alone received an explanation, are all about faith. That teaching together with their own response to Jesus' preaching has distinguished them as the new people God is gathering. Yet ever since Jesus' rebuke in 4:40 even the Twelve, to whom Jesus gave authority to preach and cast out unclean spirits, have been relegated to the sidelines. They are no more than observers when other people exercise faith. It is as though their own fear had overwhelmed their faith.

---

been the person who conducted worship and maintained the building (Schrage 1971:845-47).

What did the woman fear? She was certainly afraid that she would incur more shame. Perhaps she feared that Jesus would be angry at her impertinence, or even that he might undo the healing when he realized what she had done. Perhaps she feared the anger of the crowd if the others understood what she had done to them. Perhaps she was afraid of having the intimate details of her life revealed to everyone within hearing distance. Any one or any combination of these fears would explain the fear and trembling she displayed at Jesus' feet. To her credit she told the whole truth despite her fear.

At this point Jesus did something that is not repeated elsewhere in the Gospel of Mark. He called the woman daughter. Except for the paralytic in 2:5 Jesus had not addressed anyone, not even the Twelve, as members of his family. In fact, up to this point Jesus has not even referred to God as his father. Since this story began with Jairus begging Jesus to heal his daughter, it is all the more striking when Jesus called this otherwise anonymous woman daughter.

In what sense could she be his daughter? This was not the first time Jesus had spoken about the family. When his mother and brothers tried to exercise some measure of control over him (3:31-35), Jesus announced a new definition of the family. His family consisted of all those who did the will of God. Here was a new definition of the family in which the bond that unites people who do the will of God is set above the kinship of blood. In this woman who had suffered so much and who had violated the law of Moses, Jesus found a daughter. She had done the will of God by reaching out in faith.

Despite her fear she believed in Jesus' power to save her. This distinguished her from the disciples in the boat, whose fear had led them into sarcasm. After twelve years of searching, spending and declining health, she knew what she was facing. She also knew the risks of picking her way through the crowd to approach Jesus, but there is no hint of cynicism or resignation in her story. Fear did not prevent her from acting in hope. Surely, this is what Jesus meant when he affirmed what she had done with the words *your faith has healed you*. It was not the purity or perfection of her faith that healed her. Mark makes it clear that Jesus' power had healed her (5:30). Her faith was a response to his power, and the singular quality of her faith was acting in hope in spite of the things she feared.

If that were all Jesus had said, the implications would still be startling. In the normal course of events people of wealth and power enjoy preferential treatment. Of the two, Jairus would typically be received more favorably than the woman. He was a leader in the synagogue, and she was both impoverished and unclean. Yet Jesus called her daughter, and he held up her action as a model of faith. The subtle reordering of life in these two stories is an essential part of the Gospel (Meyers 1988:202).

We have a hint of how far this reordering extends in Jesus' final comment to the woman: *Go in peace and be freed from your suffering.* This is the kind of thing a priest would say after the proper offerings and sacrifices for cleansing had been made. Jesus, in fact, instructed the leper whom he healed in 1:43 to present himself to a priest for this very purpose. In this case, however, after his breach with the synagogues and in the presence of a ruler of a synagogue, Jesus assumed the role of the priest, required no sacrifice and blessed a woman who had made countless people unclean.

We can only imagine what Jairus might have thought of Jesus at this point. He was invested in the system of holy places, rituals and traditions that formed the fabric of first-century Jewish life. Jesus, on the other hand, had no standing with the priestly hierarchy in Jerusalem. He showed no concern with the woman's trampling of the law. And in an unhallowed place he told this woman that there was peace between her and God. It is almost as though Mark had applied the prophecy of Isaiah 40:4 to the high place on which the temple stood: "Every valley shall be raised up, every mountain and hill made low."

While the various parties in the crowd were trying to assimilate what Jesus had just said, messengers arrived to tell Jairus that his twelve-year-old daughter had died. Before the ruler of the synagogue could formulate a response, however, Jesus told him not to be afraid. Up to this point Jairus's great fear was the possibility that his daughter might die. That fear had been realized. So what did Jesus mean by telling him not to be afraid? The answer comes from the words that follow: *Just believe,* or even better: "Keep on believing" (Waetjen 1989:121). Jairus stood at the place where the dialectic between fear and faith leads to despair.

That kind of fear is a turning away from God, a decision not to take any more risks. This is the time when people may set themselves against God because they are afraid of any further disappointment. They may foreswear hope in any form because they cannot face the additional pain of having it crushed. Jesus did not ask Jairus to do anything other than what he had already been doing. He encouraged Jairus to keep on believing, and then he began giving orders.

They were a most unusual set of instructions. Jesus permitted only Peter, James and John of the disciples to accompany him. Why he chose these three is not clear. There is little to distinguish them, although they stand at the head of the list of apostles in 3:13-19. They are also the only three to whom Jesus gave names. On the other hand, none of them has emerged as a distinct character. They were indistinguishable from the other apostles except in name. If we cannot explain why Jesus chose them, though, we can appreciate the implications of his choice. He created what looks very much like a new inner circle. Even among the Twelve there were now insiders and outsiders.

Furthermore, as soon as he reached the home where Jairus's daughter lay, he told the assembled mourners to stop their wailing because the girl was only asleep, and that was a declaration he made even before he had looked at her. Then he ordered the mourners out of the house, went into the room where the girl lay, took her by the hand, told her to get up and then ordered those who had witnessed what he had done to keep absolutely silent.

It is hard to imagine a more improbable set of instructions. Was there any possibility that the mourners would not realize that the child was up and walking around? What were the odds that the rest of Jesus' disciples would not hear the story? What details of the raising of the daughter of the synagogue ruler could be kept secret even under the tightest security? All the combined details of this miracle story—that Jesus took the child by the hand, spoke to her in Aramaic and told her parents to give her something to eat—do not constitute a secret worth keeping.

There is, however, one question of overwhelming importance. Was the child only sleeping or had she actually died? Had Jesus made a correct diagnosis before he saw the child? Had Jesus really defined death as sleep, and did he have the power to awaken the dead? A curious observer might have posed many questions to test the alternatives: did the girl move before Jesus touched her; had anyone thought to check her breath; did anyone else try to wake her up by touch or by shaking; what about bright lights or sharp sounds? The objective observer, however, has no standing here. These are the questions that none of the witnesses could answer without violating the instructions Jesus had given.

This miracle looks like one of the parables in Mark 4 (Meye 1968:214). It is set against the backdrop of a large crowd, which was intentionally excluded from understanding what went on. There was a group of outsiders and a group of insiders. Jesus spoke in simple terms, but his words contained a meaning that only he could explain. And in both cases Jesus was looking for a response of some kind. A simple question distinguished the insiders from the outsiders in Mark 4. In this case no one asked what he meant by saying that death is sleep, but two people who approached him in faith received far more than they had originally sought.

It has been argued that the miracles in the Gospel of Mark were late developments in a Hellenistic environment where people believed in magic. The use of foreign words such as the Aramaic expression *Talitha koum* is cited as an example of a magical formula in favor of this interpretation (Theissen 1974:252). Whether addressing someone in her native tongue constitutes a magical formula, however, is extremely doubtful. Mark in any event made sure his audience knew what Jesus said by translating it into Greek.

The name Jairus may be a Hellenistic form of an Aramaic name (Guelich 1989:295), but even this name is missing from some of the earliest manuscripts. The fabric of the story in any event is not Hellenistic but Jewish. The implicit tension with the law, the humiliating plight of Jairus and the embarrassment of the woman all reflect the life of Jewish communities in the region of Galilee. Rather than being signs of late development in a predominantly Hellenistic environment, the details of the story speak for the faithfulness of the gospel tradition (Lane 1974:198).

Something similar must be said about those readings that advocate a primarily political reading of the miracles. There are profound implications in these texts about the structures of power in our world. Yet these implications are just that—implications. They do not stand on their own. They are secondary to the presentation of Jesus as the one who exercises faith in impossible situations, the one who elicits faith and the one who honors faith. After all, the political ramifications of the miracles grow out of the words and conduct of Jesus himself. It would be a grave mistake to read this Gospel without paying attention to the way Jesus engages the power structures of the first century. It would be a serious mistake to read the Gospels without asking how Jesus' confrontation with the power structures of his day informs us about our mission in the world. It would be a more profound mistake, however, to reduce Jesus to a set of political principles (Torrance 1992:30).

Mark does not treat miracles as events that settle arguments. The miracles in this Gospel are open-ended, and they create new possibilities that call for more faith. Both Jairus and the woman who had the hemorrhage took significant risks in approaching Jesus. After the two miracles, each of them faced a new set of challenges. Would the woman stand firmly in her new identity, or would she seek some other way to deal with the shame of her past? What would Jairus do the next time he went to the synagogue?

These questions lead inexorably to the person of Jesus. He was the one who brought the rule of God to them. The power of God that was at work in him created the new situations that they faced, and his followers could not move into them without continuing to trust him. These stories show his marvelous sensitivity to faith, but in the final analysis the fundamental question is his faithfulness. Can he be trusted to bring to completion the things he has set in motion? And if the essential question is a matter of faith, then it is impossible to reduce the movement he started to a set of principles. The person of Jesus is inseparable from the things he set in motion.

Jesus Goes Home (6:1-6) Several years after the Berlin Wall was torn down Baerbel Eccardt obtained a copy of the files that the East German Secret Police had compiled on her. She had served for thirty years as the central person in the Berlin Fellowship, an unpublicized but vital spiritual pipeline between Christians in the West, particularly in America, and Christians in East Germany. Looking through her files, Baerbel was appalled to discover the extent to which the Secret Police had penetrated the network of pastors and laypeople she had cultivated. Virtually every prayer meeting she attended in East Germany had a page in her file. Despite the intensive surveillance, however, some interesting things escaped detection.

Near the front of a file three feet thick was a report on a meeting with a group of pastors in East Berlin that had eventually led to the formation of the Berlin Fellowship. It took place about eight years after the Berlin Wall had been erected, when the full weight of their isolation from other members of the Christian family had pressed in upon them. The meeting was led by Ralph Hamburger, a Presbyterian minister who had grown up in a Jewish family in Hamburg, Germany. He encouraged them to believe that God could create a channel of encouragement, hope and reconciliation with Christians in America. Twenty years into their experience of communism that was not easy for them to believe. Ralph spoke in German, of course, and answered many questions with the assurance: "Don't worry, der Herr will take care of that." In German der Herr means both the Lord and gentleman or even sir. It is as common as the English word mister. In the margin of the typed report on this first meeting was a handwritten note: "Despite a great deal of effort and months of intensive investigations we still do not know who der Herr is or where he lives."

The account of Jesus' visit to his home is one of the more ironic miracle stories in Mark. The miracles he performed receive only the most cursory treatment. In fact, the Evangelist understates them so much that it appears as if Jesus did not do any miracles in his hometown at all. The editorial comment in 6:5, however, invites the question: *He could not do any miracles there, except lay his hands on a few sick people and heal them.* Did Jesus perform any miracles here? Were some people healed, or did nothing actually happen? This is another one of those places where Mark prods his audience to probe beneath the surface.

The answer is a resounding yes. Placing his hands on sick people to heal them lies at the heart of many accounts of Jesus' miracles. Jesus took the hand of Peter's bedridden mother-in-law and helped her up. He reached out his hand to touch the leper. The woman who touched his cloak was healed of a chronic hemorrhage. And in the preceding passage Jesus took a lifeless child by the hand and said: *Little girl, I say to you, get up!* Those healings were the source of wonder and awe. Here, though, Mark makes it sound as though virtually nothing important happened.

In this story the miracles recede into the background, and the spotlight falls on Jesus' terse comment: *Only in his hometown, among his relatives and in his own house is a prophet without honor.* By modern standards that was a poor piece of public relations; it is not the sort of thing a political consultant would advise him to say: it is neither ingratiating, solicitous nor conciliatory. It was a prickly warning that was likely to go unheeded. From a historical point of view, of course, Jesus was on firm ground. It has always been much easier to honor prophets after their death. Amos was thrown out of Israel for prophesying against the king in the king's sanctuary (Amos 7:12-13). Jeremiah was arrested on a charge of treason (Jer 26:7-11), as Micah had been a century earlier.

The intriguing feature of Jesus' parable, however, was the company of people who opposed him. He was not opposed by the king, although that is coming. His critics were the people who knew him best, and the phrasing of the parable invites the question whether Jesus was not most upset by the lack of support from his own family. The parable focuses on a steadily narrowing circle of people, beginning with his neighbors and finally zeroing in on the members of his own home. When Mark tells us that Jesus was amazed at their unbelief, his immediate family may have been the greatest disappointment.

This is not the only moment of tension between Jesus and members of his family. In Mark 3:31-35 Jesus rebuffed his mother and brothers to announce that he had a new family. The cryptic reference to this wisdom that has been given him (6:2) may have grown out of his redefinition of the family. The people who knew his family might easily have taken offense at Jesus' pronouncement about the family. Whether that strained relationship is reflected here is difficult to say. On the other hand, in a culture where the rule was to honor one's parents, this conflict between faith and loyalty to the family is quite striking.

Ultimately, however, it was not honor but faith that Jesus sought in his hometown, as 6:6 indicates. The editorial comment that he was amazed at their lack of faith brings us to a new stage in Mark's presentation of the good news. At the beginning of this Gospel, Mark summarizes Jesus' message with these words: "The time has come. The kingdom of God is near. Repent and believe the good news!" (1:15). In that context it is clear that faith is believing in the good news that the kingdom of God is near. In 6:1-6, however, the problem was not the failure of people to believe the good news about the kingdom. The problem was their failure to believe in Jesus.

The people of his hometown did not believe that there was anything unique about Jesus. He was a carpenter, a man who worked with his hands (Martin 1972:123). He was a human being just like them, whose brothers and sisters were members of the community. The sarcastic question about his wisdom reflects a suspicion of familiar people who advocate new ideas. Jesus was, in their eyes, a man who belonged near the bottom of the social world of first-century Galilee and who had no legitimate claim to anything that would distinguish him from them.

What is the import of making Jesus the object of belief? Has one person displaced the kingdom of God? Has faith in Jesus replaced faith in the reign of God? Has there been a fundamental change in Mark's proclamation of the gospel? There has been a growing interest in Jesus himself, which develops as the opposition to his proclamation about the kingdom solidifies. On the evidence of Mark 1—5, however, Mark is not replacing the gospel of the kingdom with the gospel of Jesus. He seems to be making the connection between Jesus and the kingdom as strongly as possible. We could say even in this account that wherever Jesus is, the kingdom is. The fundamental irony of this passage is that the kingdom of God was tangibly present in his hometown, but the people who knew him best could not see it.

Ever since the publication of Bultmann's *History of the Synoptic Tradition* the authenticity of this text has been suspect. Following A. J. Fridrichsen's lead, Bultmann judged this text to be a creation of the early church that purportedly explained the disappointing results of its mission (1972:31). The story of Jesus' preaching in the synagogue of his hometown, so the argument runs, shows that without faith there are no miracles. The reason that there were not more miracles and thus more converts lay in the entrenched unbelief of the people the church was trying to evangelize.

That interpretation completely misses the thrust of this story. Jesus performed several acts in his hometown that would qualify as miracles in any other setting, despite entrenched unbelief. This story is not an apology for the failure of the church's mission. The miracle that is missing here is faith, and the stumbling point was the perception of Jesus as a man of no particular importance who worked with his hands.

Mark offers no apology for Jesus' origins, social class or occupation. The text simply sets out the objections of the people who had known Jesus best and lets them stand. Evaluating people by their social class was common throughout the Greco-Roman culture, as it is in most modern cultures. The same objection to believing in Jesus would have applied wherever the gospel was proclaimed throughout the Mediterranean world. It is a fundamental misreading of this text to claim that it explains unbelief away.

Here we must also question the judgment that the lower-class peasants and artisans who transmitted the gospel of Jesus hopelessly distorted his words. The Jesus Seminar maintains that the early teachers and Evangelists failed to do justice to the historical Jesus because their "faith overpowered their memories" (Funk et al. 1993:4). This text calls this judgment into question. It preserves the memory of a community of people that was clearly at odds with the church's message—the people in his home town did not subscribe to his wisdom. On the other hand, the editorial comment in 6:6 shows Jesus as the one who brings in the reign of God. The two views of Jesus stand side by side in unresolved tension. Was Jesus the person proclaimed by the church or the country bumpkin written off by the people who knew him best? Mark leaves it to his audience to decide, and in that decision he preserves a distinction between memory and faith.

It is characteristic of Mark to treat faith as something that cannot be passed directly from one person to another. He seeks neither to prove nor to disprove. Mark invites. He beckons. He relates the accounts of Jesus' ministry with no apology for some rough edges. He prods his readers to ask questions. And as he presented the miracles as parables in 4:35—5:43, so here he presents Jesus himself as a parable. The hearers of this Gospel are left with a difficult puzzle. Is the accumulated wisdom of the Greco-Roman world correct? Could the ideas about class and wisdom and power that they had learned from birth be wrong? Could there be a common person like themselves through whom God's judgment against oppression and promise of peace are authenticated? Or are these things just so many words, so many interesting but insubstantial stories?

This is what we might call Mark's incarnational theology. It is not spelled out in the cosmic terms of the Gospel of John, nor does Mark even provide an account of Jesus' birth. He does, however, describe for us a man of low social origins through whom the power of God's reign came into history, and Mark invites us to see in him the Son of God.

The myth of the Greco-Roman world was that godliness was tied to nobility. The myth of our time is that godliness is tied to success. The person to whom Mark introduces us challenges both myths, and despite the conclusion that the canonical Gospels are so mythological that the historical Jesus is concealed in them (Funk et al. 1993:4-5, 7), we have to wonder where the power comes from to take on these two entrenched systems of value. At a mythic level the odds are heavily against the gospel of the kingdom of God. The power here is not in the ideas Mark presents but in the possibility that God actually did something in history to upset the normal scheme of things. Mark invites us to commit ourselves to the truth that God does awesome things through people and events that appear to be merely ordinary.

☐ Miracles as Parables About Faith (6:6—8:26)

The Twelve went out as shepherds to preach repentance and gather the people of God. What they called people to repent from, however, is not obvious from 6:6-13 and 6:30. Yet repentance is one of two themes that tie the mission of the Twelve to the story of King Herod and John the Baptist. The other is the use of power. Mark uses one of his favorite narrative devices here to great effect. The story of the apostles' mission starts in 6:6-13, but it does not end until 6:30. In between he has placed the story of King Herod and John the Baptist. Mark sees the implications of what Jesus did very clearly, but instead of delineating them for us he ties two stories together and invites us to explore the connections.

Repenting and Believing (6:6-30) My college roommate joined the Peace Corps and was assigned to a team of trainees who were preparing for appointments in Latin America. After weeks of intensive language study the team took a bus across the border into Mexico, where they were instructed to leave their wallets, purses, money, passports and suitcases on the bus. They were told that the bus would return for them in one week. They were expressly forbidden either to make telephone calls to the United States or to venture back across the border. It was a test of their training. Surviving for a week without access to any American privileges or money would test their readiness for working in a community where they would be the only people from *El Norte*.

The Mission of the Twelve (6:6-13) When Jesus sent the Twelve out to the villages of Galilee, he did not allow them to take bread, bag, money or extra clothes—only a pair of sandals, the tunics they were wearing and a staff. They were to find one home in each village to put them up and stay there until they moved on. If they encountered people who would not extend them hospitality or listen to them, they were to leave that town with a gesture of judgment, shaking the dust off their feet as a testimony against them.

Clearly this was more than a test of their interpersonal skills, for Jesus charged them to preach repentance. Repentance is not a popular subject on just about any conceivable occasion. Even in societies with ancient traditions of hospitality like these Galilean villages, calling people to repent could be an unpopular thing to do. It is all the more risky if the preachers have to rely for their food and shelter on the people who are supposed to repent. This was a venture of faith for the Twelve. Although they had been appointed to preach and cast out demons (3:13-19), they had been little more than witnesses, sometimes mere spectators, to Jesus' ministry. Here they moved into the spotlight and began to do the things that Jesus had been doing. In this transition from witness to preacher, their faith would be put to the test.

Each of the instructions Jesus gave might be probed for its symbolic or instructional value. We will analyze only one here: the staff. With all the things he forbade the Twelve to take, it is curious that he told them to take a . . . staff. The Greek word can mean stick, scepter or staff of a shepherd. It was probably not a scepter. None of them could have afforded one, so it was either a walking stick or a shepherd's staff. Furthermore, it was not a tool of their former occupations. It belonged to their new calling, which was something they did not yet understand. As a walking stick it would have symbolized the itinerant nature of their calling. Crossan pictures Jesus as a wandering Jewish cynic who preached a gospel of radical egalitarianism (1994:73-74). A walking stick would be an appropriate symbol for that kind of profession. A shepherd's staff, though, would have carried a completely different connotation. Ever since Jesus' withdrawal from the synagogues (3:7), he had been calling together a new people. The appointment of the Twelve was a symbolic declaration that he was creating a new Israel, and now these Twelve were to go around the villages of Galilee as heralds of the kingdom of God and proclaim that people should repent. In the Old Testament the people of God are often pictured as a flock of sheep, and their leaders are described as shepherds. Since this mission is an obvious extension of their appointment, we should understand these staves as more than walking sticks. They were tools of the shepherds who were called to gather a new flock.

Herod the Pretender (6:14-30) Mark's reference to King Herod is ironic. This Herod desperately wanted to be king, but the cruelty of his grandfather Herod the Great so disturbed the Romans that they took the title away from the family. His grandson Herod Antipas, who governed Galilee, applied twice to Rome to have the family title conferred on him but was rebuffed both times (Bruce 1972:24, 248). He never rose above the rank of tetrarch, and the juxtaposition of these two stories suggests that he might have been vexed by anyone who challenged or threatened his authority.

Herod thought Jesus was John the Baptist risen from the dead (6:16). In what Mark certainly regards as an abuse of power, Herod had beheaded John the Baptist. When Herod heard about the miraculous things Jesus was doing, he concluded that John the Baptist had returned from the other side of the grave endowed with supernatural powers. In this context, though, it might not have been only the report about Jesus' miracles that troubled him. It might also have been the fact that Jesus had sent out twelve emissaries to proclaim repentance, an act whose symbolism would not have been lost on the man who wanted to be king. The mission of the Twelve raised the stakes in the proclamation of the kingdom of God considerably.

There were competing views of Jesus. Some thought he was Elijah, the prophet whose return to Israel had been predicted at the very close of the Old Testament in Malachi 4:5-6. According to popular expectations the return of Elijah would mark the beginning of a new era in which the Messiah would rule Israel and the world. Other people saw in Jesus the return of one of the other great prophets. The role of those prophets, of course, was to call the king to live up to the conditions of the covenant. Either of these more widely held explanations was unpalatable to Herod because they both implied that God was working against him. Herod, it seems, subscribed to the one explanation he could accept: that Jesus' miraculous deeds were to be explained by the operation of magical powers from beyond the grave (Lane 1974:213).

Herod executed John the Baptist in a vain attempt to prove that he was man enough to be king. Throughout this story Herod appears as a pathetic figure, whose inept use of power led him from one difficulty into another. First came his marriage to Herodias, who had recently secured a divorce from Herod's brother Philip. That divorce was not sanctioned by Jewish law because Herodias had initiated the action, and in Old Testament and rabbinic tradition women did not have the right to divorce their husbands. Her remarriage to Herod was sanctioned by Roman law but not by the law of the covenant God had made with the people of Israel. For a man who hoped to enlist support from leaders of the Jewish state for his campaign to be appointed king, this marriage was a risky move. To make matters worse, after their marriage Herod showed great deference to the man who accused him of committing adultery with Herodias, and then, under pressure from his new wife, he imprisoned John the Baptist.

At his own birthday party Herod got carried away with himself and promised Herodias's daughter any present she should name, up to half his kingdom. That was a strange gesture from a man who did not possess a kingdom. He governed only a territory called an ethnarchy, so his offer had all the marks of a clumsy gesture designed to impress the leading citizens of Galilee with his kinglike generosity. It was a heavy-handed and ill-conceived boast. And in the end, when Herodias's daughter asked for John's head on a platter, Herod was irredeemably caught between his ambition and the words of a prophet. Not wanting to appear less than royal before his guests, he gave the order for John's execution. In the colorful language of 1 Kings 18:21, Herod limped through life tied to two conflicting opinions. Ultimately, he lost the very things he had struggled for. Although he revered and protected John, Herod became the first leader of the Jewish people to kill a prophet since King Jehoiakim (Jer 26:21-23). Not long after the events described in this passage, Emperor Gaius took away Antipas's title and gave the territory he had ruled to Agrippa, Herodias's brother (Bruce 1972:249).

If repentance is the theme that ties these events together, what light does the story about the would-be king shed on the mission of the Twelve? The largely peasant population of Galilee did not have the po-litical connections or aspirations of the Herods. If Mark were writing a Gospel that conformed to the socioeconomic models of our day, he might have been content with calling Herod to stop his oppressive be-havior. Oppression is an awful and widespread phenomenon, but the biblical concept of sin is more than a political and economic doctrine. It is radically egalitarian. Sin is not essentially a consequence of class. The poor are also capable of evil.

In their own way and on their own terms the people of Galilee faced issues like the ones Herod confronted—loyalty to family and in-decision. Jesus had traveled throughout Galilee preaching the gospel and performing miracles. His preaching had created enormous ten-sions with the two fundamental institutions of Jewish life in that area: the synagogue and the family. The situation had become increasingly polarized, as each new manifestation of the gospel accentuated the dif-ferences. When Jesus sent the Twelve out to preach, he created a mo-ment of crisis. The Twelve were going from village to village like shepherds seeking lost sheep. Would the folk of Galilee become part of the new people of God? Would they cling tenaciously to what is comfortable? Or would they put off deciding what to do?

Mark observes that Herod liked to listen to John. The Greek text says more literally that Herod heard John gladly, a translation which points back to the collection of parables in Mark 4. In the parable of the soils, the seed that falls on rocky ground represents those who hear the word, receive it gladly, but have no root (4:16-17). One parable from that collection is particularly relevant at this point: With the measure you use, it will be measured out to you—and even more. Whoever has will be given more; whoever does not have, even what he has will be taken from him (4:24-25). These words describe precisely what happened to Herod. He listened to John with considerable interest, but interest was not enough. He needed to act, but because he would not make a decision about John's words, he became someone else's pawn and killed the man he had tried to protect.

God is patient and gives us a lifetime to embrace the good news, but hearing God's word and hesitating carries a great risk. The longer we delay in repenting, the more there is for us to repent. The more we hear without acting, the easier it is to deceive ourselves. As time passes while we limp between two opinions, the more likely it is that we will do things we really do not want to do.

Five Loaves and Two Fish (6:31-44) One great myth of our time is that technology makes life easier. We have purchased sewing machines, typewriters, automatic dishwashers and computers in the hope that we will be more productive and have more time to relax. That is the dream that sells the machines. Of course, computers are not just about productivity. They are really about power, but that is another dream. Have our dreams come true? Perhaps they have in some ways, but the price is enormous. After more than a century and a half of one technological breakthrough after another, our families are in ruins, each generation is alienated from the next, and stress has become a serious public health problem. The dark side of the dream is that every gain in productivity leads to another and higher expectation of what we ought to be able to do. It is a vicious circle that leaves us empty.

After the Twelve returned from their preaching mission, Jesus invited them to go away to a place where they could get some rest. If that was what they wanted, they were surely disappointed, for Jesus did not lead them to a location where they would be insulated from the throngs that pressed upon them. A careful reading of 6:33 reveals that the boat in which they traveled was always close enough to the shore for the people from whom they wished to escape to observe. Jesus did not have them ship off to the far side of the Sea of Galilee. Their boat put out into the water and turned along the coastline. Apparently they did not travel very quickly or very far, for a crowd was waiting when they landed. All in all, this does not amount to a very convincing effort to leave the masses behind. The careful listener can almost hear the groans as the ship is beached at Jesus' instructions.

The crowd was not there by accident. The swelling throng that raced ahead to meet them had gathered in response to the disciples' preaching mission. Their mission in 6:6-13, 30 had been phenomenally successful, which Mark underscores twice when he points out that many people saw them and recognized them (6:33). The Twelve were in a situation very much like those in which Jesus had found himself in 1:21-39 and 3:20. The response to their ministry was overwhelming, but the next step was not clear. As the story develops, they recede into the background. They did not initiate any of the action. Yet Jesus' statement, *you give them something to eat,* indicates that he expected more of them.

Jesus looked at the growing crowd and saw them as sheep without a shepherd. This is a very telling comment. As the story unfolds, Mark suggests that Jesus was their shepherd. As Jesus prepared to feed the crowd, Mark describes in unusual detail a scene with green grass where the disciples arranged people in ordered groups of fifty and one hundred. It looks as though Jesus was settling the crowd down in a pasture.

These images point to passages like Ezekiel 34:22-24, where the kings of Israel and Judah are called shepherds. The leaders of God's people were often described as shepherds, and at this time there was someone else who wanted to be the shepherd—Herod Antipas, whose story precedes this text. Mark's observation that these people were like sheep without a shepherd is not the simple metaphor it might appear to be. It is a pointed reminder that God's people did not have a king. When Jesus arranged the crowds in orderly groups on the grass and fed them, he did something of enormous consequence. He enacted the role of a shepherd in a way that no Jewish king had ever done before. This is a portrait of Jesus with enormous implications. The Twelve reacted very differently to the crowd. The crowd could not get enough of them, but the disciples had apparently had enough of the crowd. In the late afternoon when the vexing question of what to do with thousands of hungry people became an inescapable problem, the disciples wanted to send them home. Woven into this account is a familiar theme in Mark—wilderness, translated in 6:31 as *a quiet place*. Earlier in Mark the wilderness was the place where John called the people of Jerusalem and Judea to repent (1:4-5), where Jesus was tempted (1:12-13) and where he went to pray (1:35). We have to wonder then whether some of these theological connotations are woven into the framework of this story. Is it possible that Jesus brought his disciples to the wilderness for repentance, testing, prayer or some combination of those spiritual disciplines?

In any event Jesus gave them an impossible task: *You give them something to eat.* Five thousand men and an untold number of women and children had followed them unbidden into a remote place, and nobody had thought to make arrangements for food. Not surprisingly, perhaps, they answered Jesus with more than a hint of sarcasm, suggesting that he adopt a more realistic view. It was purely gratuitous for them to go on to remind Jesus that there were no bakeries anywhere on the horizon. The kindest thing, they implied, would be to do what they had suggested in the first place: to send the people home. It was a test for the Twelve. At issue was the question whether the shepherds would tend the flock or look after their own interests first. Tending the flock appeared to be an impossible task because there were only five loaves and two (possibly dried and bony) fish to divide among five thousand men—to say nothing of everyone else.

The prophets had often criticized the kings of Israel for taking advantage of their people. There is no more telling indictment of the ruling families of Judah than the prophecy against the shepherds in Ezekiel 34, which stands behind this text. Yet the test Jesus set before the Twelve was not whether they intended to abuse their charges. It

6:37 *Eight months of a man's wages* is the NIV's translation into modern terms of the

had to do with the difference between being reasonable and being faithful. It would have been reasonable, perhaps even from one point of view responsible, to send the people home before it grew too dark for them to find their way. Leading the people of God, however, is not a matter of doing what is reasonable—it is a matter of faithfulness. The crowd had gathered because they had faith in the Twelve, and that faith carried the Twelve into uncharted territory. The people believed in them. Once they were all together in the wilderness, the question became in what or whom did the Twelve believe? They responded first with reason (6:35-36) and then with sarcasm (6:37).

Mark recounts this miracle, with several glaring ironies. The story begins with Jesus' suggestion that the Twelve should get some rest. They could not escape the crowd, however, and eventually they found themselves in another stressful situation. The organizing of the crowd into groups and seated on green grass, on the other hand, describes a peaceful pastoral scene. It looks like a shepherd, or in this case twelve shepherds, settling a flock down. As the story unfolds, it would be considerably longer before the Twelve themselves got any rest.

It is also surprising that there are no oohs or ahhs in the account. The statements of wonder and astonishment that Jesus' mighty acts inspired elsewhere are not found here. Neither is there any indication of hostility, bewilderment or consternation. The reactions that usually accompany Jesus' miracles are missing here. In fact, Mark reports no reaction from the crowd at all. As he describes the course of events, the crowd does not even seem to be aware that anything extraordinary happened. Within the limits of this story we cannot even be certain that anyone except Jesus and the Twelve knew what was going on.

In fact, there is reason to question whether the Twelve understood what was happening. They had seated the people on the grass. On Jesus' instructions they had checked to see if there was any food at all. They had taken the broken bread and fish from Jesus' hands and distributed it. After everyone had been satisfied they picked up twelve baskets of uneaten food. Throughout the entire account there is no indication that they understood what any of it meant, a point Mark un-

two hundred denarii specified in the Greek text.

derscores with the comment for they had not understood about the loaves; their hearts were hardened (6:52).

The Twelve began by being reasonable. Reason is a marvelous gift, but the relationship between reason and faith is often strained. It is not just that faith may require us to act beyond the stable conclusions of reason, but reason may also be a stepping stone to sarcasm and cynicism. In the guise of either sarcasm or cynicism reason undermines not just what we believe but also how we act. Ultimately, the certainty of faith comes not from our reason but from God's faithfulness. Pastors, elders, deacons, church leaders and sensitive people of every stripe ought to embrace reason as a gift. At the same time we must watch for the one who is faithful in the face of the impossible, and we need to be attentive to the voice that calls us to act.

Walking on Water (6:45-52) In the late 1940s and early 1950s America underwent one of its most shameful political ordeals: the McCarthy hearings. Senator McCarthy's investigations into the loyalty of prominent American politicians, entertainers and scientists had all the justice of a kangaroo court and ruined the careers of many people. During that same period of time FBI director J. Edgar Hoover compiled a voluminous file on Albert Einstein. Einstein was an avowed pacifist, and Hoover was suspicious of his loyalty to America. That renown physicist was not brought before McCarthy's hearings, but Hoover fomented enough concern about his political tendencies that he was not invited to work on the development of the atomic bomb. Robert Oppenheimer, who built the weapon that brought the Pacific phase of World War II to an end, was summoned, however, to answer Senator McCarthy's questions. A decade later at the beginning of the civil-rights movement Hoover compiled mountains of evidence purporting to show that Martin Luther King Jr. was a Communist. Hoover was never able to prove his case, but he engaged in a protracted campaign of harassment against King. Today the names of Einstein, Oppenheimer and King are held in great respect all over the world. Hoover and McCarthy have fallen, yet they remained unrepentant their entire lives.

In the Bible the inability to acknowledge the truth is called hardness of heart. Mark has already described Jesus' opponents as people with stubborn hearts, but it is surprising to find the Twelve tarred here with the same brush in 6:52. The series of events that led to this stunning reversal began as a search for rest. Just before it ended, as they attempted to row against the wind, Jesus came to them, walking unobstructed across the waves. They had been rowing from the late afternoon until the fourth watch of the night, about three o'clock in the morning. Although they had reached the middle of the lake by evening, hours later they had made little headway at all. It is hard to imagine two pictures of greater contrast. There is no suggestion that Jesus was tired when he stepped out of the boat and back into the welcoming embrace of the crowd. He seems to have been at peace. After rowing against the wind for most of the night, however, his followers seem to have been exhausted.

Hardened hearts, aching backs and stifled yawns are a far cry from the joy the Twelve had felt when they returned from their preaching tour of Galilee. How did the change happen? In the feeding of the five thousand men they were secondary figures. Jesus taught the crowd and initiated all of the activity. The Twelve had wanted to send the crowd home as the afternoon grew long, and when Jesus told them to feed the crowd, they replied sarcastically that it would cost too much. They participated in the miracle to the extent that they obtained the five loaves and two fish and distributed the pieces to the crowd. Except for their sarcasm when Jesus said *you give them something to eat,* there does not seem to be much to criticize.

How much should be made of that? How much we make of it depends upon what we see. If we see only one or two isolated stories we might conclude that their sarcasm was simple and almost innocent—perhaps blameless. There is, though, a broader picture. The Twelve are called the Twelve because Jesus was creating a new people, and when Jesus saw the crowd that had gathered at the shore where their boat landed, he saw them as sheep without a shepherd. If the role of the Twelve was merely to observe what Jesus was doing, they were responsible spectators. If, on the other hand, Jesus was inviting them to become shepherds of the people who were following them, their sarcasm was, wittingly or unwittingly, an impolite way of declining the role they were called to fill. In this context it would have been irresponsible to send the people home, and sarcasm would have been close to mutiny, for the people who were following them were not some random collection of individuals. They were the people of God, and to be a shepherd of God's flock requires faithfulness not only to the people but especially to God's intention. Jesus saw the people in fundamentally different terms. In a seemingly impossible situation he blessed God, and after he had broken the bread and fish he went up alone into the hills to pray.

This is another place where Mark treats a miracle as a parable. The new feature in this case is the linking of two miracles together in the sense that misappropriating the first one leads necessarily to misunderstanding the second one. When we read that the disciples were completely amazed (6:51), we are not to suppose that their amazement was the hushed awe of divine illumination. Mark explains their amazement in the next verse as the kind of amazement that accompanies hardened hearts. It was the shocked surprise of unbelief and confusion.

Not listening to and acting on Jesus' word, however, is a dangerous matter. The disciples missed something here of enormous importance, but all that is clear on the surface of the account is the disciples' fear and confusion. What they might have seen is something about which Mark only hints. What might they have seen or understood or experienced as Jesus came to them walking across the waves?

The key is the curious statement that he was about to pass by them (6:48). The Greek text is considerably stronger than the NIV translation. If Jesus intended to walk past them, what did he mean to do? Perhaps if Jesus had continued past them, he would have led them to their destination. That is an unlikely possibility, because Mark goes to some pains to point out that they did not arrive at the place they were trying to reach. Although they started out for Bethsaida, they landed at Gennesaret. Even with Jesus in the boat they arrived at a point different from their original destination. It is almost as though the wind pushed them off course geographically and spiritually.

Once before when Jesus stopped the wind from blowing on the Sea of Galilee, the disciples had been on the verge of an amazing discovery. The psalms celebrate God's sovereignty over the sea, and what Jesus did here recalls the language of Psalm 89:9: "You rule over the surging sea; when its waves mount up, you still them." Jesus did something on the Sea of Galilee that no prophet had ever attempted: he acted as though he were the sovereign Lord.

Furthermore, the words Jesus used to identify himself to the men in the boat have more than one meaning. The Greek words translated *it is I* (Mk 6:50) can also be brought into English as "I am." In English as in Greek these are the same two words that are used to translate God's name. When Jesus stood before the Sanhedrin, he uttered these same two words, and the elders of Israel declared him guilty of blasphemy (14:62).

Finally, the puzzling notion of Jesus' intending to pass by them recalls the way God appeared to Moses on Mount Sinai (Ex 33:19-22). Moses had asked to see God, and God allowed Moses to see his back as his passed by him. All these hints point to an awesome possibility. If Jesus had passed by the Twelve, they might have seen who he really was. But their hearts were hardened, and this epiphany did not quite happen. Jesus, Mark suggests, intended to reveal himself to his disciples, but their overwhelming terror stopped the revelation well before it was complete. Instead of awe and wonder they experienced only bewilderment and fear.

Several recent studies in the Gospel of Mark analyze the social background of early Christian traditions. Their explorations of the political dimensions of the gospel are helpful in many cases. It is nevertheless important not to overlook the spiritual dimensions of the text. To ignore them is to misread the Gospels. Our relationship to God is at the heart of the good news. The social and political implications of the feeding of the five thousand (6:30-44) are certainly matters of considerable interest (Meyers 1988:205-10). In 6:52, however, we see the aspect of that miracle that was most important to Mark: the disciples' hearts were hardened. Despite what they had already experienced, despite their occasional obedience, despite holding the broken bits of bread and fish in their hands, they missed the revelation that God intended to give them.

Mark's judgment needs to be taken very seriously. The observation that the disciples' hearts were hardened is obviously an editorial comment, and it was probably made by Mark himself (Guelich 1989:347). It offers an unambiguous way of assessing the relationship between the Gospel and history. On the surface, of course, this unflattering comment about the disciples shows that the early Christian Evangelists were quite capable of producing a critical reading of the material they had received. At the very least it tells us that their enthusiasm did not render them uncritical. That observation, however, does not tell us whether someone was trying to cover up an embarrassing mistake in the sources or clarify an understanding that the disciples subsequently reached, which was faithful to what actually happened.

Three observations in the text itself are very instructive. First, this interpretation was not written into the fabric of the story. Second, the disciples' conduct appears to be entirely reasonable. Their comments are a sensible response to a very difficult situation. That is to say, the person who added this editorial judgment did not change the elements of the story to make this judgment more congruent with the narrative. Third, the judgment comes to us as a surprise. It is not what we expect, and we have to sort through the larger narrative to interpret it.

This account preserves the integrity of the earlier story and holds it in tension with the judgment about the disciples. The effect of the editorial comment is to create, or perhaps highlight, what Kierkegaard calls a dialectic of faith. The tension between the source and the editorial addition is left unresolved. This is not the sort of thing we would expect from people whose enthusiasm had gotten the better of their memories. This text comes from a community that remembered the difference between what happened and what they came to understand, and the Evangelist does not try to force a conclusion on the audience. He is content to let us reach our own conclusions. This does not look at all like a case of a later faith overpowering an earlier memory; it is rather an instance where faith clarified what was remembered. The obvious and unresolved dialectical tension is an argument for the faithfulness of the event as it came to be understood. Whoever added this comment had enough confidence in the gospel not to feel the need for coercion or camouflage.

From a pastoral point of view, this account serves as both a warning and an encouragement. It is a warning about faith. To believe at some point, even to be in a position of spiritual leadership is not enough. To believe is to keep taking new risks. I know a pastor who says that something is wrong with her faith unless she is "comfortably over her head in the deep end of the pool." I think she is right. To follow Jesus is to keep venturing out past our comfort level. The encouragement is that God does not forsake us when our hearts are hardened. God continues to take the initiative, God gives us parables, God comes to us in the night when we are making absolutely no headway. God's faithfulness is greater than our fear, greater than our sin and greater than our unbelief. This portrait of Jesus and the Twelve invites us to find a place of rest in the deep end of the pool.

Clean and Unclean (6:53—7:23) If you visit a church in America, you are likely to find an American flag standing somewhere near the cross inside the sanctuary. Visitors from other countries sometimes find this disconcerting. When they ask why the flag is there, they are told, "It's not a big deal. We just want to show respect for the flag." Whether it is a big deal is a matter of perspective. To some Americans, perhaps, it is not a big deal. The sanctuary is a perfectly good place for the American flag, and they do not think too much about it. Let someone try to remove it, however, or suggest that it borders on blasphemy, and he or she would face a battle of patriotic proportions.

Cultural symbols are all the more powerful because insiders do not pay much attention to them. They are part of the spiritual landscape that insiders assume to be permanent, universally accepted and indisputably binding. In the social world of first-century Galilee, Jewish traditions about defilement and purity were deeply imbedded cultural symbols. Language may not have been a cultural distinctive. Not all Jews kept kosher kitchens, and the Pharisees and Sadducees could not agree on what books belonged in the Bible. Mark, however, does say that all the Jews washed their hands before eating according to the traditions of the elders—all Jews except the disciples of Jesus. They ate without washing their hands, even when they came from public places full of sick people. Their conduct was not only unhygienic; it was fundamentally anti-Jewish, for the traditions of purity were the basis of a powerful idea: the Jewish people could be the one clean people of the world, the one people whose worship was acceptable to God. In their worldview, every other culture was full of people who defiled themselves every day.

The Pharisees wanted to know why Jesus' disciples did not observe the purity codes. Jesus had actually done several things that undermined this cultural mandate: he touched a leper, he ate with social outcasts, and he made a habit of going into the most common places and touching or being touched by hordes of unclean people who were restored and healed outside the social and cultural structures of Judaism. If Jesus had been committed to the traditions of the elders he would have needed to undergo cleansing rituals constantly, for according to those traditions every time he went from touching one unclean person to another, he compounded what was already a serious problem of defilement.

Of course, there would have been no controversy if the people who swarmed around Jesus had not risen from the mats on which they had been carried. And naturally, if the unclean people who touched him had remained sick, there would have been no problem. No one would have cared whether he or his disciples ever washed their hands. But the unwashed crowds followed him wherever he went, and the men who watched such things could see the traditions of the elders losing their hold on the people. The problem was not whether Jesus and his disciples ate with unwashed hands. The real problem was a dynamic presence who would not conform to the boundaries of conduct and power prescribed by cultural expectations.

This was not the first time his opponents had pressed him to conform to the cultural requirements of first-century Judaism. On this occasion his opponents included a group of Pharisees and a delegation of scribes from Jerusalem, making this a confrontation of national proportions. In this case Jesus did not answer his critics with a miracle, parable or any form of indirect persuasion. He spoke directly and called them hypocrites.

It was no mild rebuke concluding with a call to repent. This was more like a warning of imminent judgment. The material Jesus quoted from Isaiah 29:13 is part of a prophecy that God would destroy the nation of Judah, which was fulfilled in 587 B.C. when the armies of Babylon destroyed Solomon's Temple and reduced Jerusalem to rubble. Isaiah had denounced the leaders of Judah for acting as though there was no God. They thought they could hide their evil schemes because God was not paying attention to matters of justice. They calculated that as long as they continued to worship God in the prescribed place with the prescribed rituals they could get away with anything.

After the exiles returned from Babylon, the law became the centerpiece of Judaism. The Pharisees were not alone in believing that adherence to the law was essential for restoration of the political independence of Israel. There were different schools of interpretation, and in some cases what Jesus called the traditions of the elders were interpretations of the commandments that scribes had developed to prevent people from inadvertently breaking a commandment. The elaboration of purity codes reflected in Mark 7:1-5 was an integral part of that trend.

The transition from 7:5 to 7:6 is abrupt. The Pharisees and scribes criticized Jesus for allowing his disciples to violate the purity codes. Jesus' response, on the other hand, was a broad attack on the traditions of the elders. It is possible to see in this transition an indication that Mark or some other editor pieced together material that did not originally belong together. As France observes about 7:10-12, however, that approach to the text is a kind of facile reductionism (2002:287). The movement in 7:5-6 is consistent with a broader pattern in Mark. Jesus did not allow his critics to define the terms of the argument. He replied to the narrowly focused objection about his disciples' impure hands with a broad attack on his opponents' hypocrisy. Nevertheless, an important thematic link ties all this material together. Unclean people were not permitted to enter the sanctuary to worship God. Their condition rendered their worship unacceptable, and their presence might have contaminated the worship of those who were clean. When he raised the issue of hypocrisy in worship, Jesus reframed the terms of the argument, but he did not change the subject. Worship was the heart of the matter.

It is no accident that Jesus chose to denounce the practice of declaring something corban. The question about his disciples implied that he was undermining the social structure of Judah. His countercharge implied that the Pharisees and scribes were undermining not only the structure of the family but the covenant between God and Israel. *Cor-*

ban means *"dedicated to God,"* and by declaring that something was dedicated to God a person excluded it from any other claim. Precisely how the practice was conducted is not clear. To declare something corban, however, did not mean that it was actually given away. It simply meant that no other claim could be made against it (France 2002:286). So, a wealthy man who was angry at his parents could declare part or all of his accumulations corban and escape the legal requirement that he care for them (Lane 1974:250-51).

Jesus charged that this practice negated the commandment to honor one's father and mother. That was a very serious matter, but corban was only the tip of the iceberg. His comment in 7:13 was not an afterthought; it was a categorical denunciation. Corban did not represent a small, isolated problem: *And you do many things like that.* This was an indictment of the entire social and religious system.

The Pharisees and teachers of the law might have objected that they were not cynics whose investment program assumed that God had lost interest in human affairs. The Pharisees in particular prayed for the triumph of the reign of God. Declaring a sum of money to be corban was not something they did in the dark. The scribes who administered the laws governing financial transactions did their work openly, and the temple would have been the safest place to deposit money that was dedicated to God.

This was a different form of hypocrisy than Isaiah had condemned. Jesus' opponents were not banking on God's indifference. Some were perhaps sincere people who believed that sin could be managed by observing the proper procedures. Yet even when they clung tightly to the traditions that were supposed to keep them pure, they sinned. Insofar as the traditions of the elders had permitted the people to get around the requirements of the law, they had even undermined the covenant that was the foundation of Israel itself. Inventive people, some perhaps with impressive credentials, had found ways to subvert the law while pretending to honor God.

How do traditions that are designed to prevent us from breaking the

---

7:7 Crossan (1994:119-22) argues that Jesus was the first Jewish cynic, but the people about whom Isaiah wrote may have had a better claim to that title. They were

law go wrong? That was the broader question Jesus addressed when he called the crowd together (7:14). The problem, he pointed out, was not the law itself or anything external to human beings. There is something fundamentally wrong inside of us. In a declaration that turns the purity codes upside down, Jesus asserted that what makes people unclean was nothing that contaminated them from outside. It was an internal problem. The new hypocrisy consisted in acting as though there were nothing fundamentally wrong with us.

The disciples had picked up something of Jesus' teaching. They did not wash their hands because they had come to understand that the traditions about defilement made little sense when Jesus could make unclean people clean. That, however, was as far as they could follow. His straightforward pronouncement that what makes people unclean comes from within was not something they were prepared to accept. So after they had left the crowd and entered a house, the disciples asked him about the parable.

Parable is a curious word to describe Jesus' declaration about clean and unclean. His statement does have form of the long parable in 4:2-20. It begins with a call to hear, moves to a general statement and concludes in a private conversation in which Jesus responds to a question from his disciples (Marxsen 1955:258-60). Yet nothing is hidden or secretive in 7:14-15. Jesus' public statement contains no obscure metaphors, vexing similes or multilayered allegories. On the contrary, it is the climax of a public argument. That declaration was supposed to be understood. Furthermore, Jesus' harsh response, *Are you so dull?* indicates that he expected them to understand. The language of the supposed parable is straightforward, and the explanation in 7:19-23 is merely an elaboration of that public statement. It does not add anything fundamentally new.

Mark 7:14-23 might be called an ironic parable. It has the form but not the substance of the other parables in Mark. At the center is a saying that may be difficult to comprehend, but the difficulty is not created by arcane language, hidden meanings or the rhetorical style of the

convinced that God was incapable of discovering their schemes to oppress the poor.

speaker. The problem lies elsewhere. In fact, the problem lies inside the disciples. Their hearts were hardened (6:52). To their credit they had come to terms with the tip of the iceberg. Their conduct was not bound by the rigid restrictions of the traditions of the elders. Yet the import and implications of the power at work in Jesus remained closed to them. In their hardness of heart they still imagined that what alienated people from God was not something inside them. The word *parable* belongs to the editorial framework of this conversation. Jesus did not introduce it. It was the disciples' unwillingness to accept his teaching that created a parable out of a direct and public teaching.

Mark's presentation of faith is remarkably egalitarian. Position does not count for much. The past is important but not determinative. Faith is not in any sense a matter of privilege. For this Evangelist, our faith is a response to God's faithfulness. It always leads us beyond ourselves and further into the kingdom of God. To balk, hesitate or resist is to risk entering that spiritual condition that the Bible calls hardness of heart. This is a gospel where insiders may unwittingly find themselves on the outside.

In verse 19 Mark moves out of the normal role of the narrator to speak directly to his audience: *In saying this, Jesus declared all foods "clean"* (7:19). This comment speaks to a later conflict in the early church about whether the law of Moses should be binding on the growing congregations of Gentile converts. It was not an easy problem to resolve. We can draw three conclusions from its inclusion at this point in the Gospel. First, Mark saw this later conflict as an extension of the debate about defilement in Jesus' ministry. Second, the debate was still going on as the Evangelist wrote. The gospel of Jesus Christ was still confronting hard boundaries of cultural and ethnic prejudice. And finally, for Mark the encounter between the gospel and cultural elitism was not incidental or peripheral. It involved fundamental matters of faith and salvation. For leaders in the early church to insist on imposing the law of Moses on Gentile converts was to risk hardness of heart.

The rabbis held a different view of the human condition. They

---

7:19 It is held in many circles that the early church not only shaped Jesus' teaching to speak to later pastoral problems, but even put words in his mouth. In this passage, for instance, the Jesus Seminar holds that only 7:14-15 might be similar to something Jesus actually said (Funk et al. 1993:36, 67-70). On balance, however, this passage taught that people possess an impulse to do good as well as one to do evil, and they believed that it was possible for people to control their impulses (Grundmann 1964:15). Yet insofar as they also held that only one group of people possessed the right to understand what God expected, their view of human nature supported the argument for the superiority of the Jewish people. In this text Jesus did not go as far as Paul did in affirming that "there is no difference, for all have sinned and fall short of the glory of God" (Rom 3:22-23). Yet he is not far from Paul in this denunciation of pious people who pretend to revere the law while inventing rationalizations for breaking it.

Surely our own recent history provides ample evidence of the extent and persistence of sin that is present in our hearts and in our social structures. People of power and influence still take advantage of those who respect and admire them, as they have since the dawn of recorded history. It may be true that babies are not born hating other people, but we learn to hate with great facility. Hatred ripens every day into racism, discriminatory laws, vindictive tribalism and secret organizations that seek to remake the world according to a bigoted vision. None of us is free from the effects of sin, and we need a Savior who will rescue us from ourselves.

Someone Speaks His Language (7:24-30) On a trip to Mexico several years ago I committed one of my more memorable cross-cultural blunders. Our translator was introducing me to several members of the church we had come to serve in the small community of Cerro Azul. After learning their names and receiving a welcome whose warmth transcended the formidable linguistic barrier between us, I felt inspired to attempt a greeting of my own in Spanish. I meant to say, "I am Ron and I am very pleased to meet you." Instead of saying *con mucho gusto*, however, I said, *me gusto*.

My declaration of goodwill was received in stunned silence. For a few awkward seconds our hosts shuffled their feet and stared at the

---

suggests that early Christian Evangelists treated the material they received cautiously. The last sentence in 7:19 is clearly a Markan addition, and it suggests that he clearly respected the distinction between his words and the tradition he had received.

ground. Then the translator snickered, and our hosts could no longer subdue the laughter that was welling up inside them. She asked me if I knew what I had just said, and taking a cue from our hosts' polite but ineffective efforts to restrain themselves, I admitted, "Apparently not." Our translator snickered again, took a deep breath and said, "You said, 'My name is Ron, and I like myself very much.'"

The Greek woman who imposed herself on Jesus near the ancient city of Tyre is the only person in the Gospel who spoke Jesus' language. She could speak to him in parables. Jesus responded to her request to exorcise the evil spirit from her daughter with a harsh, dismissive parable: *First let the children eat all they want, for it is not right to take the children's bread and toss it to their dogs.* She accepted the humiliating terms of his parable and answered him with a parable of her own: *Yes, Lord, but even the dogs under the table eat the children's crumbs.*

From a Jewish point of view this woman was the consummate outsider. She was a Gentile and a woman, and an unclean spirit possessed her daughter. The NIV describes the daughter as possessed by an evil spirit. That is not a completely inappropriate translation insofar as unclean spirits were also considered to be evil. Beelzebub (3:22), or the Lord of the Flies, was the prince of demons and ruler of the garbage dump. If we preserve the original idea of defilement, however, we underscore one of the themes that connects the accounts of 6:53—8:21: Jesus' encounters with unclean people and places of defilement.

Jesus' parable reflects the condescending view that insiders have of outsiders. He compared her to a dog, and that was not at all flattering. Jewish people of first-century Palestine did not think of dogs as the lovable pets we nurture. They saw dogs essentially as creatures that ate unclean things and spread defilement. To call someone a dog was a grave insult. The word Jesus used can be translated "house dog" (Lane 1974:261). The NIV brings it into English as their [the children's] dogs to distinguish them from the scavengers that roamed the byways and open fields unattached. Even so, this was not a kind thing to say.

The terms of this parable are distressingly blunt, and they reflect the kind of thinking that Jesus' opponents in the previous encounter would have harbored. That is to say, this woman was habitually unclean and had no right to expect anything from God. If she seeks God's grace, they might have added, she should attach herself to the people of the covenant to whom God has promised to be merciful. This is a disturbing portrait of Jesus. It bristles, and we have to wonder why this particular story is part of the Gospel.

On the other hand, this text contains several indications that there is more to Jesus' behavior than meets the eye. In the first place, he was the one who took the initiative to leave the region around the Sea of Galilee and go to the area around Tyre, a place with a predominantly Gentile population. Then he entered a house, and the Evangelist has neglected to tell us whether it was a Jewish or Gentile household, a particularly unusual omission if the point of this story is to underscore the importance of ethnic distinctions. And, we should note, this incident is connected to the previous story by the commingled themes of uncleanness and ethnic distinctions, where Jesus' treatment of ethnic issues was anything but prejudicial. In short, Mark depicts Jesus in a setting where the spiritual and ethnic issues he treated in the preceding text cannot help but rise to the surface again.

Is it possible to resolve the conflict between the difficult language of this parable Jesus used and the values he had just advocated? If the problem of becoming unclean was essentially an external one, then people could deal with it by washing themselves carefully. If, though, as Jesus maintained, being unclean was a matter of the heart, then who could be considered clean? And if being clean was a cultic necessity for worship, who was acceptable in the presence of the living God? Apart from God's grace no one was or is.

This is the context for understanding the woman's response to Jesus. She did not dispute the fairness or appropriateness of her standing as an outsider. On the contrary, she acknowledged his authority. In his own language she admitted that she had no claim on him and cast herself on his mercy. Apparently without benefit of the Hebrew Scriptures or any other prompting, this Gentile woman affirmed the truth that was implicit in Jesus' last teaching. Somehow she understood the essential and overriding truth about the relationship between human beings and the living God, a point that even the Twelve had yet to appreciate.

At the beginning of this encounter Mark observes that Jesus could not keep his presence in Tyre a secret. Apparently he had left Galilee in an attempt to be alone. Then he concealed himself in a house. Finally, he tried to put a parable between the woman and himself. As in 1:45, the secrecy motif is thoroughly ironic. Jesus could not be hidden. The secrecy motif is not only ironic, but it is also embedded in a sharp clash of values. In this instance Jesus could not be concealed from the one person who acknowledged both his lordship and her abject position before him. She did not stand on privilege or rank. She was willing to accept the crumbs that fell unnoticed from the table. The story of the Greek woman expresses in the simplest and clearest terms the way every human being comes to God. Jesus is still found at the place where we understand our need for God and realize that we have no right to expect anything at all. In fact, at this place he cannot be hidden.

How did the Greek woman know what to say? Mark does not tell us. She is one of several improbable people in this Gospel who mysteriously know what to do or say. Most of them are outsiders, just as she is, but their expressions of faith are always rewarded. When we set the conduct of people like her side by side with the dullness of the Twelve, we come to a realization that ought to inform the perceptual framework of every ardent believer: spiritual insight is not the property of a few who are in positions of privilege because of background, culture, history or social standing. This story is Mark's way of reminding us that God is at work in ways that the church may not understand.

Hearing and Speaking (7:31-37) During the summer of 1972 I helped Jim Berney, who was at that time director of the western region of InterVarsity Christian Fellowship USA, run a series of weeklong student conferences in the Santa Cruz Mountains. Collegians of the 1970s were not known for long-range planning, and by the time the last camper arrived, unannounced, we had three hundred students crammed into a facility designed to hold no more than two hundred. The frustrations of running a camp under those conditions were enormous. Several times each day we ran out of toilet paper. We needed four more large rooms than the camp possessed, and for the duration of the week the breakfast crew never managed to finish its chores before the lunch crew had to begin its preparations.

After three exasperating days Jim and I went in search of the camp manager. We found a gruff, bear of a man supervising the work of fifteen summer interns in a large field about half a mile up the mountain above our daily grind. He listened without comment as we pled our case, then crossed his bulging forearms over a barrel chest that his shirt barely covered and explained that his summer crew was hard at work raking rocks out of a field he planned to use as a horse pasture. Undoubtedly, horses would have been a nice addition to his mountain retreat, but we had more immediate problems to solve. After fifteen more minutes of pleading he agreed to let us have three interns for the duration of the week. As we left he said with vexation etched into his jowls, "You know, we could make this a real nice conference center if it weren't for these campers."

Throughout the Gospel Jesus demonstrates a remarkable ability to move in and out of different worlds. In the prolonged tour from Tyre to Sidon along the Sea of Galilee to the hills of the Decapolis, he moved squarely into someone else's territory. The places that Mark names in 7:31 were areas of predominantly Gentile population. In modern geographic terms he traveled through parts of Lebanon, Syria and Jordan.

Jesus did not seem to be in a hurry. Mark begins the next account with the words *During those days* (8:1), thus placing that story with its stipulated duration of three days in this general frame of time. In 7:31-37 Mark's account contains a linguistic subtlety about the passage of time that is easily overlooked in English. The concluding verses of this story contain several uses of the imperfect tense, indicating actions that had continued to happen over a period of time. Jesus kept on commanding the people to be silent (7:36), and they kept on proclaiming what he had done (7:37). These contextual features describe a ministry in non-Jewish areas that covered a considerable period of time.

Jesus had moved not only into the world of the Gentiles, he also moved into the world of people who could not hear. Mark's description of his behavior (7:33-34) portrays Jesus acting out his intentions for the benefit of those with whom he could not otherwise communicate. Jesus took the man who could not hear or speak apart from the crowd to demonstrate that he was about to do something for him in particular. Then Jesus put his fingers in the man's ears, spat and touched his tongue to show him that his ears would be opened and his tongued loosened. He sighed, looked up to heaven, and spoke one word in Aramaic: *Ephphatha.* Immediately the man could hear and speak correctly. This miracle is located in the Decapolis, the area where the man whom Jesus had freed from the demonic host had gone to tell what Jesus had done for him (5:20). In the Gospel of Mark it has great symbolic value because it is the one non-Jewish place where Jesus had authorized that the gospel should be proclaimed.

The man Jesus healed here was also deaf in a spiritual sense. As a Gentile, he could not hear the Word of God, and without some understanding of God's Word he could not speak sensibly. Isaiah 29:18 looks forward to the day when the Word of God would be open to the nations of the world: "In that day the deaf will hear the words of the scroll, and out of gloom and darkness the eyes of the blind will see." Mark's account has several connections with the book of Isaiah. The Gentiles are the people who walk in darkness (Is 9:2), and the Greek word translated *could hardly talk* in Mark 7:32 appears in only one other place in the Bible—in Isaiah 35:6, where the mute sing for joy.

The people who had brought this man to Jesus apparently heard him speaking and figured out what had happened. That was the point at which one of the strangest events in the Gospel began to unfold. Jesus commanded the crowd of witnesses not to tell anyone about what they had seen. When his initial instructions were widely ignored, he tried to reinforce them. The more he tried to get them to stop, though, the more they talked. Although Jesus had given instructions like this several times in the Gospel and although his instructions had been ignored before, no previous response matched this one. The discrepancy between what he commanded and what happened had never been greater. Similar prohibitions against telling what had happened appear in miracles that have some element of controversy. They are part of Mark's presentation of Jesus' miracles as parables of faith.

Several features of this account give it a parabolic flavor. First, the

---

7:33 The Greek text emphasizes that Jesus took the man apart from the crowd by in-contradiction between Jesus' instruction and the crowd's response gives a riddlelike quality to this encounter. Second, the affirmation in Mark 7:37, *He has done everything well. He even makes the deaf hear and the mute speak,* is the highest praise Jesus has received from a human being up to this point. The disciples' question in 4:35, "Who is this? Even the wind and the waves obey him?" is just that—a question. Third, the command *be opened* is ambiguous. Grammatically, it could be addressed to the man's ears or to the heavens. If as Waetjen maintains (1989:137) it is addressed to the heavens, then the way was opened for the Gentiles to hear the Word of God.

Within a Jewish context the miracles produced praise for God and questions about who Jesus was. In this Gentile context, however, the miracles produced only praise for Jesus. The phrase *kept talking about it* (7:36) is a weak translation. The Greek text does not say that the crowd went on talking about Jesus' praise. It reports that they proclaimed it. This is the same word used consistently in earlier parts of the Gospel to describe Jesus' preaching. He had proclaimed the kingdom of God. Now the Gentiles were proclaiming him.

The distinction between Jesus as the messenger and Jesus as the message is important, but it is not always easy to make. In general terms this distinction is preserved when Jesus is on Jewish soil, but as early as 1:28 people began to spread the news about him. By the time Mark describes the healing of the Gerasene demoniac, the line between messenger and message has clearly been crossed. Jesus instructed that man to spread the word about what the Lord had done, but the man broadcast the news about what Jesus had done for him (5:20). By the end of the healing of the deaf man, Jesus has become the message. From this point onward, the message and the messenger are indistinguishable. The relationship is so close that it is best described in these terms: where Jesus is the kingdom of God is.

The Twelve, on the other hand have virtually disappeared. After moving onto center stage in 6:6-52, they are suddenly nowhere to be found. Mark has not even used the word disciple since 7:17. Whether they had become studious observers trying to fathom the implications

---

cluding the words *by himself,* which the NIV omits.

of his ministry or whether Jesus was enacting parables for the sake of their hardened hearts is an open question. They do not appear, however, to have played a role in this part of his ministry. Their absence from these events is all the more curious in light of the broader context of these stories. The Evangelist perceives a larger meaning in what transpired here. The theological point of departure for Jesus' prolonged journey into someone else's homeland was an ancient prophecy found in Isaiah 29:13, which goes on to affirm: "In a very short time, will not Lebanon be turned into a fertile field and the fertile field seem like a forest? In that day the deaf will hear the words of the scroll, and out of gloom and darkness the eyes of the blind will see" (Is 29:17-18). Furthermore, since the word translated *could hardly speak* in Mark 7:32 is a rare Greek word found in only one other place in the entire Bible, Isaiah 35:6, the healing of the deaf man is cast as a fulfillment of those prophecies. On the other hand, nothing indicates that Jesus' first disciples had any inkling of what was happening.

A modern prophet might ask whether Jesus' followers in the Western world have any inkling of what God is doing today. We live at a time when massive movements of ethnic groups are the order of the day. Whether they flee from famine or civil war, whether they make pilgrimages to the centers of economic prosperity, or whether they simply want to taste the freedoms we cherish, the peoples of the world are streaming into the urban centers of North America and western Europe. Yet as people of different cultures swell into our cities, the great dream of the established population is no longer a three-bedroom house in the suburbs but a half acre of land somewhere out in the countryside where life is safer. The sad and continuing saga of the decline of the urban church raises this disturbing question: if God is bringing the peoples of the world to our shores, will there be anyone to welcome them in the name of God?

Jesus Feeds a Mixed Crowd (8:1-13) It was Friday evening on the day before our departure from a conference center for university students near the resort community of Valle de Bravo in Mexico. Our group was composed of twenty-five Anglos from southern California, and we had spent a week felling trees, whitewashing walls, chopping weeds and clearing trails at Campamento Citlali. That night as we packed up, Doña Marie came over to talk for the first time. She was an elderly woman who served as a caretaker for the camp. All week long she had been too shy to speak with us, but as we were preparing to leave she came to say goodbye. After we had exchanged a few words through a translator, I asked her what the people of the area thought about us. "Oh, they are surprised," she said. "We thought all Gringos were lazy." It was too intriguing a comment to let pass, so I asked her where the local people had gotten that idea. She looked at me strangely for a moment, as though wondering how I could fail to grasp something so obvious. "That's simple," she said. "It's because you hire Mexicans to do all your work for you."

Sometimes racial stereotypes roll so easily off our tongues that we do not think about them until we become the butt of an ethnic joke. Just about every group of people has a way of looking down upon everyone else. So it is not surprising to find the Twelve and the Pharisees voicing their own racist sentiments. Initially, the Twelve did not want to feed the crowd that had followed Jesus for three days, and the Pharisees wanted to know what right Jesus had to break bread for the four thousand. The problem for both Jesus' disciples and the Pharisees was the composition of this crowd—a gathering of Gentiles.

Mark set this event at a time when Jesus was traveling in a predominately Gentile area. *During those days* refers to the journey Jesus made from Tyre to Sidon to the Sea of Galilee and into the area known as the Decapolis. There may well have been pockets of Jewish people scattered throughout the area, but the territory described in these verses was well outside the centers of Jewish population. Besides the geographic setting, two other contextual clues support the conclusion that Jesus' audience at this point was full of Gentiles.

The first is a demonstrative pronoun translated *them* (8:4). The English pronoun *these* is a better rendering of the Greek demonstrative pronoun. Although it is certainly permissible to translate the word as *them,* retaining the demonstrative tone adds a peculiar flavor to the disciples' question. Consider what it means for Jesus' Jewish disciples to ask, Where in this remote place can anyone get enough bread to feed these? That simple change indicates that the problem was not the general impossibility of finding bread in the wilderness, but the particular affront of giving bread in the wilderness to the kind of people who were in that crowd: Gentiles.

God had fed the children of Israel manna in the wilderness more than a thousand years before, and Deuteronomy 18:15 affirms that God would send the people of Israel another prophet like Moses. The expectation of a shepherd who would tend the flock of God's people (Ezek 34:23) nurtured the messianic dreams of postexilic Judaism. When Jesus fed a large Jewish crowd in a remote part of Galilee (Mk 6:30-44), the messianic implications were unmistakable. Yet the coming of the Messiah was, first of all, a promise to Jewish people. So, for those who regarded the fulfillment of God's promises as their personal or national right, the very thought of feeding Gentiles in the wilderness would have been tantamount to sacrilege.

Second, this line of thought helps explain the dullness of the disciples at this point. How they could have been so obtuse after they had helped to feed the crowd of five thousand is a problem that has baffled students of this Gospel (Taylor 1974:359), but the problem disappears if the crowd is made up predominantly of Gentiles. Certainly, forgetting what God has done is a symptom of hardened hearts, but the subsequent interchange between Jesus and the Twelve (8:14-21) confirms that they had not in fact forgotten the details of the first miracle of the loaves. Racial prejudice is surely also evidence of a heart that is set against doing the will of God. The disciples' otherwise perplexing behavior is more understandable if it is an expression of their ethnocentrism. Their problem was not a simple recollection of the facts. It was a fundamental disagreement about the meaning and direction of Jesus' ministry.

Ethnocentrism also explains why the Pharisees demanded a sign from Jesus at this point (8:11-13). That they simply wanted to see another miracle is not convincing. Jesus' ability to perform miracles was not in question. The Pharisees objected to the implications of what he had just done. When Jesus fed the five thousand Jewish men, there was no objection from the Pharisees. They objected to the people whom he fed.

In their view of the world, God would bless those Gentiles who converted to Judaism and obeyed the law. Conversely, the Gentiles who did not come to terms with God's law could expect nothing but wrath and destruction. From their point of view Jesus was taking the children's bread and tossing it to their dogs (7:27). It was inconceivable to them that God would treat uncircumcised people just like the children of the covenant. They found the implications of this miracle as disturbing as anything else Jesus had done. So they demanded a sign from heaven because they wanted to examine his credentials and debate his authorization for something they found offensive.

The word *test* in 8:11 is the same word translated "tempted" in 1:13, when the Spirit drove Jesus into the wilderness to be tempted by Satan. The Gospel of Mark does not report any of the issues of the temptation in the wilderness. Mark simply states that Jesus was tempted by Satan for forty days. But the word *tempt* appears at several points throughout the Gospel in Jesus' interactions with other people. It is characteristic of Mark's Gospel that the concrete examples of Jesus' temptation come from his human opponents (Martin 1972:128).

Here, however, we come to another place where Mark wants to engage his audience directly. After raising the subject of Jesus' temptation, the Evangelist tells his story with such economy of language that he neither specifies what the temptation was nor why Jesus refused to provide the sign that the Pharisees demanded. Mark leaves us to sort these questions out for ourselves. It is no stretch of the imagination to conclude that the temptation was to give in to the ethnocentric view of God's grace held by both his strongest opponents and his closest followers. It is more difficult to figure out why he refused to provide a sign. Perhaps Jesus thought a sign would be useless. Perhaps he wanted to leave his detractors with a miracle that was also another parable. Perhaps in his thinking the Gentiles were not the problem. Perhaps he thought his audience needed to come to terms with their own prejudice. In any event, Jesus refused once again to allow his critics to define the terms of the debate. He had done what he had done, and he refused to argue about it. He left the Pharisees to sort it out for themselves.

It is not at all difficult to translate this story into modern terms. Think of the many hurting places in our world where people are waiting for their deliverer. Then imagine that a Savior appeared for each of these peoples who demonstrated God's power and love for them and went on to make the same demonstrations for their enemies. Consider what it would mean for Serbs and Kosovars, Hutus and Tutsis, Israelis and Palestinians to see God in these terms. We need to come to grips with our wanting to worship a god who promises good things to people just like us. It is not simply a matter of being nice to our enemies on certain occasions. We cannot follow Jesus unless we let God's grace shine upon the ethnocentrism and racism that are woven into the fabric of our lives.

A Little Yeast Goes a Long Way (8:14-21) Several years ago I was invited to speak about anger to a group of people who had recently lost their spouses. One man stared at me without blinking for the entire session. Afterward, he marched up, stood ramrod straight before me and delivered a message with an aggressive staccato: "I got nothing out of this session. I am not angry. I have nothing to forgive. And I do not need to be forgiven." He stormed away as quickly as he had come, and I just barely resisted the urge to call out: "You are wrong. You are one of the angriest men I have ever met." His wife, it turned out, had committed suicide, and he had erected an impregnable wall of denial around his pain. I did not know about his wife that evening, but I did understand that there are no answers for questions we are unwilling to ask.

We sometimes think of the Bible as a book of answers, and it does reveal a great deal about life's deepest problems. The Bible is also, however, a book of questions, and there are times when God does not speak to us if we will not live with questions. This text is full of questions, some of which are not answered anywhere in the Gospel. Jesus posed them all himself. He began by warning his disciples against the yeast of Herod and the yeast of the Pharisees. Those two metaphors were designed to prod the Twelve into serious reflection. They were supposed to think about what he meant by the yeast of Herod and the yeast of the Pharisees, but the disciples showed little interest in probing metaphors. They stepped neatly around the parabolic language and focused their mental powers on the literal facts: they had not brought any bread with them.

Trying to set them back on the right course, Jesus asked them two questions to redirect their thinking: *When I broke the five loaves for the five thousand, how many basketfuls of pieces did you pick up? . . . And when I broke the seven loaves for the four thousand, how many basketfuls of pieces did you pick up?* The disciples responded with the correct factual answers, but their minds went no further. Finally Jesus demanded: *Do you still not understand?* This provocative sequence of questions was intended to bring them face to face with the problem of their hardened hearts. There was something here that they had to sort out for themselves, something they could learn only by coming to terms with it themselves. It was not a concept he could lecture about, a sermon he could preach or a proposition he could illustrate. He left them, and Mark has left us, with the questions.

Surely, this is a place where commentators ought to tread lightly. If the Evangelist was willing to leave his readers with open questions, perhaps this is a place where we should do the same. It may be inappropriate to go further here than the Bible itself does. Accordingly, we will not attempt to resolve all the questions, but it may be helpful to pursue the story a bit further together. What did Jesus mean when he warned the Twelve about the yeast of Herod and the yeast of the Pharisees?

The clues are to be found in other passages in the Gospel of Mark. Herod has appeared only once before—in the story about the death of John the Baptist (6:14-29). Herod was a man in search of a throne, and he was a person of divided loyalties. In the end, his attempt to embrace two competing loyalties had awful consequences. He killed a prophet. The yeast of Herod, then, is a double-minded response to God's Word.

The yeast of the Pharisees is a different matter entirely. Jesus had already had several encounters with the Pharisees, and rereading any of them might produce a suitable answer. Since, however, the Pharisees had just come to Jesus demanding to see his credentials (8:11-13), it might be best to look there. Jesus had just fed a crowd of people who were not Jewish, just as he had previously fed a Jewish audience (6:35-44). The Pharisees were outraged that he would squander God's gifts on people who did not read the Bible or pretend to keep God's commandments.

When they demanded a sign from heaven, they wanted to know what right he had to share God's gifts with people who were outside the covenant. As we have seen, their hardness of heart was complicated by prejudice. In the simplest terms their yeast was hypocrisy. They were so sure of themselves and their understanding of God that they could not conceive of the possibility that God might be doing something new. The yeast of the Pharisees describes those situations in life where people are so righteously sure of themselves that they are unwilling to do the will of God. It is the consummate hypocrisy.

Those were some of the issues the first disciples had to face. When, how and to what extent they resolved them is beyond the scope of this Gospel. In fact, the Gospel of Mark is essentially a story without a resolution. Its lack of resolution is more than a curiosity; it is a fundamental part of the way Mark understood the gospel of Jesus Christ itself, and it is one of the ways Mark preaches.

For example: *The disciples had forgotten to bring bread, except for one loaf they had with them in the boat* (8:14). This editorial statement adds one more level of complexity to the text. As far as the disciples were concerned, however, there was no bread at all in the boat. In response to Jesus' warning about the yeast of the Pharisees and Herod, they said among themselves: *It is because we have no bread.* Jesus himself echoed their perception when he asked: *Why are you talking about having no bread?* Without 8:14 there would be no question about whether there was a loaf of bread on the boat. As the story stands, though, it contains a glaring contradiction. Was there no bread in the boat, or did they have one loaf with them after all?

We can frame the problem a little more precisely by observing that the question is addressed to us, and not to any of the characters in the story. The problem of whether there was any bread in the boat is part of the editorial framework. Since it plays no part in the development of the story, we might well suppose that this information is not for the characters in the story—it is for us. This is a question that the Evangelist expects us to answer.

It is not a matter of idle curiosity, nor is it merely an intellectual puzzle, for Mark uses this question to set up a thoroughly unsettling picture: the hardened hearts of Jesus' closest followers. They could not comprehend the meaning of the loaves. Can we comprehend the meaning of the one loaf? Was there a loaf of bread on the ship? It is a matter of utmost gravity, and it is a question a young child may answer as readily as a scholar. It is not, though, a question that one person can answer for another. There can be no abstract response. Every answer is personal.

Healing a Blind Man (8:22-26) In 1989 Mother Teresa visited some homeless Latino men living in a church-sponsored shelter program. Mother Teresa expressed the hope that people in Los Angeles would find housing, food and work for these men. Someone asked if she realized that it was against the law for American citizens to employ illegal aliens or offer them shelter. Mother Teresa replied, "Is it not breaking the law of God to keep them on the streets?" (*Los Angeles Times*, February 1, 1989).

The healing in Bethsaida is a curious event. It happened in stages, and its closest parallel is the healing of the Gerasene demoniac. In that encounter Jesus twice commanded the unclean spirits to leave the man. In this healing Jesus touched the man's eyes twice. At the first touch the man received his sight, but his vision was confused. He saw people who looked like trees walking around. When Jesus touched him a second time, though, he saw things clearly. This two-stage miracle is not just about the gift of sight. It is ultimately about the gift of perception.

In another respect, though, this healing fits a familiar pattern. Two of its features are connected with the theme of secrecy (Taylor 1974:368). In 8:23 Jesus took the blind man outside the village, and there is no indication that anyone accompanied the two of them. It appears that they went off by themselves. Then at the end of the account Jesus said: *Don't go into the village.* This is one of the most ironic descriptions of a secret in the Gospel. Bethsaida was no metropolitan center where someone could disappear into the anonymous masses. There was manifestly no possibility that what had happened could be kept under a shroud of secrecy.

Consider this miracle from the perspective of the residents of Bethsaida. When Jesus came to their community, some of them approached with a blind man, whom Jesus took away from them out of the village. Apparently, they did not walk away too far, or there would have been no one for this man to see later as trees walking around. From a distance then some of the villagers watched Jesus spit on the man's eyes and touch him. Jesus' disciples seem to have been among this group.

There is no indication that they accompanied him when he led the blind man outside the village. Then Jesus touched him again, and the man they knew as a blind beggar walked home without going through the village. That is to say, without any of the clues that his senses of touch, smell or sound would have provided in the village itself, without being able to count his steps along familiar paths, this man knew where he lived and went directly there. From a distance the people of Bethsaida observed more than the restoration of this man's sight. They watched a miracle of perception unfold.

This sort of event is called an enacted parable, and in the Gospel of Mark many of Jesus' miracles enact a message, theme or question. Implicit in this parable is one of the boldest claims ever put forward about Jesus: that Jesus can confer the gift of making sense of what we see. Yet the Evangelist is content to tell this story without elaboration. He simply presents the miracle in the form of a parable.

For whom was this enacted parable intended? Was it intended for the residents of Bethsaida? Or was this a parable for one or more of the disciples, whom Jesus had just accused of having eyes that did not see (8:18) and whose comprehension had become increasingly faulty? We have no clue about what perceptual problems the villagers may have had, unless it had something to do with their treatment of disabled people. We have quite a few clues about the Twelve.

When Jesus fed a Jewish crowd (6:35-44), they did not understand about the loaves, and their hearts were hardened (6:52). Consequently, when he walked calmly on the waves, they thought he was a ghost. Later on Jesus was amazed at their inability to comprehend his teaching about the radical nature of sin (7:18). Then when Jesus expressed concern for a crowd of hungry Gentiles, his disciples acted as though they had never encountered hungry people before (8:1-10). If the parable enacted at Bethsaida was directed at these men, then the problem of perception concerned their view of Jesus, their understanding of God's concern for the other peoples of the world and the nature of sin, their view of their own place in the world and their prejudice about other people. According to tradition Bethsaida was the home of Simon Peter.

People who read through the Gospel of Mark carefully for the first time often wonder how Jesus' disciples could have been so obtuse.

Again and again the people who were closest to Jesus acted as though they did not have a clue about what was going on around them. Mark's portrayal of the disciples raises several questions. Was he trying to discredit the Twelve for some reason (Trocmé 1975:120-37)? Did he think it was important to attack their standing in the early church (Tyson 1961:261-68)? Or does his unflattering portrait of the Twelve reflect a broader concern for the church? In their struggles did Mark perceive something that had a broader application?

The early association between this Gospel and Peter's preaching suggests that the early Christians, at least, did not treat Mark as the adversary of the Twelve. It is unlikely that Mark's motive for writing was to discredit the leaders of the early church. Mark's critical portrayal of the disciples points to something else—to the difficulty of knowing how to do good in a world dominated by self-interest and divided by age, gender, culture and race. It is not a simple thing to live out the values of the rule of God in a fallen world. What is good for some may be bad for others. It is increasingly clear that Jesus is not interested in a narrowly defined good.

What we see is a critical issue for every follower of Jesus. Who are, for example, those people with little or no English grouped at the curb looking for work? Are they undocumented aliens straining our already overtaxed network of social services? Are they a pool of cheap labor, working without a safety net for a third of what we would have to pay anyone else to clean our yards or tear off our leaking roofs? Or are they a sign of something God is doing? And if we are not sure, how can we make sense of what we see?

□ The Way to New Life (8:27—10:52)

Was the death of Jesus a tragic waste, an act of misguided zeal or simply an ill-conceived idea? Each of these possibilities finds an echo in the actions and saying of his disciples in the remaining chapters of this Gospel. More than any of the other Evangelists, Mark highlights the extraordinary difficulty Jesus' first followers experienced in coming to terms with his death. The section which begins in 8:27 and ends at 10:52 is the most focused collection of material about Jesus' death in Mark's presentation of the good news. The three predictions about the

Son of Man in 8:31, 9:31 and 10:33-34 present three distinct but related perspectives on Jesus' death. The events and arguments which follow each prediction are not random pieces of editorial activity, as though the Evangelist could not think of anywhere else to place them. They are stories which illustrate, explain and expand on the prediction which precedes them. There is an integral connection between each prediction about the death of the Son of Man and the material which accompanies it.

Messiah and Son of Man (8:27—9:1) The dalit who had picked up unclean things in the village for most of his life replied, "My avatar told me not to do that anymore." That was news to the owner of the estate who confronted him. It was unheard of for a member of the dalit to have an avatar. In fact, the people of the village believed that the dalit were not even human beings. This dalit, though, claimed to have an avatar who had taught him that he was made in the image of God. "Where is your avatar?" the estate owner demanded. "Someone has to remove that dead dog in front of my house." "My avatar is not here," the man answered, "but I can take you to my guru." The "guru," another dalit who served as the pastor for a growing community of faith, confirmed that the avatar would not let the dalit clean up the village waste anymore.

It was a crisis. No one could be found to take the carcass away. Eventually the pastor suggested that the village hold a meeting to decide what to do with the bloated animal. It had become a community problem, the pastor observed, and the community must decide how to fix it. After a heated discussion a solution was reached. The residents of the village returned to the sweltering street. The pastor maneuvered a loop of rope over the dog's leg, which the estate owner held up with a stick. Then one representative from each caste in the village took hold of the rope and dragged the dog away. No one was forced to touch the carcass.

Peter's Confession (8:27-30) Jesus' question, *Who do people say I am?* is a turning point in the Gospel. It brings to the fore the tension between his understanding of himself and the expectations of the people who were attracted to him. The answers—John the Baptist, Elijah or one of the prophets—have already been anticipated (6:15-16), when the things Jesus was doing and saying were brought to the attention of Herod Antipas. The suggestions that Jesus might be John the Baptist or one of the other prophets, however, move beyond the realms of prophecy and apocalyptic into superstition. The predominant idea is that Jesus was someone who had returned from beyond the grave with superhuman powers (Lane 1974:212, 290). There was clearly no consensus about who Jesus was, and the line between biblical traditions and superstition or magic was not clearly drawn in public opinion.

The conversation of 8:27-30 took place as Jesus and his disciples were on the way to the villages in the vicinity of Caesarea Philippi. This journey took them outside the region of Galilee into territory that was populated predominately by Gentiles. In light of the argument about whether Jesus had the right to feed non-Jewish people with bread in the wilderness (8:1-13), we ought to pay attention to this setting. Caesarea Philippi, known as Caesarea Panias before Herod Philip enlarged it, was one of the principal cities in the territory that he inherited on the death of his father, Herod the Great. Philip did not, however, inherit the title king. Neither did any of the other sons who had survived the suspicion and wrath of Herod the Great. That does not mean that they did not try to secure it. Philip built the city of Julias in honor of Emperor Tiberius's mother. His brother Antipas, not to be outdone, built a city in honor of the emperor's mother and called it Livias, as well as the city of Tiberias named for the emperor himself (Aharoni and Avi-Yonah 1974:140). In a family so obsessed with power it is impossible think of these construction projects and their accompanying dedications as examples of disinterested benevolence. They were teeming with political undertones. Peter's confession that Jesus is the Messiah took place in an area populated by Jews and Gentiles who had considerable experience with political intrigue.

Peter's declaration, *You are the Christ,* carried political freight of its own. Not too much later James and John asked for positions of power and prestige (10:37), and those who followed Jesus to Gethsemane were prepared to take up arms (14:47). The confrontations Jesus had had with leaders and institutions of first-century Judaism in Galilee were political as well as spiritual. There was no simple way to separate religion from politics then, just as there is no simple way to separate them today. It would be a mistake to treat Peter's confession as a purely spiritual matter. Nevertheless, as the Gospel unfolds, politics alone is too small a sphere to contain Jesus' ministry.

Peter called Jesus the Christ, and Mark introduces Jesus in the same terms, but the word never appears on Jesus' lips. In fact, he responded to Peter's confession by telling his followers not to tell anyone about this conversation. It is a surprising command that has been explained in various ways. For Wrede it was the church's rather clumsy apology for its proclamation of a messiah who never claimed to be the Messiah (1971:218-21). The Jesus Seminar, which casts Jesus as a wandering Jewish cynic, finds corroboration in the word Messiah not appearing on Jesus' lips (Funk et al. 1993:75). Aune, on the other hand, identifies a sound reason for Jesus' silence on the subject. In first-century eschatological movements it was considered God's right to designate who the Messiah would be, rather than a title that someone might claim (1969:31). Romans 1:4 presents Jesus as Messiah in precisely these terms. Therefore, anyone who claimed to be the Messiah could properly be dismissed as an imposter.

Aune's explanation of Jesus' silence, however, does not fully account for the instructions he gave to his followers. The language of Mark 8:30 places Jesus' messianic identity among the various secrecy motives in this Gospel. For Mark, secrecy, parable and conflicting values are all tied together. As this conversation unfolds, there are clearly more than enough conflicting values to account for Jesus' instructions.

The Fundamental Argument (8:31-33) The conflict began when Jesus changed the terms. He spoke of himself as the _Son of Man_, his preferred way of speaking about himself, rather than Messiah. The term _Son of Man_ appears in several Old Testament passages with different meanings. The reference to the Son of Man coming in his Father's glory in 8:38 points to Daniel 7:13, 27, where the Son of Man is a corporate figure composed of the saints who have suffered for their

---

8:33 The terms _Son of Man_ and _Messiah_ are connected, for the word that Satan took away in the parable of the sower was the word about the kingdom of God. The

obedience. It is impossible to know whether Peter and the others fully understood this reference to suffering. There is little to suggest that they did, but Peter understood enough to disagree with Jesus' next statement: *The Son of Man must suffer many things and be rejected by the elders, chief priests and teachers of the law, and that he must be killed and after three days rise again.* Since the collection of parables in Mark 4, this statement is one of the few things that Jesus had said plainly, and Peter rebuked Jesus for it. Jesus in turn rebuked him, and he spoke to Peter as though Peter were Satan.

His denunciation of Peter is so strong that we have to wonder what justifies it. After all, Peter had just answered the question of who Jesus is with insight and perhaps courage. What had Peter done to be called Satan? And of all people, why call Peter Satan? The best answer is that he was acting, unwittingly, in the role of Satan. The last time the word Satan appeared in this Gospel was in the explanation of the parable of the soils, where Satan comes to take the word away (4:15). That is what Peter did here. As soon as Jesus began to speak about his messianic role, Peter rebuked him, as though to take away the word.

The crux of the disagreement is the idea that the "Son of Man must suffer many things and be rejected . . . and . . . be killed." Behind this translation is a Greek construction called the divine passive, which conveys the idea that God is the one who is ultimately responsible for the impending death of the Son of Man. Stated simply, the Son of Man must suffer because it is God's will. This is a powerful declaration, but this is not at all a simple matter. There are times, to be sure, when God's will is presented in stark, absolute terms, but ever since the beginning of Jesus' ministry, Mark has provided hints that Jesus was going to die. If all Mark wanted to accomplish was to ascribe Jesus' death to God's inscrutable will, then he has chosen a curious way to proceed. Mark's hints invite us to understand Jesus' death as a developing theme. What is the relationship, then, between the hints about Jesus' death in the earlier parts of this Gospel and this striking

words about the Son of Man in 8:31 are also words about the kingdom of God.

declaration that these things are God's will?

The first hint of Jesus' death is the arrest of John the Baptist, which provides the background for the beginning of Jesus' proclamation that the kingdom of God is near (1:14). If the herald of the one who is to come (1:7) is rejected and killed, then we might suspect that a similar reception awaits Jesus. And although his preaching in Galilee was initially welcomed with enthusiasm, the enthusiasm was tempered by an undercurrent of tension. His first sermon provoked an outburst from a man with an unclean spirit, and a synagogue, of all places, became the setting for Jesus' first exorcism (1:21-28). The latent tension in the Galilean villagers' delay in seeking to be healed until after sundown on the Sabbath (1:32) develops into series of acrimonious confrontations about what is legal on the Sabbath, which in turn culminates in a plot to kill him (3:6).

As Jesus left the synagogues and formed a new people, he provoked a reaction from the people who had known him best. His relatives thought he was crazy (3:21), and when his mother and brothers came to assert the claims of his family, he redefined his family as consisting of those who do the will of God. The people of Capernaum rejected his wisdom about the family and ultimately rejected him (6:1-6).

Furthermore, the teachers of the law thought his healing of the paralytic was blasphemous (2:1-12), and later on the scribes from Jerusalem accused him of being in league with the devil (3:22). If this were not enough, his escalating attack on the Pharisees and teachers of the law (7:5-23) coupled with his rejection of Jewish exclusivity (7:24—8:21) have done nothing to endear him to his opponents. The wheels had been set in motion. By challenging the fundamental institutions of first-century Judaism—synagogue, nation, family, Torah—Jesus set the stage for his own death.

This is not to say that there is nothing new in 8:31. So far his major opponents have been the Pharisees and the teachers of the law. The scribes appear here, however, with two groups that we have not encountered before: the elders and chief priests. The elders are the seventy elders who sat together as the Sanhedrin and governed the affairs of the Jewish state. The chief priests presided over the programs and services of the temple. If the chief priests and elders must reject him and kill him, then Jesus has to go to Jerusalem too. Up to this point Jesus has confronted the structures of Jewish life outside the temple, which is its cultural and spiritual center. Here we see that the imperative that drove the Son of Man beyond the synagogues in Galilee also drove him to Jerusalem. The use of the divine passive affirms that it was God's will for Jesus to carry the confrontation that began in the villages of Galilee to its conclusion in Jerusalem.

In each case the conflict flared up as Jesus' preaching about the kingdom took root in this world. It was the rule of God expressed in the forgiveness of sin, the restoration of chronically and terminally ill people, the gathering of outcasts for meals and the creation of a new people that generated the conflict. The tension and opposition came not only from what might be called the little people, like the villagers in Capernaum (6:2-3), but also from representatives of the institutions of first-century Judaism, like the Pharisees, Herodians (3:6) and the scribes from Jerusalem. The opposition to Jesus is both personal and institutional, so that in pressing the claims of the kingdom of God, Jesus was also calling the whole people with its institutions and structures to repent and believe. Kim argues that the expression *Son of Man* is large enough to include the messianic identity of Jesus (1985:79-81). Here we find considerable support for his thesis, for the death of Jesus as the Son of Man is brought about by his proclamation that the kingdom of God is near and by his demonstration of its presence. The Son of Man, then, must suffer and die so that the whole people of God might be brought to repentance and faith. His preaching was a call for people as individuals and for the people as a nation, with the accompanying accumulation and delegation of wealth and power, to live and to conduct their affairs in allegiance to the reign of God.

This call to repentance and faith, however, goes far beyond the social and political confrontations that culminate in Jesus' death. There is much more than the normal forces of history at work. There is also a divine imperative that leads the Son of Man through death to a completely unanticipated outcome. The rule of God comes into history to claim our personal and corporate loyalty, but its presence in the world is not bound by our disobedience. The declaration that the Son of Man must die assumes that human disobedience will persist, but it will not prevail because death is not the end. The Son of Man must also rise on the third day.

New Terms for Life (8:34-38) The crowd that Jesus summoned came from the mixed population of the villages around Caesarea Philippi. If it is curious to find someone with the trappings of a Jewish messiah calling the peoples of the world to join him, the terms of the call are even more striking. Jesus invited people to deny themselves, take up their cross and follow him to his death. It is common in some churches to hear people speaking of having a cross to bear. In modern parlance, carrying a cross typically means doing something hard and unrewarding, like caring for a disagreeable relative or living with severe pain.

Although a great deal of later Christian tradition supports this line of interpretation, it does not fit the larger framework of Mark's Gospel. Mark does not dress Jesus in horsehair shirts. He was, on the contrary, the bridegroom whose presence negated the need to fast (2:18-22). Jesus looks no more like John the Baptist now than he did earlier in the Gospel. There is still joy and awe as the kingdom of God expresses itself in Jesus' ministry in the form of healing, reconciliation, liberation and forgiveness, but there is also suffering when the structures of culture and power oppose the claims of God.

The immediate context for the call to take up the cross is the suffering of the Son of Man. This is not a matter of austere living, but of persevering in pressing the claims of the kingdom of God. The cross was not merely an instrument of death. It was a way of executing people who were considered to be a serious threat to the rule of Roman law. Here we find an important change in emphasis. Where the first prediction of Jesus' passion (8:31) is set against a Jewish backdrop, this invitation to come after Jesus has nothing Jewish about it. There are no chief priests, elders or scribes here. Instead we encounter the word *cross* for the first time, and crucifixion was not a penalty the Jewish authorities could impose. The right to crucify was reserved for Rome (Bruce 1972:200). To take up the cross, then, means to follow Jesus in calling the world that was held together by the structures of Rome to repent and believe the gospel. The Gospel of Mark presents Jesus' death as something that happened not only because of Jesus' challenge to the structures of first-century Judaism but also to the authority of Rome. Ultimately for Jesus and Mark the Pax Romana was merely a superficial rearrangement of the powers of this world. The Pax Romana itself needed to be transformed by the shalom of Yahweh.

In this light, then, what does it mean to deny oneself? If the invitation to follow Jesus is not a call for self-denial as that is usually construed, what is it? Once again, the context provides the best solution. This is part of Jesus' response to Peter. It is an answer to the question lurking just beneath the surface of this text: How could it be God's will for the Messiah to die? Peter and presumably the other disciples were clinging to the idea that a dead messiah was of no earthly good at all. To deny oneself is to accept God's point of view about life, which has implications not just for the Son of Man, but for everyone who is drawn to him. Jesus sketched them out in parable style in 8:34—9:1. This passage begins with Jesus speaking plainly about his passion, where plainly means without parables (in contrast to 4:34). From that point on, however, his statements become increasingly less transparent. His comments about life and death in 8:34-37 resemble the pithy parables of 4:21-25, while his statement about the coming of the Son of Man in 8:38 is even less clear. And 9:1 is among the most obscure statements attributed to Jesus.

In these parables Jesus invites us to look at human life from God's point of view. We take a step forward if we admit that life belongs to God. Even that admission, though, does not take us far enough, for the assumption of these parables is not just that our lives are in God's hands, but that they are already forfeit. The disturbing question of 8:37, *Or what can a man give in exchange for his soul?* is built on this premise. According to Jesus the only real choice we have is how we give our lives up. We can try to save them ourselves and lose them, or we can give them up for his sake and the gospel's and save them (8:35).

That is not a modern view of life. In a world where the one with the most toys at the end of the game wins, we typically think that the way to save our lives is to hang onto everything that comes within our grasp. That we could save our lives only by giving them up is not immediately compelling. We might give away something we could afford to do without in a gesture of enlightened self-interest, but giving up ourselves in pursuit of God's will is quite a spiritual stretch for materialistic people. To say the least, this is an unflattering view of our predicament. Has Mark given us any evidence in support of it, or does it simply appear out of the blue? This Gospel does begin on a familiar prophetic theme—repent. Repentance was fundamental to the preaching of both John and Jesus. Despite the large audiences that they drew, however, John was arrested and Jesus had to leave the synagogues. Houses, boats and open areas became the places where people gathered to hear about the kingdom of God. Although Jesus still had to go to Jerusalem, there is nothing to indicate that the response to the kingdom of God would be any different there.

In this sort of situation Isaiah spoke of a righteous remnant that would emerge from the impending judgment as a purified people dedicated to keeping the covenant their ancestors had made with God at Mount Sinai. Mark, though, has nothing to say about a righteous remnant. Instead he has shown Jesus gathering a new people led by the Twelve. And the Twelve did not come from the ranks of the privileged and powerful. They were common folk drawn from the underclasses of small villages in Galilee. Sadly, the evidence is already in about the nature of their leadership: their hearts are hardened, and their leading voice has just spoken for Satan.

This is the bleakest assessment of Israel's prospects there has ever been. When Jesus spoke about an adulterous and sinful generation (8:38), he meant everyone—both the old people of God and the new. Lest there be any doubt that he included the new people, 8:38 can refer only to them. Who could be ashamed of Jesus' words about the suffering Son of Man except the people of the new community? They are the only ones to have heard them. There is no room for bargaining or special pleading. Everyone belongs to the generation that is characterized by terminal faithlessness and sin.

Mark 8:34-38 portrays people who yearn for deliverance but cannot comprehend how entangled they are. There would be no hope for sal-

---

8:38 Hooker demonstrates that the picture of the Son of Man coming in the glory of his Father refers not to the parousia but to the scene described in Daniel 7:13, where

vation if there were not a new standard of judgment. As part of the
good news about the king, Jesus has opened a new means of forgiveness, though we should be cautious about using the word new in this
context. This is not the first time we have heard something new about
forgiveness. John baptized people for the forgiveness of sin without
any reference to temple, cult or sacrifice. And well before the opposition to Jesus hardened into a plot to do away with him, he forgave the
sins of the paralytic. Even his disregard for the codes of purity suggests
that he was acting on a different conception of the relationship between God and people. What was only hints and glimmers now comes
to the fore. There is a way of forgiveness that is broader than the structures of Jewish life and piety. It is the company of the Son of Man. If
we are ashamed of him and his words, the Son of Man will be
ashamed of us when he ascends into his Father's presence with the
holy angels. If, on the other hand, we give up our lives for the Son of
Man, we shall receive them back.

How Peter and the others responded to Jesus' statement of the terms
of life is an open question. Their previous conduct leaves little reason to
think that they accepted it, and the pointed warning about being
ashamed of Jesus and his words suggests that they might not have been
convinced. If they could not comprehend a messiah who had come to
die, how could they acknowledge the stunning judgment about themselves? Yet they did follow him to Jerusalem. It looks as though they
were trying to believe without affirming the radical terms of repentance
that Jesus had just set out. Mark does not present Jesus' death in noble or
heroic terms. This passage contains the first prediction of Jesus' passion,
and it leaves us to ponder the kind of Messiah we would follow.

A Guarantee for the Gospel (9:1) Following Bultmann's lead
(1972:121), many distinguished New Testament scholars argue that Jesus
was convinced that the kingdom of God would arrive in all its fullness
within the lifetime of the Twelve. Mark 9:1 is frequently cited to support
that reading. Every attempt to interpret the Gospel in this way, however,
must answer a difficult question: why would a person living in the first

one like a Son of Man comes before the Ancient of Days to receive authority and dominion over all the kingdoms of the world (1966:50-53).

century bother to write a book if he were persuaded that the end of the world was at hand (Rohde 1968:139)? If the early Christian community had this understanding of this verse, why would someone take the trouble to write a gospel? Rohde originally advanced this point in connection with the prophecy of Mark 13, but his question has a broader application. Writing a book is a time-consuming task, and it is a poor communication strategy if time had nearly run out. Any vexing heresies would soon be irrelevant, and all persecution quickly ended. If this verse predicts the end of history, then the Evangelist arguably had more important things to do. That Mark wrote at a time not far from the end of the expected life span of the generation of the first disciples is itself an argument that he had a less certain, if not a longer, view of the future.

The medieval scribe who decided to begin Mark 9 at this point apparently had a different idea. By dividing the text here, he separated it from the life and death issues surrounding the Son of Man and connected it with the next event in Jesus' ministry—the transfiguration. Lane argues that the words *come with power* point to the transfiguration. He finds in 9:1 not a prophecy about the end of history but a prediction of the transfiguration (1974:313-14). There is certainly something to be said for this view, but it faces a problem of proportion. It is hard to understand why anyone would begin a prediction of an event only a short time away with the words *I tell you the truth, some who are standing here will not taste death.*

To a lesser degree that is also a problem for the possibility that 9:1 might refer to Jesus' resurrection. The resurrection is a more distant event than the transfiguration, but it is still close enough to make the language seem oddly overstated. Yet the idea that Jesus was talking about the resurrection does have something to commend itself. It takes seriously the character of 9:1 as a guarantee. The previous verse, 8:38, is a warning not to deny the words of the Son of Man. Mark 9:1, though, has an entirely different character. It sets out an assertion that is intended to be indisputable. We have no record anywhere in the gospel traditions of Jesus using an oath to vouch for the truth of something he said. Instead of an oath he introduces solemn statements with the words *I tell you the truth* to underscore their veracity.

What in the sayings of 8:34-38 requires a guarantee? There are several things that a skeptic, or even a wavering disciple, might doubt. It is not, for instance, immediately obvious that people who try to save their lives will actually lose them. That is debatable. Yet the hinge of the argument, which is also its most vulnerable and important affirmation, is the statement that people who give up their life for the Son of Man and the gospel, will receive it back again.

We are looking then for an event that confirms the argument of 8:34-38 and that happened after Jesus' resurrection, yet within the lifetime of the first generation of disciples. The only other clue is the statement that the disciples would see *the kingdom of God come with power*. Unfortunately, the exact expression *the kingdom of God come with power* does not appear anywhere outside the Synoptic tradition. There is, however, a corresponding expression in 2 Chronicles 14:9, where Zerah the Ethiopian "came out . . . with an army" (RSV). The words translated "army" in that text are the same words translated *with power* in Mark 9:1. In fact, in the Septuagint *with power* frequently means "with an army," and it can have the more particular sense of a power that defeats an enemy (similar expressions are found in Num 31:6; Judg 8:5; 2 Chron 25:10; and Baruch 2:11). Furthermore, in 2 Kings 21:5 and 23:4-5 the Greek word for power refers to the host of heaven, that is, God's army. Jesus' enigmatic words may thus refer to the arrival of an army.

A generation after Jesus' death a Roman army sacked Jerusalem. That was the moment at which the opponents of Jesus, as Mark describes them here, were overthrown. It was an event that happened within the lifetime of some of Jesus' first followers, and it is a powerful argument for the validity of 8:34-38. Those who clung to life, privilege and position, preeminently the people responsible for his death, lost what they had, while Jesus was raised from the dead.

The argument between Jesus and Peter, in the gathered company of hope and rumor, depicts a people yearning for deliverance, yet unaware of how deeply they are enmeshed in sin and self-interest. On his second visit to America just before the outbreak of World War II Dietrich Bonhoeffer criticized American preaching as self-indulgent. In a letter to his brother, Bonhoeffer commented: "Whether the church in America is free, I doubt" (Kelly and Nelson 1990:500). More recently, we have begun to call funeral services celebrations of life, succumbing to the death-denying currents in our culture. And many preachers feel that the most effective sermons are the ones that present the gospel in terms of self-fulfillment. Jesus did not think that the one with the most toys at the end of the game won. In this regard it is doubtful that much has changed in two thousand years.

The Transfiguration (9:2-13) In the cold winter of 1950 Syngman Rhee fled from North Korea to South Korea. His father, a well-known Christian pastor, had just been killed by a squad of North Korean soldiers. In South Korea Rhee enlisted as a marine to fight against the Communists. Five years later he came to the United States, enrolled in a Presbyterian college and attended Louisville Presbyterian Seminary. Rhee felt called to follow his father into the ministry. Today after serving as president of the National Council of the Churches in the USA and moderator of the Presbyterian Church (USA), Rhee no longer has the formidable bearing of a marine. His presence commands gentleness, and he describes himself as a peacemaker. A cross hangs from a chain around his neck, and he preaches the good news of reconciliation. In 1992 he was instrumental in arranging Billy Graham's visit to North Korea to meet with church and government leaders, including President Kim Il-Sung.

Syngman Rhee attributes his change of heart to two principles he learned from Dr. Martin Luther King Jr. during the civil-rights movement. First, justice and reconciliation free both the oppressed and the oppressor. Second, the oppressed have the key to bring about reconciliation through forgiveness. Rhee's transformation from warrior to peacemaker did not happen immediately. It took place gradually as the biblical message of reconciliation and the import of Dr. King's words reformed his thinking. When it happened, he was serving God in a country halfway around the world from the place where his father had been martyred.

On the Mountain (9:2-8) We do not know where the transfiguration took place. Mark does not name the mountain on which it occurred, although the last place he named, the villages near Caesarea Philippi, is located in Gentile territory. Nor have Jesus' followers had much time to come to terms with his prophecy about himself and its implications for them. Jesus was transfigured a mere six days after Peter first uttered the word *Messiah* in a burst of patriotic fervor. Peter's conception of the Messiah corresponded to the popular imagination. He wanted Jesus to get rid of the Roman oppressors. A messiah who thought it was his duty to die, however, would be little use against the armies of Rome.

The transfiguration is a unique event in the gospel traditions. It is not an expression of the reign of God breaking into history or part of a public argument about Jesus' identity and mission, nor is it a sign pointing to something else. Contrary to Bultmann (1972:259-61), the transfiguration is demonstrably different from appearances of the risen Jesus. It does not resolve doubt, nor does it tie up loose threads in Jesus' ministry. It appears unexpectedly, and if it were not here no one would realize it was missing. Its central feature is a statement about Jesus spoken by a voice from a cloud, something not found in any resurrection appearance. Furthermore, unlike the first appearance of the risen Lord to Paul, the transfiguration does not feature a blinding flash of light. Finally, none of the traditions about Jesus after the resurrection are connected with Elijah and Moses.

The closest event to the transfiguration is Jesus' baptism (1:9-11), where the words *from on high* resemble the words that come from the cloud (9:7). Yet the differences between these two events clearly distinguish them. Jesus was not transfigured at his baptism, and in this Gospel there is no indication that anyone other than Jesus perceived what had happened then. The voice at the baptism spoke to Jesus, while the voice from the cloud covering this mountain was addressed to Peter, James and John. The baptism of Jesus points ahead to the fulfillment of John the Baptist's prophecy about the coming of the Holy Spirit. Moses and Elijah do not appear there, and their presence here points in another direction.

Indeed, the presence of Moses and Elijah is one of the most puzzling aspects of this account, because they do not appear together as forerunners of the Messiah anywhere else in biblical or apocalyptic literature (Edwards 2002:264). There is, however, a connection between them at the very beginning of this Gospel. The words "I will send my messenger ahead of you, who shall prepare your way" are found at two decisive points in Israel's history. In Exodus 23:20 God spoke these words to Moses as a guarantee that the people whom God had delivered from slavery in Egypt would defeat their enemies and take possession of the Promised Land. Then in Malachi 3:1 the same words appear again to warn the people of Judah to expect a messenger of the covenant. According to Malachi 4:5-6 Elijah would return to restore the fathers to their children, and if his mission failed, God would strike the land with a curse. Moses and Elijah frame the covenant history of the people of Israel, and the connection between them is revisited in the opening verses of Mark.

This connection between the transfiguration and the covenant is strengthened by two other features in this text. One is Mark's location of the event after six days. This phrase recalls the sequence of events in Exodus 24:16 when the glory of the Lord descended on the mountain after six days. The second allusion is the word *transfigured*. Apart from the Synoptic traditions it does not occur in the Bible. In Greek literature it can be used to describe the transformation of something or someone into something else. Those stories, however, do not correspond to what is described here, and we need to probe more closely into what the word means.

The clue is found in the following event, where the crowd that ran to greet Jesus was amazed at him (Mk 9:15). Apparently, like Moses in Exodus 34:29 Jesus continued to glow after the encounter with God had ended. As Moses' face glowed because he had been in the presence of God, so we are to understand that God's glory transfigured Jesus. There is an important difference, though, between these two events. Moses glowed because he was taken up into the glory that rested on the mountain. In this encounter, on the other hand, the glory of God did not descend upon the mountain. There is no indication that Moses and Elijah were part of this radiance, nor is there anything to suggest that the appearance of Peter, James and John was changed. Furthermore, the cloud symbolizing the presence of God appeared only after Jesus had been transfigured. Everything rested on Jesus. The glory of God had became visible in him.

Peter's ill-advised suggestion to erect three shelters also points to the covenantal implications of this scene, for the word shelters describes the kind of temporary structures used in the Feast of Tabernacles, the annual celebration of the forty years' sojourn in the wilderness. Even so, his proposal was misguided insofar as it represents the same line of thought that led him to rebuke Jesus (Mk 8:32). That is to say, if the appearance of Moses and Elijah had encouraged Peter to believe that Jesus would be the kind of Messiah the patriots of Judea and Galilee expected, he was about to be disappointed once again. It was anxiety that moved Peter to speak. He did not know what to say because he was afraid.

No sooner had Peter stumbled his way to an awestruck and inept stopping point than a cloud overshadowed them and a voice said, *This is my Son, whom I love. Listen to him!* Then just as soon as the voice had finished speaking, Moses and Elijah disappeared, leaving the three men alone with Jesus. The entire episode is a stunning assertion of the authority of Jesus. This is a frequent theme in the opening of the Gospel that moves in a new direction here. In the preceding material Jesus' authority is seen in what he does. In this context, though, the voice from the cloud draws attention to Jesus' words. They are the focus of the divine affirmation.

It is well worth asking whether this is a general confirmation of everything Jesus has said or whether it has a particular application. While the words *listen to him* carry no explicit limitation, there are features of this story that direct our attention back to the argument between Jesus and Peter in 8:27—9:1. Peter's declarations run like a thread through these texts, and here for the second time the Evangelist points out that Peter's attempt to influence the flow of things was badly flawed. The voice from heaven endorsed Jesus' statement that it was the will of God for him to be rejected by the leaders of Judea, to be killed and to rise on the third day. At this point Mark's not specifying the name of this mountain takes on a new significance. If its name were known, some later follower of Jesus would have built a shrine on it, but Mark is not interested in high places. There is a great leveling going on as the Gospel unfolds (Waetjen 1989:96, 148), and the words of God, Jesus and the gospel, rather than the name of a high place, are the only suitable way to remember this event.

It would be, however, a mistake to read 9:2-8 as a mere reinforcement of what Jesus had just said, for the presence of Moses and Elijah casts a new light on what he taught. The voice that affirmed Jesus' authority to Peter also put his words above those of Moses and Elijah. As we have already seen, the Evangelist gives considerable attention to the conflict between Jesus and the law, yet there is more to the transfiguration than an argument about who was the most authoritative interpreter of the Mosaic law, for Jesus' words about salvation (8:35) take us beyond the law to a new formulation of the relationship between God and humankind: *For whoever wants to save his life will lose it, but whoever loses his life for me and for the gospel will save it.* This is the stuff of covenant, and the gospel of the kingdom of God and the person of Jesus are the fundamental criteria for life and death in the new covenant. In this covenant there is no talk of land, hegemony or privilege. The blessings of this covenant are available to anyone who follows Jesus, and they are the same for all. The transfiguration subordinates the Mosaic covenant to the judgments and promises of the Son of God.

Elijah Has Returned (9:9-13) As they walked back down the mountain, Jesus ordered Peter, James and John to say nothing about what they had witnessed. So when they reached level ground again and the crowd was amazed at Jesus' radiance, Jesus himself had become a parable. Something profound had happened. Those who had been to the top of the mountain knew something no one else did. As in the raising of Jairus's daughter, a small group of insiders could not speak about what they had witnessed, and this astounding event cried out for an explanation. The one thing they could talk about was the rising from the dead, a subject that would direct them back to the words that Jesus had spoken publicly in 8:34—9:1.

The discussion about the resurrection on the journey down the mountain led Peter, James and John to wonder about Elijah. The prophecy of Malachi had not been forgotten, and the three apparently wondered how Elijah was to return and whether he would be part of the resurrection Jesus had spoken about. Trying to sort things out, they asked him why the scribes taught that Elijah must come first, where

---

9:12 The NIV translation *Why is it written* is misleading. There is no Old Testament text which says that the Son of Man must suffer and be rejected. The suffering servant of Isaiah 41—53 is treated this way, but there is no corresponding prophecy about the Son of Man. The Greek word *pōs* usually brought into English as "how."

first means either before the arrival of the rule of God or before the culmination of all things.

Here Jesus affirmed both the scribal tradition and the ministry of Elijah as it was described in the prophecy. The teachers of the law were not wrong, and what was written in Malachi stood. Then he posed a question of his own: *Why then is it written that the Son of Man must suffer much and be rejected?* Jesus' question went to the root of the disciples' dilemma. How could Jesus speak about his own death if the kingdom of God were near (1:15) and Elijah was still to come? How, in other words, was it possible to reconcile Malachi's prophecy with Jesus' prediction? In light of all that had happened in the preceding week it was a question they dared not ask directly. Yet they had at least asked a question. They were trying to respond in some way to the word they heard on the mountaintop, and Jesus gave them something more.

Elijah had come, Jesus affirmed, and they have done to him everything they wished. Precisely who they were or what they had done Jesus did not specify. Three things, though, are implicit in Jesus' statement. First, they were people of power into whose hands God had committed the prophet. Second, Elijah's mission of restoration seems to have failed. Where we might hope to learn that they did whatever Elijah had told them to do, we read instead that the people in power did whatever they wanted to him. The final implication is that the people of power would treat the Son of Man the same way they treated Elijah.

Mark does not tell us directly when and how Elijah appeared. Obviously, Jesus was not referring to the appearance of Elijah with Moses, because Elijah was not mistreated then. Mark treats the return of Elijah indirectly. It is another parable. The meaning of Jesus' statement is not obvious at first glance, but Mark has supplied several clues. John the Baptist dressed like Elijah; his call to repentance was an attempt to restore all things; and all Jerusalem and Judea went out to him (1:4-6). Malachi 4:5-6 speaks of Elijah turning the hearts of the fathers, and the Hebrew word for *repent* means "turn." Finally, John was beheaded by

---

Why suggests that Peter, James and John were looking for clarification about a text that does not exist. *How*, on the other hand, reflects their confusion and opposition to the idea that Jesus must die.

the people in power, who did to him everything they wished. John the Baptist was not Elijah by virtue of reincarnation. He was Elijah because he fulfilled Elijah's role.

This pericope was the pivotal text for Wrede's theory of the messianic secret. For Wrede, the order for the three disciples not to disclose what had happened on the mountain until after the resurrection was the Evangelist's solution for the embarrassing fact that Jesus had not claimed to be the messiah. Here, the argument runs, Mark invented a solution for this difficulty: Jesus had instructed his closest followers to keep his true identity under wraps until after his resurrection. The best rejoinder to this assessment of Mark's intent is the observation that his account of the resurrection does not dispel all the questions about Jesus. In fact, it heightens them. Mark's presentation of the resurrection ends on a note of fear and includes a self-imposed form of secrecy: the women said "nothing to anyone, because they were afraid." That ending is impossible to reconcile with the apology Wrede proposed.

On the other hand, it is surely significant that the secrecy motifs regularly appear in conjunction with parables and stories about conflicting values. In this case the instruction not to speak about the Transfiguration comes in the midst of an argument about Jesus' messianic role, and it is accompanied by a parable about Elijah. In all probability the traditions which Mark received already contained the theme of secrecy in some form. His use of the secrecy motif adds an element of time to the mystery of Jesus' identity and mission. Neither Jesus nor the reign of God are to be understood simply or quickly. Following Jesus has never been an easy or convenient occupation. To come to terms with the gospel requires an enormous shift in thought, affection and commitment.

The various secrecy themes function in different ways. Some are ironic (7:24, 36), some cast the miracles as parables (1:43 and 5:43) and some underscore fundamental conflicts in the Gospel (8:26, 30). At several points the secrecy motifs put the audience in the position of Jesus' earliest followers, whose struggle to believe is woven into the structure of the story. Mark does not present the gospel as though he were writing a letter, essay or biography. The good news about Jesus Christ does not end when Mark's account stops. At several places the text points beyond the empty tomb. Despite the affirmation of John the Baptist, Jesus does not baptize anyone with the Holy Spirit in this Gospel. There are also points in Mark's presentation of the parables when Mark nudges his readers to ask Jesus what they mean. Ultimately, even the silence of the women in 16:8 points to a later encounter with Jesus. Built into the fabric of Mark's Gospel is the conviction that Jesus still speaks, appears and acts for his followers. The secrecy motifs are a narrative strategy which recreates for the audience the dynamics of discipleship.

Jesus' disciples and the teachers of the law had missed the significance of John's ministry. They remembered the prophecy, but they could not make sense of what they saw. Their fixation with a conquering messiah kept them from understanding the meaning of John's ministry and the significance of his death. This conversation is a word of caution for Jesus' later followers. Our dreams and aspirations must be filtered through the pivotal words of Jesus in Mark 8:34-38. It is dangerous to proclaim that Jesus is the Messiah without taking to heart his words about the cross. The danger is that we may miss not only what God is doing in our own time, but also what God offers us.

A Near-Resurrection Experience (9:14-29) At the bottom of the mountain Jesus found a disturbing scene. A large crowd had gathered to watch an argument between the teachers of the law and the other disciples. While Peter, James and John had witnessed the transfiguration of Jesus, the disciples who had been left behind had tried and failed to perform an exorcism. Jesus had given the Twelve authority to cast out demons (3:15), and they had used that power successfully on the one mission that Jesus had committed to them (6:13). Here, though, they failed completely, and their failure led to a prolonged argument with the teachers of the law. The Evangelist does not disclose what they were arguing about, but the scene described in 9:14 stands in sharp contrast to the joyful conclusion of their mission in 6:30-31.

The crowd that had gathered around the disciples at the bottom of the mountain left them as soon as Jesus came into view. The crowd that ran up to him was overwhelmed with wonder. Nowhere else in the Gospel is Jesus received with such enthusiasm. His miracles had sometimes prompted amazement, but this reception was different. Jesus had done nothing to evoke their wonder. He had simply come into view. It was his appearance that provoked their astonishment. In light of what had just transpired, the only explanation is that Jesus was still aglow with the effect of being transfigured. Like Moses who came down from the Mount Sinai after meeting God, Jesus' face still shone. Peter, James and John, however, were under a ban of silence, and Jesus offered no word of explanation. Instead he asked the disciples who had remained at the foot of the mountain what the argument had been about. None of them answered. Perhaps the ones who had been ashamed of Jesus' words in 8:34-38 were too ashamed to answer him here. Someone in the crowd, however, did speak: the father of the boy the disciples could not help. He described a child who had symptoms that were similar to epileptic seizures. Mark, however, does not treat this as a medical problem. He presents it as another instance of demonic possession.

Jesus responded to the father's desperate story with a rhetorical question: *O unbelieving generation, how long shall I stay with you? How long shall I put up with you?* These are harsh words, and they prompt the additional question of whom he had in mind. Did he mean to include the scribes, the crowd, the father or his own disciples? Was this a blanket indictment, or did Jesus have select individuals and groups in mind? If we take the narrative seriously on its own terms, the answer must be that the unbelieving generation was composed of everyone present except Jesus. Jesus believed. If everything is possible for him who believes, as he said in 9:23, then he was the only one who believed. Jesus was the one who did what everyone else found either impossible or incredible—he healed the child.

Clearly, though, the disciples had believed something, otherwise they would not have attempted the exorcism themselves. Even so, their failure stands in sharp contrast to Jesus who still glowed, something that was impossible in its own right. Whatever they believed, though, was not enough to distinguish them from the scribes with whom they had been arguing. In fact, from 6:52 onward Mark uses the same kind of language to describe the disciples that he uses to describe Jesus' opponents. They all had hardened hearts. This description is repeated in 8:17. Both Peter's rebuke of Jesus (8:32) and his ill-advised suggestion (9:5) indicate that the problem had not been resolved.

The exorcism began as the boy was brought to Jesus. Like accounts of other exorcisms, there followed an act of resistance when the spirit recognized Jesus and threw the child into another convulsion. Then when Jesus commanded the spirit to leave the child and never return, a final, violent convulsion shook the child, leaving him so still that some in the crowd thought he was dead (9:26). Jesus took him by the hand, much as he had done for Jairus's lifeless daughter (5:41), and raised him. This incident looks like another resurrection.

If faith is the belief that all things are possible, then Jesus' own disciples did not believe one fundamental thing: that it was necessary for the Son of Man to suffer and die and after three days rise again. If it was difficult to believe that Jesus could revive this seemingly lifeless child, it was even more difficult to believe in the resurrection of the dead. In a radical way Jesus placed his life in God's hands, and he believed that all things are possible with God (10:27). The disciples had not made this move of faith, and so for them the impossible was still impossible.

In the middle of this account is one man's desperate plea: *I do believe; help me overcome my unbelief!* There are many ways to interpret what the man meant, but one thing is clear. Jesus did not expect him to overcome his doubt before the child was healed. The child was raised not because his father's faith was perfect, but because Jesus believed all things were possible. Jesus helped the father's unbelief by raising the boy.

The father's cry might have been echoed by the disciples, but it was not. Their problem was not the intensity of their conviction, the strength of their passion or the firmness of their resolution. Their problem was the word of Jesus, which they had refused to accept. As later events show, they were willing to give their lives to defend Jesus in Gethsemane, until it became clear that Jesus was not going to defend his own life. The problem was not how they believed. It was what they failed to believe.

It is a mistake to read this passage as though it were a kind of divine imperative to have absolute faith. Jesus did not demand it of this boy or his father, just as he had not placed that demand on Jairus. Jesus' declaration, *Everything is possible for him who believes,* is an exhortation to come to terms with the heart of the gospel. It is not a spur for our feelings; it is a pointed encouragement to come to terms with the greatest mystery of all—that it was God's will for the Son of Man to die

MARK 9:14-29 ☐

and be raised on the third day. That truth and its implications for those
who wish to follow Jesus is the foundation of faith.
Once again the disciples missed the point. Instead of asking about
his death and resurrection, they were concerned with their impotence.
They posed the question privately, in accordance with the pattern established in 4:34, treating as a parable what Jesus had said and done.
Jesus replied: *This kind can come out only by prayer.* But care should
be taken not to interpret this statement as though he were divulging a
secret method for exorcism. Curiously, Jesus did not pause to raise his
eyes toward heaven and pray in this passage. Prayer was not the
means by which he confronted the destructive power at work in this
family. Jesus did not treat prayer as a technique or utility.
There are two ways to interpret his statement. One is to take the father's plea as a prayer. In that case, we would understand that the man
had done all that was required of him by asking—something Jesus' disciples did not do. The other possibility is that Jesus was referring to his
own practice of praying. There is no indication in Mark that the disciples prayed, although there are references to Jesus at prayer. Apart
from this father's plea, Jesus is the only one who prays in this Gospel,
and when he prayed his followers sometimes slept.
Of the several references to Jesus' praying, on only one occasion
does Mark take us inside, and that prayer begins with the affirmation
Abba, Father, everything is possible for you (14:36). It is as though
Mark were inviting his audience to follow the various references
about prayer that do not describe what Jesus prayed about to this
particular one. The prayers of 14:35-42 express a relationship in
which Jesus placed his life in God's hands and trusted God to give it
back. For Mark prayer is not primarily a way of getting what we want
from God. It is instead the space where we come to terms with God's
will. In Gethsemane Jesus reaffirmed the model of discipleship that
he had spelled out in 8:35: "For whoever wants to save his life will
lose it, but whoever loses his life for me and the gospel will save it."
We might say then that the account of this exorcism is also a parable
about the resurrection.

9:29 Some manuscripts add the phrase *and fasting,* but they represent later tradi-

The Second Prediction of Jesus' Passion (9:30-50) In *Creation and Fall* Dietrich Bonhoeffer offers a telling insight into human nature. We are locked, he observed, in a struggle for dominance from which we cannot extricate ourselves (1959:60-63). The struggle does not resolve itself quickly or easily. It often continues until relationships settle into tacitly acknowledged patterns of control and submission. The need to assert or protect ourselves each time we meet someone new says something very important about us. It reveals a fundamental insecurity at the very core of our being. Bonhoeffer traces the origin of this conflict to a fear of limits that became part of the natural order of life at the fall of humankind. Whenever we find ourselves gripped by the fear of death or betrayal we experience again this primal reality.

Arguments on the Path of Discipleship (9:30-37) The second prediction of Jesus' passion is set against the background of broken and distorted human relationships. The emphasis is not upon predictions of the future, but upon teaching for the present. Jesus taught his disciples in a closed setting, and the teaching about his impending death could not have been more relevant. This was not the first time the disciples had missed the point. They were too bound up in their own insecurities to understand what he was talking about.

Many things in this brief statement were certainly difficult to comprehend: *The Son of Man is going to be betrayed into the hands of men. They will kill him, and after three days he will rise.* The wordplay between the *Son of Man* and the *hands of men* gives this saying the character of a riddle (Pesch 1977:2.98-100). Then, too, the disciples might have expected to see a resurrection of the righteous at the end of history, although there was nothing in Jewish tradition before Jesus' teaching to indicate that there would be an earlier resurrection. Their lack of understanding is not surprising. The statement that they were afraid to ask him, on the other hand, is. It suggests that they were hesitant to engage him in conversation for other reasons. Perhaps the rebuke Peter received in 8:33 was in the back of their minds. Or perhaps Mark intends to portray them as being afraid to ask questions that would show their lack of understanding. As the story develops,

tions. The authenticity of that expansion is made unlikely by 2:19-20.

though, the impression grows that they might have glimpsed or guessed where Jesus' line of thought was leading and been afraid of the implications it held for them.

In any event as the disciples were arguing about which of them was the greatest, Jesus was trying to instill in them a whole new set of attitudes about life and death. This teaching about his death moves in a different direction than the first passion prediction. There the emphasis was on the necessity of the Son of Man's suffering and his rejection by those entrusted with the law. In this material the idea of necessity appears in connection with interpersonal relationships: *If anyone wants to be first, he must be the very last, and the servant of all.* Moreover, in this prediction the Son of Man is delivered not to the keepers of the law, but to people in general.

The disciples' argument seems to have developed out of their own recent history. Peter had first identified Jesus as the Messiah and then suffered a stinging rebuke because his thoughts about the Messiah were entirely ill conceived. Then Peter, James and John were selected to accompany Jesus up the mountainside, where they experienced an awesome event that they were forbidden to discuss with the others. At the same time the nine disciples who remained at the foot of the mountain proved to be incapable of dealing with a particularly difficult problem. Seen against this background, their argument is not surprising. It is precisely the kind of situation in which people's insecurities lead them into destructive conflict.

The teaching about the Son of Man's death addresses the things that the disciples were wrestling with: *The Son of Man is going to be delivered into the hands of men.* That is to say, the Son of Man has not come to encounter people to work out an agenda of superiority. The Son of Man has come to submit to the power of other people. That is the simple meaning of the Semitic expression "delivered into the hands of men." His life was placed in the power of those to whom he came.

9:31 The NIV's use of *betrayed* is regrettable. The underlying Greek verb can certainly be translated "betrayed," but it can also mean "handed over" or "delivered." The difference is not insignificant. To say that Jesus was *betrayed* points to a human actor behind the scene, that is, Judas. To say that Jesus was "delivered into the hands of men," however, identifies God as the agent. Thus, to say that Jesus was *betrayed*

This is a reversal of the typical pattern of human interaction. The Son of Man has not come to play subtle games of dominance and submission. He has come to undermine them. *They will kill him, and after three days he will rise.* If fear of death and betrayal lie at the root of our insecurities, Jesus did not let them govern his conduct. It was the deeply felt knowledge of God's raising him from the dead which set Jesus apart from the disciples here. For them the resurrection from the dead was too removed and too confusing to make any difference in their present conduct. For Jesus, though, the resurrection was a certainty that freed him from manipulative behavior. When Jesus said, *If anyone wants to be first, he must be the very last, and the servant of all,* he called the disciples to live beyond their means, to come to terms with life and death as he had. They were not prepared for this kind of living. It was this new world of experience, the life of self-denial and resurrection, that Jesus was trying to open up for them in the teaching about his own impending death.

Jesus brought the problem out into the open by asking about the argument they had had among themselves. When the disciples were too embarrassed to answer, he introduced a new teaching that has much in common with prophetic assertions that the Lord is against all that is high and exalted in passages like Isaiah 2:12 and 40:4. It is a theme deeply rooted in Israelite traditions, and it finds perhaps its most poignant expression in Hannah's Song in 1 Samuel 2:1-10. In the normal order of things those who are least, the poor and oppressed, serve those who are rich and powerful. Like the prophets, however, Jesus found the normal order of things woefully inadequate. To follow Jesus ultimately means that we must give up the deeply rooted desire to make other people serve us. The kingdom of God is not a power that has entered history to create a new order of dominance. On the contrary, the gospel of Jesus Christ has come to revolutionize the way we relate to each other, and the basis of this

---

into the hands of men is redundant, because that translation places him in the hands of the human being who betrayed him. The phrase *into the hands of men* is universal. He was not in the hands of men before. The RSV rendering, "delivered into the hands of men," is preferable.

revolution is his death and resurrection.

At the very heart of Jesus' teaching is a fundamentally new way of looking at people. When Jesus set the child in the middle of the disciples and said, *Whoever welcomes one of these little children in my name welcomes me; and whoever welcomes me does not welcome me but the one who sent me,* he put the matter simply and succinctly. It is an honor, for example, to receive great people, and it is hard to imagine people being displeased if their neighbors could see God walking across the doorstep into their living room. It enhances our own sense of importance to receive someone of prominence, and it increases the esteem in which our friends hold us. What greater honor could there be than to receive God? Jesus affirmed, to what was presumably a shocked audience, that we receive God whenever we receive a little child in his name.

In this context the child represents the least. If there had been a scale that rated people in Galilee according to their importance, the child would have been near the bottom. The really important people were the adult men. Children might have been valued members of their own families, but the people of prominence were the ones who had accumulated wealth and power.

How then can it possibly be true that in welcoming a child in Jesus' name we are receiving God? It is true in the same sense in which we welcome guests into our homes. Suppose a friend sends some people whom we do not know to visit us. They might be people this friend had met while traveling abroad, hiking in the mountains or studying at a university. Normally if strangers show up at our doorstep, we do not invite them in. Yet if a friend sends someone to us, there is an implied obligation. We welcome these strangers because they are important to our friend, and then in a very real sense we are welcoming our friend. So it is in this case. If we welcome people who are important to Jesus, we are actually welcoming him. He is the one who sent them, and we receive them because they are important to him. Thus it also follows that in welcoming Jesus we welcome the one who sent him, God.

What emerges is a new principle for valuing people. For Jesus, a person's value is not established by what he or she has achieved or accumulated or invented. It is established by the value God sets on the person. Because God created humankind to be God's representatives on earth, all people have the same value. And because the Son of Man was delivered into the hands of humans, all discussions about who is the greatest or most important are irrelevant. In the final analysis they are expressions of our depravity.

This is a difficult teaching to follow. The gift of life and the death of Jesus are given to us freely and in equal measure. Most Christians would say that those gifts are the most important ones they have received. Yet when it comes to the things we value, we often esteem the things we have earned and the things other people have earned above the free gifts of God. To make the things we have earned or achieved the foundation of our self-esteem is to invite back into our hearts the things from which God has saved us. Faithfulness requires that we make the death and resurrection of the Son of Man the foundation upon which we build relationships.

An Understandable Objection (9:38-41) Modern advertising often appeals to the desire for prestige. Over the last few years we have seen marketing campaigns built around themes like members only, limited edition and the mark of distinction. Their marketing power is due in large part to an overt, but clever, psychological ploy. The idea of membership is an important aspect of our self-understanding, and it is a universal part of human experience. Being part of the right circle of friends reassures us that we are ourselves the right sort of people. Having the right connections is essential for getting things done. And joining the right club is an indication that we have achieved success.

In this passage, however, Jesus exposed the dark underside of belonging to an exclusive group of people. Following his affirmation about the value of people, John stated, *Teacher, we saw a man driving out demons in your name and we told him to stop, because he was not one of us.* John offered this comment as a declaration. He did not request Jesus' approval. He seems to have assumed that this was the right course of action.

The pivotal term in this conversation is *in my name* (9:37, 41). The disciples understood this phrase in what we might call the royal sense. *In my name* is a common Semitic expression that very often means "with my authority" or "in my place." So a king, for instance, who commands one of his subjects to do something in his name gives the subject both a set of instructions and the authority to carry them out. This meaning is necessarily restrictive. The only people who can do something in the king's name would be those to whom he has specifically delegated authority. Jesus had given the Twelve the authority to cast out demons, and no one else received that commission in this Gospel. John understood what Jesus had given him in a restrictive sense, and his comment is actually an objection. It is as though he were saying, "Not arguing among ourselves is one thing, but there have to be some limits. After all, you have set us apart from everyone else."

John's objection might have been compelling if Jesus had held that view of authority, but he did not. In 9:37 Jesus used this expression in an entirely different sense. To receive a child in my name does not mean that the disciples have been given a special kind of authority for welcoming people. Likewise, if the disciples are received in my name, it is not because they possess a special power—it is because they bore Jesus' name. This is an associative concept. *In my name* means simply "because this person is important to me." Jesus used it to confer value and worth to people, not to make them submissive to someone else's authority. In short, the disciples were to do things in Jesus' name not because they had a unique and restricted authority, but because the people who benefited from what they did were important to Jesus and to God.

Pursuing the matter further, Jesus overturned the conventional wisdom about belonging to a group. That is the wisdom that asserts, "If you're not for us, you have no place among us." In this text Jesus turned that idea upside down. While the disciples wished to exclude people who were not part of their group, Jesus declared, *Whoever is not against us is for us. . . . Anyone who gives you a cup of cold water in my name because you belong to Christ will certainly not lose his reward.* This is the broadest, most inclusive language possible, and it makes membership in the group of his followers open to anyone.

Following Jesus then is not a matter of power. It is not something to do to gain influence, prestige or advantage. If it were, then Jesus could hardly speak of it as serving the least. Yet as this incident shows, there is a real danger that his followers could misuse Jesus' name in just this way. There is a profound tension between the dynamic forces of our own insecurities and fears and the power of the gospel. To follow

Jesus means to wrestle honestly with this tension, to trust the promise of the resurrection day by day to transform our deepest values and to resist the temptation to use the gospel to enhance our self-esteem.

Hellfire and Damnation (9:42-50) It is a very dangerous point in the life of an individual or a group when the capacity for self-criticism is lost. In the preceding sections of this Gospel the disciples have shown that they are perilously close to that point. Their arguments about who is the greatest and pronouncements against people who do not belong to their group were exercises in criticism directed at other people. So at this point Jesus instructed the disciples to take a hard look at themselves.

Whom did Jesus have in mind when he gave the warning: *If anyone causes one of these little ones who believe in me to sin?* It was the ones who were trying to assert their own importance at the expense of other people, his own disciples. Included among *the little ones who believe in me are* the least whom the disciples were supposed to serve (9:35), the little children whom Jesus loves (9:37) and the exorcist who was not one of the Twelve (9:38).

The word *sin* (9:42) may be misleading. In this case the Greek word might be better translated "stumble" or "scandalize" or even "be offended." In the context of 9:30-50 the idea is not that the disciples might cause someone to lie or cheat or steal. Jesus was concerned that people would take offense at him because of what his followers did to them. Jesus valued the people whom the disciples considered to be beneath them. It is not hard to imagine someone taking offense in Jesus because of what his disciples had done in their pursuit of power and prestige. He came to serve people whom the disciples wanted to dominate.

This passage is a warning to all of us who minister in the name of Jesus against using the people entrusted to us to resolve our own psychological or material needs. It is entirely inappropriate to engage in Christian ministry in order to feel important, special or powerful. That sort of thing leads to the power struggles, bickering, and insensitivity that the Twelve had just demonstrated. It creates disillusionment in people who believe in Jesus and causes them to fall away. We cannot serve other people if we are using them to meet our needs. With just this kind of situation in mind Jesus warned: *It would be better for him to be thrown into the sea with a large millstone tied around his neck.*

These are strong words, but the worst was still to come: *If your hand causes you to sin, cut it off. . . . And if your foot causes you to sin, cut it off. . . . And if your eye causes you to sin, pluck it out.* The hand represents the way we use power, the foot symbolizes the things we spend our lives pursuing, and the eye stands for the things we value. If these things cause us to sin, we are to get rid of them. For the Twelve, in particular, the words *causes you to sin* mean doing something to offend one of the little ones who believe in Jesus. These declarations are not so much a warning against personal vices as they are a warning against abusing positions of trust and leadership.

If we inquire more carefully into what Jesus wanted the disciples to cut off and pluck out, we have to be impressed by his perception of human nature, for with these words Jesus exhorted them to come to grips with those elements of sin that are part of the very structure of our personalities. Where does the desire to dominate come from? Where does the need to establish one's worth at the expense of other people originate? And what feeds the need to form exclusive associations? It is that nexus of anxieties and fears that makes us insecure about our own worth, our identity and our importance.

The consequences of failing to come to terms with ourselves are frightening. To turn our backs on this demanding exercise in self-examination is to be thrown into hell, *where their worm does not die, and the fire is not quenched.* This is the strongest language Jesus has used. Those words were not directed at people who lacked faith in Jesus. They were directed at people who believed in Jesus but were unwilling to come to terms with their own potential for harming other people.

Mark now takes us back to the argument the disciples had about which of them was the greatest. Salt is a metaphor for judgment, and the saltiness in 9:49-50 symbolizes justice. The concluding words of this conversation warn the disciples to take a hard look at themselves. They are an exhortation to see what Jesus has been trying to show them about themselves. Their critical faculties needed to be turned inward. Perhaps if they had seen themselves as they really were before God, they would have stopped arguing about who was the greatest and there would have been peace.

There is nothing more telling about us than the way we use power. Jesus' denunciation of the quest for prestige and power is universal. Those at the top of the social system and those at its bottom are capable of abusing power and liable to damnation for it. In this encounter Jesus exposed the depth of our depravity. Sin is not only a part of our social and interpersonal engagement; it has become part of the structure of our identity.

Creation, Marriage and Divorce (10:1-12) A Christian wedding has three vows. The bride and groom exchange promises in two vows, and the couple makes a third set of promises to God and the worshiping community. In each vow God plays a different role. God receives, witnesses or empowers. In both Christianity and Judaism, marriage is part of the creation account, and each new wedding is in a sense another chapter in the unfolding story of creation. In both traditions marriage is not just a matter of human love and commitment—it is also a matter of faith. When divorce comes to people who exchanged promises in a church or synagogue, it often produces both the numbing dissolution of a family and a crisis of faith.

The Pharisees' question about divorce was a trap. The Greek verb translated *test* (10:2) means either "tempt" or "test," but in 8:11 and 12:15 when the Pharisees came to test Jesus, it is clear that they hoped to discredit him. So it is here too. This was another attempt to catch him in his own words. We need to pay particular attention to the language of this question. It is not framed as we might pose it. The question is not whether divorce is permissible; it is framed in terms of first-century Judaism, in which a husband could divorce his wife, but a wife could not divorce her husband. Women did not have the right to initiate a divorce. In Jewish law divorce was a male privilege. Deuteronomy 24:1-4 sets out the terms for divorce, and it contains no provision that would help a woman who found her husband insufferable. A husband who wanted to divorce his wife, on the other hand, was required only to give her a written certificate of divorce (France 2002:387)

Since the law of Moses treats divorce in such unambiguous terms, the Pharisees' trap must lie in something outside Deuteronomy 24:1-4. One possibility is suggested by the location. The territory described in

Mark 10:1 is the region where John the Baptist's ministry took place. Presumably, somewhere in this area John denounced Herod Antipas for marrying his brother's wife, and that ultimately cost John his life. On this reading the Pharisees sought to put Jesus into a position where he must either denounce Herod and possibly lose his life, as John the Baptist had (Lane 1974:354), or denounce John and possibly lose his own following.

If that were the nature of this trap, Jesus had just given the Pharisees virtually all they could have wished for. He did not name Herod specifically, but his condemnation of divorce was unqualified. One or two more questions specifying Herod and Herodias or a word passed along to the proper authorities would have snared Jesus neatly. Moreover, although his opponents attempted to trap him later with a question about marriage (12:18-27), the subject of divorce is never raised again in Mark. If the marriage of Herod and Herodias had set the stage for the trap, then Jesus had stepped neatly into it. Yet nothing comes of it. The subject is dropped. On the other hand, after giving his answer, Jesus walked away just as though he had prevailed. The ensuing silence of the text on the question of divorce indicates that Jesus had escaped the trap.

A more convincing backdrop is the conversation about the value of human beings (9:33-50). There is a subtle contradiction between the commandment about divorce in Deuteronomy 24:1-4 and Jesus' pronouncements about greatness, the relative worth of various categories of people and the basis upon which we receive them. In that extended teaching he overturned the social hierarchy which viewed Jewish men as the most important category of people. The clear implication of 9:36-37 is that God—not a system of cultural ordering—establishes our value. We might note as a corollary that divorce is one of those things that can cause little ones to stumble.

Putting these two passages together, we might frame the problem in these terms: how do a bridegroom and bride receive each other? Do they come together to fulfill their own dreams or to serve each other? As a man's dismissal of a woman because he finds her displeasing, divorce is incompatible with Jesus' view of human worth. The trap, then, was the Pharisees' attempt to set the teaching of Jesus against the law of Moses and so discredit Jesus. At its center is the assumption of male superiority.

Jesus' response has three parts. First, he declared that Deuteronomy 24:1-4 is not an expression of God's intention for humankind, but a concession to our hardness of heart. He treated it as a subordinate part of the law, as evidenced by the implicit tension between his question—*What did Moses command you?*—and the Pharisees' response—*Moses permitted a man to write a certificate of divorce.* Jesus pressed his opponents for a reading of God's commandment that went beyond or, perhaps better, behind Deuteronomy 24:1-4. He maintained that God's intention was not honored merely by observing the letter of the law.

Second, Jesus based his understanding of marriage on Genesis 1:26-27 rather than on the account of the creation of the first man and woman in Genesis 2. His response contains a clear reference to the first creation story when God created humankind male and female. That might seem like an insignificant difference, but Genesis 2 is the fundamental justification for Jewish and Christian teachings about the superiority of men. In early Jewish expositions of the law, as in a great deal of later Christian doctrine, the idea that man was created first and woman was created to be his helper has served as the basis for male supremacy. Furthermore, the words that have defined marriage for Christians and Jews for centuries are found at the end of the second account of creation: *For this reason a man will leave his father and mother and be united to his wife, and they will become one flesh* (Gen 2:24). This was the point at which the Pharisees sought to entrap him.

In Genesis 1:26-27 no priority in the order of creation is suggested and male and female together bear the image of God. Jesus did invoke the definition of marriage found in Genesis 2:24, but he turned the trap on his opponents by grounding marriage in the affirmation of Genesis 1:26-27, which contains no hint of male supremacy. When he said *For this reason,* the reason to which he appealed was God's creation of humankind as male and female. In an argument in which so much depends upon who or what comes first, the appeal to Genesis 1:26-27 would be difficult to refute.

Third, Jesus asserted that marriage is more than a human convention. It is an example of the Creator's continuing activity. When a woman and man are married, God makes something new. The two become one, and this new act of creation is the reason Jesus went on to assert, *There-*

fore what God has joined together, let man not separate. In English this declaration is ambiguous. The words *let man not* could be construed as a wish, a piece of advice or a command. In Greek, however, there is no ambiguity. The verb is in the imperative mood: it is a command, and this command reverses the trap the Pharisees had set for him. Based on Genesis 1:26-27 rather than on the dominant assumption of male superiority, Jesus issued a new commandment, which is perfectly consistent with his teaching about the value of people and with the law of Moses. For Jesus, then, the foundation of marriage was not a human choice that could be conveniently undone by one privileged party. It was an act of creation that should not be unmade.

One other feature in this passage deserves comment: the question the disciples asked in response to Jesus' pronouncements about divorce and marriage. A house often serves as a place for private conversations between Jesus and his followers in Mark, and this depiction of a public teaching followed by a private explanation recalls the summary statement about parables in 4:34. Of particular significance is 7:17, where in a private conversation inside a house his disciples pursue what had been a public argument between Jesus and the Pharisees by asking him a question about the parable. Strictly speaking, the argument about purity in 7:1-16 does not contain a parable. It is, though, something that was unclear to the disciples because it clashed profoundly with their own views. In this Gospel parables appear in connection with controversy and fundamental conflicts of values. They are invitations to come to terms with something in an entirely new way. Like the question in 7:17, the disciples' question in 10:10 cast Jesus' teaching about marriage and divorce in the guise of a parable. This question underscored the difficulty his own followers had in coming to terms with the unsettling reevaluation of human relationships that derive from Jesus' teaching about the Son of Man (9:30-32). The question

---

10:10-12 It is interesting to consider the private teaching about divorce and remarriage in the light of the controversy about the place of the law in the early church. In the similar setting of 7:19 the Evangelist draws out the implications of the controversy of the purity codes by stating, "In saying this, Jesus declared all foods 'clean.'" There is no corresponding declaration here, but the similarity in structure and the importance of adultery in the teaching of the early church invite comment. The im-

grew out of their own entrenched assumption of male priority. Jesus' response did something the conventional wisdom about marriage did not do: it treats men and women with strict equality. He applied the same strictures against divorce to both men and women. Men and women, he affirmed (10:11-12), who initiate a divorce and remarry commit adultery against their original spouses. This additional pronouncement eliminates the possibility that his teaching about the equality of male and female might be used to expand the grounds for divorce. It precludes a reinterpretation of Deuteronomy 24:1-4 to read, "If a man or woman is displeased."

It also moves into new territory by leveling the charge of adultery against those who initiate divorce and marry again. As a legal pronouncement, perhaps, the double declaration in Mark 10:11-12 is clear enough, but the logic behind it is not so obvious. What is the rationale for treating divorce and remarriage as adultery? That judgment can be true only if the moral obligations of marriage are not discharged by divorce. As a concession to hardness of heart one might argue that divorce provides some measure of legal protection. It may limit the damage people do to each other, but Jesus, it seems, did not regard divorce as the end of the requirement of faithfulness imposed by marriage. In his teaching the certificate of divorce has no bearing on the question of adultery. What would have constituted adultery before a divorce still constitutes it afterward. It is as though the new thing God creates has a life of its own even after a certificate of divorce is delivered.

This passage raises a host of pastoral questions that are not resolved here. What about abused or abandoned spouses—is it permissible for them to file for divorce? Is divorce justified in the case of adultery? What is a wife to do if she discovers that her husband has been abusing their children? Or does the spouse who has been divorced have the right to remarry? This text does not address any of these issues. Given

plication of Jesus' teaching on divorce and remarriage is that it is perfectly possible to observe the provisions of the law scrupulously and yet sin. If a legal divorce and subsequent marriage constitute adultery, then the claim that keeping the law constitutes righteousness is further undermined. Mark's treatment of this text supports the idea that this Gospel was influenced by Pauline theology (Martin 1972:214-19).

the complexity of human relationships, the depth of our brokenness and the reality of sin, the question of God's place in our promises is not easy to resolve.

To say the least, it should be clear that spousal abuse is a fundamental violation of God's intention in creation. It is an unqualified denial that God has made the two into one flesh. In an abusive relationship there is an absolute dichotomy. Instead of one there are two—someone who habitually abuses and another who is habitually abused—so that the marriage itself is a kind of unmaking. It is a great travesty of the gospel that abusive relationships of any sort are tolerated in the church. The faithful thing to do is for pastors, lay leaders and victims to work together to see that the abuse stops. To act otherwise is to empower shame and to allow it to undermine the gospel.

The myriad of other questions about divorce and remarriage are beyond the scope of this commentary. Suffice it to say that none of us enters the kingdom by keeping the law. We enter by receiving the kingdom as a child (10:15), and once in we spend the rest of our lives learning to navigate by the compass of God's grace. Rather than view this passage as an exhaustive exposition about marriage and divorce, it is better for us to understand it as a narrowly focused argument in which the fundamental question is the value of people. That is to say, do we structure our relationships on the value God places on us or on the value our social systems place on each other? Divorce fits neatly into a system of personal relationships in which we—in this case men—do the valuing. It is much harder to justify if we acknowledge that everyone stands before God equally, that God places the same value on each of us, and that we receive God when we receive other people to serve them.

There is good news and bad news in this text. It is good news for people who have been abused, abandoned or oppressed. Their mistreatment, shame or even self-imposed guilt is not an indication of their worth. God upholds them, and the value God sets on them denies the self-appointed privilege of the abuser. On the other hand, Jesus' teaching about the nature of human relationships is bad news for people who persist in the attempt to define themselves by climbing higher in the social hierarchy.

Jesus Blesses the Children (10:13-16) Calvin Standing Bear piped a wordless invocation, turning periodically to face the directions from which the four winds blow. His invocation marked the beginning of a worship service built around the theme "A House of Prayer for All the Peoples." Sitting behind me was a Hispanic family—father, mother, uncle and three preschoolers. Next to me sat an African American pastor and his Palestinian American wife, and directly in front of us were two Anglo pastors, who in unison shot sour glances at the family the first time one of the children made a sound. The children actually did quite well with crayons and whispers for the first seventy-five minutes of the service, but when Fahed Abu-Akell, an American pastor born on the West Bank of Palestine, began to preach on hospitality, the children's whispers became more insistent and more frequent. Then the silent glances from the row in front of us also became louder, more insistent and more frequent. The message was clear: the children had outstayed their welcome.

There is no change of setting between 10:12 and 10:13. Any indication that Jesus was about to leave the house where he had just concluded his teaching about divorce is lacking. Both events appear to take place in the same setting. His disciples' attempt to turn the children away is more understandable if the children arrive as an interruption. After all, the rabbi had used houses previously as places for instructing his followers privately on several occasions, and his last comments were unlikely to have answered all their questions.

There can be no doubt that his disciples were having enormous difficulty assimilating Jesus' reversal of human valuing. Their rebuke of the people who were bringing children to Jesus in 10:13 is ample evidence that the problem persisted, and it sparked Jesus' indignation. There are few references to Jesus' emotions in this Gospel. We have seen two previously: Jesus was moved by either compassion or anger, depending upon one's reading of the textual evidence, in 1:41; and in 3:5 he was angry at the hardness of heart he found in the synagogue. Here he was indignant at least and perhaps even outraged. It is impossible to overstate the importance of this encounter between Jesus, the disciples, the children and those who brought them. What is at stake is whether one enters the kingdom of God.

There is a subtle but profound change in the language about the kingdom of God here. Nowhere else in this Gospel has Jesus spoken about the kingdom of God belonging to anyone. He had certainly not said anything like this to the men who were with him. On the contrary, he had just warned them that they were in danger of the fire of hell (9:48). What is there about children that justifies this unparalleled assertion? Is it innocence, simplicity or uncomplicated faith? Perhaps in one sense it is something like that, but none of those attributes are attested by the immediate context or by the larger context of this Gospel. Rather than this sort of association, Mark has presented children in the material that follows Jesus' second passion prediction as those who stand at the bottom of the social hierarchy. They are the ones his disciples regarded as unimportant. They are the little ones (9:42) who were in danger of being trampled upon by those who are struggling to assert their own importance. If someone had asked Jesus whom the kingdom of God belonged to, he or she might have expected Jesus to name a person like the man who ran up to him in the next incident. The idea that the kingdom of God belongs to people who are like children is a thoroughly subversive idea.

Jesus' statement that we should receive the kingdom like a child should be understood similarly. It is an ellipsis. The idea is not that the kingdom of God should be received as something of little worth in the eyes of other people, but that it should be received in the way that a child would receive it. A child would receive the kingdom as something to which he or she was not entitled. It is not a matter of right or privilege. It is not even a matter of covenant, although Mark takes pains to portray God as one who keeps covenant even with people who are faithless. The kingdom comes as a gift. We receive it in the same way we receive our worth. They both come as unearned expressions of God's love and righteousness. It is impossible to enter the kingdom of God on any other terms.

We like our spiritual leaders to have all the trappings of success—books, speaking tours, visibility in the media—and many of us are still

---

10:17 The verb translated *fell on his knees* can also be translated "worship." If, in fact,

deeply uncomfortable with having children in worship. After all, we may think silently to ourselves, children are disruptive, and the preacher or teacher needs to have the freedom to devote his or her attention to the people who can best appreciate it. One has to wonder if there is in our worship life a subversion of the gospel that is just as profound as what took place in this house.

Entitlement and Wealth (10:17-31) Poverty has been described as the one thing money cannot buy. It may also be one thing money cannot fix. In 1965 President Lyndon Johnson declared war on poverty. There were some notable gains particularly in the fields of health care and employment, but the national statistics on poverty remained virtually unchanged. In 1965 eighteen percent of Americans lived below the poverty line. In 1987, when the social welfare programs of the 1960s and 1970s were dismantled, eighteen percent of Americans still lived in poverty. Intractable social problems that prick our conscience pose the formidable question of how people with means, talent and goodwill should invest their lives. Accumulating wealth and establishing a charitable trust fund may be the most respectable option for people who make it to the top of the heap in Western cultures, but it is far from the solution Jesus put forward.

The rich man who ran up to kneel at Jesus' feet had some insight into what Jesus had been trying to teach the disciples. His appeal to Jesus as *Good teacher* may have been a piece of flattery (Nineham 1968:270), perhaps in the expectation that he would receive a favorable response. There is, however, no corroborating evidence of hypocrisy in this story, and Jesus treated him as a sincere inquirer. The comment that Jesus loved him would be out of character if he had detected anything deceptive. His response to hypocrisy was anything but affirming. *Good teacher* is a simple term of respect. It does not have the potential for manipulation that will characterize James and John's request in 10:35.

The man who fell on his knees asked how he could inherit eternal life. It is possible that his question was presumptive, but inheriting is

the man engaged in an act of worship, there would be more grounds for suspecting his motives.

one of the ways children receive things. And since eternal life was generally taken to be one of the blessings of the kingdom of God, the man has cast himself in the role of a child who wants receive the kingdom as Jesus had just described (10:15). He asked the kind of question an inquisitive child might ask who wanted to enter the kingdom of God. Both the form of address he used and the question he asked are extensions of the themes Mark has developed since the prediction of Jesus' passion (9:30-32).

The reply he received invited him to enter a place he ultimately did not wish to go. Jesus first challenged what he meant by the word *good*. There might have been several answers to the question *Why do you call me good?* The rich man might have said that Jesus spoke for God or came from God. He might even have said that God had declared Jesus to be good. That is the kind of valuing God did in the first account of creation. We cannot know what he might have said, but we can begin to see the range of possibilities that Jesus' rejoinder opened up. Jesus prompted him to pursue the matter of valuing to its proper source—God. For this man to have continued to think of Jesus as good, he would have had to affirm both that God was the proper source of values and that Jesus represented God in some way.

After this provocative reply Jesus moved for a moment onto more familiar ground and asked about his conduct. The six commandments Jesus mentioned form the second tablet of the law, the section of the Ten Commandments that orders relationships between people in the covenant community. Curiously, Jesus did not ask him about the first four commandments, whose subject is the holiness of God. It is as though Jesus were content to let the question about God's goodness stand for that part of this theological examination.

Actually, this was much more than a theological examination. It was the kind of conversation one might find on judgment day, and it covered ground a devout Jewish man of the first century would have expected. The issue was whether he had kept the provisions of the covenant. According to his own assessment (10:20), which Jesus did not challenge, he came off quite well. That, however, was not all there was to say. Jesus said that he lacked one thing, and then he told the rich man to do three things: sell his possessions, give the proceeds to the poor and follow him. Of these three things the overriding idea is the call to become a disciple. The words *come, follow me* are the same words Jesus had used to invite Simon and Andrew (1:17), and they repeat the universal invitation to become Jesus' disciple (8:34). Jesus' instructions about the disposal of the man's property are a consequence of the call to follow him.

There is a finality about the terms of this call that has not yet become obvious in the others. Presumably, Peter and Andrew could have gone back to their nets, something they actually did temporarily according to John 21:2-3. On the other hand, if this man had acted as Jesus had stipulated, there would have been no way to reverse what he had done. In principle, however, Jesus did not ask anything more of this man than he had asked of anyone else. Giving up one's life for the sake of Jesus and the kingdom of God is a radical thing to do.

Ironically, it might be said that this man was so wealthy that he could afford to turn down an invitation to enter the kingdom of God (Mk 10:22). Jesus drove home the difficulty that wealth poses with these words: *How hard it is for the rich to enter the kingdom of God!* His disciples were amazed, although stunned might be a better translation, as implied by their question: *Who then can be saved?* Their shock reflects the conviction of pious first-century Jews that the wealth of people who kept the law was actually a sign of God's favor. If the people who had earned God's favor could not enter the kingdom, they wondered, how could anyone hope to be saved? It was an abrupt and disturbing turn of things. Wealth may look like a blessing now, but in terms of the age to come it looks more like a curse. According to Jesus, wealth is an obstacle for anyone who wants to enter the kingdom of God. A more complete reversal of human values is difficult to imagine.

Jesus' pronouncement about the camel and the eye of a needle (10:25), however, was not simply a condemnation of the wealthy. Jesus was not speaking to a group of predominantly rich people. He spoke to his followers, many of whom came from the peasant population in Galilee. The tax collectors who followed him were the only people Mark describes who might be suspected of having wealth, but Jesus addressed everyone in the same way. He called them children, a reference to something they manifestly did not want to become. This warning about the difficulty of entering the kingdom was addressed to all of them, and it is preferable to take the image of a camel trying to go through the eye of a needle as part of the larger warning. That is to say, Jesus appealed to the common understanding of the place of wealthy people in God's economy to underscore his contention that entering the kingdom is extraordinarily difficult. We might put it this way: if it is so hard for someone with the material tokens of God's blessing to enter the kingdom, how much harder would it be for those who lack this sign of favor?

Jesus' answer was both reassuring and provocative: *With man this is impossible, but not with God; all things are possible with God.* This is a parabolic reply. It affirms that salvation is possible without specifically answering the question who then can be saved?

The terms of salvation, however, have already been laid out in 10:15. To enter the kingdom of God one must receive it as a child. The rich man was willing to meet Jesus halfway. He used the word inherit, which is one way children receive things, but he was only partially willing to put himself in the position of a child. He did not want to give up the things he had accumulated as an adult.

The disciples, on the other hand, were not wealthy people, and they wished to hold on to their dreams of power and prestige despite what they had left behind. The picture that emerges from the events of 9:33—10:31 is one of people who are enmeshed in a web of values, relationships and structures from which they cannot extricate themselves. Left to themselves they would have been unable to let go of the things that prevented them from becoming children who could receive the kingdom on God's terms. The hope for salvation does not lie in us. It comes from God, who is able to bring people to the point where they give these things up. The Bible presents God as the One who does impossible things—enabling Sarah to conceive when she was ninety, sending water gushing from a rock in the desert, and sustaining a widow with an inexhaustible supply of flour and oil. Perhaps helping

---

10:25 From time to time one reads that Jesus was referring to a specific location in the wall surrounding Jerusalem called the Eye of the Needle. In fact, the earliest mention of this legendary gate dates from the Middle Ages (Edwards 2002:314).

adults become children should be added to the list.

Peter followed this, at least in part, with the beginning of a protest that he and the rest of the disciples had qualified for salvation (10:28). Jesus' reply was once again both affirming and disquieting. The assurance that people will receive back one hundred times whatever they give up for him and the gospel is more than comforting, but the idea that it comes with persecution is disturbing. It would certainly have been more reassuring if Jesus had not mentioned persecution.

The assurance Jesus offered is cast in the language of family, and it recalls the encounter between Jesus and his mother and brothers (3:31-35), where he introduced the idea of a new family composed of those who do the will of God. The material in 10:29-31 expands upon the idea of this new family. It is a whole community of people with their houses and lands who have made doing the will of God the basis of their lives. Those who leave behind loved ones and property for the sake of Jesus and the gospel become part of a new community in which persecution is a consequence of the conflict between the old structures of life and this new one. This is as far as the Gospel of Mark goes in describing the church: it is a community of people who relate to each other as family, hold property as a family and order their mutual relationships around the values of the kingdom of God. In this new community, questions of priority, status, value and obligation find their shape in the life of the Son of Man who was delivered into the hands of people vested in structures of life that opposed the kingdom of God.

The Son of Man leads the way in this new social order. The innocent one who was to stand before the Ancient of Days to receive all dominion and authority was delivered into the hands of humans who killed him. That was the ultimate reversal of values, and it calls into judgment every human institution, center of power and pinnacle of privilege. A new community that sought to refurbish those values would prove to be nothing new at all, and it would be subject to the

---

10:28 The Greek verbs translated *said* are more literally translated "began to say." This suggests that Peter had more to say on the subject.

same condemnation. A community that is based on the death and resurrection of the Son of Man will be governed by a radically different set of ideas. Those who want to be great will be least of all and servants of all. Outsiders who are not against the community will be reckoned as though they were for it. All people will be treated with the dignity with which God endowed them, and there will be no entitled privileges. The coming of the kingdom of God creates a great social leveling in which the first shall be last and the last first.

To receive eternal life we must enter the kingdom of God as a child. That is no small matter. It is not a minor adjustment in our spiritual calculus of what we ought to do and how many minutes a day we ought to devote to it. Nor is it an occasion for sentimental thoughts about the spiritual child in each of us. Receiving the kingdom of God as a child means that we come face to face with the concept that the best thing in life is something we cannot earn. And if that is true, how are we to regard the things in life that we earn, like our homes, promotions or standing in the community. If the ultimate good is a gift and not a reward at all, then what value should we place on the prizes that we do win?

The Third Passion Prediction (10:32-45) For most of human history slavery was a socially acceptable institution. It was considered both a political and economic necessity. Those with the intelligence, position and influence to direct the affairs of a society required an underclass to serve their needs and enable their leadership. Two hundred years ago proponents of slavery inside and outside the church appealed to the models of classical Athens and Rome to justify slavery and colonialism as necessary and humane institutions. Today, of course, slavery is no longer morally acceptable, and descendants of the underclasses of the eighteenth and nineteenth century have raised disturbing questions about whether the people and institutions that benefited from slavery in North America should pay reparations.

A sense of approaching crisis appears in the story line: They were on their way up to Jerusalem, with Jesus leading the way, and the disciples were astonished, while those who followed were afraid. There had been hints of the coming crisis before—for example, the arrest of

John (1:14), the plot to destroy Jesus (3:6) and the heresy commission from Jerusalem (3:22)—but a specter of finality hung over this trek to Jerusalem. The previous clashes between the claims of the kingdom of God and the structures of first-century Jewish life led resolutely to an ultimate confrontation.

The mixture of fear and amazement that gripped those who followed in Jesus' wake is not hard to understand. James and John heard opportunity knocking, a thought that was apparently not far from the minds of the other apostles. There was also Jesus' disturbing teaching about how hard it was to enter the kingdom of God (10:23), the warning about those to whom it belonged (10:14) and his promise of salvation with persecution (10:30). Mark has shaped the course of events to offer several possible explanations for their excitement, confusion and fear.

On the way up to Jerusalem Jesus took the Twelve aside and told them what was going to happen to him when they arrived. In this third prediction of his passion the first problem is to identify the actors. The NIV employs the word *betrayed* in 10:33. That is a possible translation, but the Greek verb in question can also mean "hand over," which is the way it is translated later on in the same sentence: *and will hand him over to the Gentiles.* This is not an insignificant matter. At issue is the question of who the primary actor was in Jesus' suffering, death and resurrection. The choice of *betray* leads to Judas, while the choice of "hand over" points to God.

There are two important considerations here. The first is that the same Greek verb is used twice in the same sentence, and it is more consistent to translate it "deliver" in both cases. There is no justification in the context for rendering it two different ways. The second consideration is the consistency of the language in the three passion predictions. Each one begins with the verb *hand over* or *betray* in the passive voice and then moves to verbs in the active voice. In the first passion prediction the subject is indicated by the phrase "it is necessary," where it is clear that God is the one who determines what is necessary. In the active verbs that follow, human beings are the responsible agents. Since the sequence of the verbs from passive to active voice is the same in all three predictions and since there is no contextual reason to change the initiator from God to Judas, it is preferable to use the English verb *hand over*. All three passion predictions cast God in the role of the primary actor. God delivered the Son of Man to humans, who in turn seize the opportunity to kill the Son of Man.

Nevertheless, this passion prediction covers some new ground. Unlike the first prediction in 8:31, the elders are now omitted from the list of Jewish leaders. Acting as the Sanhedrin or council, the elders were responsible for administering the political affairs of Jerusalem and Judea. Here we find only the chief priests and teachers of the law, who were responsible for the administration of the temple and the interpretation of the Jewish law. The executive arm of the Jewish state is missing from this list of conspirators. Instead of the elders we find the Gentiles or nations, more particularly the Roman administration of Judea that eventually mocked, spat on, flogged and killed Jesus.

This is a curious configuration. If we follow the terms of this prophecy without consulting historical sources for the period, it looks as though the chief priests and teachers of the law will make a decision that the nations carry out. It is almost as though a line of authority ran from God through the temple to the Romans. In this text the nations appear to do the bidding of the chief priests and scribes, as though Jerusalem held sway over Rome. The hope that Israel would rule over the nations was expressed in the Psalms of Solomon 17:23-24, 33-35 (Martin 1975:111), and it was embedded in the expectations for the Messiah, who would not only free Israel from the dominance of Rome but also establish it as the first among all the nations.

That picture, however, does not accurately describe the political reality of the first century. No Jewish official or agency had the right to execute a sentence of capital punishment (Lane 1974:530). That was a privilege the Roman government reserved for itself, yet this prophecy contains no hint that the chief priests and scribes needed Rome's permission for anything. They were simply to condemn Jesus and hand him over to the Gentiles to carry out the sentence they imposed. The third passion prediction is clearly framed by messianic hopes of the

---

10:38 It is often supposed that Jesus was referring to suffering in general terms when he used the word *baptism*. After Jesus' own baptism when the Spirit descended upon him, however, the Spirit drove him into the wilderness where he confronted Satan. Later on the Holy Spirit will prompt the disciples with the testimony

day. Yet it predicts that the Son of Man would be executed as the religious leaders of Judea pursue their dreams for an exalted Israel, while God acted behind the scenes to accomplish something else.

James and John's request to sit at Jesus' right and left in his glory indicates that they share to some degree the vision of an exalted Jerusalem. It invokes a picture of Jesus sitting on a throne with one of them sitting on either side of him. They may well have been asking for a role in administering the affairs of the Gentiles in the kingdom of God.

It is not difficult to detect a certain perversity in the way they approached Jesus. The terms of their request—that Jesus do whatever they asked—transgressed the normal relationship between teacher and pupil. A subtle reversal of roles is implied here. It is as though they were asking Jesus to become their servant. They were, after all, simple Galileans whose ascent to power would have entailed a significant reversal of roles in which the last became the first. The indignation of the ten when they learned about James and John's request, however, makes it doubtful that this particular realignment of roles would have led to the larger reversal of values that Jesus advocated. Their request bears the divisive aroma of new privilege and prestige.

Reading between the lines of Jesus' reply makes us wonder whether James and John received exactly what they did not request. They asked for a share of his glory, and in the hope of glory affirmed that they would drink from his cup and undergo his baptism. The baptism and cup that Jesus promised them, however, were not badges of honor. Jesus received the baptism of the Holy Spirit (1:10-11), but that was something no one else has yet received. In fact, inside the narrative of this Gospel no one else actually does receive it, setting up an interesting tension between John the Baptist's prophecy (1:8) and the end of the Gospel (16:8). In light of the importance of this subject, it is surprising that 1:8 and 10:38-39 are the only places where the baptism of the Holy Spirit is mentioned.

With so little said about the subject in Mark's Gospel the baptism of

---

they are to give when they are tested (13:11). Suffering in this Gospel is not treated as a generalized theme. It is always suffering for the sake of the gospel, a theme that is properly connected to the empowering of the Holy Spirit.

the Holy Spirit is a difficult concept to define. There are, though, four points in this Gospel where the Holy Spirit is connected with either Jesus' ministry or that of his followers. These texts are the raw data we have for understanding what Mark means by the term. Three texts mention the Holy Spirit in Jesus' ministry: 1:12-13, where the Spirit drove Jesus into the wilderness to be tempted by Satan; 3:22-30, where Jesus accused the scribal delegation from Jerusalem of blasphemy against the Holy Spirit; and 12:35-37, where Jesus challenged the popular conception of the Messiah. One text connects the ministry of Jesus' followers with the Holy Spirit: 13:11, where he encouraged them not to worry about what to say when they were hauled before governors and kings to give an account of themselves. When they were brought to trial, Jesus affirmed, the Holy Spirit would speak through them.

These texts have several themes in common—conflict, confrontation and power. Even before Jesus' ministry began, John the Baptist prophesied about the baptism of the Holy Spirit and offered forgiveness outside the prescribed structures of worship and sacrifice in the temple. Later on we learn that the chief priests, teachers of the law and elders—who appear as a group only once before (8:31)—challenged not only Jesus' authority. As it turns out, they had also questioned John's authority from the beginning (11:27-33). In the temptation of Jesus, in Jesus' argument with the scribes about the nature of his power and in Jesus' dispute about the role of the Messiah, Mark presents the Holy Spirit as instigator, source and authority. The Holy Spirit empowers and impels Jesus into his encounters with the centers of power in that world. And in the single picture we have of Jesus' disciples and the Holy Spirit, they are pressing the claims of the kingdom of God on governors and kings (13:10). In short, the baptism of the Holy Spirit in this Gospel is both the authorization and empowerment to represent the kingdom of God before the whole world, particularly its structures of power.

Jesus' allusion to a cup is more difficult. No symbolic reference to a cup precedes this conversation. Those come later at the Last Supper (14:23-25) and during his prayer (14:36). In these later passages the cup represents suffering and judgment. In light of those texts the cup Jesus offered James and John was an invitation to share in his humilia-

tion and death at the hands of the nations. The baptism and cup then
point beyond the impending confrontation between Jesus and the
powers in Jerusalem to the disciples' subsequent confrontations with
the nations. It is doubtful that James and John would have understood
much of this. Their ready answer, *We can,* appears to have more to do
with their hope for glory than with their willingness to suffer for the
gospel. Yet this was what Jesus offered them, and it is the same thing
Jesus offers to everyone else who follows him.

The description of the uproar that followed James and John's request makes one wonder how the other apostles heard about it. The
ten were obviously not part of that conversation, and it is unclear
whether anyone overheard the three of them. It could be that James
and John announced to the other apostles that they had been granted
the privilege of drinking from Jesus' cup and sharing his baptism.

In any event Jesus seized the opportunity to expand upon his teaching about service. Some of it repeats themes he had laid out in 9:35—
10:31, but there are several new elements. The first one is the nations:
*You know that those who are regarded as rulers of the Gentiles lord it
over them, and their high officials exercise authority over them.* Why do
the nations appear here, and perhaps even more to the point, whom
did Jesus have in mind when he spoke of those who are regarded as
rulers of the Gentiles?

The verb translated *regarded* can be rendered in several ways: "supposed," "thought" or "seem." This is a strange way to speak about public officials. It is ambiguous, as if those who were regarded as rulers of
the Gentiles were different than those who actually ruled. As we have
already seen, according to contemporary messianic expectations the
people of Israel were supposed to rule over the Gentiles. Was Jesus
then speaking simply against a hierarchy of power that was common
among the nations, or was he also speaking against the hope for Jewish hegemony?

The more inclusive view is to be preferred. In the first place the hierarchical view of authority that Jesus criticized was not a purely Gentile practice, as James and John's request demonstrates. Second, the
broader view is in line with the terms of the third passion prediction, in
which the religious leaders of Judea would succeed in having the Gen-

tiles carry out their plan to execute Jesus. Third, the language of 10:42 is awkward and repetitive if Jesus had only Gentiles in mind. This verse reads much more smoothly if the words *those who are regarded as rulers of the Gentiles* refer to Israel, and *their high officials exercise authority over them* refers to the nations. Finally, the material in this passage fits together better if the context for the entire discussion is the relationship between Israel and the nations. The scope of Jesus' criticism, then, is universal. His comments to the disciples are directed against Jews and Gentiles alike. Jesus did not envision a flawed Jewish hierarchy that would replace an equally flawed Gentile one. He had a very different view of power and authority that contradicted Jewish dreams of hegemony as much as it did the practice of the nations.

Servant leadership has become a staple of the conservative evangelical church, at least in principle. There is certainly much to be said for treating church members and employees with kindness and respect, for pastors who encourage initiatives from every strata of the congregation and for communities that value meekness and humility. Yet there is a great deal of social stratification in our churches. For most of the last two hundred years Protestant churches in particular have been divided along social and economic lines. Treating people in our congregations with dignity and fairness is commendable. If our congregations are divided along economic, racial and social lines, however, the best we can do is to serve people who are just like us. That is a far cry from the vision Jesus set forth here.

The Blind Man Who Saw (10:46-52) The scene described in 10:46-48 is not the first image of wrenching poverty in this Gospel. Several of the miracle stories Mark reports reflect desperate economic conditions. Poverty is the assumed background for much of Jesus' ministry. Nevertheless, the story of blind Bartimaeus presents a scene of economic disparity greater than anything seen so far. He is the first person Mark has introduced as a beggar, and Jericho is one of the few cities or towns that Mark associates with a miracle. Jericho was the site of a magnificent winter palace built by Herod the Great. It was the eastern capital of his empire, and although none of Herod's surviving three sons was allowed to use the title *king,* Jericho was still a prominent center of affluence and power. There is only one picture of similar disparity in Mark: the portrait of the widow who put all she had into the temple treasury (12:44). It is unlikely that Bartimaeus was the only beggar. There is no way of telling how many might have been there, but for a first-century audience this story would have invoked the mental picture of a number of beggars sitting outside a city of conspicuous wealth along the road that led to Jerusalem. Thus, as Jesus approached his final confrontation in Jerusalem, Mark underscores the contrast between the people who are disenfranchised and the social concentration of influence and wealth.

The story of Bartimaeus does not appear in this setting by accident. It repeats the motif of *being on the way* (10:32, 52), and Jesus asked Bartimaeus the same question he put to James and John: *What do you want me to do for you?* He granted Bartimaeus's request, while he seems to have given James and John something they did not really want at the time. Bartimaeus received his sight, and the Sons of Thunder received a share in Jesus' suffering. If the healing of the blind man at Bethsaida (8:22-26) is a parable for Peter, then the healing of Bartimaeus may be a parable for James and John.

This story has at least one feature that is parabolic. Bartimaeus called Jesus *Son of David*—a messianic title. Up to this point whenever messianic language had appeared on someone's lips, Jesus had commanded silence on the subject. As soon as Peter had said the word Messiah, Jesus warned the disciples not to say anything about him to anyone else. The unclean spirits who cried out in recognition of him received the same treatment (3:12). Yet Bartimaeus called Jesus the *Son of David* repeatedly and at full volume. The story of Bartimaeus presents two puzzles: How did he of all people perceive who Jesus was, and why did Jesus not order him to be silent?

Bartimaeus is one of several people in this Gospel whose amazing perceptions about Jesus are not explained. For example, the Greek woman in 7:24-30 is the only person who spoke Jesus' peculiar language. She heard the parable he gave her, understood it and answered him with a parable. The unnamed woman in 14:3-10 anointed him with a very expensive perfume to the indignation of some of those with whom he ate. In some way what she did symbolized the gospel, for

Jesus said: "Wherever the gospel is preached throughout the world, what she has done will also be told, in memory of her." Finally, at the foot of the cross the Roman centurion who watched him die declared: "Surely this man was the Son of God!" (15:39). None of these people belonged to the circle of disciples who were close to Jesus, and two of them were Gentiles. They were all people who could not have been expected to have these kinds of perceptions. How they understood what to say or do is a mystery, but it is a mystery that is consistent with the gospel, for in Mark the rule of God is always greater than our expectations.

The lack of a secrecy motif is also fitting in this account. Mark uses the miracles as enactments of the good news that the kingdom of God is at hand. They are demonstrations of Jesus' preaching and teaching, and as such they play a role in the escalating conflict between the rule of God and the people and structures that resist its claims. The secrecy motifs accentuate this sense of conflict. Here the conflict of values lies right on the surface. Jesus was on his way to Jerusalem, where his disciples hoped to see the power of Rome overthrown. The Messiah, however, had not come to overthrow the Romans but to serve the least and give his life as a ransom for many. Surely the blind beggar—whose name is a mixture of Aramaic *bar* ("son") and Greek *Timaeus*—is one of those for whom he came.

In this connection there is one other facet of Bartimaeus's story to explore: Jesus' pronouncement *your faith has healed you*. Jesus had used these words once before when he healed the woman with the hemorrhage (5:34). Some in the church today treat these words as a kind of entitlement. That is to say, people who have enough faith can be healed of anything. Faith in the sense of expectation is a good thing, but what do we say when people with high expectations do not receive the healing they had hoped for?

In the story of the woman with the hemorrhage the details do not support a theology of entitlement. Her faith was not bold or daring. There was a furtive, frightened quality about the way she approached Jesus. Her faith was mixed with a sense of shame. She knew that she was breaking the levitical laws of purity, and she did not want anyone to know what she was doing. On the whole, her story is a poor argument for faith as entitlement.

Bartimaeus, on the other hand, was bold and insistent. Some in the crowd found his loud persistence offensive and told him to be quiet. That the same words have already appeared in a healing that does not support a name-it-and-claim-it faith should give us pause here too. The larger context of this story provides a better explanation. Bartimaeus's faith was not only insistent, it was insistent on one particular point: he wanted the son of David to interrupt what he was doing to attend to the plight of a man who lived on the margins of society. That the greatest should serve the least has been an article of faith since 9:35, and Jesus had just underscored it in 10:45. Bartimaeus perceived not only that Jesus was the son of David, but also that the son of David had come to serve him. His insight into Jesus' identity is no less amazing than his insight into what Jesus came to do. Once again we cannot discern how Bartimaeus achieved these remarkable insights, but his perception of Jesus is more clearly focused than that of even the Twelve. In short, it was not how he believed, but what he believed that made the difference.

Bartimaeus's amazing perception did not stop there. After his vision was restored, his penchant for asserting himself suggests several diverse possibilities. He might have gone on to ask for a small amount of money so that he could get properly situated in his new life. He might have asked for a set of new clothes, a gift that would have removed the stigma of being a beggar. Or having successfully publicized Jesus' identity, he might have applied for a position as the herald of the son of David. Bartimaeus did none of these things. Instead, when Jesus gave him the freedom to go his own way, he followed Jesus on the road to Jerusalem.

In some unexplained way Bartimaeus knew who Jesus was, and he had an appreciation of what Jesus came to do. He knew what to ask for, and he knew what to do when his request was granted. His story presents an example of faith as discernment. That the Son of Man came to serve is a liberating thought. It is also a dangerous one, especially given the modern credo that self-interest is a good thing. It is easy to think of things we would like someone with power to do for us, many of which might ultimately prove to be destructive. Bartimaeus's plea for mercy shows the way. That request is always appropriate, and it puts us in a position where we can best appreciate what to believe, how to believe and what to do.

□ Faith in the City (11:1—13:37)

The ancient city of Jerusalem has been a flashpoint for conflict for generations. First mentioned as Salem, or Peace, in Genesis 14:18, Jerusalem later became the personal property of David who discovered how to breach its defenses. In 587 B.C.. the city was sacked and burned by the Babylonians. It was rebuilt after the Exile and then destroyed again in A.D. 70. A thousand years later Muslims and Christians fought for control of the city during the Crusades. Today Jerusalem is a city revered by three faiths. It is the home of Christian churches which date from the Middle Ages and the thirteen-hundred-year-old Islamic shrine known as the Dome of the Rock, but there is no Jewish Temple in the city. Modern Jerusalem is a city divided not only by international treaty, but even more fundamentally by competing visions for peace. The events of 11:1—13:36 offer tantalizing insights into Jesus' vision for the city.

The Entry into Jerusalem (11:1-11) In the spring of 2003 as the major fighting in Iraq was winding down, a commencement speaker at a major Christian university expounded the theme of America as the hope of the world. Many people in the congregation warmed to his oration, although a steady trickle of people left their seats and walked out. The graduation ceremony had many elements of a worship service, including communion, and although there was no Scripture lesson, his address was a sermon. The speaker was a congressman and a lay preacher. Listening to him preach, I thought about people I knew who had gone to Iraq just before the outbreak of the war as part of Christian peacemaking teams. Many of them were Mennonites, some were pacifists of no particular denomination, and they had a very different sense of what hope looked like. I remembered a gathering of pastors and development workers from around the world who spent an evening in Bangkok praying fervently that war would not break out. And then I thought about the beggar who accosted me on Pradipat Road, pointed an arthritic finger in my face and declared in halting English, "War no good!"

Each year Christians celebrate Jesus' entry into Jerusalem on Palm Sunday. The palm branches we use that day symbolize victory and triumph. Some Bibles even title this passage "The Triumphal Entry." The Gospel of Mark, however, is not interested in palm branches. In fact, Mark makes no mention of palm trees at all. The branches that people spread before Jesus in this Gospel were simply branches. Furthermore, this was no victory parade. The procession came to an inconclusive end when Jesus entered the temple, looked around and left (11:11). Mark's interest lies elsewhere. Of the eleven verses in this passage the first seven are devoted to an unlikely event: borrowing an animal.

It is an unusual story. The procurement of the beast that no one had ridden before is told from a peculiar point of view. It contains a great deal of descriptive material that only a few people on the inside knew about. Jesus sent two of his disciples into the next village, told them they would find a colt there that no one had ridden before, and instructed them to say if they were questioned: *The Lord needs it.* The two disciples found things just as Jesus had told them, replied as instructed and returned with the colt. It is not clear that anyone other than the two disciples overheard Jesus' instructions, nor does the account stipulate that they said anything to anyone except the people in the village who wanted to know what they were doing with the colt.

The word *Lord* in 11:3 is a point of interest. Jesus had used that title on only two other occasions. The first occasion was his conflict with the Pharisees about the Sabbath when he declared, "The Son of Man is Lord even of the Sabbath" (2:28). Later when he exorcized the legion of unclean spirits from the demoniac, Jesus said, "Tell them how much the Lord has done for you" (5:19). On the surface the reference to Lord in 5:19 is ambiguous. It could refer either to God or Jesus, although the man who had been possessed understood it as a reference to Jesus. That incident occurred in a demonstrably Gentile area, while Jesus used the term here just outside Jerusalem. In this case, however, it is not certain that anyone except the two disciples knew that he had used the term *Lord* about himself.

That the colt had not been ridden before receives the same treatment. It is not apparent that any people except the two disciples were aware of this detail. Questions about who knew what are lost in the wave of excitement that followed the return of the disciples with the colt. One of two things can be said about the way this incident is framed. Either the details about the colt are included for the benefit of Mark's audience, or they were things to be remembered and reflected upon after the events in Jerusalem had reached their climax.

Perhaps both possibilities are true, but from this point on, remembering becomes an important theme in the passion story, particularly for Peter (14:72). In retrospect, one thing is clear about the way Jesus entered Jerusalem. It began with a series of instructions that turned out exactly as he had predicted. The first seven verses remind us that Jesus is someone with a singular authority. He spoke and set in motion a series of events that seem small against the larger issues that overshadowed his entrance into the city. Yet they show that he entered Jerusalem on his own terms, and they underscore the things that he had predicted about his reception in Jerusalem.

It is more difficult to know what significance to attach to his use of the term *Lord*. At the very least this claim to authority corresponds to the idea that he entered the city on his own terms. It also corresponds to the description of his visit to the temple (11:11). Psalm 118:25-29 portrays the temple as the traditional destination for festive processions, but Mark contains no indication that Jesus engaged in an act of worship there. He entered Jerusalem, went to the temple, looked around, then left. His trek to the temple has more the character of a tour of inspection, an impression that is strengthened by the events of the next day, when he cleared the temple of people selling animals and changing money. Jesus' abrupt visit to the temple looks very much like a prelude to judgment and may contain an allusion to Malachi 3:1.

The story line becomes much more complex after the two disciples returned with the colt. Most pilgrims walked to Jerusalem (Jeremias 1975:59), and a close reading of Mark 11:7-10 makes it appear that their return ignited an outburst of messianic excitement. They came back, threw their cloaks over the colt, Jesus sat on it, many more people spread their cloaks and cut branches on the road, and those who preceded and followed him cried out: *Hosanna! Blessed is he who comes in the name of the Lord! Blessed is the coming kingdom of our fa-*

ther David! Hosanna in the highest! The word *hosanna* can mean either "save us now" or "God save us," so these exuberant cries express a deeply rooted expectation of salvation. Given the close sequence of events and the picture of Jesus in the center of everything, it almost looks as though this procession had become a parade in his honor. Yet if this were a procession escorting the Messiah into Jerusalem, we would expect some climactic event after Jesus had entered the city. Nothing remotely like that happened. Once inside the city, the crowd seems to have dispersed. The procession sputtered to an anticlimactic end. It almost looks as though Jesus went to the temple by himself. Furthermore, it would be difficult to explain the lack of any reaction from the Roman authorities if this were a public declaration of the Messiah (Lane 1974:393). By the time we reach the end of this passage, the procession looks much more like a typical pilgrimage for a high holy day in which the crowd engaged in customary activity as it approached Jerusalem, chanting from the Psalms of Ascents and spreading branches along the roadway. From this perspective Jesus appears to be only a figure of some unspecified distinction against the background of the popular hope that God would save Israel by restoring David's kingdom.

This account of Jesus' entry into Jerusalem is fraught with tension. It begins and ends with descriptions of Jesus making gestures of authority, although it is unclear who besides the reader and a handful of his followers perceives them. In between is a procession in which Jesus was treated as a figure of some prominence as the pilgrims celebrated their dream of a messianic kingdom. Mark does nothing to resolve the tension. On the contrary, he seems interested in highlighting it.

For example, in the description of the animal the Greek word translated *colt* is ambiguous (11:2). It often appears with the word *horse* or *donkey,* and in those cases it is appropriately rendered "the colt of" a horse or donkey. When it appears alone, however, it often means simply "horse" (Bauer 1953:222). If Mark were thinking of Zechariah 9:9, we would be justified in hearing messianic fervor in the pilgrims' chanting, but it is doubtful that the pilgrims were proclaiming Jesus as the Messiah, as we have just seen. Thus the argument for understanding this animal as a horse is weakened. In this Gospel the best reason for translating the word as "colt" rather than "horse" is the description of it as one that no one has ever ridden. Even so, whether it is the colt of a donkey or a horse is unresolved.

Is this description simply a reference to the animal's age, or is Mark pointing to something else? That Mark is content with an ambiguous description indicates that he was concerned with something other than nailing down this particular fact. This is a suggestive description, which might point in several directions. It could be part of an attempt to portray Jesus in the guise of a Second Adam or New Human Being, to use Waetjen's term (1989:180). That the colt was tied up indicates that it was already domesticated, and this makes it difficult to sustain a comparison between Jesus and Adam here. That the animal had not been ridden before may be taken as an allusion to Jesus' kingship (France 2002:431). Yet the ambiguity with which Mark presents the entry into Jerusalem raises the question whether something more complex is going on.

Another possibility is suggested by the verb *sat on* or *ridden* 11:2, 7. That verb appears at two critical junctures later in the passion story. In an argument Jesus pressed about the nature of the Messiah, he quoted Psalm 110:1: "The Lord said to my Lord: 'Sit at my right hand until I put your enemies under your feet'" (Mk 12:35-37). The point of this argument is that the Messiah is greater than David. Later Jesus declared to the high priest: "You will see the Son of Man sitting at the right hand of the Mighty One" (14:62). Both of these texts belong to a larger argument about Jesus' authority and identity, and the colt on which Jesus sat is part of that argument. It points to a throne Jesus would claim on which no one else had sat.

The crowd was looking for a messiah to liberate David's city, sit on David's throne and reclaim David's kingdom. Jesus, though, came not only as Messiah, but also as the Son of Man. As the Son of Man, Jesus did things David never dared to do, like claiming the authority to forgive sin. The connections between Jesus and David are not to be underestimated, but the throne on which Jesus was to sit had never been occupied before. The root of the tension in this passage is the difference between the Savior the crowd wanted and the Savior who came.

As in other sections of the Gospel of Mark, there is something parabolic in this text. Jesus' entry into Jerusalem is a complex contrast between his authority and the expectations of first-century Judaism. To paraphrase the words of the pilgrims we might state the matter this way. Who came that day in the name of the Lord? Was it the Messiah the crowd expected to restore the kingdom of David? Or was it Jesus, who came to judge, to be judged and to open a new path of salvation? In short, Mark presents Jesus' entry into Jerusalem as a parable about salvation.

Jesus Condemns the Temple (11:12-25) Baerbel Eccardt's commitment to ministries of reconciliation and peace date from her childhood in Nazi Germany. Her father was a respected judge, although he was not a member of the Nazi party. He decided not to join the Confessing Church movement, as Baerbel and her mother had done, in the hope that he could use his position to provide some measure of protection for people who were at risk under Hitler's regime. Baerbel's disabled brother and sister were among many people who lived precariously in a nation committed to producing a pure race.

During the Cold War Baerbel was one of the principle figures in a ministry called the Berlin Fellowship. Based in First Presbyterian Church of Hollywood, the Berlin Fellowship sustained channels of hope and reconciliation between churches in America and churches behind the Iron Curtain. As much as she loved Americans, Baerbel often found it uncomfortable to worship in American churches. Once upon entering a church in southern California she noticed an American flag displayed prominently on the dais, not far from the pulpit. Baerbel stopped for a moment before whispering, "Is this a church for me, too?"

It is common to refer to Jesus' confrontation with those who changed money and sold animals as the cleansing of the temple, as though he intended to sweep out something objectionable and restore it. What happened in the temple is so dramatic and decisive that cleansing seems a very tame description. From a historical point of view this is the event that provoked the chief priests and elders to have him crucified. In that light, cleansing is either the wrong word to describe what happened or it describes an event that was woefully deficient. Perhaps a more appropriate description can be found.

Mark provides a significant clue in the story of the fig tree, which is interwoven with the story of the events in the temple. In 11:11 Jesus inspected the temple and left. In 11:12-14 he cursed the fig tree. In 11:15-19 he drove out the people who trafficked in sacrifices and taught the crowd, as his opponents sought to kill him. Then in 11:20-25 he returned to the fig tree on his way back to the temple and used its withered remains as an occasion to teach about faith and forgiveness. This narrative technique is called intercalation or sandwiching, and Mark uses it to suggest connections between what would otherwise be read as unrelated material.

The cursing of the fig tree is a disturbing event (Anderson 1976:265), especially so because Mark clearly states that figs were out of season. Some try to soften this story by claiming that Jesus expected to find first fruits on the tree, the few figs that would have appeared in advance of the full crop which would come later (Gundry 1993:636). While the story might be read in that way, the unqualified statement because it was not the season for figs cannot be reconciled with this line of interpretation. The plain implication of this simple statement is that there was nothing wrong with the fig tree. The fig tree, then, is a sign or symbol of something else, and Mark's intercalation points to the temple.

The setting for what Jesus did in the temple is the days leading up to Passover, perhaps during the Festival of Sukkoth. Both Passover, which celebrates God's deliverance of the Jewish people from Egypt, and Sukkoth, which commemorates God's provision in the wilderness, were celebrations of national pride. In the first century when the Jewish people lived under the administration of Rome, these festivals were also a flash point for patriotic hopes. They brought out the deepest religious and patriotic feelings of the people, yet as Jews from around the world streamed into Jerusalem to celebrate their day of liberation, foreigners held the reigns of power in the Promised Land.

There was one place, however, where the Jewish people were still in control—the temple. Caesar permitted them to practice their religion unhindered by the politics of Rome. In Ephesus the temple of Artemis housed statues of the goddess Roma and Caesar Augustus. Temples in Athens, Corinth and Alexandria held similar statues. Throughout the Mediterranean world, houses of worship displayed tokens of their allegiance to Rome, but it was not so in Jerusalem. The temple in Jerusalem housed no statues of any kind. It was unpolluted by the trappings of foreign gods, and the keepers of the temple were committed to keeping it pure.

Rome's tolerance and a Jewish commitment to keep the temple pure help to explain the presence of the moneychangers. Church governing boards and pastors often cite what Jesus did in the temple as a reason to prohibit the sale of anything on church patios on Sunday mornings. There is very little in this Gospel to support such a prohibition. Despite efforts to prove otherwise (Anderson 1976:266), Mark contains no hint that the animals offered for sacrifice were overpriced or that the rate of exchange was artificially inflated. In fact, an argument might be made that the sellers and moneychangers were providing an important service. The pilgrims who streamed in from all parts of the Roman Empire to celebrate Passover needed a ready supply of animals to sacrifice, and the money they brought with them was typically inscribed with the image of a god or goddess. It would not do to have pious Jews purchase sacrifices for the one true God with idolatrous currency, so the temple authorities authorized the striking of money that contained no offensive symbols. Those who came to Jerusalem to worship were required to use this currency to purchase their sacrifices.

This is the background for appreciating Jesus' condemnation of the temple: *Is it not written: "My house will be called a house of prayer for all nations"? But you have made it a "den of robbers"* (11:17). Jesus' description of the temple as a den of robbers is an allusion to Jeremiah 7:11, where the prophet asks: "Has this house, which bears my Name, become a den of robbers to you?" For Jeremiah the robbery in question had nothing to do with the purchase of sacrificial animals or inflated exchange rates. The leaders of Jerusalem whom Jeremiah denounced were guilty of oppressing foreigners and widows and orphans, shedding innocent blood and following other gods. Their sin was twofold: they were robbing the people of justice, and they were robbing God of true worship.

Mark's account contains something not found in the other Gospels. It is a quotation from Isaiah 56:7: "My house will be called a house of prayer for all nations." The nations figured less prominently in Jeremiah's prophecy, but they were still present. In Jeremiah's condemnation of Solomon's Temple the nations were present as foreigners whom the leaders and legal system of Judea oppressed. In Mark, however, the question is not oppression but access to the temple. What Jesus found wrong with Herod's Temple was the absence of the peoples of the world. They were not there praying.

Furthermore, if the stalls for animals and tables for changing money were set up in the Court of the Gentiles, Jesus had even more grounds for concern. The Court of the Gentiles was the one place within the temple precincts where foreigners were permitted. If, however, that area was dominated by the commercial activity leading up to Passover, then the nations were effectively denied access to the temple. In Mark the problem was not the commercial activity in the temple as such; it was the set of practices that denied the nations access to the house of prayer. In Jesus' adaptation of Jeremiah's prophecy, robbery in the temple assumes international dimensions. If we ask who was being robbed of what, we would have to say that God was robbed of the worship of the nations and the nations were robbed of their place in the house of prayer.

In studies of Mark's account one verse is often given scant attention: *He . . . would not allow anyone to carry merchandise through the temple courts* (11:15-16). In this case merchandise includes animals for sacrifice. Thus Jesus' prohibition extended not just to the one place where buying and selling took place but to all the temple courts. Jesus did not simply put an end to some commercial activity. The inescapable implication is that he also stopped the offering of sacrifices for the duration of the day. Isaiah had demanded: "Who has asked this of you, this trampling of my courts?" (Is 1:12). Jeremiah declared: "Add your burnt offerings to your other sacrifices and eat the meat yourselves!" (Jer 7:21). Both these prophets had also acted out prophecies about the impending destruction of the land (Is 20; Jer 27:1-15). Neither of them, however, had gone so far as to arrest the whole system of sacrifice. It is no wonder then that the chief priests and teachers of the law sought a way to kill Jesus. His words and actions were a formidable threat to their administration of the temple.

The next day as Jesus and his followers walked from Bethany to the temple, Peter noticed that the fig tree had withered to its roots. It would never sprout branches or produce figs again, and Peter remembered what Jesus had said. The verb *remember* becomes an important term from this point on in Mark's Gospel. Throughout the passion story Jesus' disciples witness events whose meaning is much larger than they could comprehend at the moment. Their meaning becomes apparent only in retrospect. So it was with the fig tree. They had heard Jesus' words in Mark 11:14, but they had not expected the fig tree to wither overnight. It would also be so with the temple. They had seen what he had done in the temple, but their reverence for the temple was so entrenched (13:1) that they did not perceive what it meant.

Peter's exclamation in 11:21 reflects surprise and even shock at what had happened to the fig tree, but Jesus did not address Peter's feelings. He replied as though he were continuing a lesson that had begun the day before. *Have faith in God,* he affirmed, and *if anyone says to this mountain, "Go, throw yourself into the sea," and does not doubt in his heart but believes that what he says will happen, it will be done for him.* The critical question is what Jesus meant by the words this mountain. It was not simply any mountain. It was the mountain that lay before them as they approached Jerusalem. It was the mountain on which they had stood the previous day, and it was their destination that day. It was the temple mount (Bird 1953:177).

The fig tree then is an enacted parable about the temple. When Jesus denounced the temple as a den of robbers, drove out the merchants and customers, overturned the tables of the moneychangers and stopped the offering of sacrifices, he was not trying to purify the temple. His actions amounted to a curse. And if the fig tree, which he also cursed, had withered away to its roots, what would become of the temple? The destruction of the temple is the event to which 11:23 points. In cursing the temple, Jesus had not doubted in his heart. He had absolute confidence that what he had said would be done for him. And if we ask what the basis for his confidence was, it is to be found in the opening clause of 11:22: *Have faith in God.* His certainty was grounded in God's integrity and justice. Jesus had not cursed the temple on a whim. It was his conviction that Herod's Temple stood in the way of God's purposes, just as Solomon's Temple had become a sanctuary for robbers centuries before. As the rule of God drew near in history, the temple could no longer stand—not only because it opposed him, a theme that is developed comprehensively through the rest of the passion story, but because it stood against the reign of God.

Jesus did not invite his first followers to join him in cursing the temple, but he did encourage them to pray with the same unwavering faith that he had demonstrated when he put an abrupt end to the sacrifices of the previous day. We must be careful though, because a careless reading of 11:24 might create the impression that Jesus thought of prayer as a license for selfishness. His bold declaration about believing *that you have received it, and it will be yours* is easily misunderstood. This Gospel provides, on the contrary, several counterexamples of heartfelt requests that were denied, as illustrated by the manipulative request of James and John (10:37). Furthermore, the Greek word for *you* is plural throughout 11:24, suggesting that these prayers are corporate petitions rather than personal requests.

The similarity in the language about faith in 11:23-24 indicates that the context is unchanged, and the word *therefore* at the beginning of 11:24 points back to God's faithfulness and integrity. The overarching issue is the same: entrenched opposition to the rule of God. The line of thought connecting these two verses could be stated this way. If the temple in Jerusalem was not immune to judgment, then neither is any other enclave of power. God can be trusted to judge impartially. The promise of 11:24 is not a blank check that Jesus' followers could draw upon to fulfill their own aspirations. It is an instruction about how they are to confront the centers of power that oppose the kingdom of God. The word *whatever,* then, should be taken in the sense of no matter how formidable, rather than in the sense of anything and everything.

Why then did Jesus place so much emphasis on believing in prayer? The best answer is that the encouragement to believe is not so much a call for pure faith as for enduring faith. Looking back on the events of the first century, we can appreciate the need for constancy. The judgment of the temple did not fall immediately like a thunderbolt from heaven. A generation later, as God worked through the forces of history, Jesus' followers were still waiting for it to happen. In 11:23 Jesus took the stand of a prophet who knew that God's judgment was certain, yet he also understood that God's judgment often operates through the unfolding events of history. The call for enduring faith is a directive for his followers to adopt the same prophetic stance.

The promises of 11:23-24 are based on God's commitment to act with justice through the events of history. Overturning the tables of the moneychangers and merchants in the temple was not a call to violence or armed revolt. There is no evidence that Jesus bore arms or encouraged his followers to do so. Shutting down the system of sacrifice was an enacted prophecy that God would act to redress an abuse of power. In the verses that follow that act, Jesus gave his disciples instructions about how to deal with entrenched, unyielding opposition to the rule of God. This intransigence was not merely the unfaithfulness of a few people: it was institutional opposition. Throughout the Gospel of Mark Jesus confronts individual people, spiritual powers and human institutions with the claims of the kingdom of God. As he began his ministry in Jerusalem, Jesus encountered not only the disobedience of the high priests and scribes, he also confronted the temple as a system of worship that was robbing God. In the final analysis Jesus' teaching about prayer outlines a strategy for pressing the claims of the rule of God against unresponsive enclaves of power. He did not encourage his followers to take up arms. He encouraged them to pray with the enduring faith that trusts God to act in and through the events of history.

After the two strong statements about confronting systems of power that resist the rule of God, the transition to the theme of forgiveness in 11:25 seems abrupt. In fact, it is so abrupt as to appear out of place to some scholars. Several commentators (Bultmann 1972:25; Schweizer 1970:235; Nineham 1968:305) maintain that it is a late addition rather poorly related to the preceding material, and if it is taken as a purely personal matter, the transition from 11:24 to 11:25 is all the more jarring. The transition is certainly abrupt, but abrupt insertions and transitions occur with enough frequency in this Gospel to be considered part of the Evangelist's style. And if the setting for prayer in 11:25 is still corporate, then the tension between the two verses is considerably lessened. Since the Greek word for *you* is plural throughout 11:24-25, it is better to infer that the same setting applies. Both verses are concerned with the gathering of a group or community for prayer.

To pursue this line of thought further, we might ask when in the days leading up to Passover a group of people might gather for prayer and what they would ask God to do. One thing comes immediately to mind: a prayer for deliverance from the nations that oppress the people of God, in which case the acts of injustice done to them need to be forgiven. This reading fits well with the theology of the broader passage. If the nations of the world are to have a place where they pray with the people of Israel, then forgiveness of the wrongs that one people suffer at the hands of another is essential. If forgiveness is not part of the prayers of the nations, then their prayers might easily become a hopeless litany of revenge.

It is possible then that 11:25 describes a corporate prayer by an oppressed community that is asking God to rectify the injuries it has suffered. In that case the request for justice is to be tempered by forgiveness. It must be tempered also by the recognition that oppressed groups can injure other people as well, a concern that the disciples' own conduct justifies (9:34; 10:13, 37). Viewed in this light, a prayer for justice is also ultimately a prayer for reconciliation.

Of course, the personal interpretation of 11:25 is still possible. If it is preferred, then the scope of forgiveness is obviously smaller, although the granting of forgiveness is not necessarily less difficult. In either case this verse affirms that prayers of faith are not prayers for revenge. It establishes forgiveness as the framework in which prayers about opposition to the gospel are offered. And in light of the underlying theme of this passage it presents reconciliation as the point where justice and forgiveness meet.

Finally, Jesus' use of the word *father* at the end of 11:25 should not be overlooked. This is the first time in the Gospel of Mark that God is described in this way. Jesus has been described as God's "son" in 1:11 and 9:7, but heretofore no one has referred to God as *father*. One of the major themes in the previous sections of the Gospel is the creation of a new family (3:31-35), in which the will of God is the defining factor. The reference to God as father here is entirely consistent with that passage. We might wonder then why we have not seen it before or why it appears here. The best answer is that in this passage the will of God is startlingly and clearly revealed. Against the backdrop of nationalistic dreams and all the roiling patriotic fervor, forgiveness and reconciliation are revealed to lie at the very center of God's will. Forgiveness may be the costliest gift to give, as well as the most overwhelming to receive. As the engines of war drove inexorably forward in the late 1930s, Sandor Meretey gave in to the relentless peer pressure at his school in Budapest and joined in the beating of a Jewish boy in his class. This child was not only Sandor's classmate. He lived in an apartment upstairs from Sandor, and the two boys had often played together. Wracked by remorse that day, Sandor could not hide what he had done from his father. So on his father's orders Sandor trudged upstairs that evening. The boy he had played with would not come to the door, so Sandor delivered his apology to the child's father, who received it in silence. A few days later Sandor and the other classmates watched in shock as a contingent of Hungarian soldiers escorted all the Jewish children from the school. That night the apartment upstairs was empty, and Sandor never saw his former playmate again.

Sometime after the war ended Sandor looked up to see a bedraggled, emaciated figure shuffling toward him down one of the rubble strewn streets of Budapest. Sandor recognized the man at once. He was the father to whom he had apologized years before. Sandor did not wish to risk a meeting. He looked for some avenue of escape, but it was too late. The man had recognized Sandor too. Sandor stood stock-still as the man approached, put his arms around him and wept. His wife and son had disappeared in the concentration camps. He was the family's only survivor. "Thank you," the man whispered through his tears. "You were the only one who ever said you were sorry."

A Question of Authority (11:27—12:12) "The thing you fear the most is what you worship," observed a colleague in a Bible study. In many churches this pastor's comment would be highly offensive. In popular Christian culture where God is honored as our friend and where the fear of God has been reduced to a comfortable respect, such a comment is either heresy or nonsense. After all, the counterargument runs, when we gather to praise God we are not worshiping our fears. Yet if we fear the loss of health, a job or a personal relationship enough, we will do just about anything to secure what we do not want to lose. If our fear is great enough, we will cast aside all sense of propriety and transgress any boundary. Paul encourages us to "work out [our] salvation with fear and trembling" (Phil 2:12). The question is not whether there is a place for fear in worship. The question is what place we give it.

Fear and Authority (11:27-33) The chief priests, scribes and elders have been mentioned once before as the people who would put Jesus to death (8:31), but this is the first time they appear on stage together. They were the most powerful people in Jerusalem. They controlled the temple, oversaw the resolution of legal disputes and administered the political and financial affairs of the Jewish people. They had not come to conduct a disinterested inquiry about Jesus' credentials. His actions in the temple on the previous day were a direct affront to their leadership. Ultimately, they were the ones he had accused of robbery. A delegation composed of these people indicates how deeply he had shaken things up. Precisely what they hoped to get from him is impossible to say, but the questions they posed about his authority were not objective theological inquiries. They were legally and politically charged.

Jesus refused to become entangled in a debate about his credentials. Instead he turned the spotlight on theirs, by asking about John the Baptist. The masses had believed that John was a prophet, but the leaders of Judea had found him to be a troubling presence. He did not encourage the masses to present offerings or make sacrifices in the temple. Instead John summoned the citizens of Jerusalem and Judea to have an encounter with God that was not mediated by the temple or its leaders. His death at the hands of Herod had provided an apparently happy solution to their dilemma, but there was to be no convenient solution in the case of Jesus. Jesus pressed the engagement in Jerusalem by asking them to declare themselves: Was John a prophet?

There was more to Jesus' question, however, than a challenge to their authority. He was the second prophetic figure to appear within a very short span of time. For hundreds of years there had been no prophets in Judah. Then two charismatic figures appeared suddenly, and the leaders of the temple had not known how to respond. Something dynamic had begun to happen, and they found themselves on the outside and in the opposition. By asking them about John, Jesus invited them to go back to the place where something new had begun to happen and affirm what God was doing. It was an opportunity to repent. Jesus' question offered the chief priests, elders and scribes two possibilities. They might affirm that John was a prophet, or they might stipulate that John was merely a popular figure whose claim to authority was no larger than the following he had attracted. They chose to do neither and answered: *We don't know.* As Mark describes their deliberation (11:31-32), however, that was not a true statement—it was an evasion. They did not think John's authority came from God because they had not believed John. They thought his authority had purely human origins but were afraid to say so because they feared the people.

Mark refers to their fear of the crowd twice in this engagement. In 12:12 their fear also prevented them from acting against Jesus on the spot. This double reference is particularly significant in the context of an argument about who was acting for God. Psalm 111:10 and Proverbs 1:7 affirm that the fear of God is the beginning of wisdom, but in this confrontation about worship the leaders of Jerusalem were constrained by their fear of people. Any claim they might have made to act for God had been undermined by the fear that actually governed their conduct.

A Parable About Judgment and Vindication (12:1-12) Empty buildings stripped bare to their concrete walls can be found around the world. Many of them were erected by well-intentioned charities and mission organizations. They were supposed to be schools, churches, hospitals or secure offices from which to do relief and development work. Sadly, these structures are casualties in a conflict of values that Western organizations have been slow to understand. Unbroken cycles of war, famine and grinding poverty rendered them useless, unless they were rooted in the fundamental values of the social system where they were built. For Westerners buildings are sound investments, and it was easy to believe that pouring lots of money into constructing them would help address some pressing problems for which donors had given money. It turned out to be an ironic kind of help. In many cases the buildings turned out to be helpful only for individuals who needed a ready supply of copper wire, doors and windows. The buildings had a different value for us than for the people for whom they were supposedly constructed. Today few charitable organizations will have anything to do with a erecting a building. Doing good is a complicated matter, and the most difficult challenge is deciding what appropriate good to do.

Jesus had declined to give the leaders of Jerusalem a direct answer about his authority, but as he began to speak in parables, he gave them an indirect one. In this Gospel parables are often a sign of judgment. They indicate that someone has stopped listening to God. A parable is the first consequence of a persistent failure to listen. A parable makes understanding what God is saying more difficult, and the parable brings with it a set of new conditions. In order to understand God it is necessary to see oneself through the lens of the parable, something that is typically unflattering. Parables are a witness that a profound alienation has occurred, and repentance in some form becomes a requirement for understanding what God says. Speaking in parables was not, then, a concession to Jesus' opponents. It was an escalation of the argument.

The parable of the tenants is a revision of the parable of the vineyard found in Isaiah 5:1-17. In the original parable the vineyard represented the people of God. When God came to gather fruit from the vineyard, there were no sweet grapes to pick—only bitter ones. The bitter grapes symbolize the bloodshed and oppression that the people of Israel and Judah had produced instead of the justice and righteousness God had hoped to harvest. Isaiah's parable ends with a pronouncement of judgment against the people; the fertile land of Judah would become a wasteland.

Although Jesus borrowed the themes of the vineyard, the beloved, the winepress and the watchtower from Isaiah's parable, he made three fundamental changes that give his parable a different focus. Isaiah's parable is set as a song to the *beloved* one, that is, to God. In Jesus' parable the beloved one is the son of the owner of the vineyard. In the Gospel of Mark the term beloved occurs in two other places. At both the baptism of Jesus and on the Mount of Transfiguration God called Jesus the *son whom I love*. Reading the parable in the broader context of Mark, it appears that Jesus has put himself inside this parable.

Second, Jesus did not charge the rulers of Judah with exploiting the poor, as Isaiah did. The thrust of this parable is not that the vineyard produces bitter fruit. The problem is that the tenants will not give the owner any of the vineyard's produce. These tenants refuse to recognize the owner's rights and the authority of his representatives. They are guilty of robbery, the same charge Jesus made in Mark 11:17, and ultimately of murder. There is plenty of bloodshed in this parable, but this violence is not exercised by the rich and powerful against those beneath them. In killing first the servants and finally the beloved son, the tenants attacked the owner. This is more like a rebellion—violence from the bottom upward.

Third, Isaiah's parable ends with a warning that the vineyard would become a wasteland. His parable was a prophecy of doom for the people of Judah. Jesus' parable ends with a different scenario: the owner will destroy the tenants and give the vineyard to others. This parable envisions the destruction of only the tenants. The vineyard is not to be destroyed, but the tenants will be replaced.

Like the parable of the soils in chapter four this parable is allegorical. The comparison of the owner to God, the beloved son to Jesus, and the tenants to the leaders of Jerusalem seems obvious (Gundry 1993:684). What other comparisons may reasonably be drawn is not so clear. The servants might represent the prophets, and the servant who was wounded in the head might represent John the Baptist (6:27). Yet pressing the details of the parable too far leads into a confusing quagmire. Jesus' opponents, for instance, perceived correctly that he had told this parable against them, but they were not responsible for killing any prophets. Their opposition to John took the form of indifference, not overt hostility. Isaiah 5:7 provides a clear guide to sorting out the references in the Song of the Vineyard. The Gospel of Mark, on the other hand, does not. Jesus' parable ends instead with a cryptic quotation from Psalm 118:22-23. What light does it shed on the parable?

The first point is the way the quotation is introduced: *Haven't you read this Scripture?* It is not cited as a prophecy, nor is there any language about fulfillment here. This text is used descriptively, not prophetically, and its focus is God's activity. Psalm 118:22-23 describes a scene that is still familiar to people throughout the developing world. When a building is destroyed or abandoned, the local people salvage whatever they can to use in other building projects. The author of

Psalm 118 would have us imagine the picture of desolation that the armies of Babylon left behind after sacking Jerusalem in 587 B.C. They had turned the city of David into a rubbish heap. Over the years, as the people who remained in the area struggled to carve out a new life, they pulled out of the rubble the stones that were still suitable for building. Years later when a Jewish delegation returned from Babylon with permission to rebuild the city and the temple, they found only a pile of broken stones that the builders had rejected. The task of rebuilding looked impossible. Psalm 118 celebrates a striking accomplishment: from the fragments of stone that the local builders had thought unusable God built another temple.

Obviously, this setting is different. Mark does not invite us to envision a pile of broken stones on the temple mount. Herod's Temple was built from newly hewn stone, and its major structures had been completed by the time Jesus cursed the temple. The juxtaposition of the parable of the tenants and Psalm 118:22-23 points to something other than the temple buildings. The parable describes a group of rebellious tenants who reject the owner's authority. The quotation from Psalm 118 indicates that the temple is the location of the rebellion and robbery. The temple building was not the issue. The problem was what happened in the temple. The leaders of Jerusalem were using the worship of God for their own ends.

This is the point at which it is particularly important to appreciate the descriptive rather than prophetic use of Psalm 118. The Jesus we meet in the Gospel of Mark was not interested in the hopes for restoring the glorious buildings of Solomon's Temple and the political hegemony of Israel. His vision included the reconciliation of the nations rather than their subjugation. What Jesus perceived in this conflict was a fundamental disagreement about the way God acts. He saw that God was doing something in history that the leaders of Jerusalem had rejected. The chief priests, elders and scribes had a vision for Mount Zion that did not take into account the marvelous capacity of God to act outside of our expectations in ways that are perfectly consistent with God's character. Jesus, on the other hand, saw God doing the same sort of thing that God had been doing in Jerusalem hundreds of years before. God was acting again to reconstitute worship. In the final analysis, Psalm 118:22-

23 was Jesus' answer to the challenge to his authority.

Over time the places where we worship are statements of our deepest values. Today the urban centers of North America are populated by church buildings that are sparsely attended on Sunday mornings. Once they were homes for spirituality and community life, but as different ethnic groups moved into the cities, the people who built the churches moved out. They may still work in the city or depend upon it for their economic livelihood, but they do not live or worship there anymore. Demographers used to call this phenomenon "white flight," but the same process can now be found in nonwhite groups too. These buildings are monuments to the past, and their empty presence leads one to wonder who the owner was. Was it God's house, and did God leave? Or did it belong to someone else all along?

Land and Loyalty (12:13-17) Set against the background of her American Jewish husband's kidnapping by Hezbollah, Sis Levin's *Beirut Diary* describes the plight of a Palestinian Christian who lost her home in Jerusalem. She and her husband returned one day to find that a Jewish family had simply moved into their home. There was no recourse. No one in the Israeli government listened to their plea for justice, and that day the Copti family joined the thousands of other Palestinians whose homes the Israelis have confiscated (1989:26). *Beirut Diary* raises a number of penetrating questions about the prospects for peace in the Middle East. For people of faith perhaps the most disturbing one is the simple lament: "Whose side is God on?"

The Pharisees whom the chief priests, elders and scribes sent to trap Jesus might very well have applauded this policy. They were ardent nationalists who nurtured the hope that God would send a messiah to defeat the foreign powers and expel them from the land. The Herodians who accompanied them lived at the other end of the political spectrum. They were in many ways collaborators with Rome. They were not an official political or religious party. Herodians is a loose term that designated a range of Jewish people attached to Herod's court. In the world of first-century Judea it is difficult to imagine a stranger political alliance than the ad hoc committee of Pharisees and Herodians sent to Jesus. It was the same strange pairing that first plotted to destroy him in 3:6.

They came to trap him in his own words, and despite their flattery they posed a particularly thorny question: *Is it right to pay taxes to Caesar or not? Should we pay or shouldn't we?* If Jesus had said that Caesar had a right to collect taxes in Judah, the Herodians would have been satisfied, but the Pharisees would have denounced him to the crowd as a man who sided with their oppressors. If, on the other hand, he had denied Rome's right of taxation, the Herodians would have had everything they need to denounce him to the Roman authorities in Judea. That was an interesting dilemma, but it was only the tip of the iceberg.

Two parts of this encounter point to a deeper issue. One is the comment that Jesus knew their hypocrisy. The Pharisees themselves paid taxes to Caesar, and the Herodians could not have cared less about the way of God. Their hypocrisy suggests that the issue they brought was not the issue that was of fundamental importance. The second indication that something larger is at stake is the language the Pharisees and Herodians use to approach Jesus. The flattery of 12:14 recalls the prophecies of Isaiah 2:2-4 and Micah 4:2-3, where the nations come to the Lord's temple to learn to walk in his ways and God judges for them with impartiality. This language indicates that the real issue was Jesus' vision of the place of Gentiles in the temple. Beneath the question about paying taxes to Caesar was a more fundamental concern about sovereignty. When the nations come to Jerusalem, who makes the rules? This question lay at the heart of Jesus' dispute with the leaders of Jerusalem, and neither he nor they have shown any sign of backing away from it.

Jesus deftly avoided the trap by refusing to argue whether Caesar had justifiable rights in Jerusalem. His declaration to give to Caesar what is Caesar's contains an implicit recognition that Rome provided some public services such as roads, aqueducts and systems of commerce that ought to be respected. It is consistent with exhortations in other parts of the New Testament to honor the emperor.

More importantly, Jesus framed the question of what God expected in a way that transcended the neatly drawn categories of his opponents. Giving to God what is God's is a broad statement that invites the Pharisees and Herodians to reassess what they were giving to God. It certainly includes the tithes that the Pharisees dutifully gave as well as any offerings the Herodians may have brought, but its ramifications are much broader. If Caesar's image symbolizes the things that belong to Caesar, what image denotes the things that belong to God? That is the image of God that every human being bears. Neither the Pharisees nor the Herodians nor anyone else in Jerusalem, however, gave God the things that properly belong to God—people without regard to race, culture or gender. By posing the question of what belonged to God, Jesus brought to the fore once again what he had charged the leaders of Jerusalem with earlier—that they were robbing God (11:17).

In a world dominated by sectarian divisions Jesus announced a decidedly inclusive principle: whatever bears God's image belongs to God. This would have been a particularly troublesome idea for the Pharisees, who were obsessed with keeping the Promised Land holy. The basic meaning of holiness is belonging to God, and their passion for it was evident in the countless things they did to keep themselves, their temple and their land pure and undefiled. The Jesus we meet in this Gospel, however, defined holiness in terms that come from the creation of the world. For him holiness was not fundamentally a matter of personal, ethnic or cultic purity. It was essentially a commitment to extend the rule of God to everyone and everything that belongs to God.

The God of the Living (12:18-27) Several years ago I conducted a funeral for a young man who had died of diabetes. He had had the disease since childhood, and by the time he placed his faith in God, he had already lost his eyesight. God filled his life with joy. He had an in- . candescent spirituality that radiated hope and courage. Toward the end, though, when his kidneys failed and he slipped into a coma, his friends wondered where God was. And when he died, it felt to some as though God had abandoned him.

That question where is God when nice people die? is the key to understanding this confrontation between Jesus and the Sadducees. The Sadducees were the most conservative of the religious parties in first-century Judaism. Their Bible contained only the five books of Moses. They did not accept the Prophets or the Writings. It was their convic-

tion that the resurrection was a late addition to Jewish thinking found
only in books like Ezekiel and Daniel. They maintained that it was not
part of the spiritual legacy of Moses.

The Sadducees approached Jesus with another question designed to
embarrass him as he taught in the temple. It is not easy for modern
readers to understand the various dimensions of the question. It was
based on an ancient tradition that predated the Mosaic covenant called
the levirate law. According to the levirate law if a married man died
and left no children, his brother was obligated to marry his widow and
raise up a child for him who would continue the first brother's family
line (Deut 25:5-6). What would happen then, the Sadducees asked, if a
man had six brothers and he died leaving a wife without any children
(Mk 12:20-23)? And then suppose that all six brothers accepted the obligation of the levirate law, and each in turn married the same woman
but died without leaving any children? If people really did rise from the
dead, whose wife would she be after the resurrection?

It was an apparently insoluble problem conceived to demonstrate
that the resurrection was an absurd idea. The levirate law was a well-
attested part of the books of Moses. And as the Sadducees were at
pains to point out, the idea of a resurrection did not make any sense in
the context of that law. So, if the resurrection could not be reconciled
with the clear teaching of Scripture, then the new doctrine had to be
discarded. In good rabbinic fashion Jesus responded to their question
with another question: *Are you not in error,* he asked, *because you do
not know the Scriptures or the power of God?* That was a two-pronged
attack on their logic, and each tine merits our attention.

Jesus began by asserting that there would be no marriage after the
resurrection. His choice of words is particularly interesting. To marry
was a male role. To be given in marriage was a female role. According
to Jesus neither role is to apply after the resurrection. Both men and
women will be like the angels in heaven, he affirmed. Apparently, then,
neither marriage nor the sexual stereotyping that is so much a part of
this world has any place in the next. Beneath that assertion lay a very
serious issue. The Sadducees' expected the future to be like the past.
That expectation was the premise for the vexing little problem they had
invented. Jesus maintained, however, that the future would not be like

the past. It would be so different that the levirate law could not apply. Expecting the future to be just like the past is certainly a natural thing to do, but it limits our faith. It keeps us from being open to new things. It restricts God to the boundaries of our experience. This was the heart of the matter. The God of Jesus, on the other hand, does new things like creating a means of forgiveness at the Jordan River. The Sadducees, like the other religious leaders in Jerusalem, did not see God's hand in the ministry of John the Baptist, and they did not recognize God in the things Jesus did either. Their God was bound by their view of the past.

In point of fact, their God had done new things in the past. In the passage to which Jesus called their attention (12:26) God did several new things. God appeared in a bush that burned without burning up. God appointed Moses to lead a group of slaves to freedom. And God gave Moses a leprous hand and healed it within the space of a few minutes. The God of Moses did new things.

The passage to which Jesus referred, Exodus 3:6, is particularly interesting in this connection. It was, of course, part of the canon of Scripture that the Sadducees accepted, and it was the cornerstone in their understanding of the future. God had promised Abraham and his descendants a country of their own. When God appeared to Moses, that promise was renewed. The exodus was the next step toward fulfilling it. The Sadducees expected God to do the same thing for them. There were Roman troops quartered in the land God had promised them, and a Roman governor held the reigns of power. The Sadducees believed that God would act again to set them free. Their hope for the future was tied firmly to the land, and this passage was a crucial part of its foundation.

In this story where God did so many new things Jesus put his finger on something else that no one had seen before. When Moses heard the voice coming from the burning bush, Abraham, Isaac and Jacob had been dead for hundreds of years. How could God still be revealed as their God so long after they had died, Jesus asked in effect, unless they were still allied with God? If God were really their God, Jesus argued, then death had not ended their relationship.

God had made a covenant with the patriarchs in which God promised to be their protector. It is impossible to pursue this line of thought very far without confronting this question: how could God be their protector and abandon them when they faced their greatest opponent—death (Lane 1974:429-30)? For Jesus, the argument for the resurrection did not depend upon which books were admitted into the canon of Scripture. The resurrection was not for him a late and therefore dispensable addition to the faith of Israel. The resurrection was inherent in the very character of God. He perceived that belief in the resurrection grows out of the character of God. The God of Abraham, Isaac, Jacob and Jesus is the God of the living.

This was a stunning interpretation of an Old Testament text that was a cornerstone of first-century Judaism. While it did not deny that God promised the land to Abraham's descendants, it did open a much broader vision of the future. The traditional reading, which focused so narrowly on the question of land, did not have much room for other peoples. The Gentiles had to be expelled from the land for those promises to be realized. Jesus had already made his differences with that ideology quite clear, and precisely here in one of the definitive texts of that dogma Jesus opened up a vision of the future that could be large enough to include the nations. His vision was not tied to a piece of real estate that only one people could possess. It was not tied to the hope that Israel would reemerge as a major political and military power. His vision was inclusive, and nothing in his teaching in Mark supports the idea that the nations would be subjugated to Israel.

Does the resurrection replace the land as the focal point for the future? And if it does not, how are the two ideas related? Mark leaves these two questions unresolved at this point. He has, however, given us an important clue and invited us to pursue it. In the previous controversy the Pharisees hypocritically said that Jesus taught the way of God in accordance with the truth (12:14). Despite their hypocrisy they were right. That is a form of irony that appears increasingly in the second half of Mark. Unfounded accusations, hypocritical testimony and the mockery to which Jesus was subjected often unintentionally contained a great deal of truth. In the final analysis even hypocrisy and unfaithfulness may confirm the sovereignty of God.

The Greatest Commandment (12:28-34) Festo Kivengere was the archbishop of Uganda during the awful days of Idi Amin. Idi Amin was one of the most savage tyrants in recent history. During a brutal reign from 1971 to 1979 the man who claimed to be "Lord of all the beasts of the earth and fishes of the sea" orchestrated the torture and execution of hundreds of thousands of people, many of whom belonged to the Anglican church that Bishop Kivengere led. Before Idi Amin was driven from power, Bishop Kivengere was asked what he would do if he found himself with a loaded gun in the presence of Idi Amin. The bishop replied: "I would hand the gun to the President and say, 'I think this is your weapon. It is not mine. My weapon is love'" (Coomes 1990:397).

The sympathetic scribe who approached Jesus in 12:28 posed what appears to be a much safer question. It does not have the complexity of modern questions about the dynamics of love and oppression, nor was it one more attempt to discredit Jesus in the temple. His question was posed without guile or hypocrisy, and there was no hint of antagonism. This question was not the sort of thing for lesser minds to take up. Some of the great rabbis in Judaism had addressed themselves to this weighty question. To ask this question of Jesus in the temple was to recognize his status as a great teacher.

Even as a friendly question, though, its consequences were far-reaching. At the conclusion of this interchange Jesus stated that this scribe was not far from the kingdom of God, an affirmation that he gave to no one else. Mark adds the tantalizing comment that no one dared to ask him any more questions. Both statements are provocative. They invite Mark's audience to engage in further reflection. What was there about the scribe's answer that brought him close to the kingdom of God, and what was there about this conversation that intimidated Jesus' opponents? Those two questions frame the interpretation of this passage.

Jesus' answer to the scribe has three distinctive features. In the first place it begins not with a commandment, but with a statement of faith, with the foundational creed of Jewish life and thought: *Hear, O Israel, the Lord our God, the Lord is one,* quoting Deuteronomy 6:4. The Shema, so-called from the Hebrew verb to hear, was recited daily in prayer by pious Jews in the first century and is a profound affirmation of God's covenant love and character. The scribe wanted to know what was the single most important thing to do. Jesus, however, did not take conduct as his point of departure. He began with the character of God. His affirmation of this creed grounds the question of conduct in God's love for humans, which is the only appropriate framework for our affections and actions.

Second, when Jesus quoted the commandment that follows the Shema in Deuteronomy 6:5, he specified four ways of loving God: heart, soul, mind and strength. The Hebrew and Greek versions of Deuteronomy 6:5 each contain only three—heart, soul and strength. Jesus added a fourth, mind (dianoia), to create a kind of supertotality. From the affirmation that *God is one* there follows a requirement for an integrity which exceeded that of the erudite people who had tried to trap him. If God is one, there should also be a oneness about each man and woman. Nineteen centuries later Danish philosopher Søren Kierkegaard pursued a similar theme when he penned a reflection on the Beatitudes titled *Purity of Heart Is to Will One Thing*. For Jesus, purity of heart or authenticity, to use a contemporary term, is found in loving God completely.

In a Jewish understanding of human nature it is impossible to make tidy distinctions between heart, soul, mind and strength, yet each of these four terms finds an echo in the charges and countercharges that Mark presents in Jesus' disputations in the temple. The unwillingness of the chief priests, elders and teachers of the law to commit themselves on the question of John's authority (11:33) betrays their divided hearts and strength. The teachers of the law who devour widows' houses and make long prayers (12:38-40) represent another manifestation of the same problem. The hypocrisy of the Pharisees and Herodians (12:13-17) is a matter of the soul, and Jesus had just charged that the Sadducees did not understand either the Scriptures or the power of God. Here then is one explanation for his opponents' failure of nerve. Any further questions might have proven to be self-incriminating. Indeed, there was a twofold risk. On the one hand Jesus' opponents ran the risk of exposing their divided loyalties. On the other hand, if they continued to pose questions that Jesus answered well, they would only heighten his standing before the crowd as one who loved God with his whole being.

The third distinctive feature about Jesus' reply is that it contains not one but two commandments. In addition to Deuteronomy 6:5 Jesus also cited Leviticus 19:18: Love your neighbor as yourself. In his exposition of the greatest commandment it is impossible to love God completely without loving our neighbors in the same way we love ourselves. History is replete with zealous figures who claimed to love God even as they mistreated and oppressed the people who lived near them. The controversies in the temple provide an example from the first century: the teachers of the law who devour widows' houses (12:40). Loving our neighbors as ourselves is an essential part of loving God. Without it people who claim to love God fervently can become an awful, destructive presence in the community of faith.

Several commentators seek to connect this section of Mark's Gospel with the broader injunctions in other parts of the New Testament to love one's enemies. One possibility is to suppose that the term *neighbor* actually includes the broader human family. On balance, though, the word *neighbor* in Leviticus 19:18 refers more narrowly to members of the community of faith and foreigners who may live with them (Edwards 2002:372). No linguistic reason justifies a larger interpretation (France 2002:480). A better approach is suggested by the sympathetic scribe's response in Mark 12:32-33.

The scribe declared that Jesus had spoken truly, and in good rabbinic fashion he restated and amplified Jesus' main points. He affirmed that God is one and added the comment and *there is no other but him,* a statement that reflects the universality of Jesus' declaration in 12:17: "and to God what is God's." If God is truly one and there is no other, then all people, Jews and Gentiles alike, owe their allegiance to the One who is true.

That affirmation, of course, was not new in Jewish thought, but in the context of the temple controversies it offered grounds for leading his critics back to places where they did not want to go. It is only one small step from this affirmation to the question of what belongs to God. What is at stake here is the implications of the Shema. Is it a confession that defines one people against the rest of humankind, or is it a confession that summons one people to live in some sense for the rest of the human race? Isaiah had envisioned Israel as a standard rallying the nations to their true loyalty (Is 11:10). Jesus described the relationship between Israel and the nations as one of service (Mk 10:42-45), and he found the existing practices of the temple to be a catastrophic violation of that relationship (11:17). The disturbing implications of this fundamental confession of God's people provide one more reason that Jesus' opponents did not wish to pursue an open debate with him any further.

The scribe's other amplification in 12:33 ventures even further into uncharted territory. Loving one's neighbor, he affirmed, is more important than all burnt offerings and sacrifices. This statement contains implicit grounds for criticizing worship in the temple, and whether this sympathetic man intended it to serve this function, Jesus pursued the issue a few verses later in his condemnation of the scribes (12:38-40). The implied critique of worship recalls the incident that touched off these controversies: Jesus' cursing the temple. In 11:17 the issue is the inclusion of the nations in the worship of God in the temple. Here the question is the place of love and justice within the covenant community of Israel.

This would certainly have pointed the way toward a discussion the chief priests, elders and scribes would have been loath to reopen, but even more importantly it provides a yardstick for gauging Jesus' statement that this particular scribe was not far from the kingdom of God. To put the matter simply, if the scribe understood so much about the relationship between love, justice and worship within the boundaries of his own community, what did he understand about the other peoples of the world? Could he have affirmed what Jesus had done, or would he have preferred to stop somewhere short to maintain his standing within his particular community? That is, not surprisingly, another matter that Mark leaves unanswered. It is a question on which Jesus' closest disciples might well have faltered at this stage, and it is a question for Mark's audience to ponder. If we love God with all our heart, soul, mind and strength, is there any human being who lives beyond the implications of that love?

David's Lord in the House of God (12:35-44) Two thousand years ago there were many ways to judge a city: the reputation of the gods and goddesses who protected it, its traditions and history, the beauty of its architecture, the wealth it generated, the military might it could muster, the security of its water supply and the defensive position it enjoyed. By any of these measurements Jerusalem was an impressive city, but when Jesus looked at the city he used a different set of criteria. He was naturally concerned about the reputation of the God for whom the temple had been built, and he had already prophesied about one particular item—the place of the nations in the worship of Israel. In his concluding public comments about the city the concern for worship appears again, as well as two other items which are not reflected in the list above—the aspirations of the people and the administration of justice.

Probing the Fabric of the City (12:35-40) As Jesus taught in the temple he turned the tables on his opponents by asking them a pointed question: *How is it that the teachers of the law say that the Christ is the son of David?* The meaning of this question is not apparent to us because the word *son* in Western cultures does not carry all the meaning that it did in Jesus' day. At one level *son of David* means a man who had descended from David, the archetype Israelite king. In accordance with texts like 2 Samuel 7:11-16, which promises that David's line will never be without an heir to his throne, the popular expectation was for the Messiah to be a descendant of David's. Accordingly, *son of David* was a messianic title. Curiously enough, this was one of the few titles that Jesus accepted (Mk 10:46-52). At the very least when Bartimaeus addressed him as the son of David, Jesus did not order him to be silent. The Gospel of Mark, however, makes almost no mention of Jesus' birth, nor does it attempt to prove Jesus' credentials as one of David's heirs. With characteristic irony Mark introduced the idea that Jesus is the son of David as a blind beggar called out for help from the roadside.

In first-century Palestine, however, the word *son* also carried the idea of being secondary or lesser. If the Messiah were the son of David in this sense, he would be a person of secondary or derivative stature. If Jesus had thought of David as the archetype for the Messiah, then Jesus would have viewed the Messiah as the person who came to fulfill the hopes and promise of David's kingdom. The enemies of the Messiah would look like David's enemies. The Messiah would engage them as David had engaged his enemies, and his triumph would look like David's. These are the implications that prompted Jesus' question. It was not the Messiah's line of descent that Jesus called into question. It was the nature of the Messiah's rule. The dilemma Jesus posed for the scribes was this: how could the kingdom of David be the model for the Messiah's rule, if David called the Messiah his lord (12:37)? If the Messiah is David's lord, then the expectations associated with the restoration of David's kingdom might well prove to be an inadequate measure of the messianic kingdom. Put in simplest terms, it is a question whether David's rule is the model within which the Messiah would reign or whether David's kingdom was itself a signpost pointing to a larger and different kind of sovereignty. Would the Messiah fulfill the scribes' expectations or would he exercise his rule according to a different set of values?

Psalm 110, which Jesus used to pose this question, points away from the popular hopes for a messiah, for it goes on to affirm that the lord who stands between David and the psalmist would be a priest forever, in the order of Melchizedek (Ps 110:4). Melchizedek, a name that means king of righteousness, was not an Israelite. He was the Canaanite priest-king of ancient Jerusalem to whom Abram paid a tithe (Gen 14:20). So when Jesus used this psalm to talk about the Messiah, he set in motion two ideas that distinguish the Messiah from David. First, if the Messiah was to be a priest as well as a king, then he would fulfill a role that God had denied to all previous Israelite kings: he would be a priest-king himself. Saul had forfeited his claim and his family's claim to the kingship because he intruded on the role of a priest (1 Sam 15:23). Subsequently, the distinction between priest and king was absolute, as Uzziah found to his horror in 2 Chronicles 26:16-20. Second, if the priest-king to whose order the Messiah belongs was a Gentile, then the implications of his rule far exceed those of a strictly Jewish messiah.

It is difficult to know how far to pursue the implications of Psalm 110:4. Mark does not use this psalm to present a systematic exposition of the nature of the Messiah's rule. He uses it explicitly only to raise a question. Nevertheless, there are some features about the way Psalm 110 is used that invite Mark's audience to draw out the implications of the surrounding controversy stories. That the question about the Messiah's role arose at the turning point in these controversies is one point. Previously Jesus had been the examinee, as the leaders of Jerusalem put him to the test. This pericope brings a shift in roles. This is the place where Jesus became both interrogator and accuser. In the questions and accusations that follow this turning point there are clear echoes of his opponents' shortcomings.

One more question grows out of Jesus' use of Psalm 110: In the temple controversies, who appears as the enemies of the rule of God? Who were the ones God would subdue so that David's Lord could rest his feet on them? In the popular imagination the enemies of the Messiah would be the nations or, more particularly at this time, the Roman Empire. Throughout the Gospel of Mark, however, opposition to the kingdom of God comes not from the Gentiles but from Jewish leaders. So here, too, the people Jesus singled out for the most severe punishment (Mk 12:40) were not Roman governors and generals, but Jewish scribes.

After the exchange between Jesus and the sympathetic scribe (12:28-34), it is surprising to find Jesus denouncing the teachers of the law categorically (12:38-40). Mark has, of course, already implicated the scribes as a group in the plot to do away with Jesus (11:27; 12:12), but the conversation between Jesus and that one scribe went so well that the Evangelist leaves us wondering whether some form of reconciliation might not be possible. There is by now in the Gospel a divine inevitability about the role of the chief priests, elders and scribes in the death of Jesus. Close examination of this passage, though, reveals both another dimension of their estrangement, as well as a path with some potential for reconciliation.

The teachers of the law held fundamental positions in the spiritual, political and economic infrastructures of Jerusalem. They were a part of the city's foundation in ways that modern ministers and religious teachers are not. Jerusalem was not a secular city. The separation of church and state that we take for granted was unimaginable in the first century. Our civil servants and elected officials must be very careful not to step over the line that distinguishes public duties from private religious or moral convictions. In that day, however, civic life worked according to a very different principle. It would have been inconceivable for community leaders not to order public affairs according to their religious traditions. The teachers of the law were the people who interpreted the Word of God, pressed and resolved legal disputes, derived public policy from the Scriptures and oversaw the administration of justice. The roles of spiritual guide, civil servant and lawyer were all incorporated into the activities of this one profession. When Jesus denounced the teachers of the law, he probed the fundamental set of personal, economic and legal relationships that made Jerusalem a city.

Jesus censured the scribes for the things they loved and for their failure to secure justice for widows. They devoured widows' houses, made pretentious prayers, sought out the prominent seats in civil and religious meetings and liked to be recognized in public. The things they liked cannot be reconciled with the two commandments that Jesus and the sympathetic scribe had just discussed: it is impossible to love your neighbors as yourself when you are constantly seeking to put yourself in a position above them. Furthermore, the words *most important seats* and *places of honor* are particularly telling. Both are compounds formed from the Greek word for "first." The teachers of the law, in Jesus' critique, were people who sought to be first rather than last and servant of all (10:45). Their personal agendas also set them against the rule of God. In short, the very ones who were charged with guarding the Word of God were people of divided loyalties who did not love their God with the singular integrity that Deuteronomy 6:4-5 requires.

Equally damning is the practice of devouring widows' houses. It reduces the scribes' prayers to a cultic pretense. Devouring is a term of oppression. What is described in Mark 12:40 is not a few isolated instances in which one or two people trapped in poverty lost their homes, but an entire set of legal practices like foreclosing the mortgages of widows who could not repay loans their husbands had taken out. Jesus viewed these practices as a form of oppression that was enabled and justified by the keepers of the law. It was perfectly legal, and it was systemic. Devouring widows' homes was embedded in the economic fabric of the social order.

Of particular interest is the combination of personal sin and systemic evil. Typically, we think of personal sins as a discrete category of wrongdoing, and if we confess our sin when we worship God, personal transgressions are the things we specify. In Jesus' denunciation of the scribes, however, personal sin was inseparably connected to social evil. In failing to love God with all their heart, soul, mind and strength, the scribes had created a platform for oppression. In this Gospel faithful love of God is inseparable from faithful love for one's neighbors. It is the foundation for social justice.

True piety also requires the love of justice. To love God is to do more than create a level playing field, where everyone starts with an equal opportunity. The most gifted and cunning have a permanent advantage. If their love of God is mingled with the love of success and social prominence, then the emergence of disenfranchised people is inevitable. To love justice is to make the commitment that there will be no disenfranchised underclass. A lack of concern for justice demonstrates a failure to love our neighbors as ourselves, and it is a sign that our love of God is fatally flawed.

Finally, the teachers of the law were stewards of the social imagination, just as they were supposed to be stewards of justice. The scribes were the people Jesus blamed for the idea that the rule of the Messiah would follow the pattern of David's rule. Their interpretation of the Psalms and Prophets shaped public expectations about the Messiah, and the flaw that turned piety into pretense also subverted their vision of the future. That flaw was the quest for a cozy position of dominance. The privileged seats that their oppression of the poor made possible are mirrored in the hope that Israel would subdue the nations. Like their administration of the laws of the day, their vision of the future was grounded in the pursuit of power and privilege. Jesus' condemnation of the scribes is not an abrupt departure from his probing question about the nature of the messianic kingdom. It is an extension of that critique. There was a profound link between their hope for Israel's future and the oppression of their own people.

Jesus' denunciation of the scribes was not formulated to win any friends from that quarter. He did not cajole, coax or extend an olive branch, and there is nothing to indicate that he sought to reduce the tension. His comments have the conciliatory tone of a cannon shot fired across the bow of an opposing ship. And yet the possibility of a change of heart was not withdrawn. The path that brought the sympathetic scribe near the kingdom of God was still open to all the scribes, but it required repentance. It required a turning away from the social prominence they sought and a turning toward God with an undivided love. Ultimately, the arguments that seem to focus on Jesus were not simply about him. The telling point was the meaning of the Shema, the oneness of God and the oneness required of those who claim to love God. This was a conflict about the covenant.

The Widow's Offering (12:41-44) Generations of children have learned about the widow's two coins in Sunday school, where it is still a staple in the endeavor to teach them about giving. I remember wondering as a child whether it was really necessary to give the whole quarter that was in my pocket, or whether it might be more prudent to come back the following Sunday with change. Adults are naturally more calculating. After all, besides what we give to God we have to account for food, clothing, housing, home insurance, transportation, car insurance, education, medical insurance, community causes, vacation, life insurance, retirement, entertainment and, of course, taxes. The most calculating question of all, though, is this one: was it wise for the widow to put into the temple treasury all that she had?

She put in two copper coins that might have been enough to sustain her for another few days. Mark contrasts her gift with the contributions of the many wealthy people who gave large gifts from their abundance. They could afford to make generous gifts. Their generosity was predicated on something the widow did not have—affluence. She, on the other hand, gave what she could not afford. Seated across the way, Jesus observed the unfolding scene and commented: *But she, out of her poverty, put in everything—all she had to live on.*

How is it possible that the widow's offering was greater than any other gift? Certainly on a monetary scale the contributions of the wealthy people would count for much more than her two coins. Jesus' observation makes sense only if he were using a different scale entirely, and the scale he used brings to mind two previous moments in the controversy stories. One is the debate with the Pharisees and Herodians (12:17) about what belongs to God. In offering all she had to live on, the widow was giving herself to God. She bore God's image, and in the language of the parable that brought that argument to an end she gave what belonged to God. Her story also reminds us of the discussion of the greatest commandment (12:28-34). The widow's gift demonstrates her undivided love for God, and so it is also greater than whole burnt offerings and sacrifices. Unlike the scribes whose hypocrisy Jesus had just denounced, this disenfranchised woman worshiped authentically. If the proper worship of God comes from people like her, then the system that has disenfranchised her stands condemned.

Set against this touching picture of worship is the widow's prospects for the future. Her outlook is bleak. The most distressing aspect of her plight is the thought that the wheels of justice were set in motion against her, for if the keepers of the law devoured widows' houses, then the poor were trapped in poverty. Things could only get worse. Alms from the temple may have kept the poor from starving, but charity then as now did not provide a way out of poverty. All too often charity serves to sustain poverty. It makes it a bit more tolerable. This story ends on a very disturbing note. The widow had given her life to God, but there was precious little hope for her within the system of law and temple upon which the city of Jerusalem was built.

The Sadducees' hope (12:18-27) offered little comfort to her. They saw the great hope of Israel as the continuing survival of the nation based on the law of Moses. The description of this woman as a poor widow, however, suggests that there was no family member who could provide for her. If that were so, then the most she could have hoped for was the survival of a permanent underclass. This is the point at which Jesus' critique of the Sadducees has particular poignancy. They did not, Jesus asserted, understand either the Scriptures or the power of God. Certainly the resurrection holds out a hope for the poor that goes far beyond what the Sadducees could offer. Yet even beyond that great hope, the power of God was already at work in history to create a new set of relationships in which those who gave things up in true worship are bound together by a renewed sense of justice and love (10:29-31). His was a vision for all of life that went far beyond what we typically mean by charity. For Jesus, justice and charity meet in a radical commitment to do the will of God.

A Prophecy About the Temple (13:1-37) The temple in Jerusalem was a spectacular construction project. This enormous building project was begun by Herod the Great, and the last structures on the complex were completed just a few years before Jerusalem was sacked in A.D. 70. Its first stage was the placement of enormous blocks of stone to fill in a valley and create a plaza where thousands of people could assemble for worship. The temple itself was a palatial building, which Josephus claims was covered in gold plate. His description is disputed, but after Jerusalem was plundered the price of gold throughout the province of Syria reportedly dropped by 50 percent (Jeremias 1975:23-24).

It is sometimes called Herod's Temple because King Herod the Great underwrote the cost of construction. His ruthless use of power is remembered in Matthew's account of the slaughter of the children, and even as the temple was being built Herod's financing of it was a source of controversy. The moral failings of Herod the Great, however, do not figure in Jesus' condemnation of the temple. Building on earlier prophecies found in Jeremiah 7:12-14 and Isaiah 5:1-7; 56:7, Jesus had denounced the temple as a den of thieves who robbed God of the worship of the nations.

Magnificent Buildings (13:1-4) It is no wonder that the unnamed disciple was so impressed by the buildings. Perhaps it is not going too far to say that he was awestruck. Yet his misplaced sense of wonder indicates that he had failed to comprehend what Jesus had done when he stopped people from carrying anything through the temple (11:16). This outburst of religious enthusiasm became the occasion for Jesus to state unambiguously the meaning of what he had done: *Not one stone here will be left on another; every one will be thrown down* (13:2).

Jesus' tone is predominantly pastoral. His teaching is punctuated by a series of warnings: "be on your guard" (13:9, 23, 33) and "watch" (13:5, 34, 37). There are words of encouragement as well: "Do not worry beforehand about what to say. Just say whatever is given you at the time" (13:11). As well as several reassurances that God is in control (13:19-20, 34-36) and the promise that Jesus has told the disciples everything before it happens (13:23). On the whole, Jesus seems to have been more interested in preparing his disciples for the future than he was in predicting it.

Jesus' statement put an abrupt end to any euphoria about the beauty of the temple. But later as he sat on the Mount of Olives in sight of the temple, the first four disciples he had called asked him about the prophecy privately. There are really three issues tied up together here. The first one is: *When will these things happen?* The term *these things* refers to the destruction of the temple stone by stone.

In the minds of these men the destruction of the temple was an event of such cataclysmic proportions that it would lead to the end of history and the beginning of a new age—the messianic age. The second question reveals their curiosity about the end of the age: *And what will be the sign that they are all about to be fulfilled?* This question actually has two components. The words *all about to be fulfilled* refer to events which might accompany the destruction of the temple and inaugurate the new age. A similar expression is found in Daniel 12:6. The request for a sign, however, points to a different event, something that would indicate when the end of the world, as they knew it, was about to come upon them. The key to understanding this passage is to keep these three issues in mind: the destruction of the temple, the end of the age and the sign accompanying the end. This prophecy is an answer to these questions, and as we work through Mark 13:5-37, we will try to discover where and how they are answered.

This is a long and complex prophecy, and it will be helpful to divide it into smaller sections. Clues to the structure of this material are found in the repetition of warning phrases like "watch out" (13:5), "be on your guard" (13:9), "so be on your guard" (13:23) and "learn this lesson" (13:28); in summarizing statements like "these are the beginning of birth pains" (13:8) and "I have told you everything ahead of time" (13:23); and in thematic statements like "the gospel must first be preached to all nations" (13:10), "when you see the abomination that causes desolation standing where it does not belong" (13:14), and "at that time men will see the Son of Man coming in clouds" (13:26). Using clues like these, we may break the text into six units: 13:5-8; 13:9-13; 13:14-23; 13:24-27; 13:28-31; and 13:32-37. These are not discreet, sequential units, and there is a considerable amount of overlapping material from section to section. In some cases the same events are looked at from different perspectives. The structure of this prophecy is dictated by Jesus' pastoral concern rather than by an interest in precise chronology.

Watch Out for Yourselves (13:5-8) Occasionally Jesus answers a question that has not been asked. That appears to be true here. The disciples wanted to know the details about the destruction of the temple and the end of history. Instead, Jesus told them to be concerned about themselves, to take care that they were not led astray by people pretending to be him: *Many will come in my name, claiming, "I am he," and will deceive many.* That was not a comforting beginning. Its unstated assumption is that Jesus would be absent for a considerable period of time. During that time there would be wars, earthquakes and famines. These are the kind of events that might lead apocalyptic enthusiasts to believe that the end of all things had come upon them. The pretenders would apparently be convincing, for many people would be deceived.

What might this deception look like? There are two possibilities, depending on how the phrases *in my name* and *I am he* are understood. *In my name* can be understood either as a title like Messiah or more literally as the name *Jesus.* And the phrase translated *I am he* could also be translated "it is I." One possibility then is that people would appear with the announcement "I am he," claiming to be the Messiah themselves. The other possibility is that people would appear saying, "it is I," claiming to be Jesus. The difference is considerable. It is a "question" of whether Jesus was warning his followers against the appearance of false messiahs or against the appearance of people who claimed that they were actually Jesus returning after a prolonged absence.

It is difficult to know for certain which of the two possibilities is intended because this Gospel provides material that can be used to support either interpretation. The argument for messianic pretenders is supported, for example, by Jesus' affirmation that "I tell you the truth, anyone who gives you a cup of water in my name because you belong to Christ will certainly not lose his reward" (9:41), which posits a close association between the title *Christ* and the phrase *in my name.* Second, Mark contains no unambiguous reference to the return of Jesus, although 2:20 may allude to it, and in this Gospel the only picture of the relationship between Jesus and his followers after the resurrection is the image of a shepherd leading his flock (14:27-28; 16:7). That picture offers a different kind of comfort than the parousia. Third, since the term birth pains occurs often in apocalyptic literature in connection with messianic expectations, its appearance in 13:8 might indicate that Jesus was concerned about messianic pretenders throughout this discourse.

On the other hand, *birth pains* also appears in prophetic literature without any particular reference to messianic expectations. It is, for instance, part of the Day of the Lord motif in Isaiah 13:6-8. Second, with the one exception of Mark 14:62 Jesus' acceptance of the title Messiah was indirect at best, and even the affirmation in 14:62 occurs in his condemnation before the Sanhedrin, a public setting that would have confounded popular messianic hopes. It would be curious to find it used so forthrightly here. Furthermore, when Jesus referred explicitly to false messiahs in 13:21-22, the phrase *in my name* does not appear. There are two precedents for identifying someone who has already died with another person who appears on the scene later. According to 8:28 some people thought Jesus was John the Baptist returned from beyond the grave with miraculous powers. And in 9:13 Jesus affirmed that Elijah had already returned in a veiled reference to John the Baptist. Within the conceptual horizon of this Gospel it is certainly feasible that some later figure might claim to be Jesus.

Finally, the textual evidence in Mark for "I am he" or "it is I" is indecisive. The Greek expression behind them is a common one, and Mark uses it in both senses. A good case can be made for "I am he" on the basis of 14:62, just as a good case can be made for "it is I" on the basis of 6:50. There is no clear resolution. The most that can be said with certainty is that the Jesus the disciples had known would not be physically present when the events described in 13:5-8 transpired. Yet a further implication is that those who remained true to their calling would expect to see him again in some way and that expectation would make them vulnerable to imposters.

What is clear is the threat that the pretenders would pose. To embrace one of them would lead to the conclusion that the end of all things had arrived, and to accept that conclusion would lead Jesus' followers away from their mission. Their task was neither to escape into apocalyptic fervor nor to become passive observers of the final events of this age. Their calling was to be faithful witnesses to Jesus and the reign of God throughout the difficult series of events by which God would bring something new into being. And this would not be a brief, sudden process. Jesus' statement these are the *beginning of birth pains* indicates a longer period of time.

Wars, rumors about war, earthquakes and famines signify only the beginning of the end. These events are governed by two overriding considerations: they do not signify the end of history, and there is a divine necessity about them. They must take place because it is God's will for them to happen. The Greek verb translated *must* also appears in the first prediction of Jesus' passion (8:31) and later in this prophecy (13:10). In both cases the context for the things that must happen is suffering, conflict and confusion. So here Jesus spoke pastorally to his followers. These are words of assurance. He affirmed that God had ordered time, and he set the stage for them to understand that God would be working purposefully through their sufferings in the same way that God was at work in his own suffering.

In the centuries that have passed since Jesus spoke these words, there have been wars, earthquakes, famines, false messiahs and even a few who claimed to be Jesus. The assurance that God orders history has been a marvelous comfort to the church through the ages. From time to time pretenders still appear, but today the church faces a new type of uncertainty: the challenge posed by the postmodern world. Today the threat does not simply come from those who claim that the Messiah has finally arrived. Some voices within the church argue that Jesus is not the only Savior. Either claim can be profoundly disturbing. Yet Jesus has not abandoned the church, nor has God left us to our own devices. Jesus' words of assurance are still trustworthy. In spite of these unsettling developments, God continues to order the events of history. We should understand these things as another component of the events that must take place. Neither the end of the church nor the end of the world has arrived. Events like these are part of the birth pains, and God is still acting in history for the salvation of the world.

Preach the Gospel First (13:9-13) Jesus issues a second exhortation to be alert. The opening of 13:9 is almost identical to that of 13:5, with one exception. In 13:9 Jesus tells his disciples to watch out for themselves. In this case it would not be a pretender who posed a threat to them. This would be a threat of a different kind. The problem addressed in 13:9-13 is not the possibility that Jesus' followers would be misled, but that they would fall away under persecution. In the context of floggings and trials the words be on your guard might convey something like get a good lawyer or beware of people trying to entrap you. Yet there is nothing in Jesus' comments to indicate that the disciples should attempt to avoid any of the things described in 13:9-11. On the contrary, they should expect to be treated this way. The disciples would be handed over, and this is the same kind of language that has been used about Jesus. The verb *handed over* is a distinctive component among the ideas of this Gospel. Throughout Mark 14—15 the same Greek verb is translated "handed over," "arrested," "betrayed" and "delivered." This one verb describes the entire course of Jesus' arrest and trial. Like Jesus, then, the disciples are to be arrested, perhaps even betrayed to councils and synagogues and handed over to stand trial before governors and kings. Jesus' prediction about his disciples is very similar to what he had predicted about his own death (10:33-34). The prophecy's second warning is a vivid extension of the words by which Jesus originally invited these four men to become his disciples: "Come, follow me" (1:17).

Suffering for his sake is the fundamental component of Jesus' teaching that the disciples had yet to grasp. Their lack of understanding was precisely why they must be on their guard. The course of events that they expected to accompany the destruction of the temple was not going to transpire. There would be no immediate vindication of the sacrifices they had already made to follow Jesus. Instead, more would be asked of them, even to the point of giving up their lives. That is implicit in the statement he who stands firm to the end will be saved. The end in this case means the end of their lives. This paradoxical remark is another affirmation of the radical idea that Jesus first declared in 8:35: "Whoever loses his life for me and for the gospel will save it."

In the cataclysmic days to come there would be many other paths to choose instead of the one that Jesus and John the Baptist had taken. Messianic pretenders would appear to proclaim other ways to save Judea and themselves. There would possibly be periods of discouragement and disillusionment like the one John the Baptist faced in Matthew 11:2-3. For these reasons Jesus told his disciples to pay attention to themselves. They needed to accept the implications of Jesus' death and follow him resolutely.

What was ultimately at stake was not only the way they saw themselves but also the way they perceived God acting in history. Their suffering would serve a purpose. It would be the way in which the gospel was proclaimed to the nations. In the appearances before synagogues and councils and in the trials before governors and kings, the gospel would be preached and God's purpose would be worked out. What would appear to be trials before imperial magistrates would actually be something else. They would be evangelistic events. The trials were to be preaching events where the good news would be proclaimed to people of power.

The proclamation of the gospel is the essential thing. The word *first* should be understood as a declaration of priority rather than chronology. Preaching the gospel is more important than securing one's own safety, which is the normal human response to danger. To interpret Mark 13:10 as implying "first before the end of all things" falters on the evidence of 13:32, where Jesus stated: "No one knows about that day or hour . . . only the Father." It is one thing for Jesus to say, *The end is still to come* (13:7). That is a pastoral comment that does not imply a particular sequence of events that must transpire before the end of the age. To construe the word *first* in 13:10 as a statement about time, however, is to establish a chronology, something that contradicts Jesus' statement that he did not know when the end of history would come. As with 13:5-8, the primary purpose of this section is pastoral and parenetic.

This is the context in which we are to understand that the Holy Spirit would give the disciples the words to say when they were placed on trial. It would make no sense to suppose that the Spirit of God was giving them the keys for their legal defense. Preserving their lives was not the point. The point was the proclamation of the gospel. At the moment when it might appear that God had left them on their own, they were

---

13:11 The NIV's translation *beforehand* for *en ekeinē tē hōra* obscures the connection

not to worry. Jesus offered the assurance that the Holy Spirit would inspire their proclamation of the gospel as their lives hung in the balance. Is it possible to discover anything more about the substance of their proclamation? The apostles would, of course, preach the gospel. The basic meaning of the word *gospel* in this document is stated in 1:15: "The kingdom of God is near." This early statement is the only summary of Jesus' preaching that Mark provides, so it constitutes the one certain point of reference for understanding what the gospel is. Furthermore, it is characteristic of Mark that when the good news about the reign of God is proclaimed there is conflict. This conflict emerges very early in Jesus' ministry, and as it escalates Jesus' death becomes the goal of his opponents. The source of this conflict is the competing loyalties that Jesus' preaching creates. The claim that the kingdom of God makes upon people surpasses any other allegiance, even to the point of establishing a new sense of family (3:31-35). It is not surprising then that the proclamation of the gospel would create the kind of severe distress in the family that 13:12 describes: brother betraying brother, fathers betraying children, and children betraying their parents. It is the kind of conflict to be expected when the family is redefined around a new center, and it is the counterpoint to the family members whom the disciples have left for the sake of the gospel (10:29).

It is unlikely that the proclamation of Jesus as Messiah would provoke the hostility described in 13:13. There is nothing in 13:21-22, where the idea of messianic pretenders appears again, to indicate that someone could incite such animosity by claiming to be the Messiah. A much more likely candidate is the title *Lord.* It has already appeared in some of the miracle and controversy stories. Most notably, Jesus introduced *Lord* in the dispute about the Sabbath (2:28), where it constitutes one of the boldest assertions of his authority. It is also the title that Jesus raised before the temple crowd in his parable about David (12:35-37). The lordship of Jesus was a cornerstone of the early church's preaching, and from Acts 7:59 onward it is associated with hostility toward Jesus' followers. It is entirely consistent with this text to

---

to other periods of testing and judgment when the same word is translated *hour.*

conclude that the theme of Jesus' lordship is intended to be a component of the apostolic preaching before the imperial powers.

There would be more at stake in these trials than we typically associate with evangelism. We usually think of evangelism in strictly individual terms: passing out tracts, inviting friends to evangelistic services or sharing our personal faith. The proclamation of the lordship of Jesus and the kingdom of God, however, assume stunning proportions when they are expounded before the centers of power. These trials of the disciples were to be confrontations about the nature of authority. Evangelism here is not simply a matter of personal faith. In the apostolic preaching the authority of Jesus as lord and the claims of the kingdom of God confront the power and authority of Jewish culture and the Roman Empire. This kind of confrontation can have only one purpose—to summon the political powers to acknowledge the authority of Jesus and align themselves with the kingdom of God. Consequently, preaching the gospel before the representatives of Rome is nothing less than kingdom rising up against kingdom. As Mark 13:13 makes clear, the disciples are to pursue this confrontation with the ruling powers to the end.

One other implication may be drawn from this material. The word *end* appears in 13:13 for the second time in this prophecy. Earlier in 13:7 it referred to the end of history. In this case, however, it follows immediately on the warning that children would have their parents put to death. The end to which 13:13 refers is the end of one's life. What does the juxtaposition of these two ends suggest? It implies that the disciples would carry out their mission and die before the end of history arrived. Otherwise, the exhortation to persevere to the end of their lives would make little sense. This is then the second time within the opening sections of his prophecy that Jesus distinguishes his teaching from the apocalyptic expectations of his own followers.

In sum, Jesus' concern for the way his followers conducted themselves was paramount. They were not to be led astray by people who appeared to announce that the end had come. They were not to be misled by concerns for their own safety. Their lives were to serve a larger purpose. He wanted them to stay on task. They were to persevere when their hope for glory brought them into court. They were to stand firm to the point of death as faithful witnesses to a person and message they were just beginning to understand.

The Abomination That Causes Desolation (13:14-23) Neither Jesus nor Mark was the first to use the term *abomination that causes desolation*. Virtually identical language appears in Daniel 9:27 and 11:31. In simple terms an *abomination that causes desolation* is an act of sacrilege that results in widespread destruction. The two passages in Daniel refer to the slaughter of a pig on the altar in the temple at the order of Antiochus IV Epiphanes in 165/164 B.C. That inflammatory act led to the Maccabean Revolution, the expulsion of the Syrians and the first independent Jewish state after the exile. When the term reappears in this prophecy, it strikes an ominous note.

There is, however, one important change in the language of Mark 13. This abomination that causes desolation is followed by a mismatched word. The Greek participle translated *standing* is masculine, while the word *abomination* is neuter. In English, of course, this distinction is lost. Most English Bibles ignore it, as though it were simply a grammatical mistake. That is the sort of judgment that comes from treating a text as primarily a written communication. This Gospel and this prophecy, on the other hand, were intended as oral communication. The effect of mismatched words that are heard is harder to ignore. It is striking to hear one word when we expect to hear another.

Consider, for example, the dramatic impact of former First Lady Barbara Bush's commencement speech at Wellesley College on June 1, 1990. Wellesley College is a prestigious liberal arts college for women, and her invitation to address the Wellesley graduates was controversial. In 1947 the First Lady had dropped out of college to marry George H. W. Bush, foregoing the opportunity to have a career outside the home. The audience Mrs. Bush faced that day was full of young women who were making very different choices about the courses of their lives. Barbara Bush silenced her critics when she closed her speech with these words: "Who knows? Somewhere out in this audience may even be someone who will one day follow in my footsteps, and preside over the White House as the President's spouse. I wish him well!" (Bush 1990).

The First Lady's use of *him* instead of *her* created a memorable moment. Mark 13:14 creates a memorable warning when a masculine word appears where it is not expected. A better translation of 13:14

would begin this way: "When you see 'the abomination that causes desolation' standing where he does not belong." The distinction between *he* and *it* is critical. *He* points us in an entirely different direction than *it* does.

There are no mismatched words in the passages in Daniel. That abomination is clearly a thing—the slaughter of a pig in the temple. Mark's use of *he* instead of *it*, then, suggests that this abomination has to do primarily with a person. Furthermore, the destruction of the temple is the immediate background for this prophecy, and the borrowed language about an abomination that causes desolation indicates that Jesus' warning has specifically to do with the temple once again. The desolating sacrilege to which Mark 13:14 refers then is most probably a person whose appearance or presence in the temple resulted in widespread destruction.

The abomination that causes desolation might have been the appearance of the antichrist (Edwards 2002:399), the image of a god or deified ruler erected in the temple (Gundry 1993:741), the standards of the Roman army displayed in the temple as soldiers offered mock sacrifices (Hooker 1991:314), and the illegitimate investiture of Phanni by the Zealots as high priest shortly before the sack of Jerusalem (Lane 1974:469). On balance, the most likely candidate to have fulfilled this prophecy is Phanni. The other proposals are more problematic.

In the first place, Mark does not look for the appearance of a single antichrist, but for several false messiahs. Neither in this prophecy nor anywhere else in this Gospel does Mark give any indication that he was concerned about the appearance of a single antichrist. Furthermore, the imagery Jesus evoked is so closely connected with Daniel 9:27 and 11:31 that it implies another act of sacrilege in the temple. The temple that Herod built is the background for this prophecy, and it is the most likely place where the abomination would appear, to stand

---

13:14 The NIV to its credit preserves the masculine pronoun *he* in a footnote. It does not, however, pay enough attention to the oral nature of this Gospel. That the Gospel of Mark was intended to be read aloud in worship is underscored by the editorial insertion *let the reader understand*, where the reader is a member of the early Christian community who read the text out loud. The reader was charged to tell the

where it ought not to be. Finally, both the possible placement of a statue in the temple and the parading of Roman standards in the temple courts are things. Either could properly be referred to by the pronoun *it*. The investiture of Phanni, on the other hand, was an event that was centered on a person.

What is the scope of the destruction that follows the abomination that causes desolation? Occasionally this passage is called "The Great Tribulation," a title in which some interpreters find a link to the end of history. The four men to whom Jesus gave this prophecy may well have thought that another act of sacrilege in the temple would presage the end of the world, but the abomination described in Daniel refers to an event well before the end of history. It is not obvious that Mark 13:14-23 should be taken as a sign of the end of all things.

Much of the description of the ensuing destruction points directly to events of local rather than global significance. The concluding part of 13:14, let those who are in Judea flee to the mountains, and the opening of 13:18, pray that this will not take place in winter, make little sense unless the distressing events take place in Judea. Even the ominous language of 13:19-20 recalls events in Israel's past. It has a well-attested background in prophetic literature, often in prophecies against Judah and Jerusalem: "How awful that day will be! None will be like it" (Jer 30:7); "it is close at hand—a day of darkness and gloom . . . such as never was of old nor ever will be in ages to come" (Joel 2:1-2). The idea of an act of judgment that would be unlike anything that had ever been or ever will be is an established motif in the prophetic concept of the Day of the Lord. Furthermore, these two prophecies about the Day of the Lord declare that God's ultimate purpose is not utter destruction, but salvation. Even the assurance given in Mark 13:20—"but for the sake of the elect . . . he has shortened them—fits the pattern."

---

story about Jesus, to read the signs of the times and to warn the community when it was time to flee.

13:15-17 The summons to flee when the moment comes is given to both men and women, a feature of the prophecy that corresponds well with Mark's concern to include women in the rest of the Gospel (see 5:34; 10:6-12; 15:40-41).

What are we to make of language like this? Is it simply hyperbole, or does it make an substantive contribution to the judgment that these prophecies announce? On the one hand, poetry is often a component of prophecy, and hyperbole is a common poetic device. So the possibility that statements like these are poetic exaggeration cannot be summarily dismissed. On the other hand, though, these words suggest a very striking idea. The key to recognizing it is the broad historical context of the prophecies. Jeremiah and Joel predicted the imminent destruction of Judah and Jerusalem at a time when the northern kingdom of Israel had already been destroyed by the armies of Assyria. After Judah and Jerusalem were destroyed there would be no nation or temple devoted to the worship of the God of Israel. It was an unprecedented event for Yahweh to destroy the land and people who had built the sanctuary where the glory of the Lord dwelled. Not only was it unprecedented, except for the prophets it was unthinkable. There never had been nor would be another day like it.

An allusion to a third Old Testament text, Daniel 12:1, is often seen here as well: "At that time Michael, the great prince who protects your people, will arise. There will be a time of distress such as has not happened from the beginning of nations until then." There are obvious similarities in the description of the time of distress, but Daniel 12:1 is a much more problematic passage. This is clearly apocalyptic rather than prophetic literature. Rather than being connected with the prophetic Day of the Lord, this time of distress is associated with apocalyptic themes such as the resurrection of the dead and the archangel Michael, who is the great prince and protector of the people of Israel. The deliverance promised at the end of Daniel 12:1 is salvation through resurrection, a prominent theme in Daniel 12:2, not the end of a period of distress during which the present age would continue.

The distinguishing feature of Daniel 12 is the role of the archangel Michael, for if Michael the protector arises (Dan 12:1) and "the power of the holy people" is destroyed (Dan 12:7), then what does Michael rise to do? It appears that Michael stands up not to protect his people from distress, but to inflict it upon them. That too would be an unprecedented event. In apocalyptic literature the angelic protectors of nations are sometimes absent and so leave their people open to persecution. Except for this text, though, there is no hint of an angelic protector ever turning against the people assigned to his care.

To summarize, the ominous language of Mark 13:19 is not without precedent. Jeremiah, Joel and Daniel use similar language to describe catastrophic events that were of local rather than universal significance. The distress that those books prophesy is not to be measured solely in terms of physical suffering. The events to which those prophecies point were not unique because more people were killed, taken into slavery or left destitute than at any other time in history. The grief and hardship that accompanied the first destruction of Jerusalem were undeniably awful, but what made that suffering unprecedented was its spiritual component. The nation that God had created out of love and faithfulness was no longer a historical entity. The temple was a pile of rubble. There was no house in which the name of the Lord could dwell, nor was there a place for priests to offer sacrifices for sin. It was not the defeat of Yahweh by the gods of Babylon that had brought this disaster upon the people of Judah. The people of Israel had turned their backs on the God of the covenant, and the Lord of hosts had turned against the people of Israel.

In light of these texts, what can be said about the days of distress described in 13:19? What makes the period of tribulation in Jesus' prophecy unique? The explanation lies in recognizing the role that the people of Judah and Jerusalem played in prophetic schemes of history. They were the remnant, the people who were to be purified by their suffering under the previous act of judgment. As a righteous remnant, they were to be the people who offered God an acceptable worship. Yet the controversy stories of Mark 11—12 indicate that the worship offered to God in the temple was not acceptable. The opposition to the rule of God that first surfaced in Galilee was entrenched in the structures of Jerusalem. John the Baptist had been executed, and Jesus was about to be crucified. God's messengers had been received with contempt, and the temple would be destroyed again.

If it was unprecedented for God to destroy the land and people of Judah in 587 B.C., what words could describe an act of judgment against this remnant? It, too, would be an act without parallel. It makes perfectly good sense to understand this text as an extension of the prophetic Day of the Lord. The supposed tension between the universal and local motifs disappears. Mark 13:14-23 is not a prophecy about a global conflagration. The scope of this text is clearly fixed upon Judah and Jerusalem. Furthermore, 13:20 is perfectly consistent with this line of interpretation. If God has turned against the remnant that was supposed to be righteous, who could be saved?

Mark 13:20-23 contains two important reassurances for the elect. Not only has God shortened the period of destruction for their sake. Jesus also warned them ahead of time against false prophets and messiahs who would try to deceive even the elect. As the interjection *if that were possible* indicates, however, God will not allow them to be led astray. Even so, these are surely two of the more curious affirmations in the entire Gospel. To put the matter simply, why would the elect need to be spared? A popular Christian belief regards salvation as a kind of insurance against the fires of hell. If that were what concerned Jesus in 13:20, we might well wonder why God would want to shorten the days. After all, once the elect had died their insurance would become effective and they would be received into heaven. Furthermore, we may conclude from 13:10 that some of the elect would actually die as witnesses to the gospel. So if neither the prospect of death nor one's reception into heaven is the issue, what is the point of God's limiting the time of distress?

Two observations are in order here. First, from the opening pages of this Gospel there has been a tension between calling or election and salvation. Jesus called Peter, Andrew, James and John (1:16-20). Presumably, they are to be numbered among the elect. Yet Jesus spoke to Peter as if he were Satan (8:33), and he warned John with the other eleven against a sin they may well have committed that might have led them to hell (9:38-50). Even if one takes the position that Jesus was speaking in hyperbole, the fact remains that it was extraordinarily difficult for the apostles to come to terms with the depth of their own sin and the full implications of the gospel. Salvation in this Gospel carries the sense of being made whole as well as the idea of deliverance, and Jesus' followers are made whole as the gospel they hear reshapes their lives.

13:20 Both the English words *elect* and *chosen* derive from the same Greek word,

Second, salvation in Mark is both personal and corporate. The corporate dimension appears early in the table fellowship of sinners (2:13-17), the calling together of a new nation or people (3:13-21) and the creation of a new family (3:31-35). These themes recur with some frequency, notably in the discussion of leaving one's family (10:24-31), the image of a new flock that the risen shepherd will lead (14:27-28) and the description of the women who served the crucified Jesus (15:40—16:2). The gospel creates a new community of people. It is consistent, then, with the theological distinctives of Mark to see the same two themes at work in the foreshortened time of affliction. God has limited the days of distress to create a period within history so that the people whom God has chosen may be transformed by the gospel and shaped into a new community.

Both themes are reflected in the description of the time following the days of unparalleled distress. That would be a time of testing and sorting out. False prophets and messianic pretenders would appear, and in this context it is most likely that they would proclaim that God would save Jerusalem in a fruitless attempt to rally the inhabitants of Judah to its defense. Jesus indicated that the pretenders would be extremely persuasive. They would produce signs and wonders in support of their claims to induce even the elect, who should know better, to stay and aid their cause. Jerusalem, though, was not to be saved this time. The followers of Jesus were not to be deceived by these claims. His followers were not to give their lives in the hopeless defense of a lost cause. They were to commit themselves to the proclamation of the gospel. In this time, the hopes and dreams of the elect would be tested and refined in a manner not unlike what the original disciples experienced during Jesus' earthly ministry.

Moreover, throughout 13:20-23 the elect are treated collectively. Every time the English word *elect* appears here, the Greek word it translates is plural. And the term is used absolutely. There are no qualifying adjectives or indefinite pronouns. It is not a question of some of the elect being led astray. The messianic pretenders do not arise to entice a few individuals away. The threat would be extended to all. The

eklegō, "to choose."

elect appear in these verses as a group. The false Christs and false prophets would be a threat to a community that looked for the return of its Savior and the culmination of its salvation.

The reassurance Jesus offered in 13:20-23 makes most sense if the elect are understood as a community of people who are still being gathered and formed. For Mark salvation and survival are not the same things. Those whom Jesus called and all those who wish to follow him are expected to give up their lives for his sake and the gospel's, a point that is clearly underscored in 13:13. Accordingly, the shortening of the period of tribulation points back to the overriding priority of this prophecy—the proclamation of the gospel to all the nations. That is to say, if the days of distress had not been shortened, the gospel would have been silenced, its witnesses killed or muzzled. Because of the elect, whom God chose, however, the gospel could not be silenced.

It is virtually impossible to overstate the impact that the impending destruction of Jerusalem would have. For hundreds of years the well-being of this city had been the focal point of Jewish hope. The disciple who exclaimed, "What massive stones! What magnificent buildings!" expressed the popular confidence of the community God had gathered to repopulate Galilee and Judea after the destruction of Jerusalem in 587/586 B.C. Yet once again Jerusalem was about to be destroyed, and Jesus' prophecy contains no hint that the city would be rebuilt. Not long before the armies of Babylon destroyed Jerusalem, the prophet Jeremiah bought land as a gesture of confidence that the remnant of Judah would be restored to the land (Jer 32:7). There is nothing comparable in Jesus' ministry. The reordering of faith that the second destruction of Jerusalem would entail would be unlike anything that had happened before. The only reassurance Jesus offered had nothing to do with the hope of a restored Jerusalem. It is grounded in the sovereignty of God who acts not only to judge, but more importantly to save. Despite the fact that Mark 13 contains no reference either to a return or a holy remnant, Jesus did affirm that God would still act to save the elect. Contemplating the enormous spiritual upheaval that loomed in the not-too-distant future, Jesus declared: *So be on your guard; I have told you everything ahead of time.*

The Son of Man Sends Out His Angels (13:24-27) Many sincere

Christians believe that these verses predict three events that come at the end of history: the darkening of the sun and moon and the falling of the stars is thought to describe the end of history and the collapse of the universe as we know it (13:24-25); the coming of the Son of Man is thought to depict the return of Jesus Christ (13:26); and the gathering of the elect to their eternal reward from the ends of the earth and the ends of heaven is thought to represent the summoning of the people who have been saved to their eternal reward (13:27). Furthermore, it is understood in this line of thought that these three events would happen in a short span of time, one after another, on the heels of the great distress just described in 13:14-23.

There are, however, several reasons for not accepting this interpretation. In the first place, it is doubtful that the language about the darkening sun and falling stars depict the end of the world. In the Bible this kind of language has a very different meaning. The image of the stars falling from the sky is part of a prophecy of judgment against the nations in Isaiah 34:4: "All the starry host will fall like withered leaves from the vine." In this prophecy God judges the nations by destroying their armies (Is 34:2), and the object of God's particular wrath is the kingdom of Edom, which is completely destroyed and turned into a wasteland (Is 34:8-13).

Isaiah 34 is clearly not a prediction of the end of the world. The prophet only foretells the vindication of Zion, and it is apparent from Isaiah 34:16-17 that the peace that comes upon Zion is a blessing that happens in that historical era. The picture of the stars falling from the sky is part of the description of a complete realignment of the power structures of that era. In the new political economy Judah would no longer be a pawn in the politics of the ancient Middle East. God would restore its prosperity and security. But Edom and the armies that had marched against Zion would be utterly destroyed. The idea of the stars falling from the heavens then is part of the description of a complete reversal in the power structures within history. It is as though the heavens reflect what transpires on earth.

Similarly, the specter of the sun and moon being darkened appears in Isaiah 13:10 in the judgment against Babylon and in Ezekiel 32:7-8 in the prophecy against Pharaoh. Once again, rather than signal the end of the world, these images describe a major disruption in the world's political structures that was about to occur within the framework of history. In the worldview of the Old Testament the destruction of a nation is an event of such proportions that even the powers of heaven— the sun, moon and stars—are disturbed. There is good reason then to think that Mark 13:24-25 does not describe the end of history, but a change in the powers in this world.

Second, the Son of Man does not come to earth, as the idea of Jesus' return requires. On the contrary, the Son of Man comes before the Ancient of Days to receive power and dominion in Daniel 7:13 (Hooker 1966:53). In Hebrew the word that the NIV translates "approached" in Daniel 7:13 is the verb *come*. Although there is no indication in any biblical text about the Son of Man returning to earth at the end of history, the picture of the Son of Man coming in clouds with great power and glory in Mark 13:26 is clearly drawn from Daniel 7:13. In fact, Daniel 7:13 is the only biblical text (other than Mark 13:26 and its parallels) that speaks about this event. Consequently, it may be concluded that Mark 13:26 describes the ascension of the Son of Man to a position of great power and glory in the presence of the Ancient of Days rather than the return of the return of Jesus to earth.

Third, there are important differences between the appearance of the Son of Man in Mark 13:26-27 and in Daniel 7:13-14. The idea of the Son of Man sending angels to gather the elect is absolutely unprecedented. Nowhere in the Old Testament is there any mention of the Son of Man sending out angels to gather the elect. As a matter of fact, except for this passage and its parallels there is only one other mention in the New Testament of Jesus as the Son of Man doing this: Matthew 13:41. The sending of the angels to gather the elect is an idea that appeared after the composition of the book of Daniel.

Furthermore, the very idea that the elect are still to be gathered conflicts with Daniel 7:10, 14, where the nations are already assembled before the Son of Man appears on the scene. In the vision described in Daniel the space before the throne of the Ancient of Days is filled with multitudes; and when the Son of Man receives authority,

---

13:27 Although it is less well attested in early manuscript traditions, the expression

glory and sovereign power, all peoples, nations and men of every language worshiped him. In Mark 13:26-27, however, the multitudes are not present. The elect are still to be gathered.

Another significant departure from Daniel's vision is the idea that the Son of Man appears in those days, following that distress. As we have seen, the distress described in 13:14-20 is the judgment of Jerusalem, and God is the one who would bring destruction to the holy city. In Daniel's vision the appearance of the Son of Man marks the vindication of the saints of the Most High over the foreign powers who have unjustly persecuted them (Dan 7:21-22). There the saints of the Most High are the faithful people of God, the residents of Judah and Jerusalem who have been oppressed by foreign powers. The background for this appearance of the Son of Man, however, is not the unjustified persecution of the righteous. It is an act of judgment upon a faithless and unbelieving generation that robbed the nations of their access to God's house. The contexts of Mark 13 and Daniel 7 are quite different. Apart from the image of the Son of Man coming in the clouds, these are two very different scenes.

Gundry's objection (1993:783-87) that the language of verses 24-27 should be taken literally is not persuasive. His appeal to Acts 1:9-11 presupposes that both passages refer to the same event, despite the fact that the term *Son of Man* does not occur in that text. Given the differences between the scenes described here and in Daniel 13, it is highly problematic to speak of a literal reading of Mark 13:24-27. The interpretation that has been developed in this commentary takes the symbolic character of the Markan text seriously and attempts to explore its internal logic.

Although derived from the language of Daniel's vision, Mark 13:24-27 describes a new scenario. The events sketched out in Mark move in a direction that Daniel 7:13 does not anticipate. An unexpected scene has been inserted into the Son of Man imagery that originated in the book of Daniel. This new scene separates the ascension of the Son of Man from the final judgment at the end of history. Therefore, the pop-

---

his angels is best understood as the messengers sent by the authority of the Son of Man.

ular interpretation founders because it misrepresents the symbolism of the heavenly powers being darkened, and it misconstrues the events associated with the coming of the Son of Man. We will have to look elsewhere for a convincing explanation of this passage, and the place to begin is with the question of who will see what in Mark 13:26.

The NIV reads *at that time men will see,* which may be misleading, for the Greek text says literally "and they shall see," without specifying who *they* are. It is possible to suspect that behind the Greek text stood an Aramaic passive construction, which could come into English as "the Son of Man will be seen." The difficulty here is the scenario described in 13:27, which indicates that the elect have yet to be gathered. They apparently are not present when the Son of Man comes with the clouds. In fact, it is not clear from 13:26-27 that any human witnesses are standing before the throne of God when the Son of Man ascends to his position of great power and glory. Yet there is one place later on in the Gospel where a group of men are identified as witnesses to this event. In 14:62 Jesus said to the chief priests and elders who sat as his judges: "And you will see the Son of Man sitting at the right hand of the Mighty One and coming on the clouds of heaven." Within the framework of this Gospel the one group of people who are specifically addressed as future witnesses of the Son of Man's coming is his enemies (France 2002:611), not his elect, which Hooker (1991:319) and others overlook.

If these people are the ones who see the Son of Man coming in the clouds, what would they see? Mark 14:62 extends the imagery of 13:26 so that the members of the Sanhedrin are told not only that they would see the Son of Man coming with the clouds, but also that they would see him seated at the right hand of God. The picture of Jesus' sitting at God's right hand recalls the concluding condemnation of the leaders of Jerusalem (12:35-37) in which Jesus quoted from Psalm 110:1: "The Lord said to my Lord: 'Sit at my right hand until I put your enemies under your feet.'" That image of judgment and condemnation does not appear explicitly in Mark 13, but it is consistent with the central theme of this prophecy—the destruction of the temple. Indeed, since Jesus entered Jerusalem in 11:11 his condemnation of the temple has been the catalyst for every other event. The best answer then to the question of what they would see is the destruction of the temple. That event would be the corollary of the Son of Man's exaltation. The exaltation of the Son of Man in heaven would be an event that the chief priests, elders and scribes could not actually see because it would take place before the throne of God. The exaltation of the Son of Man, however, would also mean the destruction of the temple. In its destruction they would see the vindication of the Son of Man.

We come now to 13:27. How are we to understand the sending of the angels to gather his elect from the four winds, from the ends of the earth to the ends of the heavens? Traditionally, the gathering of the elect has been seen as an event that happens at the end of history when Jesus returns. First Thessalonians 4:16-17 provides the clearest picture of Jesus' return, but it is not clear that Mark 13:27 describes the same event. For in Mark the Son of Man does not return to earth. He remains with God while the gathering takes place. Furthermore, there is no mention of Jesus as the Son of Man in 1 Thessalonians 4:13-18. Mark 13:27 may represent a new event in the heavenly reign of the Son of Man rather than the return of Jesus to earth.

Several other Markan features point to the same conclusion. One is the way the word *angel* is used in this Gospel. It can certainly refer to heavenly beings (8:38). Yet the same term is translated "messenger" in reference to John the Baptist (1:2-4). And at the empty tomb where Matthew records the appearance of an angel, Mark mentions only the appearance of a young man. Those examples are sufficient justification for asking whether *angelos* should be translated "angel" or "messenger" in 13:27. The cosmic imagery of 13:24-27 suggests to many commentators that "angel" is to be preferred. That is an assumption that needs to be tested. At issue is the question whether this assumption takes the imagery seriously enough, for in the vision of Daniel 7 the one like a Son of Man receives authority over people, but there is no indication that this figure receives authority over divine beings. In Mark 2:10, 27 Jesus has already claimed to exercise authority as the Son of Man over people. It is entirely consistent then with both the earlier part of the Gospel and the vision of Daniel 7 to translate *angelos* as "messenger" here.

Then, too, we might ask who the elect are and where they are gathered. The lack of a promise about either a purified remnant or the restoration of the Jewish people to the land after the destruction of

Jerusalem suggests that the elect comprise a larger group than the biological descendants of Abraham and Isaac. The judgment of the temple itself points in the same direction. Jesus condemned it because it was not a house of prayer for all the nations. Finally, the one overarching imperative in this prophecy occurs in 13:10—and the gospel must first be preached to all nations—where nations probably means peoples rather than the various countries to which Jewish people had been dispersed. It seems clear, then, that the elect of this prophecy includes the peoples of the world (Hooker 1991:319).

The question of where the elect are gathered is more difficult to determine. There are two possibilities: the elect might be gathered to Jesus as in 2 Thessalonians 2:1, or they might be collected into a community as when the people of God gather in Hebrews 10:25. By itself the language of Mark 13:27 is inconclusive. Three considerations, though, point to this gathering as the formation of a new community on earth. In the first place, forming the elect into a new community is one of Mark's fundamental themes. Those who are drawn to the Son of Man are variously described as a new nation (3:13-21), the family of God (3:31-35) and sheep without a shepherd (6:34). In this prophecy it is clear that the peoples of the world are also to be counted among the elect, but up to this point there has been no explicit reference to their being gathered into the new community. The description of the elect being gathered from the four winds, from the ends of the earth to the ends of the heavens speaks nicely to this otherwise glaring omission. It is worth observing that gathering the elect into a new community would not be the only expression of the heavenly Son of Man's authority on earth. The early church believed that the heavenly Son of Man continued to forgive sin, just as it viewed worship on the first day of the week as an extension of his lordship over the Sabbath (Rev 1:10).

Second, the expectation for a new community is set up by Jesus' prediction of the temple's destruction. Yet, as we have already noted, Mark 13 lacks any mention of a purified remnant. If 13:27 outlines the formation of a new community on earth, then 13:24-27 describes three interrelated events: the destruction of the temple as an obstacle to God's purposes, the vindication of the Son of Man, and the sending of messengers to do what the temple did not accomplish. There is a logic to this sequence of events that the idea of a heavenly gathering lacks. Third, this interpretation helps to explain the curious reference to *his elect*. This term might be understood as those whom he chose or those who belong to him (Gundry 1993:745), both of which are impossible here since 13:20 underscores that God has chosen them. *His elect* then refers to those people who are gathered by the authority of the Son of Man. That would be an awkward and strange way of describing the gathering of the elect before the Ancient of Days, but his elect makes perfectly good sense as a description of what happens in history after the destruction of the temple. That is to say, if his elect refers to those who are gathered by his authority, then they do not encompass the entire number of the elect. Moses, Elijah and John the Baptist, for example, would have to be numbered among the elect in this Gospel, yet none of them was gathered by the authority of Jesus. And if his elect is not an exhaustive term, then 13:27 does not depict the end of the world. It describes the gathering and forming of the community of the elect in history by the proclamation of the gospel.

Lane offers a differing and widely held view that the Son of Man comes to earth, and upon his arrival, or parousia, the elect are gathered to him (1974:476). Although he recognizes the dependence of Mark 13:26 on the vision of Daniel 7 where one like a Son of Man comes before the Ancient of Days, Lane maintains that in this prophecy the Son of Man comes to earth. There is, however, no directional indication in Mark 13:26. The text does not specify whether the Son of Man comes to earth or comes before the Ancient of Days. Without a clear indication that the prophecy has changed the imagery upon which it is based, it is safer to assume that the movement is once again toward God. The Son of Man in 13:26 comes not to earth, but to appear before the throne of God.

We find then that 13:24-27 describes a vision of the future that Jesus' disciples had not expected. If they had supposed that the destruction of the temple would lead to the end of the age, they were to be disappointed, for the judgment that was about to fall on Jerusalem would not signal the end of history. It was to mark the end of the temple's stewardship of God's promises to the nations. That responsibility would be entrusted to the Son of Man. The priority that Jesus announced in

13:10—the preaching of the gospel to the whole world—would be accomplished, but it would not be realized through the agencies and activities of worship that were bound to the temple. The gospel would be proclaimed by the messengers whom the Son of Man would send to gather a new community from all the peoples of the world.

A Parable of Judgment (13:28-31) If a credible person forecasts a catastrophe, people want to know how certain the prediction is and when it will happen. The four disciples' questions in 13:4 convey the same concerns: "When will these things happen? And what will be the sign that they are all about to be fulfilled?" Having sketched out the events leadings up to the destruction of Jerusalem, Jesus turned to address those particular issues.

How would Jesus' followers know that the destruction of Jerusalem was certain and imminent? Once again Jesus used a fig tree as a parable. The Greek word translated "lesson" in 13:28 is actually the word for "parable" and could be justifiably translated so in this case: *As soon as its twigs get tender and its leaves come out, you know that summer is near. Even so, when you see these things happening, you know that it is near, right at the door.* The lesson or parable of the fig tree is that the destruction of Jerusalem will be imminent when the events Jesus has just described happen, that is, the wars and rumors of war, earthquakes, famines and the appearance of the desolating sacrilege. The sign the four disciples requested turns out not to be a single event: it is a series of events leading up to the destruction of the city, and the most important of these events would be the investiture of Phanni as high priest. That was the indication that it was time to flee.

The NIV broke new ground with its translation of 13:29. Other versions read "he is near," which indicates that those translators thought this verse describes the return of Jesus. On the other hand, the NIV's rendering, *it is near,* is consistent with this prophecy not describing the end of history, but the judgment of Jerusalem. Clearly, a great deal is at stake in the way 13:29 is translated, and there is no simple or literal solution since neither "he" nor "it" appears in the Greek text. The clause in question is elliptical, and the pronoun must be supplied by the translators.

"It" is preferable to "he" because summer, a common symbol for judgment, is the closer antecedent. The argument for "he" traces the antecedent back to the Son of Man in 13:26. The Son of Man is more distant grammatically. Furthermore, the expression *at the door* (literally "at the gates") is appropriate to describe the arrival of the armies of Rome, but it does not belong with the images that describe Jesus' return. The New Testament does not portray Jesus' returning to the gates of Jerusalem or to any other gates for that matter. He will appear with the clouds of the air to summon the faithful, living and dead, to be with him. In short, both the imagery of this verse and its grammar require a translation that put a judgment in history at center stage.

The answer to the second question about when judgment will fall is simpler to resolve. It would happen within the lifetime of Jesus' earliest followers: *This generation,* he affirmed, *will certainly not pass away until all these things have happened.* And in fact Jerusalem was destroyed in A.D. 70—well before that generation has died. Simple and direct as it is, though, 13:30 has been the subject of a great deal of debate, since it carries the implication that Jesus was mistaken for those who hold that the subject of 13:28-31 is the return of Jesus. If the description of *the Son of Man coming in clouds and glory* (13:26) refers to the return of Jesus and if the elliptical clause in 13:29 is translated *he is near,* then Jesus predicted an event that did not transpire within the time frame he set forth.

Some of those who maintain this position argue that the phrase *these things* in 13:29 refers only to the events described before the Son of Man sends out his angels (13:27), but this is an arbitrary piece of exegesis, as Lane shows (1974:478-80). Several explanations for the problem are offered. The most notable are the possibilities that God changed the order of events after Jesus spoke or that Jesus foresaw distant events as though time had been truncated. And yet if *these things* includes the parousia, why is the assurance of 13:30 given at all? What is the point of assuring people who have already witnessed the gathering of the elect that *he is near, right at the door?* The purpose of 13:28-29 is to provide encouragement in difficult times, but such a reassurance would be meaningless if those disciples, together with the rest of the elect, have just been gathered to their eternal reward. On the contrary, the thematic structure and pastoral concern of 13:28-32 are the confirmation that the subject of this prophecy is not the return of Jesus, but the judgment of Jerusalem and the mission of his followers.

The parousia is an event that lies largely outside the concern of Mark's little apocalypse. It is referred to only once, when Jesus says: "No one knows about that day or hour, not even the angels in heaven, nor the Son, but only the Father" (13:32). The parousia is an event that the followers of Jesus still expect with great hope.

So, then, are these words a simple, straightforward lesson, or are they more properly a parable? The affirmation that judgment would come upon Jerusalem within a lifetime is uncomplicated and direct, and if that affirmation resolved everything there would be no reason to speak about a parable. Knowing the time frame for the destruction of Jerusalem, though, does not resolve everything. Like the other sayings and events in the Gospel that are called parables, this material involves a conflict of values, for as the judgment of Jerusalem approached, the followers of Jesus would find themselves harassed and brought to trial. And in the risking of their lives they were to see the unfolding of God's purpose to preach the good news to every nation. That would be a considerable stretch for people who had yet to agree with Jesus' declaration about saving and loving one's life (8:34-38). Although they had spent a considerable amount of time with Jesus, the reordering of their lives around the gospel was far from complete.

A Parable About Watching (13:32-37) It is characteristic of Jesus as we meet him in the Gospel of Mark that he would conclude his remarks about the future with a parable. Parables are his standard teaching device, and unlike the preceding parable about the fig tree, he delivers this one without an accompanying explanation. This parable is of particular interest because the times that are mentioned in 13:35—evening, midnight, when the rooster crows and dawn—are in fact the times of the major events leading up to Jesus' crucifixion: the Last Supper happens during the evening; the prayer in Gethsemane and arrest of Jesus at midnight; the denial of Peter when the rooster crows; and the trial before Pilate at dawn. It is almost as though Jesus or Mark had set the reader a puzzle by concluding this section with an open-ended parable that tantalizes with hints of an even larger meaning.

At one level the parable requires no explanation. Its meaning is clear: the master of the house will return unannounced so the servants should be ready at all times. But to say this much neither explains what being ready entails nor accounts for the way time is structured in the passion story. To probe those issues requires more reflection.

The crucial point here is to understand that the events Jesus discusses inaugurate a new sense of time. Earlier in the Gospel the words *day* and *hour* simply marked the passing of time. Their meaning was merely chronological. From this point on, however, these two words describe time that is distinguished by features of special significance. We find the word *day* in expressions like *days of distress unequaled from the beginning* (13:19), *in those days* (13:24) and the day in which heaven and earth will pass away (13:31-32). The word *hour* also becomes invested with a special meaning. An hour is an event when faith is put to the test (13:11). Besides the hour when Jesus' disciples will be placed on trial for their faith, there is the hour of testing in Gethsemane (14:37), the hour of his betrayal (14:41), the hour of his crucifixion (15:25) and the hour when he dies (15:33, 37). It is apparent that both these words refer to events that are charged with meaning.

From a chronological perspective the day of the owner's return is more important than the hour. To say that the owner will return at 9:00 a.m., for instance, is not to say anything of particular importance. But to say that the owner will return on Easter Sunday in A.D. 2000 is to make a statement of great significance. It is important to note that this parable does not refer to the day when the owner will return, but to the hour.

The time to expect the owner is at evening, midnight, cockcrow and dawn, and the distinctive meaning of hour in this prophecy is a time of testing or trial. As it turns out, evening, midnight, cockcrow and dawn correspond to the times when Jesus' disciples were put to the test. This parable then directs the disciples' attention away from speculations about when this age will end. They are instead to look for God to be present with them in the moments of testing, as the Holy Spirit, according to Jesus' promise in 13:11, would be with them when they go to trial. For the disciples the day is not as important as the hour. The implication of the parable is that if the disciples are not ready for the hour of their testing, they will certainly not be ready for the day of his return.

It is often argued that Mark 13 interrupts the narrative structure of Mark by introducing a set of ideas that are poorly, if at all, related to the rest of the Gospel. That conclusion is unwarranted. Many fundamental themes connect this discourse with the rest of the Gospel: the conflict with the centers of power in the world, the authority of Jesus, the proclamation of the gospel, the place of suffering in the life of Jesus' disciples and Jesus' persistent efforts to refocus their vision from dreams of apocalyptic glory to the call to follow him. In fact, given the dual Markan emphases on the centrality of Jesus' death and the inability of the disciples to come to terms with it, the Gospel would be incomplete without Mark 13. This chapter is the text that relates the great themes of Jesus' ministry to the task of his disciples after his death and resurrection.

☐ The Cross as the Gateway to the Future (14:1—16:8)

The Passion of Jesus is one of the best known stories in the world. Among its cast of characters are several well-remembered figures like Judas, Peter, Pontius Pilate and the high priest, whose name Mark does not record. It is also, however, punctuated by a series of unlikely characters. There are, for example, brief references to two men named Simon. The first is identified as Simon the Leper in 14:3, a name which suggests someone who has come to terms with the shame of his past. The second is Simon from Cyrene in 15:21, whose two sons are also mentioned by name even though they do not play any role at all in the story. There is an anonymous woman who preached the gospel without saying a word, an unnamed centurion who first gave voice to the truth about Jesus and a largely anonymous group of women who did more to embody Jesus' teaching than any of the Twelve. Careful attention to the smaller figures in the Passion story opens up a wealth of new meaning.

At the Home of Simon the Leper (14:1-11) Mark's transitions are often abrupt. This one, however, is smooth. The statement that it was now two days before Passover and the Feast of Unleavened Bread creates an easy movement from the parable at the end of Mark 13 to the beginning of Mark 14. If the sequence of events flows evenly, though, the thematic transition is jarring. It is hard to imagine a greater contrast than the one between the prophecy Jesus had just delivered about the destruction of Jerusalem and the nationalistic dreams associated with the Feast of Unleavened Bread. This festival was immediately preceded by the celebration of Passover and nourished the hope that God would deliver the Jewish people from the yoke of Rome. Popular expectations about the kingdom of God held that the nations would be defeated and the people of Israel liberated from the yoke of Rome. Yet four of the disciples had just heard Jesus predict that Jerusalem would be devastated within a generation. This seemingly simple transition turns the spotlight on two competing visions for Jerusalem.

Looking for an Opportunity (14:1-2) The chief priests and teachers of the law perceived a different crisis—the threat that Jesus posed to their authority. The confrontations in the temple had gone badly for them. Each engagement with Jesus had led to another defeat, while his popularity with the crowd soared. It looked as though the leaders had lost control of the situation, and Jesus displayed absolutely no interest in accommodation or compromise. The timing of this growing crisis could not have been more problematic. Passover was at hand, the masses were looking for a new deliverer, and the city was rife with rumors about Jesus. The chief priests and scribes needed to do away with him, but if they acted publicly, they risked the wrath of the crowd.

The answer to their dilemma appeared later in 14:10, when one of Jesus' inner circle approached them with an offer to betray him. What is missing from the story, however, is an explicit motive. It is clear why the religious and political leaders of Judea were opposed to Jesus, but it is not clear why Judas turned against him. What moved Judas to hand Jesus over to his enemies? Where we might expect to find a comment about Judas's motive the story line is interrupted by the account of the unnamed woman who anointed Jesus with nard. Weaving two stories together is a frequent Markan narrative technique. It opens lines of interpretation that either story taken by itself would lack, and it invites us to interpret what we see. So here Mark presents two otherwise unconnected events and prompts his audience to consider the meaning of Jesus' death.

The Anointing at Bethany (14:3-9) The anointing at Bethany took place in a curious setting: the home of Simon the Leper. Simon, we may presume, was still alive; otherwise it is unlikely that the house would be called his home. We might also suspect that Simon was the head of the household and that he was no longer a leper. Whether Jesus had healed him is unclear, although the hospitality extended to Jesus and his entire retinue certainly points to that possibility. What is clear, though, is that this man still had a home. In some way that we are not told about, Simon had been healed and spared the financial devastation that often accompanied leprosy. The anointing of Jesus is thus set between the abyss of poverty and the hope of salvation.

Whether the unnamed woman in 14:3 grasped the full implications of what she was doing is unclear. She may have brought the flask of nard, a spice often used in funeral preparations, with the thought that Jesus would die in Jerusalem. On the other hand, she may have intended to do nothing more than to present him with a gift of gratitude and devotion. It is impossible to say with certainty what her intention was, but she did the right thing. She is one of several people who appear without explanation to say or do something surprisingly appropriate. Like the woman with the hemorrhage (5:25-34), the Syrophoenician woman (7:24-30), Bartimaeus (10:46-52) and the centurion (15:39), she is someone who perceived a truth that others could not or would not express. It is all the more surprising that Mark does not explain how she knew what to do, but it is striking that the disciples, who symbolize the church for Mark, rarely possess this intuitive understanding. In the framework of this Gospel it is usually someone outside the expected circle of leaders who has it, and Mark always treats this intuition as faith.

In any case she acted extravagantly. The three hundred denarii specified in the Greek text, which someone in the house set as the value of the oil and alabaster flask (14:4-5), may have been half again as much as what it would have cost to feed the five thousand (6:37).

That could have done a lot for the poor, and for someone at the table of Simon the Leper the woman's gift was not simply extravagant—it was a shocking waste. This concern for the poor was not something new, and from one point of view it demonstrates that the disciples had been paying some attention to their teacher. In Mark the vast majority of Jesus' ministry was spent with people in the small towns of Galilee. They were mostly peasant farmers, fishermen and small craftsmen who lived at or near the bottom of the local economy. These were the people Jesus fed because they were like sheep without a shepherd (6:34). Furthermore, Jesus had declared that his ministry to those who lived at the bottom of the social order was not incidental (2:17; 10:44-45). He had come to serve the least.

Jesus accepted her gift and rebuked her detractors. He set her gift in a category of acts in which expense does not matter. He viewed what she had done as the sort of thing people do when someone they love has died. At that time no expense is too great to express their sense of loss. In this case, Jesus asserted, the woman had simply expressed her feelings before he died: *She has poured perfume on my body beforehand to prepare for my burial.* Jesus had come to Jerusalem to die, but that was a feature of his ministry the disciples had yet to acknowledge. They had begun the journey to Jerusalem in the hope of benefiting from a change in regimes. That Jesus had come to Jerusalem to die had not impressed itself upon them. Their incomprehension and resistance to his impending death mitigates the harsh tone of his response: *Why are you bothering her? She has done a beautiful thing to me. The poor you will always have with you, and you can help them any time you want. But you will not always have me. She did what she could.* It is almost as though he were accusing the woman's critics of hypocrisy, and we might well wonder whether their concern for the poor was still laced with dreams of power and glory. His followers had understood part of what he had come to do, but they were still missing the fundamental point. Jesus took this gesture of extravagant devotion as an opportunity to press the lesson home.

There is more to this story, though, than the forging of a teachable moment, for Jesus went on to say something about this woman that he had not said about even the Twelve: *I tell you the truth, wherever the gospel is preached throughout the world, what she has done will also be told, in memory of her.* In this Gospel the occasions on which the disciples are singled out for attention do not usually cast them in a favorable light. Yet what this anonymous woman did was so important that her story would be told wherever the gospel is proclaimed throughout the world. What is there about this anointing to warrant such an affirmation?

First, Jesus had already drawn a connection between the anointing and his death. That connection is echoed at the Passover Seder, when he uses the words *broken* and *poured out* to describe his own death. The language about breaking and pouring in 14:3 is very close to that of 14:22, 24. What she did, in other words, not only gave Jesus an opportunity to drive home the point that he had come to Jerusalem to die; it also symbolized it. Her extraordinary act embodied the gospel. Wherever they told this story after his resurrection, Jesus' followers would proclaim the gospel.

Mark does not provide a systematic exposition of Jesus' death. Brief statements and small vignettes interspersed throughout the larger story interpret it. Among other things, the death of Jesus is foreshadowed by the arrest of John the Baptist (1:14). It is also an expression of the will of God (8:31), a consequence of Israel's continued rejection of the prophets (9:13) and a ransom for many (10:45). This incident opens up a new perspective that might be attributed to either God or Jesus or both. The death of Jesus is compared here to an act of exquisite beauty. More precisely, it is an exquisite act of reconciliation.

No one expected it. The chief priests, elders and teachers of the law were not looking for it. The nations had no idea it was about to be offered. Even Jesus' disciples did not realize it was coming. They had their minds set on other things, and it was these other things that made Jesus' death necessary: the quest for privilege, struggle for dominance, fixation with money, smug self-deception, oppression of conquered people—in short, sin. Yet the scope of his death is universal. It was a gift for the nations that oppressed the people of God, just as it was a gift for those who repeatedly demonstrated that they were preoccupied with their own concerns rather than with the things of God. This marvelous gift is not forced on the intended beneficiaries. It is offered irrespective of the way it is received. It was offered to his disciples who had hardened hearts. It was offered to the one who was to betray him. It was offered to the leaders of Jerusalem who opposed him. And it was ultimately offered to all the peoples of the world whether they had any inkling that it was even being offered. That is the nature of reconciling gestures. They are made without demanding a particular response, but they are costly. Mark 10:45 presents the death of Jesus as a ransom that frees people from their bondage to sin. This passage presents it as God's gift to an estranged world.

A Plot Is Hatched (14:10-11) One indication of the world's estrangement is Judas's reaction, and it is significant that Mark identifies him not only by name, but also by function: he was *one of the Twelve* (14:10). In this Gospel Judas is mentioned only three times: in the list of apostles (3:19), here and in the betrayal scene (14:43). Both here and in 3:19 Judas is also identified by his family name, and in all three cases his place among the Twelve and his role as the one who betrayed Jesus are recounted. This was not the act of a casual opportunist. The man who betrayed Jesus was one of those who could have said with Peter, "We have left everything to follow you!" (10:28). It was a calculated treachery committed by one of the inner circle. There is no doubt about who betrayed Jesus, just as there is no doubt about the enormity of the betrayal. The one thing that is not specified, however, is Judas's motive.

The money mentioned in 14:11 is not a convincing motive. It is no more than an afterthought. Mark gives no hint that Judas asked for it. The idea of giving Judas money came from the chief priests, as though they thought it a fitting reward. Even so, there is no indication that Judas approached them with the proposal that they reward him for betraying Jesus. He did not betray Jesus in order to get a reward. On the contrary, something else in the story of Jesus' anointing prompted him to act.

There is one specific link between the report of Judas's decision to betray Jesus and the story of the woman who anointed him: the word *then* at the beginning of 14:10. It must be given its full weight. There is no indication that Judas waited until the meal had ended or that he stayed in the house until he could leave unobtrusively. His decision to betray Jesus came immediately after Jesus' declaration about the significance of what the woman had done.

Several aspects of that story, taken individually or collectively, could explain the betrayal. In the first place, Jesus had raised once again the subject of his death. Judas may have finally understood what Jesus intended to do in Jerusalem. He may have felt that he himself had been betrayed, and he may have considered delivering Jesus to the chief priests to be a fitting response to the one whom he thought had betrayed him. Second, Jesus' pronouncement about the woman would have been a further irritant to a man whose hopes for the kingdom of God were mixed with dreams of personal glory. None of the men had received a commendation like hers. In fact, the Twelve are more often criticized than praised in Mark. Moreover, Jesus' open declaration that the good news of the kingdom of God would be preached throughout the whole world might have been deeply troubling to a patriotic Jew. Mark's Gospel contains several indications that the gospel was for the nations as well as the Jews: the healing of the deaf man (7:31-37), the second feeding story (8:1-10), the description of the Son of Man's death as a ransom for many (10:45) and the enacted parable against the temple (11:20-25). In commending what this woman did, however, Jesus made the first explicit, public declaration that the gospel would be preached to the entire world. To someone who had nurtured the belief that the kingdom of God would see the Jewish people elevated to a position of supremacy over the nations, that would have been a profoundly disturbing thought.

It may bring things into sharper focus to frame the question this way: What good is a dead messiah? The Jewish belief in resurrection envisioned a resurrection at the end of history, and the witness of the New Testament is clear. The resurrection of Jesus came as a complete surprise to his followers. Once his intention to die in Jerusalem became clear, as it finally did to all of them in the Garden of Gethsemane, it shook them to the core. They did not expect him to die and they certainly did not expect him to rise on the third day. In Gethsemane most of them reacted with shock and fear. In this passage Judas's reaction bears the stamp of anger, and anger might easily motivate a betrayal. If money was not the motivation for what Judas did, why is it mentioned in 14:11? The reference to money points the reader back to the complaint about doing good for the poor, and it sharpens the question about Jesus' death. What good would Jesus' death do for the poor? A skeptic might observe that the poor do not need anyone to die for them—they do that quite nicely for themselves.

As we have already seen, from one point of view his death is an extravagant waste. If it is not a waste, though, if it is an extravagant gift, what does it accomplish?

The death of Jesus accomplishes two things for the poor. First, it judges the structures of society that elevate a few to positions of power and privilege and subordinate the rest of humanity. The hierarchical ordering of society is one of the things that keeps some people poor, and for much of human history it has been an assumed fact of life. Aristotle, for example, held that slavery was part of the natural order of life: "For that some should rule and others be ruled is a thing not only necessary, but expedient; from the hour of their birth, some are marked out for subjection, others for rule" (1984:1990). The death of the Son of God at the hands of the ruling elite in Jerusalem exposed the bankruptcy of social hierarchies.

Second, Jesus did not seek to condemn one hierarchy only to replace it with another. Jesus' conception of life in the kingdom of God stands in stark contrast to any system of privilege. Jesus came to give his life as a ransom for many so that the first would be last and the last would be first (10:45). His death implies the leveling of all human institutions. In the world Jesus envisioned, greatness is not a matter of being served, but of serving those who would otherwise be considered least.

The clearest picture we have of that world is found in 10:29-31, just after Jesus had invited the rich man to give up all his wealth and the trappings of privilege that accompanied it. It is a new picture of society with a broadened view of the family and a radically restructured relationship between people and property rights. The family is expanded to include all those who do the will of God, an idea Jesus introduced in 3:35. And the relationship between people and property is defined not by what they hold title to, but by what they give away. Acts 2:42-47 and 4:32-37 and James 2:2-4 portray the early church's implementation of these ideas. Luke describes the followers of Jesus in Jerusalem as a community characterized by open sharing, and James insists that the poor be treated with the same dignity as everyone else. This restructuring of values and relationships is the second thing Jesus' death accomplished for the poor. It not only condemned the old order, it created a new one in this age.

Over the last two thousand years the church has struggled with the social implications of Jesus' death. The convents, monasteries and abbeys of the medieval church were one expression, but by the time of the Reformation some had amassed so much property and wealth that they created their own positions of privilege. Most Protestant experiments in communal living have proven to be short-lived and have had limited appeal. Even the manse held in trust by the congregation is almost a thing of the past. Most Protestant pastors own their homes, and for many Christians the right to own private property has become an article of faith. The last one hundred years have seen a proliferation of Christian charities, but the poor are still marginalized.

As she pulled into the restaurant parking lot with her two children, Kathy Arai glanced at the disheveled woman standing next to the garbage bin with three small children. As Kathy got out of her car, a voice near the garbage bin said, "They serve big portions in there. If you have any food left over, would you bring it out for us?" As an activist for the homeless and a member of Pasadena Covenant Church for many years, Kathy smiled at the woman and said, "Yes, of course." Then she thought to herself, "That could be me and my kids." So she invited the four of them into the cafeteria and paid for their meals.

As they all sat down to eat and talk, Kathy learned that the woman and her children had been living on the streets for several weeks. Her husband had lost his job and then abruptly disappeared. Her story was not unusual. Many Americans are only one month away from living on the streets. Kathy had heard stories like hers before, and she was accustomed to the ambience that accompanies people who cannot wash regularly. The other patrons, however, were not. Sitting two tables away was a group of well-dressed people who stared at them, rolled their eyes and shook their heads. Eventually a large man in a neatly tailored suit came over to their table to deliver an ultimatum: "We're the missions committee of a major church in this city, and we're trying to hold a meeting here. You're making it very difficult for us to get anything done."

As he turned back to his committee, the homeless mother whispered to Kathy, "Maybe we should go." "No," Kathy declared, "let's finish our food. Maybe they should be the ones to go." The missions committee finally came to the same conclusion. As they were leaving, a woman who had invested a considerable sum in her appearance stopped to vent her aggravation. "Don't you know what it says in the Bible?" she demanded. "The poor you will always have with you!"

Jesus and God's Covenant (14:12-31) Early in our marriage I learned the danger of making impromptu arrangements for dinner. My wife makes plans with careful deliberation, while I have always held that spontaneity was one of the highest virtues. On more than one occasion the clash of these two worldviews has inspired conversations that are remembered more for their great energy and conviction than for any sense of mutual affirmation. So it was with considerable interest that I studied the preparations for Passover in this passage. It almost appears that everything was done at the last possible moment.

Preparations for Passover (14:12-16) It was the day of the Passover Seder, when the animals that were to be eaten that evening were sacrificed. The disciples did not know what arrangements Jesus had made, so they asked him. He replied with an improbable set of instructions that included finding a man carrying a jar of water who would take them to another man who had a furnished guest room ready for the Teacher. That the population of Jerusalem swelled from 55,000 to perhaps 180,000 people during Passover (Jeremias 1975:83) makes this scenario even more unlikely.

This is the second set of implausible instructions Jesus gave about his sojourn in Jerusalem. He had previously given instructions to two disciples about obtaining a colt that had never been ridden (11:2-7). In both instances things turn out just as he described, and that is just the point. In the events leading up to his death, Jesus gave his disciples two sets of improbable tasks that transpired just as he said they would. These instructions reaffirm the authority of his words.

The authority of Jesus' words is one of the fundamental themes of a meal that is celebrated in the Christian community not as a Passover Seder, but as the Last Supper. Despite attempts to identify connections between the blessing, thanksgiving and cup of this meal with the ritual for the Passover Seder (Bowman 1965:264-72), it must be said that Passover has receded so far into the background that we cannot locate anything that Jesus said or did at that meal with any certainty in the ritual of the Seder (Bahr 1970:200-202). We cannot even specify at what point in the traditional liturgy Jesus gave his disciples the bread and wine. Except for the introductory comments (14:12) and the casual comment *when they had sung a hymn* (14:26), there are few explicit connections. It is as if the Seder formed only the framework of the evening. The words of Jesus rather than the liturgy of Passover give the evening its substance. Jesus did not come to Jerusalem to celebrate a feast. He came to die, and everything he said during the meal points to his death.

Jesus Predicts His Betrayal (14:17-21) One feature of the Last Supper is particularly noteworthy: Mark pays more attention to the idea of Jesus' betrayal than to any other part of the meal. When we celebrate the Lord's Supper in our churches, the minister makes a passing reference to the night he was betrayed and spends much more time presenting the bread and cup. Here the situation is reversed. Jesus talked about his betrayal at some length (14:17-21) and made only brief references to the bread and cup (14:22-23). If Jesus' death eclipses Passover, his betrayal is the predominate theme in this presentation of his death.

Given the enormity of the betrayal, it is not surprising that Mark devotes so much space at the Last Supper to it. Yet the way he presents it is surprising. Judas is not named here, although the clear implication of the text is that Jesus knew who was about to betray him. Consequently, each of the disciples who was present asked, *Surely not I?* Jesus responded by stating that his betrayer was one of the Twelve and by issuing the severest warning imaginable: *It would be better for him if he had not been born.* This warning, the anonymous reference to his betrayer and the introspection of all the disciples create a space for repentance. Mark's presentation of the Last Supper is an invitation to repent not only for the Twelve, but for everyone who follows Jesus, and it recalls the first words that appear on the lips of Jesus in this Gospel: "Repent and believe the good news!" (1:15).

Yet his betrayal was inevitable. Jesus affirmed that it was written that the Son of Man would be betrayed (14:21). In part this sense of inevitability comes from the Evangelist's reflection on Jesus' death, as his early identification of Judas as the betrayer suggests (3:19). More to the point, however, are Jesus' own words. The second passion prediction introduces the theme of betrayal in the timeline of events leading to the crucifixion (9:31). There his betrayal is presented as the sort of thing people do when God does not intervene to stop them.

Here, too, the theme of inevitability is grounded in Jesus' words, for, strictly speaking, no particular Scripture predicts that the Son of Man will be betrayed. The description *one who dips bread into the bowl with me* is an allusion to Psalm 41:9, which does not mention the Son of Man. If that psalm, which comes the closest to the themes of the Last Supper, does not predict the betrayal of the Son of Man, then how is his betrayal written? This is a case where an Old Testament passage is viewed from the perspective of what happened to Jesus and then appropriated, and the justification for applying this text to him is the image of Jesus as the Son of Man who identified himself with the least of all in order to be the servant of all (Mk 10:45). That is to say, Psalm 41 describes the worst thing that can happen to people who give themselves in love and trust. They can be betrayed and become the objects of ridicule and scorn. In taking on the role of a servant, Jesus identified with those, who from the point of view of love and faithfulness, are treated as the least, and he served even his betrayer by inviting him to repent. Other texts in Mark treat the death of Jesus as a divine necessity (e.g., 8:31; 9:31). At the Last Supper, though, his betrayal is treated as a matter of human inevitability. This is the sort of thing people do to each other unless they are restrained by something—culture, law or even God. It is an aspect of human nature that is well attested in the Scriptures.

The Bread and the Wine (14:22-26) Bread symbolizes life and salvation. When Jesus fed the five thousand men, he not only sustained their lives. He also enacted the role of the messianic shepherd who would faithfully lead the people of God. Later the Pharisees demanded to know what warrant Jesus had to feed a predominantly Gentile crowd as well. They objected to his inclusion of unholy, unclean outsiders in the eschatological promises of God. The flat, unleavened bread of Passover, which Jesus broke and gave to his disciples, also symbolizes salvation. It recalls the hasty flight from slavery in Egypt and sustains the hope that God will act again to save a people in bondage.

In this setting, however, bread carries another set of meanings as well. It symbolizes not only life and salvation, but also intimacy and betrayal. Jesus identified his betrayer as one of the Twelve who was dipping bread in the same dish. Then he took bread, gave thanks, broke it, gave it to them and said, *Take it; this is my body.* Blessing and breaking bread are part of the ritual of Passover, but there is nothing in the Seder service that corresponds to Jesus' word about himself or his betrayer. At any other observance of Passover the table conversation would lead naturally from reflections about the defeat of Pharaoh's army to hope for the defeat of Israel's current oppressors. Here, though, the opposition to the rule of God was not the Romans or even the chief priests and Pharisees. It is someone from the new community. It was one of the Twelve, a consummate insider.

Judas's betrayal was the first step in the defection of all the disciples. There was only one betrayer, but all the others were to fall away that night as the events leading to the crucifixion unfolded. This is not a new theme in Mark. As early as 6:52 the Evangelist describes the Twelve in the same terms he had employed about the Pharisees: "their hearts were hardened." Then in 8:33 Jesus rebuked Peter: "You do not have in mind the things of God, but the things of men." There is very little in what follows those passages to speak for them. There is no righteous remnant in this Gospel unless it is Jesus himself. There is no group of insiders who are fundamentally different and should be saved from the unique threat posed by those who are outside the community. Mark has a strictly egalitarian understanding of sin and righteousness. Jesus' words at this Passover meal recast the dynamics of salvation, for it is one thing to take comfort in the thought that what we need to be saved from lies out there beyond us. It is another thing entirely to con-template the possibility that we might be allied with the forces that are set in opposition to the rule of God.

Furthermore, Jesus' declaration, *this is my body,* makes something explicit that has been implicit since the feeding of the five thousand. He himself is life and salvation. In Aramaic this statement refers not merely to his physical body, but to the whole person (Behm 1965:736). Jesus himself is the bread and all it symbolizes. These simple words constitute a paradigm shift that comes with two fundamental conse-quences. First, as Passover has receded into the background of this meal, so too have the dreams of nationalistic supremacy. There is no holy community here to be delivered. The people who were called to be set apart for God have shown themselves to be opposed to God's rule. Ultimately, this is true not only of the chief priests, elders and scribes; it is also true of Jesus' own followers. Except for Jesus, no one at this Passover faithfully embraces God's purposes in history.

Salvation comes at someone's expense. In the exodus the armies of Egypt were defeated, and as the people of Israel moved into the land the defenses of city after city were overthrown. At this time, too, the popular hope for the salvation of Judea hinged on the defeat of Rome's armies. Here, however, the one who bears the cost of salvation is nei-ther the enemy of popular expectations nor the unfaithful generation of Jewish leaders nor even the confused and unstable disciples. No one community, nation or group of nations is defeated for the salvation of an entitled people. The one who is our salvation is also the one who was betrayed and died. Jesus bore the cost of salvation himself so that no nation or people is excluded. His salvation is salvation for all.

It would have been natural at such a moment for Jesus to identify his betrayer and either put an end to it or let him become the butt of all the anger, hostility, shame and guilt that the disciples would feel as the night progressed. It would have been convenient for his followers to have had an easy target for the conflicting passions that would inevita-bly well up from within. But Jesus was not interested in catharsis at someone else's expense. As 14:27 suggests, he wanted his death to be an occasion for them to come to terms with themselves and with God.

The festive celebration of the defeat of the enemies of Israel is replaced by the somber thoughts of betrayal and defection, an enigmatic allusion to Jesus' resurrection and an equally cryptic reference to another meal. In the description of this meal we find no "us against them," no victory of the persecuted over the oppressor. The people whom Jesus died to save are not a righteous minority. If the Last Supper is to be understood as a kind of Passover Seder, then it is a Passover without nationalism or triumphalism. In its Markan form salvation is not presented in the traditional terms of Passover, that is, who God is and what God has promised us. The meal and its meaning have been transformed. Instead of when will we be delivered from our enemies, the fundamental question has become how God is for us.

In all probability this was not something that any of his followers would have understood then. They had still not come to terms with the idea that Jesus was going to die. Yet after Judas's betrayal and their own falling away, Jesus' words would nourish them. These words will enable them to come to terms with themselves. They help Jesus' followers of all ages accept that God understands us before we understand ourselves. The profound love that is the foundation of this understanding feeds us when our illusions have turned to ashes.

The idea of Jesus' death may be only implicit in the symbolism of the bread, but it comes to the fore after the disciples have drunk from the cup when Jesus said, *This is my blood of the covenant, which is poured out for many*. The *blood of the covenant* is an allusion to the blood from the sacrifice of young bulls that was sprinkled on the altar and on the people to institute the Mosaic covenant (Ex 24:6-8). And the thought of his death is underscored with the words *which is poured out for many*. The covenant that Jesus talks about here is instituted by his death.

What is the covenant about which Jesus spoke here? A number of New Testament passages speak about a new covenant. In fact, the term New Testament itself is an archaic way of saying new covenant. Undoubtedly, these various texts are all related. Our task, however, is to determine the meaning of Jesus' covenant in this context. Several points can be gleaned by paying careful attention to the particular language of this text. In the first place, as we have already observed, this covenant is instituted by Jesus' death. The first step toward its establishment was not the defeat of Pharaoh; it was an act of betrayal.

Second the centerpiece of this covenant is an oath that Jesus takes not to drink any wine again *until that day when I drink it anew in the kingdom of God.* This is an oath of abstinence, and it comes as something of a surprise, because up until this point Jesus has insisted that his ministry is an occasion for joy rather than a time for fasting (2:18-22).

A comparison with 2:18-20, though, is instructive, for the parable about the bridegroom ends with the statement "but the time will come when the bridegroom will be taken from them, and on that day they will fast." Unexpectedly, at the end of this parable Jesus added an ominous pronouncement: the joyful celebration that had characterized his ministry would be cut short. His vow of abstinence in 14:25 sounds the same note. It too is an unexpected and ominous statement which implies that a joyful celebration lies ahead at some unspecified time in the future. The celebration of the kingdom of God, which the disciples thought to be imminent, has been postponed.

If this correlation between the parables about the bridegroom, the wineskins and the unshrunk cloth on the one hand and the promise Jesus makes at the Last Supper on the other is appropriate, then we have a very important clue about the meaning of the covenant, for the parables in 2:18-22 are all expressions of the tension between the old and the new. The old represents those values, traditions, loyalties, ways of looking at the world and centers of power that conflict with the ministry of Jesus. The new symbolizes the kingdom of God that has drawn near and has begun to make its presence felt. Ultimately, of course, the forces of the old are the ones that conspired to kill Jesus.

Third, this covenant assumes that Jesus will be resurrected. After his death the idea of Jesus' drinking wine new in the kingdom of God is possible only if he is alive. Disembodied spirits, or ghosts as we would call them, have no place in the teaching of Jesus. His teaching points consistently to the resurrection as the goal of our salvation.

Thus, the day when Jesus drinks the wine anew in the kingdom of God marks the time when the tension between the old and new no longer exists. That will be the day when the new has come completely and the old has passed away. This meal is a forerunner of another festal meal at which the triumph of the new will be celebrated. It is a preliminary event, a sign pointing from the betrayal of Jesus to the eventual disappearance of the old. It is supremely ironic that the death of Jesus, which from one point of view marks the victory of the old, is actually the institution of a new covenant that guarantees the demise of the old.

Two related issues need to be addressed in this context: what is the role of God in this covenant, and with whom is the covenant made? God's role is unstated but implicit. God is the one who raised Jesus from the dead. Since the death of Jesus marks the triumph of the old, his resurrection reverses what would otherwise have been an insurmountable defeat. In the resurrection of Jesus God is revealed as the one who destroys the power of the old and vindicates the new.

For whom does God do this? For whom is the new covenant instituted? According to 14:24 Jesus' blood is poured out for many. There is a similar expression in 10:45, where the Son of Man gives his life as a ransom for many. Both passages have a similar theology in that salvation is provided for many by the death of a Savior. In 10:45 the many are the nations over whom the few, that is, the Jewish zealots and religious leaders, think they are entitled to rule. God's concern for the nations is a subject of special importance in the later part of this Gospel. It finds poignant expression in Mark's justification for Jesus' cursing of the temple (11:17). Later in 13:27, following the tribulation that is visited upon Judah, the Son of Man gathers the elect from the ends of the earth, and it appears that the elect includes the gentiles.

In 14:24 the *many* seems to have a similar meaning. It is inclusive, not restricted to one group of people. This covenant is also for the nations. It is a covenant for the many, not the few. It does not exclude the Jewish people, for the next promise Jesus makes is to his own Jewish disciples: *But after I have risen, I will go ahead of you into Galilee.* By the same token, however, neither is it limited to them. A good argument can be made that the disciples represent the whole people of Israel. At this point in the Gospel their hearts are hardened (6:52; 8:17-21), they belong to an unbelieving generation (9:19) and they would all fall away (14:27). Except for their association with Jesus there is little to distinguish them from the crowds in Galilee or Jerusalem which were attracted to Jesus. Furthermore, the fact that Jesus singled out twelve of them to share his authority points to his continued concern for the entire Jewish people. It should also be observed that Jesus inaugurated this covenant before even the Twelve understood who he was. This line of thought leads to a concluding point for reflection. The covenant Jesus confirmed at the Last Supper was established with a group of people who were unable to keep its terms at the time it was made.

The meal Jesus spoke about in 14:25 looks very much like the meal prophesied in Isaiah 25:6-9, where the nations are invited to a feast in Jerusalem that God has prepared: "On this mountain the LORD Almighty will prepare a feast of rich food for all peoples, a banquet of aged wine. "On that day death will be destroyed, and the nations will say with Israel, Surely this is our God." Like the covenant, this meal is inclusive. The feast of Isaiah 25:6 celebrates the defeat of death, a theme that is implicit at the meal Jesus keeps with his disciples. And the feast of Isaiah 25:6 is the kind of eschatological celebration that Jesus' covenant anticipates. It appears then that in the Last Supper, as presented in this Gospel, the prophecy of Isaiah 25:6-9 has become the basis for a new covenant between God and the nations. It would be well, however, to exercise caution in speaking of something new. In light of this prophecy and the place of the Jewish people in the covenant, it might be more accurate to think of the Last Supper as a evening of covenant renewal rather than as an event which inaugurated something completely new.

The Shepherd and the Sheep (14:27-31) The Passover Seder concludes at Mark 14:26 with the singing of a hymn, probably one of the psalms. Whatever there was to say and remember about God's salvation in the exodus from Egypt had been said. But the centerpiece of the meal Jesus had celebrated with his disciples, his approaching death and its meaning, was still before them: *You will all fall away,* he declared, *for it is written: "I will strike the shepherd, and the sheep will be scattered." But after I have risen, I will go ahead of you into Galilee.*

The statement *I will strike the shepherd, and the sheep will be scattered* is a quotation from Zechariah 13:7. This is a dour prophecy about a judgment that would fall first upon the shepherd, the leader of God's people, and then upon the flock. It is particularly appropriate in this context because this shepherd appears to be blameless. Other prophecies use the same imagery of shepherd and flock, like Ezekiel 34:7-10, where judgment falls upon God's people because the nation's leaders have been more like robbers than shepherds. In that case the wickedness of the shepherds is the reason destruction falls upon the flock.

In Zechariah 13:7, however, there is no hint that the shepherd is guilty of anything. On the contrary, he is the one who is close to the Lord! In fact, a careful reading of Zechariah 13:7-9 indicates that the problem lies with the sheep. The flock would be refined: two thirds of them would die and the rest will be tested like gold. The clear implication is that something is wrong with the sheep. But unlike other Old Testament passages that use the idea of a condemned flock as a metaphor for judgment, there is really nothing in these verses to suggest that the shepherd has violated God's trust in any sense. It seems rather that judgment falls on the shepherd as a prelude to the destruction of the flock. When the shepherd has been struck down, the sheep are defenseless and ready for slaughter. Putting all of this together then, we have here the picture of a shepherd who suffers with the flock despite his innocence. The shepherd's suffering is a consequence of his identification with the sheep rather than a result of his own iniquity.

What is the relevance of this quotation to the passion story? Why is it here? It is suggested that this quotation was added at a later time when the church was interested in proving that the events leading up to Jesus' death all happened according to the Scriptures. The early church certainly had a keen interest in showing that Jesus' death transpired according to God's will, but there is much more to be said.

This passage has more than one level of meaning, and we have already touched upon the first—the idea of an innocent shepherd being struck down with the flock. This is a fascinating and perhaps unexpected picture of God's judgment. Judgment is the predominant theme in the span of material that begins with Jesus' entry into Jerusalem and concludes with his teaching about the future. Here on the eve of his own death he did not rail against those who opposed him. Rather he saw his own death as the first step in the judgment of the flock like the shepherd of Zechariah 13:7. He did not set himself apart but identified with those who were about to be destroyed.

Two related themes converge at this point. Jesus had instructed his disciples to forgive when they pray that God will bring justice so that they too may be forgiven (11:22-25). Then in his teaching about the days of distress (13:9-23), Jesus did not suggest that his followers would walk through those events unscathed. On the contrary, they would be arrested, flogged, put on trial before local councils, governors and kings, and be universally despised. They would be part of the world in which brother will betray brother to death, and a father his child (13:12). More to the point, they were the ones who would be betrayed. Both in the way they pray about justice and in their participation in the unfolding events of God's judgment, Jesus' followers are to identify with the people who suffer.

This brings us to another level of meaning: one of the consistent themes in Mark is that salvation is not the avoidance of danger or suffering or harm. People are saved when they endure to the end (13:13). Salvation ultimately means resurrection in this Gospel. Even Jesus talked about his own salvation in these terms. He was going to die according to the prophecy in Zechariah 13:7, but his death would not be the final word: *But after I have risen,* he added to the quotation from Zechariah, *I will go ahead of you into Galilee.*

The way of salvation leads through suffering and death to the resurrection. What Jesus asked of his disciples in the teaching about the days of distress in Mark 13 is nothing more than what he asked of himself. When they face the ultimate test of their faith, they will already have seen him in Galilee. Meeting the risen Jesus, seeing the promise come true, would help sustain their faith in God when they face death.

On a third level, it is a matter of considerable interest that Mark specifies Galilee as the place where the disciples would see the resurrected Christ. In much of contemporary Jewish expectations the promises of God were so closely tied to Judea and Jerusalem that it is surprising to find the hope of the resurrection leading away from Jerusalem to Galilee. Why is this so? Why does Mark ignore Jerusalem and focus the hope of seeing the risen Jesus in Galilee?

The answer lies in the connection between the resurrection and the new covenant. The resurrection is one of the fundamental elements in the covenant Jesus had just confirmed, and this covenant is an inclusive one. It is not for one people or group of people. It is for Israel and the nations. Jerusalem is the place where Jesus came expecting to find the nations worshiping God (11:17), and judgment has come upon the temple because that expectation was not met. Galilee, on the other hand, is the place where Jesus' ministry extended beyond the ethnic boundaries of Judaism and touched the nations. It was during his Galilean ministry that Jesus exorcized the Gadarene demoniac and the daughter of the Syrophoenician woman. It was during the Galilean ministry that he healed the deaf-mute in the Decapolis and repeated the miracle of the loaves. And Galilee itself contained an ethnically diverse population. In short, Galilee symbolizes the inclusiveness of the covenant.

Despite the rich theological texture of these statements, the disciples heard only one thing: the prediction that they would all fall away. The rest of what Jesus had to say seems to have passed right over their heads. Perhaps their ears were still ringing with the accusation that one of them would betray him. But where the earlier prediction led them into a period of introspection, this time they felt the need to protest their loyalty. Peter objected, *Even if all fall away, I will not.* When Jesus pressed the point by predicting that Peter would deny him three times before the rooster crowed twice, Peter insisted that he would die rather than disown Jesus. The others, not wanting to be slighted, all made the same promise.

Sadly, their loyalty was completely misplaced. They wanted to be loyal to Jesus without being loyal to the one whom Jesus followed. They had not come to grips with the identity of the one who would strike the shepherd. We might say that what they have not heard is more important than what they have heard. They have heard and rejected the idea that they would fall away, but they did not understand that God was the one who would take Jesus' life.

Their protestations of loyalty must be taken with complete seriousness. When Peter led the disciples in declaring that they were ready to die for Jesus, he was not making an idle boast. The loyalty they offered Jesus was put to the test when he was arrested, and one of them grabs a sword to defend him (14:47). They were in fact ready to die to save his life, but Jesus did not want his life saved. It is simply not possible to give your life to save someone who goes willingly to his own death. Jesus had embraced the idea that it was God's will for him to die. This affirmation is something the disciples could not make until after the resurrection. It was impossible for them to be loyal to Jesus at this point because they did not share his faith in God.

To say this much, however, is to raise an even larger question: Did the disciples have a choice or were they merely following a predetermined path? There are two conflicting clues in the immediate context. On the one hand, this is the second time that evening that Jesus had quoted from the Old Testament to explain the actions of his disciples before they transpired. And, as we have already seen, Mark's recounting of the Last Supper begins with an impressive display of Jesus' predictive power. Everything, it seems, happened just as he has said it would.

On the other hand, however, this story is not told as though people had no choice. When Jesus quotes Psalm 41:9, it is part of a veiled warning to Judas. Even the quotation from Zechariah 13:7 ultimately offers more in the way of hope than inescapable fate, for it is not the final word; it is a preliminary statement. The final word, the note in fact on which this Gospel ends—"there you will see him, just as he told you" (Mk 16:7)—is an open invitation to follow the risen Jesus to Galilee. Despite the emphasis on events transpiring according to Jesus' words and the words of the Old Testament, there is still an element of human choice present in this story.

How are these two disparate points of view held together in the narrative? It is obvious from the rest of Mark 14 that these predictions and their outcome are of more than passing interest. They form the framework for the subsequent accounts of Jesus' arrest and trial before the Sanhedrin. In the final analysis the passion narrative is not only Jesus' story; it is also the story of his disciples.

The text has a few obvious features. In the first place, there is no way to determine what might have happened had the disciples acted differently. Even with the elements of the story that seem to indicate that choice is possible, nothing in the text encourages us to pursue this line of thought. Second, the fundamental theme underlying the entire passage is that God was about to act. Finally, we note that the only person who acted with any degree of freedom was Jesus. His freedom is poignantly expressed in the prayer: "Abba, Father, everything is possible for you. Take this cup from me. Yet not what I will, but what you will" (14:36). Jesus expressed his freedom by confessing that all things are possible to God and asking God to let events transpire differently. In the end, however, he surrendered his wishes and affirmed what God was doing.

The disciples fulfilled the prophecy of Zechariah 13:7 in spite of themselves. Despite their protestations of loyalty and their actual attempt to rescue Jesus, they did in fact fall away. The difference between Jesus who exercised his freedom and the disciples who futilely protested theirs is that Jesus affirmed God's will while his followers did not.

These observations lead to the following reflection. The arrest, crucifixion and resurrection of Jesus was a time during which human choice was possible only within the framework of what God was doing. It was a time when there was no absolute freedom for people, and in that time the only way to exercise freedom was to affirm what God was doing. To choose against what God was doing, as Judas did, or to ignore it, as the other disciples did, is to act out against our will the very things we would choose not to do.

The Son of Man in the Hands of Sinners (14:32-42) By any normal definition of the word it is heroic to prevent someone from being beaten or killed. On the night he was arrested Jesus' disciples tried to assume the mantle of heroism. They were clearly willing to fight to save his life. Their willingness to risk their lives cannot be doubted, yet before the sun rose the next morning they had all deserted him. Something much more demanding than defending an unarmed man was required of them that night, and they failed the test. Nineteen centuries later when Kierkegaard wrote about Christian heroism, he said that it was something so private and personal that no one else would know about it. Kierkegaard saw the struggle of faith as essentially an inner contest. That night, perhaps for the last time, Jesus' first disciples turned a blind eye to the inner dynamics of faith. They thought the struggle lay with his opponents. So on that Passover night Jesus' followers were prepared sincerely and mistakenly to strike a blow against the enemies of God.

Jesus at Prayer (14:32-36) Jesus certainly had something different in mind when he told Peter, James and John to keep watch, after telling his other followers to stay behind and pray. Keeping watch is an obligation of faith prescribed by Exodus 12:42. Yet just as Passover recedes into the background of the cross at the Last Supper, so here the obligations of the traditional Passover vigil are refocused on the events that were to transpire that night. Mark has already prepared his audience for this transition. The Greek word translated "keep watch" (14:34) is the same word that appears in the parable about the absent owner of the house (13:33-37). The references to evening, midnight, cockcrow and dawn in that parable correspond to the major events of this night. What Jesus warned his disciples about in the parable happened to them here. When they should have been watching, they fell asleep.

For what should they have watched? On that night keeping watch meant looking for God to act again decisively to save the people of the covenant. Despite his private and public teaching about the cross, though, Jesus was the only one who had come to terms with what God intended to do. On this night the armies of Rome would not be driven out of the land. Instead, God would strike the shepherd who was also the Son on whom God's favor rested. Curiously, in this appropriation of Passover themes there is no question of the shepherd's sin. On the contrary, God was about to strike the only one who had exercised faith in every setting. This was to be an act of judgment directed against a man who had done no wrong, and its consequence would be the scattering of the flock.

Furthermore, God's judgment would not mean the end of the flock. The death of the shepherd and the scattering of the flock would create a new possibility for the sheep to be saved, because it was God's intention to raise the shepherd again. The scattered sheep were to be regathered as they followed the risen shepherd into Galilee. The death of the shepherd would seal a covenant that included both Israel and the nations, and it would be fulfilled when the rule of God is completed.

The covenant sealed by the shepherd's blood does not annul any of the earlier covenants that God has made. Like the prophecies of Isaiah and Jeremiah, this act of salvation depicts a loving God who continues to be faithful even when God's people persist in disobedience. Unlike those prophecies, however, there is no hint that the people are purified by the judgment that they would suffer. The Gospel of Mark contains nothing like the words of Isaiah 40:2. In this case the shepherd bears the weight of judgment, and his suffering opens a new path into the future.

This was the act of salvation that Jesus expected when he told his disciples to watch and pray. He kept the Passover vigil himself by praying. The words of his prayer in Mark 14:36 are both simple and profound. They express the honest struggle of a human being who stands before a terrible and awesome event, suffering an act of judgment that he does not deserve. Jesus faced the prospect of his imminent death, and he felt the universal human desire to save his life. Yet as the Son on whom God's favor rested, he also struggled to keep faith with the One he served.

Jesus kept watch by praying: *Abba, Father, everything is possible for you. Take this cup from me. Yet not what I will, but what you will.* There have been several earlier references to Jesus' praying, but this is the first time Mark states explicitly what Jesus prayed about. It is a deeply moving prayer, distinguished by its simplicity, honesty and trust. It is more than an anguished petition. It also affirms what and how Jesus believed about God. It is both an objective and subjective confession of faith.

The prayer begins by calling upon God with a term of intimacy, love and trust that was not part of the standard temple liturgy. *Abba* is a word whose precise meaning has been much debated in modern scholarship. It is, on one hand, a term of affection young Jewish children might use to address their father. In that regard it suggests intimacy and a deep bond between parent and child. *Abba* also appears in settings that require a sterner interpretation, where obedience and reverence are the predominant connotations (Kittel 1964). In this context both meanings are appropriate. God had addressed Jesus as Son on two occasions. At the baptism of Jesus the voice from heaven confirmed him as the one on whom God's favor rested, and at the transfiguration God clothed him with an unearthly splendor and gave him a place of distinction above even Moses and Elijah. *Abba* is the fitting response to the voice from heaven that called Jesus the beloved Son. At the same time Jesus' prayer concludes with a statement of profound reverence. This prayer employs both the language of intimacy and obedience, and it would be wrong to argue for one at the expense of the other.

Jesus' use of *Abba* is a particularly impressive introduction for his next affirmation. "Lord," "Lord of Hosts" or even "God Most High" would certainly have been appropriate ways of addressing the One for whom all things are possible. *Abba* personalizes what might otherwise be a formal confession of faith and sets the stage for the request that follows. *Abba* tells us something about how Jesus believed in God's omnipotence. The one to whom he prayed was not distant or aloof. The God for whom all things were possible, the God to whom Jesus was about to give his life, was faithful and loving.

The second aspect of this confession is the affirmation that *everything is possible for you*. Jesus had previously made two similar statements: "Everything is possible for him who believes" (9:23) and "all things are possible with God" (10:27). On those two occasions it was ultimately the resurrection that Jesus had in mind. Jesus' teaching since Peter's confession (8:29) has been based upon the fundamental paradox that the only people who can be saved are those who give up their lives (8:34-38). This teaching itself is based upon his faith in the power of God to do the impossible—to raise people from the dead. His confession was not something new. It was the foundation of his proclamation about the rule of God. In the Garden of Gethsemane, however, Jesus did not ask God for reassurance that he would be raised from the dead. When Jesus asked, *Take this cup from me,* he wanted God to change what was about to happen. In this prayer Jesus applied the same confession to another impossibility.

What precisely did he want God to do? Narrowly understood, the cup could represent the crucifixion (Kelber 1976:51). In that case Jesus would simply have been asking God to spare his life, a request that is certainly understandable, yet that by itself is strangely at odds with 8:34-38. Alternatively, the cup might be a symbol for what he suffered on our behalf. That interpretation cannot be dismissed out of hand, but the larger narrative framework of this Gospel lacks the details about vicarious suffering that typify this point of view. A more likely possibility is suggested by the two previous occasions on which Jesus spoke symbolically about his cup (10:38; 14:23-24). In each of those texts the cup signifies not only his death, but also the salvation that his death achieves. On this reading we might paraphrase his petition in the following way: is there not some manner for salvation to be accomplished other than through the death of Jesus? Or in the broader terms of the passion story we might ask whether there was a way for the people of God to be reformed other than through his death and resurrection, something perhaps like a purified remnant. It may seem surprising to think of Jesus asking God if there were not some other way for his mission to be accomplished. Yet this picture of Jesus at prayer is entirely consistent with Mark's emphasis on the humanity of Jesus. Of all the Gospels this one is particularly concerned to show the human face of the Son of God (Martin 1972:120-26).

The concluding words of this prayer are another clue about how Jesus believed. The words *yet not what I will, but what you will* stand in sharp contrast to what is often called our fixation with creature comforts. Our culture is preoccupied with the need to have more. The daily parade of advertisements in the media has convinced us that whatever we have is not enough. There is no more penetrating critique of the pursuit of excess than Jesus' prayer. It underscores the truth that self-denial and suffering are inescapable parts of following Jesus.

Yet it must also be said that not all suffering is befitting. Tragically, victims of abuse sometimes believe that it is necessary for them to accept the abuse. Some even believe that it is God's will for them to be abused. Jesus' prayer is not meant to suggest that victims of abuse should resign themselves to it. His suffering was a consequence of the gospel he preached. It was inflicted upon him by people in positions of power who opposed him and his message, and, as this Gospel makes perfectly clear, he was not silent about his suffering. His words about his own suffering and his denunciation of those who imposed it upon him are also part of the good news. The God whom Jesus called Father was not abusive, nor did he require that Jesus be silent.

Several years ago I heard a sermon on this text in which the pastor affirmed that it was not God's will for people to suffer abuse or be imprisoned in abusive relationships. By noon the following day the church staff had received twenty-four telephone calls from people within the congregation who asked for counseling about abuse. For those twenty-four people that sermon was good news, and their requests for help were the first step in their release from captivity.

This prayer is the second confession of faith we find on Jesus' lips. The first one is the Shema, which Jesus recited in 12:29-30: "Hear, O Israel, the Lord our God, the Lord is one. Love the Lord your God with all you heart and with all your soul and with all your mind and with all your strength." The two confessions have much in common, but where the Shema is corporate, Jesus' prayer is intensely personal. His personal confession goes beyond the Shema insofar as what the confession for all of Israel treats as a commandment, this prayer treats as an inner reality. Jesus called God Father, and in his willingness to affirm God's will above his own Jesus lived out this commandment. It was not a goal or ideal; it was the essence of life for him. The oneness of God in the Shema finds its reflection in the oneness of Jesus' love. To call God Father is to make loving God the foundation for all of life. Loving God is much more than a feeling. It is also a lifetime of choices and actions.

The Testing of the Disciples (14:37-42) The accounts of Jesus' praying and the sleeping disciples are woven together in an interesting way. Jesus prayed the same prayer two and possibly three times. Mark supplies no information about what Jesus did just before he returned to find Peter, James and John asleep for the third time. In fact, as the story line goes back and forth between Jesus' prayer and the disciples taking their rest, we read less and less about what he did and, by contrast, more and more about what they did—or rather what they did not do. These interwoven stories create two contrasting portraits of the testing of faith.

The disciples' test of faith hinges on the competing claims of flesh and spirit. This is the inner struggle that sets our desire to preserve and enhance our lives at all costs against that part of us that responds to God. The tension between flesh and spirit had already emerged with startling clarity when Jesus rebuked Peter for being on the side of humans rather than on the side of God (8:34). We should understand Jesus' rebuke in 14:37-38 to mean that their desire to be faithful to Jesus was genuine. Their spirits were willing in some sense to follow him, but the part of them that clung to dreams of life, power and glory was not strong enough to follow the lead of the spirit. When he came a second time to find them asleep, Mark tells us that their eyes were heavy, a pointed way of saying that they were giving way to the pull of the flesh.

When Jesus returned a third time to find them asleep, the NIV brings his opening comment into English as a question: *Are you still sleeping and resting?* In the Greek text behind this translation, though, it is not clear whether this should be a question or a declaration. In the earliest manuscripts the text is transmitted without punctuation marks or even spaces between words. In the 2001 edition of the Nestle-Aland Greek New Testament all the various clauses in 14:41-42 are treated as statements. The difference is not trivial. A question casts Jesus' opening comment in gentler terms. That is to say, a question could imply anything from a mild inquiry to a rebuke. A direct statement, however, casts this comment as an indictment. It is a declaration that they had failed the test of faith. On balance, it is better to understand this as a statement. There is little justification for reading it as a question, and in the context of Jesus' earlier commands to watch and pray, there is a finality about what happened when he returned for the third time. The time for watching had passed, and they were not up to the task.

His next comment, which the NIV renders "enough," is more problematic. This reading is essentially a translation from later Latin texts, and the most that can be said is that it is compatible with one of the possible meanings of the original Greek verb "to pay in full." This translation, however, is not supported by other Greek texts. There are no contemporary parallels for translating this verb in the absolute sense it has in the NIV's rendering of 14:41.

On the other hand, this verb can also mean to be far away or distant, and what has just been demonstrated is that watching was far from them. A similar metaphorical use of this verb occurs in 7:6: "But their hearts are far from me." Here the text moves easily from the charge that the three were still sleeping to the verdict that they had failed to keep their covenant obligation. Watching was far away. It was the furthest thing from their hearts.

From this point onward Jesus' death is treated as a foregone conclusion, an observation that raises the question of how Jesus received an answer to the request he made in 14:36. We might wonder if God spoke to him. Did he receive a vision of the future without his death? Was God silent, and did Jesus find his answer in the silence? Did he hear the approach of Judas with an armed guard? Any of these things might have happened, but the text has little to say about any of those possibilities. On the other hand, there is at least the curious juxtaposition of Jesus and the three he took apart. The interwoven pictures of Jesus at prayer and the three sleeping disciples suggest that he received an answer in their failure to keep watch.

Jesus declared: *The hour has come. Look, the Son of Man is betrayed into the hands of sinners.* Two of these terms, *Son of Man* and the verb *delivered,* appear in all three passion predictions. "The Son of Man will be delivered to the chief priests, elders and scribes" (8:31), "into the hands of men" (9:31), and "to the chief priests and scribes, who will in turn deliver him to the Gentiles" (10:33). The term *sinners,* however, is not mentioned in any of the passion predictions. In fact, it has appeared only once before, when Jesus was accused of eating with tax collectors and sinners (2:17).

In 2:17 *sinners* refers to Jewish people who did not adhere to the strictures of the law. Among other things, they did not wash their hands when they came from the marketplace, they associated with Gentiles, and they did not keep kosher kitchens. Here the term has a broader application, and it is broader in two ways. First, in this setting it has the sense of those who stand against the rule of God, for these sinners will share in the responsibility for Jesus' death. Second, *sinners* is now a universal term because there was no one, not the Twelve or even the three who represented the inner circle of Jesus' followers, who stood with Jesus in affirming God's will. Even Peter, James and John have proven themselves unfaithful. In the language of the passion predictions, there was no human being to whom God could have delivered the Son of Man other than sinners. Everyone except Jesus stood for a vision of salvation that undervalued the depth and ramifications of sin. Jesus alone embraced the salvation that God offered for sinful humankind. The failure of Peter, James and John to keep watch undermines the idea of a privileged inner circle whose members are somehow fundamentally different from everyone else.

There persists in some Christian circles a naive nostalgia about Jesus' first disciples. It is sometimes expressed as a desire to have been with them: "If only I could have heard what they heard, seen what they saw and felt what they felt." Stated in those terms, it reveals a fundamental confusion between being a fan and being a disciple. If it were not clear before, it is certainly clear in this grove of olive trees that what the three disciples closest to Jesus heard, saw and felt did not translate into a privileged kind of spirituality. Mark's presentation of the original disciples shows that physical proximity to Jesus did not make the challenge of following him any easier.

Judas's Betrayal of Jesus (14:43-52) Betrayal comes in many forms. It may be anonymous so that the identity of the betrayer is concealed. It may be conceptual as when a student professes the principles of his or her mentor, but undermines them behind the mentor's back. Betrayal may be motivated by the desire to humiliate or seek revenge, or can be direct and personal. Whatever its form betrayal is the antithesis of love and faithfulness.

The Gospel of Mark does not specify a motive for Judas's betrayal of Jesus. Very little is said about Judas. He is identified very early as the one who betrayed Jesus (3:19), but even at the Last Supper when Jesus predicted that one of the Twelve would betray him Judas is not mentioned by name. Judas appears as an actor in this Gospel only in this passage and in the material that comes just before and just after the anointing at Bethany (14:1-2, 10-11). There is little here to suggest what led him to betray Jesus, which leaves the story of Jesus' anointing as the one place in this Gospel to search for a motive.

The Moment of Betrayal (14:43-47) Although Mark treats the mo-

---

14:43 The sequence of statements about Judas's arrival appears as a witness to Jesus' authority even as he goes to the cross, rather than as an indication that he heard Judas's coming. Jesus' words *here comes my betrayer* are followed by the

tive indirectly, he presents the betrayal itself in the most direct terms. Judas had given his new companions a sign. They were to arrest the one he kissed. When he arrived on the scene, he went immediately to kiss Jesus and said, *Rabbi!* The breach of intimacy here is more disturbing even than the language Jesus used to predict his betrayal (14:18). It is impossible to imagine a more personal form of betrayal. In fact, to betray Jesus and call him *Rabbi* at the same moment is tantamount to accusing Jesus of teaching him how to consummate a betrayal. It is as though Judas were saying, "You taught me to do this."

Typically when a betrayer succeeds, he or she has managed to exercise a high degree of control behind the scenes. In this case, however, despite Judas's apparent success there are clear indications that he was not in control of what happened. Judas's arrival was not a surprise. Jesus announced that Judas was about to arrive even before the others realized what was happening. At the moment of his arrival Judas is again identified as one of the Twelve, a reference to Jesus' prediction that one of the Twelve who was dipping bread with him would betray him. And in the unfolding story the word *immediately,* a key term associated with Jesus' authority and with the rule of God, appears twice in 14:43, 45, where it is translated "just as" he was speaking and going "at once." Despite Judas's seeming triumph this betrayal takes places according to the Scripture and to Jesus' words. Someone else was in charge of the events that night.

The Scriptures Must Be Fulfilled (14:48-52) Interpreting the prophecy of Zechariah 13:7, Jesus had also predicted that his other followers would all fall away. Their protestations of unfailing loyalty come inevitably to the reader's mind when one of them struck at the head of the high priest's servant. It was not a disabling blow and succeeded only in cutting off the ear of one of the party that had come to arrest Jesus. It symbolizes perhaps the futility of a handful of peasants and fishermen taking on a squad of trained and disciplined guards, and it was futile in more than one sense, for it demonstrated a sincere but

---

words *just as.* The description of things happening immediately after Jesus speaks has been a sign of his authority since the earliest parts of this Gospel.

misplaced loyalty. That is to say, Jesus' followers were prepared to die *for* him, but they were not prepared to die *with* him. On this night salvation would come to God's people not through the defeat of their enemies but through the death and resurrection of the Savior.

Jesus put an end to the hostilities by saying: *Am I leading a rebellion that you have come out with swords and clubs to capture me?* It is an ironic accusation in the form of a question, for in asking whether they thought he was leading a rebellion, Jesus used the same word that he had employed to compare the temple to a den of robbers (11:17). He pointed back to that encounter specifically when he went on to observe: Every day I was with you, teaching in the temple courts, and you did not arrest me. What he said and did took place openly, in broad daylight, while the course of events that enabled them to arrest him required secrecy and stealth. Despite the official sanction that cloaks their actions, they look more like robbers than he does. Nevertheless, his final comment in this scene—*but the Scriptures must be fulfilled*—signifies even to his followers who tried to remain faithful that Jesus would not oppose the mob that had come to arrest him.

But the Scriptures must be fulfilled, however, is more than a gesture of submission. It is a powerful theological affirmation whose import has been the subject of a great deal of debate. Should it be interpreted narrowly, as an apology for Jesus' death (Bultmann 1972:282)? That is to say, is its purpose to assure the believing community that Jesus' death was actually the fulfillment of a divine plan despite the argument that no one anointed by God should have suffered such a cursed and shameful death? Does it apply primarily to the events attending the Last Supper and crucifixion (Lane 1974:526)? Or does it have a larger significance (Anderson 1976:324; Hooker 1991:352)?

This Gospel certainly presents the death of Jesus as an expression of God's will. The divine-passive construction of 8:31 and the heavenly voice of 9:7 are clear statements of the relationship between God's providence and Jesus' death. On the other hand, there are some problems with holding tightly to a narrow interpretation of this text. This Gospel begins with the phrase "It is written in Isaiah the prophet," a reference that is in fact a conflation of texts which stretch out in time from the occupation of the land to the intertestamental period. This sweeping historical reference in itself serves as a caution against a narrow reading of Old Testament texts. That is to say, the Evangelist's first use of Scripture is expansive. Second, the juxtaposition of John's arrest (1:14) and the beginning of Jesus' ministry casts the shadow of the cross over the entire Gospel. Third, a wide variety of Old Testament texts feature prominently in the development of the conflict between Jesus and the institutions of Israel. These texts constitute a much broader witness than those that could be used as proof texts for Jesus' death. The preeminent place of the cross in this Gospel and Mark's use of Scriptures in the escalating conflicts about Jesus argue against a narrow view.

Furthermore, the competing ideas about salvation present throughout Mark's passion story support a broader view of the fulfillment of Scripture. Jesus' entry into Jerusalem and the celebration of Passover itself contrast the popular hopes for a messiah with the hope that is rooted in a shepherd who dies and rises from the dead. In the immediate context Jesus' followers were prepared to fight for him, a clear reflection of the hope that the Messiah would lead Israel in a mighty triumph over its enemies. Thus the story of Jesus' betrayal and arrest sets one kind of hope against another. In light of the conflicting views of salvation and Mark's use of the Scriptures it is more appropriate to understand the statement *but the Scriptures must be fulfilled* as an invitation for the hearers of the Gospel to locate their own hope for salvation in his death and resurrection.

The account of the young man who ran away naked (14:51-52) should be understood in this light. It is suggested that this is Mark's signature—that this young man is actually the Evangelist himself (Taylor 1974:562). This is an interesting possibility, but there is little to support it. Even the observation that none of the other Gospels include this incident is insufficient to justify identifying this mysterious young man as Mark. An explanation for why the Evangelist included it has to be sought somewhere else.

Nothing in the text suggests that the Evangelist attached any particular importance to the young man's identity. In addition to the lack of a name, none of the other specific identifiers that are important in the larger passion story are used. There is no mention of his being one of the three or one of the Twelve. He is simply identified as one who followed Jesus. There is an "everyman" quality about this story. He could have been almost anyone who followed Jesus. There are, on the other hand, two salient points in his description: he was wearing a linen garment, and he ran away naked. The linen garment points ahead to Jesus' burial, when he was wrapped in a linen cloth (15:46). The same Greek word is used in both places. On more than one occasion Mark has introduced a term whose significance becomes apparent only later in the story. John's baptism (1:7), for instance, points forward to the baptism of the Holy Spirit rather than backward to any precedent. Similarly, the cup of 10:38 points forward to Jesus' prayer in 14:36, where its meaning is revealed. So the significance of what this young man did is to be found in its connection to Jesus' death.

The picture of naked abandonment is stated twice in 14:52 with the phrases *he fled naked* and *leaving his garment behind*. This image serves as a marked contrast to Jesus, who at that moment set everything aside to do the will of God. Jesus gave up his own life to affirm God's will. In contrast, 14:51-52 describes someone who left literally everything behind in order to save his life (Meyers 1988:369). This is a vivid denial of the call to become disciple, for his disciples are called to do what Jesus did: If anyone would come after me, he must "deny himself and take up his cross and follow me" (8:34). At precisely this point the universal aspect of this incident becomes apparent: it is impossible to follow Jesus without acknowledging that his death is an act of unselfish obedience. This anonymous man symbolizes a profound truth. Ultimately, there is only one way to follow Jesus—to give up one's life for his sake and the gospel's (8:37-38). All other attempts to follow Jesus lead to disillusionment, defection or betrayal.

We live in the age of the consumer church, where salvation is couched in terms of wealth, power and success. The mantra in much of the Protestant church for the last generation has been, "If we want to grow, we have to meet people's needs." As an organizational principle, perhaps, there may be some wisdom in this dictum. Churches that do not help people make connections between the gospel and their lives will struggle to claim the loyalty and commitment of members and visitors. Yet we must be very careful about the kinds of connections we try to make. The consumer approach to congregational life is based on the needs people feel. The story of Jesus' arrest and betrayal, on the other hand, reminds us that none of his followers felt the need for a Savior who would die for them. The foundation of the church is the death and resurrection of the Son of God, and we cannot forget that the salvation Jesus brought is much more comprehensive than the relief of the needs we feel. It is no small matter for the church; it is a question whether our congregational life will be built around our assessment of ourselves or around the mission of God.

Jesus' Trial Before the Elders of Israel (14:53-72) The principle of presumed innocence is one of the foundations of modern civil life, as is the right to be tried without undue delay. In most cases people who are suspected of breaking the law can count on two things: their guilt will have to be proven in a court of law, and they will not be arbitrarily confined. In recent history, though, these fundamental human rights have been overridden when the threat to national security was deemed very grave. From 1939 to 1944 approximately 120,000 Japanese Americans were removed from their homes and held in internment camps without trial. It was done legally. At the highest levels of government, actions were taken that suspended the rights for this one group of American citizens. In war or in times leading up to war, basic human rights are often compromised. Now that terrorism has moved from the fringes of life to the center of democratic societies, labeling someone a terrorist threat has sometimes been sufficient justification to deny his or her basic human rights.

False Testimony (14:53-65) Jesus was certainly brought to court expeditiously, but this trial is so prejudiced against the defendant that there is some question that it actually happened. The trial took place late at night. It would have been impossible to give proper notification. Jesus did not have the opportunity to call any witnesses on his behalf. And the trial opened, it seems, without a specific charge against him. The procedure itself has no claim to objectivity since the chief priests and the whole council attempted to gather evidence against him (14:55). Their clumsy efforts create the impression that this defendant was presumed guilty. Judged by modern standards of human rights, Jesus' trial was a farce.

Jesus' innocence is the subject of the next trial, something that also underscores the difficulties with this one. Pilate was clearly reluctant to condemn Jesus to death, and his reluctance casts this procedure as a caricature of justice. The irregularities in the trial at the house of the high priest ought to be taken seriously, but they are not in themselves sufficient justification for asserting that it never took place. They are consistent with a rush to judgment, and history is replete with examples of how far the law can be bent when the threat to the structures of power seems great enough (Meyers 1988:372-74).

The evidence that led to Jesus' conviction did not come from the testimony marshaled by the court. In 14:56-59 Mark states three times that the evidence against him was false and did not agree. Two Old Testament texts stand behind Mark's description of the witnesses. Deuteronomy 17:6 stipulates that the consistent testimony of two witnesses is required to sustain a legal indictment. The charge specified in Mark 14:58 may have come close to the truth: *We heard him say, "I will destroy this man-made temple and in three days will build another, not made by man."* The editorial comment in the following verse—*yet even then their testimony did not agree*—suggests that there was some substance to this testimony. Jesus had in fact prophesied against the temple (11:17-23) and predicted its destruction (13:2). The words he was accused of saying, however, do not appear in this Gospel. The statement that comes closest to this accusation is found in John 2:19: "Destroy this temple, and I will raise it again in three days." But even that prophecy omits the terms *man-made* and *not made by man,* and it lacks the claim that Jesus himself would destroy one temple and build another.

It is not difficult to understand why such a charge would have appealed to the court. The prophecy in Mark 11:17-23 is parabolic, and it does not seem that even Jesus' own disciples understood clearly what it meant. Furthermore, Jesus had not made the prophecy of 13:2 in the temple courtyards before large crowds of witnesses. He had given it to a smaller group of his followers. If, however, it was established that he had predicted the destruction of the temple, his opponents would have had a

---

14:56 There are enough departures from what may be reconstructed about court procedures at the time of Jesus to raise the question whether a trial such as Mark describes could have happened at all. For a defense of the integrity of Mark's account,

compelling tool for discrediting him. They could have cast him as another Jeremiah, whose prediction of the temple's destruction also included the destruction of Jerusalem and conquest of Judea. Denouncing Jesus as a prophet who predicted the destruction of Jerusalem would have gone far to reestablish the authority of the chief priests and elders when their judgment saw the light of day. More to the point, that Jesus had asserted his own power to destroy the existing temple and build another not made with hands raises the specter of blasphemy. Thus, convicting him on the one charge that is specified would also substantiate the chief priests and elders' claim to be the guardians of orthodoxy. Mark's record, though, is clear: the testimony was false, and it did not agree.

It would be enough to establish the testimony as false to say that the witnesses did not agree. Yet Mark repeatedly says that the testimony was not only inconsistent but false. This repetition leads to the second relevant Old Testament text: "You shall not give false testimony against your neighbor" (Ex 20:16). Giving false evidence in a court of law is a violation of the Mosaic covenant. God's covenant with Israel forms a major part of the structure of this Gospel. Isaiah's understanding of the covenant is the starting point for Mark's story of Jesus. The covenant lies behind the account of the transfiguration, and a few hours before this trial began, Jesus had inaugurated a new covenant. Yet here in the highest court of God's people, the chief priests and the ruling elders solicit false witnesses and break the covenant in the name of preserving orthodoxy and order.

It is a bitter irony that those so preeminently entrusted with the covenant should violate it so flagrantly. It is not, though, the only irony in this passage. Mark's passion story is full of irony, and another important point of irony in this scene is that Jesus did not conduct himself as a person who is on trial for his life. Jesus offered nothing in the way of a defense. Even under the hostile prompting of the high priest he remained silent. His studied silence leaves the impression that the whole proceeding was about something else.

---

see Gundry 1993:893.
14:58 The terms of the accusation raise the question of contact between the pre-Markan and pre-Johannine traditions.

There are two ways to understand Jesus' statement in 14:62: *I am.* *And you will see the Son of Man sitting at the right hand of the Mighty One and coming on the clouds of heaven.* It is either an admission of guilt or a prophecy against his opponents. If it were an admission of guilt, it would be hard to explain his persistent silence before his accusers. There is no hint that he had been worn down by the testimony and questioning. Even when his accusers came near the truth, Jesus held his tongue. It is as though he had chosen the moment to speak, and his response to the high priest was not couched in terms of confession or admission of guilt. His words bristle with challenge and confrontation. The form of mockery that follows Jesus' statement indicates that the court had heard his declaration as a prophecy. His face was covered, he was beaten, and some of those present challenged him to prophesy (14:65), to identify who had struck him. This kind of mockery is most intelligible if Jesus had just prophesied against them. It is as if they were saying, "You claim to be a prophet? Very well then, prove it."

The first words Jesus addressed to the court, *I am,* are a direct reply to the high priest's question: *Are you the Christ, the Son of the Blessed One?* Their authenticity has been challenged on the grounds that Jesus did not make a direct claim to be the Messiah anywhere else in the Gospel and preferred to refer to himself as the Son of Man, even when Peter called him the Messiah (8:29). Why would Jesus call himself the Messiah here, when he had invariably avoided the term up to this point? The answer lies in the observation that the chief priest and members of the Sanhedrin were the ones who by virtue of their own authority needed to recognize his claim. From this perspective it was less important what the masses in Galilee and Judea thought. Although he had proclaimed the good news of the rule of God by the sermons he had preached and the miracles he had performed in Galilee, Jerusalem was the place where his identity and authority had to be recognized. And these were the people who ought to have done so. If they rejected him while the masses acknowledged him, the people of Galilee and Judea stood on the brink of

---

14:62 Some commentators treat Jesus' response as though it contained only a single, unified image (Nineham 1968:407-8), but that interpretation founders on a significant discrepancy. If only one scene was described here, the logical sequence of events

civil war. There is no indication anywhere in the Gospel traditions that Jesus intended to incite armed conflict among the people of God. It is entirely consistent with Mark's presentation of Jesus that he should claim to be the Messiah before this audience.

There may be more here than a claim to be the Messiah. In Greek the simple expression translated *I am* can also serve as the name for God, so it is possible to see in these words a further claim to be divine (Ladd 1974:168-69). There are two reasons for being cautious in pursuing this idea. In the first place, a great deal depends upon what language would have been used in the court. A dual reference is certainly possible in Greek, but it is unlikely that a conversation in either Hebrew or Aramaic could have produced this conjunction of terms. In the second place, when Jesus went on to say *the right hand of the Mighty One,* he referred to God indirectly. The high priest did the same thing when he asked if Jesus was the Son of the Blessed One. Referring indirectly to God was considered to be a way of avoiding blasphemy. It is difficult to imagine Jesus putting forward a claim to be divine, something that would certainly have been considered blasphemous by the court, and in the very next moment using the kind of language about God that was designed to keep a person from committing blasphemy. The argument would be more convincing if the text read something like "at the right hand of my Father." On balance, it is not impossible that Jesus or Mark also intended to advance a claim to divinity, but the matter is ambiguous, perhaps intentionally so.

His claim to be the Messiah, nevertheless, was also a claim to have authority over the elders of Judea, but it is not the only such claim in Jesus' testimony before the court. The two others contained in his prophecy are even more sweeping. For those of us steeped in traditions of Western thought it may not be easy to appreciate the import of his words: *You will see the Son of Man sitting at the right hand of the Mighty One and coming on the clouds of heaven.* This statement was addressed to the whole court, and it invoked two Old Testament

---

would be for the Son of Man to come in glory and then be seated at the right hand of power. That the Son of Man is seated first, and as it were out of sequence, indicates that we are not dealing with one event to which both images refer.

scenes to which Jesus has already referred on different occasions.

In 12:35-36 Jesus had appealed to the picture of someone seated at God's right hand when he posed the question: "How is it that the teachers of the law say that the Christ is the son of David?" That is a Semitic way of asking whether David was greater than the Messiah. In answering his own question Jesus invoked Psalm 110:1: "The LORD said to my Lord: 'Sit at my right hand until I put your enemies under your feet.'" On the basis of this text Jesus argued that the Messiah was David's Lord. This was a matter of no small consequence, for if the Messiah is greater than David, then the rule of God that the Messiah ushers in need not follow the expectations for the Davidic kingdom. It would be the Messiah who interpreted David's reign, and not the other way around. That is to say, the expectations aroused by the hope for the restoration of David's kingdom need not define the rule of the Messiah.

In order to appreciate fully the prophetic element in this image, we need to keep the court scene clearly in mind. The court considered itself to be in a position to judge any claim about Jesus and any claim he might make. The prejudice of the court is manifest, however, and its members are accordingly cast in the role of Jesus' enemies. To be seated thus at the right hand of the Mighty One is to take a position above David and to wait while God vindicates the one who has been so wronged by his enemies. This part of the prophecy is therefore both an assertion that they do not have the right to pronounce judgment on his messianic authority and a prophecy that God would judge the witnesses and members of the court.

What authority did Jesus specifically claim to have? That is the subject of the second image, for the Son of Man who is seated at the right hand of power is also the Son of Man who comes in the clouds of glory. This scene is taken from Daniel 7:13, where "one like a son of man" appears before God to receive authority over all people. It seems from Daniel 7:27 that the "one like a son of man" is a corporate figure, composed of those among the people of God who have suffered unjustly. It is also clear that those righteous ones suffered oppression at the hands of the other peoples of the world. In Daniel's vision the scales of justice are finally righted when the people of Israel who have suffered so horribly are finally given the authority to judge those who persecuted them. On Jesus' lips, however, the term *Son of Man* had both a more specific and a broader meaning. He treated it as a title and applied it to himself. As a title, the term *Son of Man* has a narrower focus. It refers to Jesus himself. At the same time, though, his authority has a broader application, for what comes clearly into view here is not only the oppression of the Gentiles, but also the abuse of power by the leaders of the people of God. The first passion prediction in Mark 8:31 laid the responsibility for his death at the feet of the chief priests, elders and scribes. The third passion prediction in 10:33 indicted the nations for this miscarriage of justice. He is the Son of Man who was delivered into the hands of men (9:31). This trial would certainly qualify as an abuse of power so that Jesus is shown to be the quintessential *one like a son of man* who suffered unjustly at the hands of Israel and the nations. This Son of Man is the innocent one whom the whole world condemned to death.

Jesus claimed as the Son of Man an authority that was much greater than the court's. In the imagery drawn from Psalm 110:1 he asserted both the right to define the role of the Messiah and the expectation of waiting for God to judge his enemies. In the second scene he asserted that he would judge not only them but all humankind. This is then both a declaration about the role of the Messiah and a pointed prophecy against the chief priests and the elders.

We ought not to overlook that the first time Jesus claimed the title *Son of Man* in this Gospel, he asserted his right to forgive sin on earth (2:10), and the accusation of blasphemy lay just beneath the surface of the passage. Then he gathered disenfranchised people from the margins of society (2:17) and claimed the right as the Son of Man to return the Sabbath to its original purpose as a day set aside for humankind (2:28). The Son of Man appears initially in Mark to reconcile and restore. Then follow the passages about the Son of Man giving up his life and suffering at the hands of the leaders of Israel and the nations. The last theme to emerge is the picture of the Son of Man as the judge of history. It is surely no accident in Mark's Christology that the one who will judge the nations and right the wrongs of the past came first to heal.

Forgiveness emerges in an intriguing way in Jesus' prophecy against the temple. Whether we read 11:25 as a late and somewhat clumsy insertion into the text or as an integral element of the good news Jesus preached may depend upon how we interpret his final declaration before the court. Was it merely a prophecy against the self-serving stewards of Herod's Temple? Or did the Son of Man, who had already claimed the right to forgive sin, also proclaim his authority over the chief priests and elders in order to open another pathway to reconciliation with God?

In the Gospel the quest for justice and the forgiveness of sin are inextricably linked. Such a connection stands in contrast to social systems where justice is primarily punishment or retribution. In the Gospel the goal of justice is restoration, and the goal of forgiveness is reconciliation. Justice is not a form of social revenge, nor is forgiveness permission to do harm again. There is a dynamic tension between the two, and what holds them together is the suffering and authority of the Son of Man. Jesus is the hope for those who need to be forgiven and restored.

In this regard the long witness of the African American church is instructive. Jesus has stood at the center of its faith through the brutal years of slavery, the grinding years of legal segregation and the numbing poverty of urbanization. It has not preached revenge or retribution. It has welcomed white folks into worship when black folks were not welcome in white churches. In the face of massive discrimination it has consistently sought restoration and reconciliation, yet it has never abandoned the pursuit of justice. Forgiveness and justice are inseparable components of its communal life, and the African American church's experience of Jesus holds the two together.

The high priest had heard enough. He tore his robes in a gesture of horror and declared that Jesus had committed blasphemy. The Sanhedrin followed suit and condemned him to death. What precisely the high priest considered to be blasphemy is less certain. Was it the invocation of the divine name, the claim to be the Messiah or the assertion that chief priest and elders would be judged? It is difficult to decide which part or parts of Jesus' declaration the high priest had in mind, and it is also doubtful whether this court had the right to pronounce a capital sentence (Taylor 1974:570). What is clear, though, is that Jesus had so offended the court that its outraged members felt he deserved to die.

Peter's Denial (14:66-72) The mocking that followed Jesus' condemnation serves as a bridge to the account of Peter's threefold denial.

The jeering cries of "prophesy!" are reflected ironically in 14:66-72, which culminates in Peter's breakdown. During that night Jesus made two predictions. The prophecy about Peter and the other disciples was fulfilled in stages before dawn. The fulfillment of the other prophecy lay beyond the ending of Mark's Gospel. Here again Jesus perceived things about people that they did not want to face in themselves, and that perception underscores his claim to be the judge of all humankind.

Prophecy is not the only ironic connection between these accounts, for Peter, who followed Jesus nearly into the court itself, gave false testimony. He lied three times. The scene in the courtyard of the high priest unfolds as a counterpoint to Jesus' trial. The maid confronted Peter directly at first and later accused him before a group of bystanders of following Jesus. They in turn pronounced something like a verdict, when they insisted that Peter was surely a Galilean. It is as though there were two trials that night. In Jesus' trial the witnesses spoke falsely, while the accused alone spoke the truth. In Peter's, the witnesses spoke the truth while the accused swore falsely.

According to 14:71 Peter both cursed and swore that he did not know Jesus. The Greek says only that Peter cursed. It does not say that he cursed himself, as the NIV indicates. It is possible, of course, that he did curse himself, but in the typical Semitic way of swearing Peter would have said something like this: "May God strike me dead if I know the man." That is itself a kind of curse, and it would be strange for Mark to depict Peter cursing himself twice. It is impossible to rule out the more startling thought that Peter cursed Jesus (France 2002:622).

Mark twice describes Peter warming himself by the fire (14:54, 67), but after the maid's first question he moved away from the fire into a darkened gateway. The symbolism here is intriguing. Peter was not only moving away from the light. As his denials became more and more forceful, he also moved further away from Jesus (Waetjen 1989:225). Ever since his confession that Jesus was the Christ (8:29) Peter had been of two minds. Despite this insight he was nevertheless on the side of humans rather than God (8:33). Previously that night despite his deepest protestations of loyalty he was unable to keep watch with Jesus in the Garden of Gethsemane, and he was oblivious to Jesus' own struggle. Here, however, Peter's protestation of loyalty came unraveled. He denied the one he had tried to follow even at a distance, just as he had denied Jesus' teaching that it was God's will for him to die. In the final analysis there is no way to follow Jesus without coming to terms with his death and resurrection.

Peter's behavior illustrates a fundamental theme in this Gospel: hardness of heart. The words *understand* (14:68) and *remembered* (14:72) recall the exchange between Jesus and the Twelve in 8:17-19, where Jesus asked whether the disciples had hardened hearts. Sadly, after the flight of his followers and Peter's denials, the question must be answered in the affirmative. Ultimately, even his own disciples had hardened hearts. Faith is not a matter of privilege, membership in an inner circle or the possession of arcane secrets. It is fundamentally a matter of hearing the word of God, accepting and acting on it. To hear the word of God and to ignore or reject it at any point is to risk the judgment of God. Peter's story makes it clear that the same dynamics apply to everyone.

For Mark sin and hardness of heart are two sides of the same coin. Sin is not merely, as we so often suppose, a matter of breaking a commandment. In the courtyard of the high priest Peter broke one commandment three times, but to think of sin as simply trespass or transgression does not explain Peter's downward spiral. Peter was trapped in a pattern of behavior that his best intentions and most devout protestations could not alter. Sin is a power that people cannot break themselves. Its counterpoint is the love of God that hardens our hearts, for God does not judge to destroy but to save.

In this case we might say that God hardened Peter's heart in order to break it, and in its breaking a new possibility emerged that Peter could not have created himself. Here we return to the opening scenes of the Gospel. It was the fulfillment of a prophecy that brought Peter to this point, and prophecy is the note on which the Gospel of Mark opens. First there is the conflation of texts that Mark attributes to the prophet Isaiah. Then John the Baptist, a prophet, preached a message of repentance, leading to Jesus' proclamation to repent and believe the gospel (1:1, 4, 15). At the end of this passage Peter has been brought face to face with a truth he did not want to acknowledge. In many ways this Gospel is the story of how Peter, who symbolizes the best efforts of pious people to be faithful, is brought to the point of repentance. Peter's new possibility is also a matter of prophecy, but it could not be realized until after Jesus' resurrection. Even as Jesus invoked Zechariah 13:7 to predict that his disciples would fall away, he promised to go before them into Galilee after his resurrection (Mk 14:28). Before Peter swore the oath that culminated in his own denial of Jesus, the Son of Man had already laid out the path of salvation for Peter as well as for everyone who would follow him. This characterization of prophecy as the word of God that both judges and saves is the foundation of Mark's Gospel. Only God's grace could save Peter from what he invoked upon himself, and only God's grace can break the power of sin in us. C. S. Lewis observes: "To love at all is to be vulnerable. Love anything, and your heart will certainly be wrung and possibly be broken" (1960:169). Love is a wonderful gift to give and receive, but we often hold closest to our hearts the things that bring us into great peril. Grace is the power of God's love that comprehends our vulnerability and rescues us from the peril into which we fall.

Jesus, Pilate and the Crowd (15:1-15) Traffic school is an amazingly fertile ground for irony. Several states in America have enacted laws that delete one minor traffic violation from the record of licensed drivers who complete an authorized session at traffic school. Since cleaning up their driving records may prevent sudden spikes in the cost of automobile insurance, hundreds, if not thousands, of motorists grudgingly graduate from traffic school every week. It is not, by all accounts, a refreshing or stimulating experience, especially since many of the people who attend traffic school do not think they deserve to be there. That is to say, they do not think they have really done anything wrong—they have simply suffered the misfortune of having been caught. The brooding boredom of one eight-hour session was relieved when the instructor asked a student who repeatedly challenged his interpretation of the law, "What is the source of your information?" The student replied, "I'm, uh, a policeman," at which point the entire classroom—with one notable exception—expressed its thunderous appreciation for the officer's presence among them.

Mark's passion story is laced with irony. Jesus' trial before the Sanhedrin revolved around a prophecy he gave to the high priest and for which he was mocked, even as the prophecy he had given about Peter was being fulfilled. In that trial the crux of the irony is the question of who spoke for God. Did Jesus speak for God when he denounced the chief priests and elders as enemies of God? Or did the high priest speak for God when he labeled Jesus' testimony blasphemy? In the trial before Pilate and the ensuing scene with the crowd, however, the irony revolves around Pilate's attempt to exercise the authority of his office. He resisted the maneuvering of the chief priests, elders and scribes, yet ultimately found himself doing exactly what they had wanted. Jesus did not behave like a person whose life was in Pilate's hands, a matter at which Pilate himself was amazed (15:5). Finally, what seems to be Pilate's attempt to exercise both mercy and justice ends in a farce. He released a guilty man and condemned an innocent one. Pilate is also the one who finally made Jesus' identity as Messiah public (Hooker 1991:376), but other than Jesus no one—including Pilate himself—believed it to be true. These points of irony indicate that some authority much greater than Pilate was behind the course of events.

The Trial of Jesus Before Pilate (15:1-5) The second phase in the legal maneuvering against Jesus began *very early in the morning* when the chief priests, elders and scribes handed Jesus over to Pilate. There are three words of particular importance in 15:1, and the phrase *very early in the morning* contains two of them. One is a Greek word usually translated either "immediately" or "as soon as." Since the opening verses of Mark this particular word has been associated with the in-breaking reign of God. It signifies that the time of waiting is over and God's action is at hand. The second word, often translated "dawn," appears in the parable of 13:33-37. Dawn is one of the times that the parable specifies for watching. The third term, *hand over*, is well known from the three passion predictions, and the sequence of actions in 15:1 closely follows the third prediction in 10:33-35. These terms are a further confirmation that God was at work in the events leading up to Jesus' death.

There can be little question that the chief priests, elders and scribes sent Jesus to Pilate because they did not have the right to carry out a capital sentence themselves. It is also probable that they wanted Jesus to die in a way that would bring as much reproach on him as possible. The chief priests seem to have been the ones who stirred up the crowd to demand a crucifixion. To die on a cross, of course, was to incur a curse according to Deuteronomy 21:23. Later while Jesus hung on the cross, some of the false testimony from the first trial had apparently leaked out to the crowd, which mocked him as the one who would destroy the temple. Jesus was thus cast as a pariah (Waetjen 1989:227) who had spoken against the temple, and the crowd called for him not only to be executed but to die in such a way that he was cursed.

In the face of all the machinations that went on around him, Jesus was an island of silent resolve. It is true, of course, that Jesus was also silent except for one reply in his trial before the Sanhedrin, but his conduct is more puzzling here. Before the Sanhedrin he gave a straightforward answer to the question "Are you the Christ, the Son of the Blessed One?" That retort provoked the court to act. In this case, however, his response was ambiguous.

Jesus' reply to Pilate's question, *Are you the king of the Jews?* is variously translated "you have said so" (RSV) and *yes, it is as you say* (NIV). The difference between these two renderings is considerable, and the Greek text can support either translation. Lane (1974:551) and France (2002:628) take his statement as an affirmative response, while Gundry (1993:924) and Hooker (1991:367-68) regard it as intentionally ambiguous and noncommittal. Which one more accurately translates the flavor of his response is difficult to say. On the whole, however, the context suggests that the RSV's "you have said so" is preferable. If Jesus had claimed unambiguously to be the king of the Jews before Pilate, there would have been no need for his opponents to make other accusations. That one charge would have supplied the grounds to sustain a verdict of guilty of the capital offense of insurrection. But in 15:3-4 the chief priests, apparently recognizing the weakness of their case, present a series of other charges. If Jesus had meant to say *yes, it is as you say,* it is difficult to see why his accusers felt the need to shore up their case.

What is clear, however, is that the entire character of his response was different. In the trial before the Sanhedrin Jesus not only claimed to be the Messiah, he also prophesied against the very powers that had orchestrated the trial. There is no corresponding prophecy, though, in the trial before Pilate. Furthermore, before the Sanhedrin his own testimony was the evidence that convicted him, but before Pilate he gave his accusers nothing that helped their case. Yet it is also clear that Jesus did not contest the charge. If he did not explicitly affirm it, neither did he make any effort to protest his innocence. Pilate, it appears, gave him every opportunity to refute the charges against him, but except for his ambiguous statement in 15:2 Jesus simply refused to testify. He appeared before the Sanhedrin as a man unjustly accused. Before Pilate, though, Jesus appeared as someone who had chosen not to defend himself.

On the surface Jesus' vastly different testimony at these two trials is quite puzzling, and as long as we view the trials as events whose purpose was to establish the truth about him there is little hope of solving the puzzle. Mark's passion story, though, is full of irony, and the broader context of this Gospel offers a very different way of understanding these two scenes. Under any normal set of circumstances the purpose of a trial is to establish guilt or innocence by evaluating the evidence. These were not normal circumstances, as the parade of false witnesses before the Sanhedrin demonstrates. For Mark, the trials of Jesus and subsequently those of his followers serve another purpose. Courtrooms are the places where the good news of God's reign is proclaimed to the peoples of the world and the powers that govern their lives.

Mark's presentation of the gospel is grounded in a corporate conception of life. If Jesus had preached only to crowds in Galilee and Judea, he would not have proclaimed the gospel to the Jewish people. To proclaim good news to individuals is also to press the claims of God on the organizations, institutions and powers in which and under which they live. Jesus' proclamation of the gospel began in the villages of Galilee, but it led step by step to his trial before the Sanhedrin in Jerusalem where he challenged the chief priests and elders to recognize the authority God had given him. In the Gospel of Mark evangelism and prophecy go hand in hand, and the trial of Jesus was no simple court proceeding. It was a call for the leaders of Israel to repent and believe the gospel.

Mark 13:9-11 describes Jesus' followers proclaiming the gospel in the same way to the peoples of the world. That, too, is a matter of prophecy both in terms of what Jesus said about them and in terms of what they would say to governors and kings. He encouraged these simple folk not to be intimidated by the trappings of power and money because the Holy Spirit would tell them what to say. That is the stuff of prophecy. So also, in their testimony evangelism and prophecy were to be inseparable.

From this point of view Jesus' conduct at the two trials makes perfectly good sense. In neither case was he concerned to defend himself. Before the elders of Israel he claimed to be the Messiah and fulfilled the role of evangelist by giving a prophecy. He had come when the time had been fulfilled to proclaim the kingdom of God, to call the people of Israel to repent and believe the gospel (1:14-15), but he was not an evangelist to the nations. That was the role his disciples were to play. When his followers preached the good news to the peoples of the world, they would prophesy to governors and kings. So for all practical purposes Jesus stood mute before Pilate. He did not deny his identity, but neither did he utter a prophecy. He had already proclaimed the gospel to the people of Israel in faithful obedience, and now he watched quietly for God to act.

If Jesus did not declare himself to Pilate, neither did Pilate declare himself on the question of Jesus' guilt or innocence. Nowhere in the extended proceeding of 15:1-15 did Pilate pronounce a verdict. He delivered a sentence without finding that Jesus was guilty. With ironic cruelty Pilate simply acceded to the will of the crowd, ordered Jesus whipped and sent him off to be crucified. In this way the full claims of the gospel were not yet brought against Rome. Jesus did not challenge Rome with an open claim to have authority over Caesar, and Rome did not reject him, even though it authorized his execution at the will of the crowd.

Jesus and Barabbas (15:6-8) Other than the Gospel traditions there is no record of Pilate customarily releasing one prisoner at each Passover. Lane argues, nevertheless, that 15:10 describes the kind of political act that was not only possible, but even probable (1974:555). On the other hand, it has been argued that the specter of Pilate pleading with the crowd for the life of an innocent man does not in any way correspond to his reputation as a ruthless politician (Hooker 1991:366, 369). Another way of reading 15:6-15, however, corresponds to Pilate's well-attested character. Pilate's appeal to the crowd is believable if his goal was to embarrass the chief priests, elders and scribes rather than to save an innocent man.

The editorial comment *knowing it was out of envy that the chief priests had handed Jesus over to him* indicates that Mark was under no illusions about Pilate's character. It was not the thought of Jesus' innocence that prompted Pilate to act, but the perception of a weakness on the part of those who were trying to force his hand. If, as the text suggests, Pilate had come to the conclusion that he was being manipulated by the chief priests and elders, Jesus' recent popularity with the crowd presented him with an opportunity to embarrass the Jerusalem establishment. His appeal to the crowd may well have been designed to exploit an apparent rift between the Jewish leaders and the Jewish people. Pilate's first words certainly do not sound like an appeal for objective justice. They are an arrogant display of power: *Do you want me to release to you the king of the Jews?* This inflammatory question assumes the crowd's right to choose its king as well as Pilate's power to decide a king's fate. As it turned out, however, the chief priests outmaneuvered Pilate, and on this reading he would also have been embarrassed. So he took out his frustration on the easiest target—a man who had already demonstrated that he would not defend himself. In the final analysis, Mark's depiction of Pilate rings true.

In 15:5 Mark points out again that Jesus' passion took place during Passover. The expectation that God would send someone to deliver the people of Israel ran high, and in that highly charged atmosphere Mark contrasts two very different saviors. On the one hand, there was Jesus, a prophet who denounced, provoked and healed but did no violence. He did not condemn the peoples of the world as the enemies from whom Israel had to be delivered. On the contrary, he treated the chief priests, elders and scribes as though they were the enemies of God's rule. The crowd was alive with the rumor that he had spoken against the temple (15:29), and at this point he stood alone. Barabbas, on the other hand, was a man of violence. He had been arrested with a group of insurgents in one of the numerous small uprisings that characterized Judea at that time. It is impossible to determine which particular armed conflict he had been part of, but Rome was clearly the enemy of this would-be savior.

Twice Pilate called Jesus king (15:9, 12). The first time he simply used the title to refer to Jesus, but the second time Pilate called Jesus *the one you call king.* Curiously, the crowd did not contest Pilate's use of the title, but in calling for Jesus to be crucified the chief priests and the crowd made it clear that Jesus was not the Messiah they wanted. The dialogue between Pilate and the crowd is an ironic conversation about what kind of king this crowd and its leaders would accept.

Barabbas is a representative figure with a symbolic name. Mark's description of him (15:7) places him among a group of people without singling him out in any way except by his name. Barabbas is an Aramaic name, easily recognizable as "Son of the Father" since Mark has already given us a translation for Abba (14:36) and a similar patronymic in Bartimaeus (10:46). Mark provides a translation for Bartimaeus but not for Barabbas, as though he expected us to figure it out for ourselves. Abba, of course, is the term Jesus used to address God, but it is not the way anyone else in this Gospel speaks to God. The contrast between Jesus and Barabbas raises the question of who the true son of God is: the one who would solve Israel's problems by the use of violence or the one who called the nation and its leaders to repent. Like the name Barabbas itself, Mark does not tell us the answer; it is something he leaves for his readers to decide for themselves.

The Outcome of the Trial (15:9-15) The outcome of this trial is decidedly anticlimactic. It lacks a conclusion. Pilate did not make a decision in his chambers, and even after his interaction with the crowd Pilate never actually pronounced a verdict. The real confrontation had already occurred between Jesus and the Sanhedrin, where the ultimate question was whether the leaders of Jerusalem would acknowledge the authority of the Son of Man. They did not and asserted instead their own authority by condemning him on the charge of blasphemy. The rest, including the trial before Pilate, is presented almost as a foregone conclusion. Incited by the high priests, the crowd asked for the release of Barabbas. At this point it appears that Pilate's hand is forced. To release Jesus would be to put himself in the difficult position of having to explain, perhaps to other Roman officials, why he could not successfully prosecute a messianic pretender whom the leaders of Jerusalem themselves had condemned.

From the Evangelist's point of view this is pure irony. The Sanhedrin has condemned Jesus and then managed the appearance of Jesus before Pilate so that the representative of Rome carried out the sentence of death it had declared. Jesus' death was the result of a manipulative strategy by which the clients of Rome forced their foreign overlords to carry out their wishes. Pilate, on the other hand, made sure that the elders of Israel bore the responsibility for condemning *the king of the Jews.* Twice in 15:9-15 he called Jesus *the king of the Jews,* and the cross itself bore an inscription that read THE KING OF THE JEWS (15:26). The leaders of the Jewish people and the representative of Rome used each other for their own ends.

This is an ironic and damning portrait of authority. Ultimately, there was no justification for his execution, as the Evangelist is at pains to point out. His crime, if it could be called that, was defying the authority of the leaders of Israel as the prophets had done. The chief priests, elders and scribes had found a way to deal with the threat he posed, and Pilate had neither the courage nor the inclination to stop them. So the king of the Jews was handed over to a squadron of Roman soldiers for crucifixion. If there were nothing more to these events than political intrigue, the death of Jesus would be little more than fodder for cynics. Yet in the generation after his death Jesus' followers continued to press the claims of the kingdom of God in Jerusalem, throughout Asia Minor, Rome and even into Spain and India. The book of Philemon offers one small, but telling insight into the relationship between the proclamation of the gospel, issues of justice and the interface between the emerging church and the world. There was more at work in the death of Jesus than politi-

5:11 If, as Gundry thinks, the crowd that called for Jesus to be crucified was the same crowd that had listened gladly to his teaching in the temple (1993:926), the depiction of Jesus as someone who wanted to see the temple destroyed explains a great deal. The crowd that had welcomed him into the city was looking for the liber-

cal intrigue. Jesus died in the final analysis because it was the will of God for him to die.

Jesus' Humiliation and Death (15:16-39) Humiliating a condemned prisoner is prohibited today by laws against cruel and unusual punishment. What happened to Jesus would be illegal in the modern democracies of the Western world. In the Mediterranean world of the first century, however, humiliating a deposed or despised ruler was not at all uncommon. Defeated kings and generals were routinely paraded before the people of the city or nation with whom they had been at war. This is in fact the explanation for Paul's metaphor in 2 Corinthians 2:14-16: the very smells of the triumphal procession remind the victors of their salvation and the conquered enemies of their condemnation.

The Soldiers Mock Jesus (15:16-20) History contains many parallels for the kind of mockery to which Jesus was subjected. An entire company of soldiers, perhaps an exaggeration, assembled to dress him in the royal colors, strike the head on which a crown of thorns has already been placed and spit upon him. The purple robe was a caricature of his royal splendor, and the crown of thorns may have served the same purpose. If, as is often supposed, the thorns pointed down and were pressed into his head, the crown would have been another instrument of torture. If, on the other hand, the thorns pointed up and away from his head (Hooker 1991:370), they would have mimicked the radiating splendor of a real crown. The cane or reed was a parody of a royal scepter, and with consummate cruelty the soldiers used it to beat Jesus, who had just suffered a flogging. The mockery reached its climax as the soldiers knelt before him, hailed him as king of the Jews and spat at him. Mark is careful to point out that the whole affair took place within a palace. There could be no more ironic place to make sport of a king.

This is the second time Jesus has been humiliated and mocked. The first mocking took place after his trial before the Sanhedrin. Common to both events are the reports of spitting and beating. Apart from that,

---

ation of Jerusalem. But if the temple was to be destroyed, Jerusalem would fall. The mockery of Jesus in 15:30 offers a possible explanation for how the crowd might have turned against him.

these two shameful incidents take very different forms. In 14:64-65 the elders made fun of him because of the prophecy he had given in 14:62. Despite the ridicule, however, one of Jesus' predictions came true in the very next incident when Peter denied him. In this context the soldiers displayed their scorn not for a prophet but for a king who had no following. This comparison leads us to ask whether there are any signs of his true kingship in what follows.

The Crucifixion (15:21-39) Two signs point to Jesus' kingship at the very beginning of the account of the crucifixion. The first appears in 15:21 when the soldiers force Simon to carry his cross. Simon was a member of a Jewish family that had some unspecified connection with Cyrene in North Africa. By itself Simon's service might be taken as another form of ridicule, as though the soldiers thought it was not right for a king to be burdened with his own cross. The reference to Alexander and Rufus, however, points in another direction. Alexander and Rufus play no role at all in the story, unlike the previously unmentioned women in 15:40 who served Jesus. The mention of Alexander and Rufus makes sense only on the assumption that they were people the Evangelist expected his church to know because they were part of the early Christian community. This text points beyond itself to the later experience of the early church. Jesus' first exercise of authority was calling disciples, and just before the crucifixion Mark introduces as followers of Jesus the sons of the man who carried his cross. What begins as mockery becomes a sign of Jesus' messianic authority.

The second sign of his kingship is found in the subtle statement that he refused the wine and myrrh offered to him just before he was crucified (15:23). The wine laced with myrrh was supposed to act as a drug to deaden the pain of being nailed to the cross. His refusal to drink the concoction is sometimes taken as an indication that Jesus

---

15:21 Waetjen (1989:231) advances the intriguing idea that Mark's brief description of Simon indicates that he was a laborer with few rights in an oppressive economic system. That is difficult to see in the NIV's translation of *erchomenon apo agrou* as "passing by on his way in from the country," but it is certainly possible if the phrase in question is translated more literally "coming in from the field." If Waetjen is correct, then the soldiers had devised an additional way to mock Jesus. They turned his

chose to experience the full extent of the suffering set before him. Jesus may have wanted to keep whatever sharpness was left to him (Lane 1974:564), although there is no particular reference in the passion story to that idea either. On the other hand, Jesus had taken a vow not to drink wine again until God brought the kingdom to its fulfillment (14:25). That vow is the best explanation in this Gospel for his refusal to drink the wine mixed with myrr and it is another sign of his true kingship.

This silent gesture is a powerful statement. In rejecting the drug, Jesus affirmed his faith in God to bring to fulfillment the good news with which his ministry began. Jesus did not cast aside the messianic implications of everything that he had done up to this point. Although he continued to be speechless until the lonely cry in 15:34, his silence was not the despondent abdication of a man who had tried and failed to become king. It was a silent testimony to his faith in God and to his role as Savior and Messiah.

The story of the crucifixion is built around a series of references to time in a way that is unlike anything else in the Gospel. At the third hour after dawn (15:25) Jesus was crucified between two robbers and mocked again. At the sixth hour (15:33) darkness covered the land. And at the ninth hour (15:34) Jesus called out to God, uttered a last cry and died. Time is a fundamental part of the structure of Mark. From the opening prophecy until the crucifixion the words *at once, as soon as, suddenly* and *immediately* have all signaled the fullness of time and the approach of the kingdom of God. The words *very early* in 15:1 are also part of this familiar narrative device. They remind us that the trial and crucifixion of Jesus were not an aberration in God's plan. The time of waiting has been fulfilled, and the rule of God was breaking into history through these events. Yet there is more to the hours that frame the crucifixion than the fulfillment of God's prom-

---

death into another symbol of oppression. The resurrection, however, turned everything upside down by opening the way for a new community in which there were no distinctions of class.

15:27 Lane points out that the word translated "robbers" could also be used of rebels like Barabbas (1974:568). Robbery was not a capital offense, but rebellion against Rome was.

ises. The word *hour* is invested with new meaning in the apocalyptic discourse of Mark 13. In 13:11, 32-36, an hour becomes something more than a measurement of time. It signifies the presence of a special kind of time, a time of testing and judgment. The third, sixth and ninth hours of the crucifixion are times of judgment.

The third hour. Three processes of judgment are at work in the crucifixion of Jesus. At the surface level, of course, is the judgment executed against Jesus for which Pilate, the chief priests and elders were primarily responsible, and it is the subject of the events that are recorded from the third to the sixth hour. At first it appears to be the only judgment that was taking place, but there was a profound irony at work that they did not perceive.

Irony runs through virtually every detail of the account of the crucifixion in 15:24-32. The soldiers who had mocked him (15:16-20) and divided his garments at the foot of the cross (15:24) were acting out the script of Psalm 22:7, 18. Mark portrays what seemed to be an indisputable expression of Rome's authority as a series of acts dictated by a sovereign God. The indictment against Jesus, THE KING OF THE JEWS (Mk 15:26), is similarly laced with irony. He was a king whom the leaders of Israel had rejected, yet he was the one who resolutely looked to God for deliverance (Ps 22:8). God had called him Son (Mk 1:11; 9:7), and his deliverance was not too far away. He was the king of the Jews despite the taunts of the powers assembled in Jerusalem.

Furthermore, his crucifixion between two robbers was not a mark of shame but an indication of his glory. The reference to *one on his right* and *one on his left* points back to 10:37, where James and John asked to sit on his right and left when he came into his glory. This Gospel lacks a picture of the risen Christ appearing in his glory, and the one scene that might otherwise be taken as a representation of Jesus in his glory, the transfiguration (9:7, 9-13), points away from itself to the crucifixion. These considerations raise the question of whether Jesus appeared in his glory on the cross. Is it not the very essence of his ministry that he identified with sinners and placed his life irrevocably in God's hands? The stunning glory of the Messiah is that he gave his life to ransom sinners. Once again what appears to be further mockery turns out to be an ironic statement of the truth.

On the other hand, the taunts directed at Jesus were a denial of the truth. Those who passed by wagged their heads at him, another enactment of Psalm 22:7, and said: *So! You who are going to destroy the temple and build it in three days, come down from the cross and save yourself!* Jesus had not said he would destroy the temple. That particular accusation was part of the false testimony presented at his trial before the Sanhedrin, and its repetition here helps to explain how the crowd had turned against him. It is hard to imagine a resident of Jerusalem or Judea who would have rallied to the support of someone who claimed that he would destroy the temple. More to the point, though, is the misunderstanding behind the jeer: *Come down from the cross and save yourself!* Jesus could not save himself by coming down from the cross. According to Mark 8:34-38 the only way for Jesus to save his life was to give it up. To have come down from the cross would have been to turn his back on God and cast his lot on the side of humankind.

In 15:31 the chief priests and scribes ridiculed him as though he were an impotent pretender to the throne: *He saved others but he can't save himself! Let this Christ, this King of Israel, come down now from the cross, that we may see and believe.* Despite their smug derision, the King of Israel hung on the cross, and the condescending gibe *that we may see and believe* was an utter misconception. It was not a question of seeing and believing. They needed to believe what they saw. Their salvation, not his, hung in the balance.

The two men who were crucified with him also joined the mocking. Although Mark has not recorded any of their insults, he has used a pregnant word to characterize what they said. The Greek verb translated "insult" can also be translated "blaspheme." In this context insult is certainly not a bad translation, but to Mark's Greek-speaking audience the description of their words as blasphemy would have been very significant. Those who saw the truth in what Jesus said to the high priest would have appreciated the blasphemy of the two thieves. Jesus had come to serve the least, and as he hung on the cross he was certainly the servant of all (10:45). It was the most perverse kind of blasphemy to insult the one who was giving his life as a ransom for many, particularly for two men who could be numbered among the many.

The sixth hour. At the sixth hour darkness came over the whole land. This scene depicts a time of utter silence. Mark records no gibes, insults or mockery. There is only darkness. It is as though Jesus had been abandoned in the darkness, and this sense of being cut off from everyone sets up the lonely cry of 15:34. With stark simplicity Mark leaves his readers to contemplate the mystery of the Son of God hanging on a cross, cursed by God (Deut 21:23) and utterly alone.

The darkness was not an accident of nature. It came from God, and it symbolizes God's judgment on sin. Many Old Testament texts show the connection between darkness and judgment (e.g., Zeph 1:15; Mic 3:6; Joel 2:2). Throughout the prophets darkness and judgment go hand in hand. In the death of Jesus alone on the cross, then, we are invited to see God's judgment on sin. The innocent Son of God, the Messiah, the King of Israel died while a man of violence escaped death. Jesus did not die in the place of only Barabbas; he died in the place of Pilate, the chief priests, scribes and elders who abused their power; he died in the place of the mob who rejected the Savior God had sent; he died in the place of everyone who is caught in the power of sin. His death opened a new avenue of salvation. No longer are people delivered from God's judgment because they have suffered enough for their sin. They are now saved by their identification with the one who suffered on their behalf. Jesus gave his life as a ransom for many, so that many could be freed.

God's judgment for sin fell on Jesus, but Mark does not intend for us to understand that this particular act of judgment suspended all others. The temple, for example, still stood under God's judgment, and its destruction was not far off. The punishment that fell on Jesus did not compromise God's holiness or change in any way God's opposition to sin. It did, though, open the way for those who follow Jesus and believe the gospel to escape the eternal consequences of their disobedience and be forgiven for their sin.

The ninth hour. The depth of suffering Jesus endured on the cross is evident when he cried out with a loud voice: *My God, my God, why have you forsaken me?* There is no lonelier cry in all the Bible. The physical suffering from the flogging, mockery and crucifixion is almost unimaginable for us. The gibes and insults are perhaps closer to our experience, but it is impossible for us to comprehend the sense of abandonment Jesus felt. At the beginning of the Gospel Jesus is the one on whom God's favor rests (1:11). He is the one who should be heard even above Moses and Elijah (9:7). And now near the end of the Gospel God abandons him (15:34). This was not a pretense, nor was it something done for effect. His cry of despair was authentic, and it came from a kind of pain that no other human being can understand. God had turned away from the innocent one who bore the sin of the whole world.

We cannot comprehend what was in Jesus' heart as he uttered this awful plea, but Mark has shaped the story so that we see more than Jesus' agony. There is hope in the God on whom Jesus still called. The reference to Alexander and Rufus (Mk 15:21) offers a glimpse of the flock that will follow Jesus into Galilee. Jesus' refusal to drink wine (15:23) points to the final consummation of the kingdom of God. And Psalm 22, which has so many echoes in Mark 15:16-34, moves finally from despair to deliverance. Its high point is the salvation of all the families of the nations (Ps 22:27), which anticipates the exclamation of the centurion in Mark 15:39. Thus Mark's presentation of the crucifixion does not diminish Jesus' suffering and death in any respect, but it does encourage us to remember that each of the three passion predictions ended with a prediction that God would raise him from the dead.

There was also judgment between the sixth and ninth hours, and this judgment falls on the leaders and people of Israel. After Jesus' exclamation in 15:34, one of the people in the crowd said: *Listen, he's calling Elijah*. There was a tradition that Elijah would come to rescue the innocent sufferer (Jeremias 1964:935-36), but another tradition about Elijah is closer to the story line of the Gospel—the expectation that Elijah would return before the inauguration of the age to come (9:11-13). Jesus knew that Elijah had already returned, and in the awful realization that God had turned his back on him Jesus knew that Elijah would not return to take him down. In any event, he had not called out to Elijah. Jesus had called out to God. At this point the people in the crowd could not make sense of what they heard, just as they did not make sense of what they had seen in the ministry of John the Baptist. Like Peter their hearts had been hardened.

That judgment foreshadows the tearing of the curtain in 15:38. There were two curtains in the temple that Herod built: an inner curtain separated the holy of holies, the temple's inner sanctum, from the rest of the temple, and an outer curtain separated the temple itself from the courts beyond its walls. Only the high priest could proceed past the inner curtain, and only Jewish men could proceed from the courts into the temple proper. Mark does not specify which of the two curtains was torn, but the centurion's confession, which follows immediately afterward, suggests that it was the outer curtain that kept Jewish women and all Gentiles from the center of worship. The verb translated "torn" in 15:38 is another form of the verb rendered "torn open" in 1:10. At the beginning of his ministry the heavens were torn open and the Spirit of God descended on Jesus. At the end of the Gospel the curtain of the temple was torn from top to bottom, and the Gentiles were granted full access to the worship of the living God.

How did the centurion perceive who Jesus was, and what precisely did he mean by the confession: *Surely this man was the Son of God?* According to 15:39 the centurion heard his cry and saw how he died. Jesus died in a very unusual way. Crucifixion ended in suffocation as the victim's body weakened and collapsed upon itself until the condemned person could no longer breathe. Jesus did not die like that. He uttered a loud cry and expelled his last breath. Every soldier knows one simple rule of conflict. If you do not try to save your life, you will lose it. Jesus did not live by that rule. He had done nothing to save his life, and at the end he gave one last cry as though he were giving it up.

Perhaps something like that was the sequence of thought that led to the centurion's confession. In the final analysis, though, we simply cannot be certain how he arrived at his momentous conclusion. Mark does not give us access to the centurion's mental processes. He is like the Syrophoenician woman who spoke to Jesus in parables (7:24-30) and the woman who anointed him for burial (14:9-10). They are people who say or do the most profound things, yet they are the most unlikely instruments of revelation. It is one of the integral themes of Mark that the people who should understand do not, while the people who seem to be outsiders perceive things with startling clarity. Mark's God is the God of surprises, even as psalms and prophecies from the Old Testament are being fulfilled. To believe in this God is to learn to expect the unexpected. What the centurion meant when he exclaimed that *surely this man was the Son of God* is difficult to pin down. The Greek text lacks the definite article before the term *Son of God,* and it is doubtful that this Gentile would have understood the connection between the terms *Son of God* and *Messiah.* Given his own cultural background, we might conclude that he thought Jesus was a divine man or a deified hero. In the context of this Gospel, however, the term *Son of God* has a much larger meaning. Yet even if the centurion's confession was bounded by the forms and meanings of his own culture, what he said points to something greater. He perceived the truth, even if he did not understand it (Lane 1974:576). Mark leaves his audience at the foot of the cross after showing us what the centurion witnessed and what he said, as though to ask, "What do you believe?"

The Empty Tomb (15:40—16:8) An energetic young man stepped forward one Sunday morning after the conclusion of the program for single adults and said to the pastor who had spoken, "I really love this program and I would like to join the leadership team." The pastor pointed over to the coffee urns and said, "That's great! Come early next week and make the coffee." The young man looked puzzled and replied, "Perhaps you didn't hear me. I am volunteering to be a leader." The pastor pursed his lips and said, "I did hear you, but perhaps you do not understand what it means to be a leader in the church. If you're not willing to serve, you're not qualified to lead."

Waiting for the Kingdom of God (15:40-47) Watching the crucifixion from the distance were the only followers of Jesus who stayed with him to the end, a group of women who had *cared for his needs* during his ministry in Galilee: *Among them were Mary Magdalene, Mary the mother of James the younger and of Joses, and Salome.* The Greek verb translated *cared for his needs* (15:41) is the same word Mark uses to describe the ministry of the angels to Jesus in the wilderness (1:13) and the word Jesus used to describe the mission of the Son of Man (10:45)—*diakoneō* ("to serve"). Here we learn for the first time that women had been part of the group of disciples who followed him in Galilee. Their presence at the crucifixion with the other women who joined them was another form of service, as was their subsequent attempt to prepare his body for burial.

The picture of these women caring for Jesus' needs and watching him die is very moving, but by itself it may be misleading. The NIV's translation lacks the specific connections with the idea of service in 1:13 and 10:45. It is no small point. It is a question of whether we read 15:41 as a touching piece of sentimentality or perceive the deeper significance of what the women did. Were they simply the ones who did the work that was beneath the men's dignity? Or were they doing the work of angels? Did they enact the mission of the Son of Man? Did they realize what the men preferred to avoid, that the most important thing is serving?

It is surely no accident that the women are described here for the first time in the language of discipleship. They followed Jesus. In the hierarchy of first-century Galilean life their presence had gone unnoticed. Now that delusions of power and glory had led the men to desert Jesus, however, the women who had followed him remained. If we say that Jesus died for our sin, we must also say that his death exposes the convoluted nexus of human motivations and sweeps all of them away except for one—love. The men's affection for Jesus was tainted by their ambition. When their dreams crumbled to dust, they ran away. The women, whose affection was expressed in acts of service, remained. Even though they too had not come to grips with the divine necessity for Jesus' death and resurrection, they did remain, if from a distance, with him. Their service is held up at the cross and compared favorably to his. What follows from this comparison in Mark's Gospel is a complete overturning of the existing social hierarchy, for two of these women were the first ones to be entrusted with the news that Jesus had risen.

Someone else was also present on the periphery, but Mark does not mention him until after he has introduced the women as disciples. Joseph of Arimathea went to Pilate to claim Jesus' body. Mark describes Joseph as a member of the Council, which is generally taken to mean that he was a member of the Sanhedrin that had condemned Jesus the night before (Lane 1974:579; Gundry 1993:984). If he was a member of the Sanhedrin, then we must assume either that he was not present at the trial or that he kept his silence. The one point about him that Mark does make clear is that Joseph was waiting for the kingdom of God. This is the first time that this description appears in Mark, and its late appearance implies two things. First, Joseph expected the kingdom of God to come through someone like Jesus, rather than through a figure like Barabbas. Second, he was willing to take some risks on Jesus' behalf, for he went to Pilate as evening drew near on the Day of Preparation, the day before the Sabbath.

Mark's description of what he did indicates that he handled Jesus' body himself (15:46). It is hard to imagine that he could have purchased a shroud, taken Jesus' body down from the cross, wrapped it, placed it in a tomb and sealed the tomb before evening fell. Furthermore, Joseph had to get Pilate's permission to remove Jesus from the cross. Pilate did not believe that Jesus had already died, so he sent for the centurion to check Joseph's report. That was a great deal for Joseph to accomplish between three in the afternoon and sundown, and sundown signified the beginning of the Sabbath. Mark presents us with the possibility that a Jewish leader of considerable standing handled a corpse on the Sabbath. The Sabbath was a holy day, and touching a corpse was a very unholy thing to do. What drove his action was the fear that the soldiers would take Jesus' body down from the cross and discard it unburied outside the walls of the city, which was the usual outcome and final humiliation of crucified rebels (Crossan 1994:123-27). There was little chance that Joseph could have been sure of finishing everything he had to do before the start of the Sabbath. It was at the very least a risky thing to do, and it was, in any event, hardly a course of action that would have endeared him to other leaders in his community. For Joseph, waiting for the kingdom of God meant denying himself in some sense and honoring Jesus.

Waiting for the kingdom of God is often a dangerous matter. Jesus drew a lot of criticism for associating with outcasts. Many of the people he healed lived at the lower levels of the social order. His following included at lot of people from the underclasses of Galilee and Judea, and he died—in the language of 10:45—serving all. Ministering to the poor and marginalized is still dangerous, as the witness of six priests in Latin America demonstrates. Very early in the morning of November 16, 1989, a small company of uniformed figures forced them out of their beds at the Jesuit Central American University in San Salvador and marched them outside the dormitory to execute them. A few days after their deaths Mauricio Colorado, then attorney general of El Salvador, warned Pope John Paul II that the Salvadoran government could not guarantee the safety of priests and bishops "who have persisted in keeping alive this questionable ideology of the church of the poor" (*Los Angeles Times,* November 26, 1989).

Joseph of Arimathea stands out as a person of distinction who took a great risk as he waited for the kingdom of God. What he did for Jesus recalls the confrontations in the early part of the Gospel about how to keep the Sabbath. Jesus had asserted that the Son of Man was lord of the Sabbath (2:28). The controversy stories in Mark 2—3 illustrate the conflict between the new, which the kingdom of God brings, and the old, representing the traditions of the culture that opposed the kingdom. In Joseph's conduct the tension between the old and the new appears dramatically once again. At the very moment when the powers opposed to the kingdom of God seemed to have triumphed, the hope of the kingdom of God moved this man to take a great risk.

The Women at the Empty Tomb (16:1-8) The conflict between the old and the new is evident at one other point in this story: the identity of the women who served Jesus. They were clearly concerned to observe the Sabbath traditions, so they watched Joseph place Jesus in the tomb (15:47) and then waited until the Sabbath had ended before attempting to anoint his body for burial (16:1). The second woman named *Mary* appears here in the passion story for the third time. In 15:40 she is identified as *Mary the mother of James the younger and of Joses;* in 15:47 she is *Mary the mother of Joses;* and in 16:1 she is *Mary the mother of James.* Mary the mother of James and Joses appears earlier in Mark (6:3), where she is also identified as the mother of Jesus (Waetjen 1989:240).

Based on a comparison of this text with the passion story in John,

15:47 *Joseph* is a variant rendering of *Joses.* In the Greek text the name is spelled in

Wenham argues that this Mary is not the mother of Jesus (1975:8, 10). It is true that Mark introduces several new figures in the account of Jesus' crucifixion. Neither Mary Magdalene, Salome nor Simon of Cyrene have appeared in Mark's Gospel before. It is possible that the Mary of 16:1 is not the Mary mentioned in 6:3 (Edwards 2002:485-86). Yet this is a place where we might expect to find Jesus' mother, and Mark treats Mary the mother of James the younger and of Joses differently than the other women listed here. Mary Magdalene and Salome are referred to in exactly the same way throughout the story of Jesus' burial. Their names remain unchanged each time they are mentioned. On the other hand, this Mary is identified in three different ways in these few verses. No other person in this Gospel is treated in this way. It is as though the Evangelist were inviting his readers to think more carefully about who she might be.

Jesus' mother first appears in this Gospel at the door of the house where he was teaching (3:31-35). That interchange between them prompted Jesus to give a radically new definition of the family: his family consisted of all those who do the will of God. That statement would have come as a considerable shock to his natural family, and it follows another major surprise—reconstituting the people of God around the ministry of the Twelve (3:13-21). In that section of Mark new structures of life emerge that take their form and meaning from the rule of God. The family is redefined. The nation is redefined. Even the relationships among his followers are changed. From that point on, whatever resists or opposes the authority of the kingdom of God is part of the old order. In the old order prestige, privilege and position count for a great deal. Relationships in the new order, though, are built upon service and sacrifice for the rule of God.

Mary appears as a disciple who served Jesus faithfully even after the men had forsaken him. Even though the Gospel was written well after the resurrection, there is no claim of privilege for the mother of Jesus. There is no struggle for influence or control. There is no contest between mother and son about his place or hers in the family. If Jesus' glory was his death on the cross, then her glory is her service to him. By not describing the role of Jesus' mother and the other women ear-

the same way each time he is mentioned (6:3; 15:40; 15:47).

lier in the Gospel, Mark holds up the cross as the place where the most fundamental restructuring of human life takes place.

As soon as possible after the Sabbath had ended, the three women went to the tomb to anoint his body for burial. Jesus was anointed for burial, however, before the crucifixion (14:8), and when they arrived they found the stone rolled away, the tomb open and the body gone. Instead of Jesus' body, they found a young man sitting inside, waiting to give them a message: *Don't be alarmed. You are looking for Jesus the Nazarene, who was crucified. He has risen! He is not here. See the place where they laid him. But go, tell his disciples and Peter, "He is going ahead of you into Galilee. There you will see him, just as he told you."*

The resurrection is portrayed in stunning understatement. There is no celebration of the victory over death, no joyful reunion between Jesus and his followers, no demonstration of supernatural power. In fact, even the messenger in the tomb is described only as a young man. This is not to say, of course, that Mark was unaware of the accounts of the risen Jesus. The message that the women receive in 16:6-7 clearly demonstrates that Mark was aware of those events. There could be no gospel without a resurrection. Yet Mark treats the resurrection obliquely. There is a message from Jesus but no appearance of the one whom God has vindicated.

As the narrative stands, the words of Jesus rather than the resurrection itself occupy center stage. The message from the risen Lord is not a new word. It is the same message he gave them on the night of his betrayal: "But after I have risen, I will go ahead of you into Galilee" (14:28). These are words of repentance and faith. For the disciples who forsook him and especially for Peter, who struggled in vain to keep his pledge of faithfulness, this message is a summons to turn their backs on the past and follow Jesus into a new future.

The Gospel ends where it began. The opening summary of Jesus' preaching is: "The time has come. The kingdom of God is near. Repent and believe the good news" (1:15). Repentance and belief are two overarching themes that tie this Gospel together. At the end of the story they have a fullness of meaning that was not possible earlier. At the beginning of the Gospel the disciples repented and believed when they left their nets beside the sea to follow Jesus. Now, however, they have come face to face with something that seemed absolutely unthinkable—that it was God's will for Jesus to die and rise again.

The resurrection of Jesus established the validity of a fundamental, new truth about human life. Life is not about acquisition, accumulation, privilege and power. On the contrary, that is ultimately death: "Whoever wants to save his life will lose it, but whoever loses his life for me and for the gospel will save it" (8:35). The resurrection of Jesus is the vindication of both his person and his word.

Perhaps in this we find an explanation for the indirect way in which the resurrection of Jesus is handled. This account of Jesus' teaching and ministry is written for an audience that is considerably removed from the original events. The audience has not seen the risen Jesus, nor is there much in this Gospel to foster the hope that later disciples would see him in their lifetime. How then would they understand the good news? How would they know the truth of the apostolic preaching that the rule of God had come? The approaching kingdom of God is so closely tied to the person of Jesus that we have to wonder what has become of it since the resurrection.

Mark's answer is apparent in 16:7-8, where he focuses the reader's attention upon Jesus' words. As the first disciples knew the truth of the gospel in following Jesus, so too the kingdom of God can be experienced and understood as later disciples follow his words. As the Evangelist has been at pains to show, it was not a lack of loyalty to the person of Jesus that led to the falling away of the Twelve. It was their failure to accept and act upon his words about the cross. For later generations of his followers, the kingdom of God is present as people follow Jesus' words, in the same way that it was present during his earthly ministry. We do not have to see the risen Jesus to know the power of the kingdom of God. We encounter, recognize and welcome it as we obey his teaching.

None of this, however, should be taken to mean that the rule of God is bound by what we experience. The rule of God was present through Jesus as a power that challenged the other centers of power in first-century Galilee and Judea, whether his followers felt or discerned it. The gospel that Mark proclaims is much greater, much more substantial than our experience. It is still shaping life and history, even if we do not perceive it. The kingdom of God is greater than the sum of people who believe in it.

This Gospel is addressed to people who have profound choices to make, and Mark presents the resurrection through their eyes. He treats the resurrection of Jesus in the same way that he treats the other miracles in this Gospel, as though it were an enacted parable. It contains several similarities to the raising of Jairus's daughter (5:35-43). Except for Jairus's immediate family the only witnesses were Peter, James and John. Jesus enjoined them all to silence. They were to say nothing about what they had seen, and yet the child was alive. Those who had not been allowed into her room were left to wonder at the profound implications of Jesus' statement that the child is "not dead but asleep" (5:39). So, at the end of the Gospel we are in a position like theirs. We do not see what happened in the tomb, but there must have been more to the story or there would be no story at all. Like the women who were left trembling and bewildered (16:8), the empty tomb confronts us, and we are invited to come to terms with its disturbing implications. For the resurrection of Jesus means that people who cling to life will lose it, while those who deny themselves for the sake of Jesus and the gospel will save it.

The miracles in this Gospel come as both gift and crisis. They point to the God who offers us new life, and they challenge the deepest values and structures of our existence. The resurrection of Jesus is the greatest gift and the profoundest challenge of all. Mark does not attempt to persuade us of its truth or to defend it against its critics. The good news of the resurrection is an invitation to follow Jesus and a promise that those who follow him will see him.

APPENDIX: The Longer Ending of Mark (16:9-20)

There is one question left to be considered: the ending of this Gospel. The NIV has a break after 16:8 before printing 16:9-20, as do the RSV and most other recent translations. Some Bibles like the KJV seek to preserve a narrative flow from 16:1-8 to 16:9-20. Most modern translations, however, treat 16:9-20 as a late addition to the original Gospel. There are good reasons for not accepting 16:9-20 as part of the original manuscript. In the first place the earliest manuscripts simply stop at 16:8. Moreover, 16:9-20 does not follow the logic of the account of the empty tomb. Mark 16:9 contradicts 16:8, and the longer ending contains no mention of Jesus meeting the disciples in Galilee. Galilee in fact is not mentioned there at all. The longer ending denies the expectation that the young man's message sets up. In fact, the longer ending itself does not appear to have been composed at one time (France 2002:687). There seem to have been several stages in its development, as indicated by the apparent break at the end of 16:11 and the awkward and unspecific beginning of 16:12.

There are two other possibilities. One is that the original ending may have been lost. In favor of this suggestion is that 16:8 by itself would seem to be a strange ending. In Greek the last word of the Gospel is *for*, and there is a very real question about whether this ending would even be grammatically correct. Gundry observes that 16:9-20 reveals such a great dissatisfaction with the ending at 16:8 as to indicate that the early Christian community thought the original ending had been lost (1993:1012). On the other hand, it is difficult to imagine how the original ending could have been lost without any convincing attempt to reconstruct it. One would have to argue that not only the ending but any memory of it was also lost. Apart from the earliest manuscripts all ending at this point, this is a problematic thesis because Mark is the first of its kind. It is difficult to argue how the first Gospel should have ended.

The other possibility is that 16:8 is the intended ending (Marxsen 1968:140-42; Meyers 1988:99). An important point is to be found in the idea that the women did not say anything about what they had seen because of their fear and astonishment. This is the ironic counterpoint to the injunction Jesus gave his disciples after they had witnessed the transfiguration: "Jesus gave them orders not to tell anyone what they had seen until the Son of Man had risen from the dead" (9:9). Now that the Son of Man has risen from the dead, however, the followers of Jesus who knew about it were speechless. Their silence underscores Mark's presentation of the resurrection as a parable.

In conclusion, then, it is simply implausible that the Evangelist was unaware of the accounts of the resurrected Jesus. There is little except conjecture to support the idea that the original ending has been lost. The longer ending conflicts with 16:7 and 16:8, and negates their parabolic character. On the other hand, something is to be said for the idea that Mark intended for the Gospel to conclude in this enigmatic way. If this is so, then the Gospel of Mark ends on the same note with which it opened—a call to repent and believe.

Bibliography

Aharoni, Yohanan,
and Michael Avi-Yonah
1974   *The Macmillan Bible Atlas.* New York: Macmillan.

Anderson, Hugh
1976   *The Gospel of Mark.* New Century Bible. London: Oliph-
                ants.
Aristotle
1984   *The Complete Works of Aristotle*, vol. 2. Edited by Jonathan
                Barnes. Princeton: Princeton University Press.
Aune, David
1969   "The Problem of the Messianic Secret." *Novum Testamen-
                tum* 11:1-31.
Bahr, Gordon J.
1970   "The Seder of Passover and the Eucharistic Words." *No-
                vum Testamentum* 12:181-202.
Bauckham, Richard
1998   "For Whom Were the Gospels Written?" In *The Gospels for
                All Christians*, pp. 9-48. Edited by Richard Bauckham.
                Grand Rapids: Eerdmans.
Bauer, Walter
1953   "The 'Colt' of Palm Sunday." *Journal of Biblical Literature*
                72:220-29.
Beasley-Murray, G. R.
1986   *Jesus and the Kingdom of God.* Grand Rapids: Eerdmans.

Behm, Johannes
1965   "κλάω κτλ." In *Theological Dictionary of the New Testa-
                ment* 3:726-43. Edited by Gerhard Kittel and Gerhard
                Friedrich. Translated by Geoffrey W. Bromiley. 10 vols.
                Grand Rapids: Eerdmans.
Best, Ernst
1965   *The Temptation and the Passion.* Cambridge: Cambridge
                University Press.

Bird, C. H.

1953   "Some γάρ Clauses in St. Mark's Gospel." *Journal of Theological Studies* 4:171-87.

Bonhoeffer, Dietrich

1959   *Creation and Fall*. Translated by John C. Fletcher. London: SCM.

Bowman, John

1965   *The Gospel of Mark*. Leiden: Brill.

Bruce, F. F.

1972   *New Testament History*. New York: Doubleday.

Bultmann, Rudolf

1972   *History of the Synoptic Tradition*. Translated by J. Marsh. Oxford: Blackwell.

Bush, Barbara

1990   "Remarks of Mrs. Bush at Wellesley College Commencement." <www.wellesley.edu/PublicAffairs/Commencement /1990/bush.html> (accessed April 28, 2006).

Carlston, Charles S.

1975   *The Parables of the Triple Tradition*. Philadelphia: Fortress.

Coomes, Anne

1990   *Festo Kivengere*. Eastbourne, U.K.: Monarch.

Cranfield, C. E. B.

1963   *The Gospel According to St. Mark*. Cambridge Greek New Testament Commentary. Cambridge: Cambridge University Press.

Crossan, John D.

1994   *Jesus: A Revolutionary Biography*. San Francisco: HarperSanFrancisco.

Dahl, Nils A.

1952   "Parables of Growth." *Studia Theologica* 5:132-66.

Dodd, C. H.

1961   *The Parables of the Kingdom*. New York: Scribner.

Edwards, James R.

2002   *The Gospel According to Mark*. Pillar New Testament Commentary. Grand Rapids: Eerdmans.

Eusebius
1989   *The History of the Church from Christ to Constantine.*
                        Translated by G. A. Williamson. Revised and edited by An-
                        drew Louth. London: Penguin.
France, R. T.
2002   *The Gospel of Mark.* International Greek New Testament
                        Commentary. Grand Rapids: Eerdmans.
Funk, Robert W.,
Roy W. Hoover, and
the Jesus Seminar
1993   *The Five Gospels: The Search for the Authentic Words of
                        Jesus.* New York: Macmillan.
Greeven, Heinrich
1968   "προσκυνέω κτλ." In *Theological Dictionary of the New
                        Testament* 6:758-66. Edited by Gerhard Kittel and Gerhard
                        Friedrich. Translated by Geoffrey W. Bromiley. 10 vols.
                        Grand Rapids: Eerdmans.
Grundmann, Walter
1964   "ἀγαθός κτλ." In *Theological Dictionary of the New Testa-
                        ment* 1:10-18. Edited by Gerhard Kittel and Gerhard
                        Friedrich. Translated by Geoffrey W. Bromiley. 10 vols.
                        Grand Rapids: Eerdmans.
Guelich, Robert A.
1989   *Mark 1:1—8:26.* Word Biblical Commentary 34A. Dallas:
                        Word.
Gundry, Robert H.
1993   *Mark: A Commentary on His Apology for the Cross.* Grand
                        Rapids: Eerdmans.
Hooker, Morna D.
1966   "The Christology of the New Testament: Jesus and the Son
                        of Man." In *The Finality of Christ,* pp. 32-54. Edited by
                        Dow Kirkpatrick. New York: Abingdon.
1991   *The Gospel according to St. Mark.* Black's New Testament
                        Commentaries. Peabody, Mass.: Hendrickson.
Jeremias, Joachim
1955   *The Eucharistic Words of Jesus.* Translated by Arnold
                        Ehrhardt. Oxford: Blackwell.
1964   "Ἠλ(ε)ίας." In *Theological Dictionary of the New Testa-
                        ment* 2:928-41. Edited by Gerhard Kittel and Gerhard
                        Friedrich. Translated by Geoffrey W. Bromiley. 10 vols.
                        Grand Rapids: Eerdmans.
1975   *Jerusalem in the Time of Jesus.* Translated by F. H. Cave

and C. H. Cave. Philadelphia: Fortress.

Kähler, Martin

1988   *The So-called Historical Jesus and the Historic Biblical Christ.* Translated by Carl E. Braaten. Philadelphia: Fortress.

Keener, Craig S.

2000   "Family and Household." In *Dictionary of New Testament Background,* pp. 353-68. Edited by Craig A. Evans and Stanley E. Porter. Downers Grove, Ill.: InterVarsity Press.

Kelber, Werner H.

1976   "The Hour of the Son of Man and the Temptation of the Disciples." In *The Passion in Mark.* Edited by Werner H. Kelber. Philadelphia: Fortress.

Kelly, Geffrey B., and
Nelson, F. Burton, Editors

1990   *A Testament to Freedom: The Essential Writings of Dietrich Bonhoeffer.* San Francisco: HarperSanFrancisco.

Kim, Seyoon

1985   *The Son of Man as the Son of God.* Grand Rapids: Eerdmans.

Kittel, Gerhard

1964   "ἀββᾶ." In *Theological Dictionary of the New Testament* 1:5-6. Edited by Gerhard Kittel and Gerhard Friedrich. Translated by Geoffrey W. Bromiley. 10 vols. Grand Rapids: Eerdmans.

Ladd, George F.

1974   *A Theology of the New Testament.* Grand Rapids: Eerdmans.

Lane, William L.

1974   *The Gospel According to Mark.* New International Commentary on the New Testament. Grand Rapids: Eerdmans.

Levin, Sis

1989   *Beirut Diary.* Downers Grove, Ill.: InterVarsity.

Lewis, C. S.

1960   *The Four Loves.* New York: Harcourt Brace.

Lohse, Eduard

1971   "σάββατον κτλ." In *Theological Dictionary of the New Testament* 7:1-35. Edited by Gerhard Kittel and Gerhard Friedrich. Translated by Geoffrey W. Bromiley. 10 vols. Grand Rapids: Eerdmans.

Markus, Joel
1999   *Mark 1—8.* Anchor Bible 27. New York: Doubleday.

Martin, Ralph P.
1972   *Mark: Evangelist and Theologian.* Grand Rapids: Zonder-
                    van.
1975   *New Testament Foundations,* vol. 1. Grand Rapids: Eerd-
                    mans.
Marxsen, Willi
1955   "Redaktionsgeschichtliche Erklärung des sogenannten
                    Parabeltheorie des Markus." *Zeitschrift für Theologie und
                    Kirche* 52:255-71.
1968   *Introduction to the New Testament.* Translated by G. Bus-
                    well. Philadelphia: Fortress.
Mauser, Ulrich
1963   *Christ in the Wilderness: The Wilderness Theme in the Sec-
                    ond Gospel and Its Basis in Biblical Tradition.* Naperville,
                    Ill.: Allenson.
Meye, Robert P.
1968   *Jesus and the Twelve.* Grand Rapids: Eerdmans.

Meyers, Ched
1988   *Binding the Strong Man: A Political Reading of Mark's
                    Story of Jesus.* Maryknoll, N.Y.: Orbis.
Nineham, Dennis E.
1968   *The Gospel of St. Mark.* New York: Seabury.

Oepke, Albrecht
1964   "βάπτω κτλ." In *Theological Dictionary of the New Testa-
                    ment* 1:529-46. Edited by Gerhard Kittel and Gerhard
                    Friedrich. Translated by Geoffrey W. Bromiley. 10 vols.
                    Grand Rapids: Eerdmans.
Payne, P. B.
1978   "The Order of Sowing and Ploughing in the Parable of the
                    Sower." *New Testament Studies* 25:123-29.
Pesch, Rudolf
1977   *Das Markusevangelius.* 2 vols. Freiburg: Herder.

Rohde, Joachim
1968   *Rediscovering the Teaching of the Evangelists.* Philadel-
                    phia: Westminster Press.

Schnackenburg, Rudolf
1971   *The Gospel According to St. Mark.* Translated by Werner
                     Kruppa. London: Sheed and Ward.

Schrage, Wolfgang
1971   "συναγωγή κτλ." In *Theological Dictionary of the New Tes-
                     tament* 7:798-852. Edited by Gerhard Kittel and Gerhard
                     Friedrich. Translated by Geoffrey W. Bromiley. 10 vols.
                     Grand Rapids: Eerdmans.

Schweizer, Eduard
1970   *The Good News According to Mark.* Translated by Donald
                     H. Madvig. Atlanta: John Knox.

Soulen, R. Kendall
1996   *The God of Israel and Christian Theology.* Minneapolis:
                     Fortress.

Stephens, Mitchell
1998   *The Rise of the Image and the Fall of the Word.* New York:
                     Oxford University Press.

Taylor, Vincent
1974   *The Gospel According to St. Mark.* London: Macmillan.

Theissen, Gerd
1974   *Urchristliche Wundergeschichte.* Göttingen, Germany:
                     Gütersloh.

Torrance, Thomas F.
1992   *The Mediation of Christ.* Colorado Springs: Helmers &
                     Howard.

Trocmé, Étienne
1975   *The Formation of the Gospel According to Mark.* Trans-
                     lated by Pamela Gaughan. Philadelphia: Westminster
                     Press.

Tyson, Joseph B.
1961   "The Blindness of the Disciples in Mark." *Journal of Bibli-
                     cal Literature* 80: 261-268.

Vermes, Geza
1967   "Appendix E: The Use of נשׁ בר/בר נשׁא in Jewish Ara-
                     maic." In Matthew Black's *An Aramaic Approach to the
                     Gospels and Acts,* pp. 310-30. 3rd ed. Oxford: Clarendon.

Waetjen, Herman C.
1989   *A Reordering of Power.* Minneapolis: Fortress.

Weeden, Theodore J.
1971   *Mark—Traditions in Conflict.* Philadelphia: Fortress.

Wenham, John W.
1975   "The Relatives of Jesus." *Evangelical Quarterly* 47:6-15.

White, K. D.
1964   "The Parable of the Sower." *Journal of Theological Studies*
                15:300-307.
Wrede, William
1971   *The Messianic Secret.* Translated by J. C. G. Greig. Cam-
                bridge: Clarke.